GOOD GOVERNANCE ISSUES AND SUSTAINABLE DEVELOPMENT
The Indian Ocean Region

Editors

ROBIN GHOSH
RONY GABBAY
ABU SIDDIQUE

ATLANTIC PUBLISHERS AND DISTRIBUTORS

Published by
ATLANTIC PUBLISHERS AND DISTRIBUTORS
B-2, Vishal Enclave, New Delhi-110 027
Phones 5413460, 5429987

Sales Office
4346/4C, Ansari Road, Darya Ganj,
New Delhi-110 002
Phones 3273880, 3285873, 3280451
Fax 91-11-3285873
e-mail : gupta.atlantc@axcess.net.in

ISBN 81-7156-821-1

Typeset at
APD Computer Graphics, Delhi
Printed in India at
Mehra Offset Press, Delhi

FOREWORD

This book is the result of an international seminar held at The University of Western Australia in October, 1996. The purpose of the Seminar was to bring together leading experts from many disciplines and professions to discuss "Governance Issues and Sustainable Development in the Indian Ocean Rim Countries".

The papers presented in the Seminar were assessed by independent reviewers, who recommended publication of only a select group of papers, which are included in this volume. As editors, we regret the long delay in the publication of the volume, which was caused by circumstances beyond our control.

We wish to record with thanks the generous financial support from AusAID, Canberra, that made it possible to invite several eminent persons from overseas to attend the Seminar in Perth.

The initial typescript was prepared by Mr Ratan Kumar Ghosh of the Centre for Migration and Development Studies. Mrs Glenys Walter, Administrative Officer in the Department of Economics at The University of Western Australia, prepared the camera-ready copy with her usual professionalism. We wish to record our thanks to both Mrs Walter and Mr Ghosh.

A word of thanks to Dr K R Gupta, Managing Director, Atlantic Publishers and Distributors, New Delhi is also appropriate here. Dr Gupta, who was trained as a professional economist, has made his name in India as a reputable publisher. The publication of this volume at short notice became possible because of the efficiency of Dr Gupta's office in New Delhi.

Finally, we wish to record our appreciation of support from Professor Paul Miller, Head of the Department of Economics at The University of Western Australia, who has always taken a keen interest in the research activity of the Centre for Migration and Development Studies.

Editors
R Gabbay
Perth *R N Ghosh*
Abu Siddique

List of Contributors

BEAHAN, MICHAEL, University Fellow and Former President of the Senate, Centre for Development Studies, Edith Cowan University, Perth, Western Australia, Australia

BENTLEY, NOKOME, Fisheries Scientist, Trophia, Claremont, Western Australia, Australia

BOTHA, D J J, Emeritus Professor of Economics and Managing Editor, South African Journal of Economics, University of Pretoria, Pretoria, Republic of South Africa

CHWEYA, LUDEKI, University of Nairobi, Kenya

GABBAY, RONY, Senior Honorary Research Fellow, Department of Economics, The University of Western Australia, Nedlands, Perth, Australia

GHOSH, R N, Senior Honorary Research Fellow, Department of Economics, The University of Western Australia, Nedlands, Perth, Australia

GUPTA, SUBRATA, Principal, Jogamaya Devi College, Department of Economics, Calcutta University, Calcutta, India

HALAIS, CHRISTINE, Consultant, Trophia, Claremont, Western Australia, Australia

HAMID, M A, Professor, Department of Economics, Rajshahi University, Rajshahi, Bangladesh

LOUW, H A, Professor, Department of Sociology, Vista University, Welkom, Republic of South Africa

KEHREN, TATJANA, Research Assistant, Department of Economics, The University of Queensland, Brisbane, Queensland, Australia

MUTORO, HENRY, University of Nairobi, Kenya

NASONG'O, WANJALA, University of Nairobi, Kenya

PORTER, PAIGE, Executive Dean, Faculties of Economics & Commerce, Education and Law, The University of Western Australia, Nedlands, Perth, Australia

RAY, PRADEEP, Associate Lecturer, Department of Organisational and Labour Studies, The University of Western Australia, Nedlands, Perth, Australia

ROY, KARTIK C, Associate Professor, Department of Economics, The University of Queensland, Brisbane, Queensland, Australia

SCHRIRE, ROBERT, Professor, Chair of Political Studies and Director, Institute for Study of Public Policy, University of Cape Town, Cape Town, Republic of South Africa

SIDDIQUE, M A B, Director, Centre for Migration and Development Studies, Economics Department, The University of Western Australia, Nedlands, Perth, Australia

TALUKDAR, T K, IPS (RETIRED), Formerly, Commissioner of Police, Calcutta, India

TISDELL, CLEM T, Professor and Head, Department of Economics, The University of Queensland, Brisbane, Queensland, Australia

YASMEEN, SAMINA, Senior Lecturer, Department of Politics, The University of Western Australia, Nedlands, Perth, Australia

ZACARIAS, AGOSTINHO, Senior Lecturer, Department of International Relations, University of the Witwatersrand, Johannesburg, Republic of South Africa

ZHUGE, REN, Department of Forestry, Southwest Forestry College, Kunming, People's Republic of China, and Visiting Vellow, Department of Economics, The University of Queensland, Brisbane, Queensland, Australia

TABLE OF CONTENTS

Part I

GOOD GOVERNANCE ISSUES

1 GOOD GOVERNANCE ISSUES AND DEVELOPMENT

R N GHOSH, R GABBAY AND M A B SIDDIQUE

INTRODUCTION

For several decades since the end of World War II, the economic literature on development of the Third World had almost exclusively focused attention on the key economic and demographic variables which were supposed to initiate and sustain development. For example, it was argued that low income countries did not generate sufficient domestic savings for investments. Hence the ability of such countries to reach the "take-off" stage was largely dependent upon the inflow of foreign capital and/or foreign aid that would fill up the domestic savings gap. Again, economic wisdom in the 1960s and 1970s pointed towards the need for population control measures to effectively enable the Third World countries to overcome what is known as the "poverty trap". Despite, however, massive injections of capital from the World Bank and the OECD countries during the 1960s and 1970s, many countries of Africa and Asia failed to record a significant improvement either in their GDPs or in the standard of living of their population at large. Injection of foreign aid and capital from developed countries over a number of years had of course significantly benefited minority groups in each country who used their incomes on "conspicuous" consumption of imported goods, and also encouraged corrupt governments to spend capital on military hardwares and the "monument-building" activity such as ultra-modern luxury buildings and skyscrapers in cities. In other words, the flow of foreign capital in developing countries was in many cases associated with little or no development at the grassroots but with the growth of a corrupt bureaucracy and a corrupt minority group that derived direct benefits from foreign aid and capital. Moreover, foreign capital imposed a burden on the future generations who were faced with the responsibility of repaying the debt. Many of the sub-Saharan African countries are currently faced with unsustainable debt-repayment burden, because of foreign debt, contracted in the 1970s and 1980s, that went into wasteful and unproductive expenditure.

In 1992 the World Bank published its first report on *Governance and Development* in which it focused its attention on the topic of governance. In that report, the World Bank explored the meaning of governance and why it was important for development. The Bank defined governance to mean the manner in which power was exercised in the management of a country's economic and social resources for development. The World Bank Report on *Governance and Development* concluded that if sustainable development was to occur, a predictable and transparent framework of rules and institutions for the conduct of private and public business must exist. In a subsequent report entitled *Governance: The World Bank's Experience* (1994), it was stated that "Good governance is epitomized by predictable, open, and enlightened policymaking (that is, transparent processes); a bureaucracy involved with a professional ethos; an executive arm of government accountable for its actions; and a strong civil society participating in public affairs; and all behaving under the rule of law."

Following the lead of the World Bank, a general consensus has now emerged among economists that good government is an important element in the complex process of economic change in a country. Savings and investments, and population control measures cannot initiate sustainable development without efficient management of resources. To achieve a long-term process of development it is therefore very important to have an open, transparent and accountable administration that is free from corruption. In other words, good governance is the key to sustainable economic development.

THEORY AND CASE STUDIES

The present volume contains a total of eighteen papers, most of which were presented in an international conference on "Governance Issues and Sustainable Development in the Indian Ocean Rim Countries", held in Perth from 28 to 30 October 1996. The papers included in the volume were all refereed and selected after several revisions.

In her Opening Address to the Conference, Paige Porter drew attention to the dynamic context for development research in the Indian Ocean Region. This is followed by a very important paper by K C Roy and C A Tisdell on "Good governance in Sustainable Development: The Impact of Institutions". Roy and Tisdell have argued that good governance would depend on institutional structures and the economic resources available for ensuing governance. In some cases centralised governance structures are inefficient. In other cases, decentralised structures turn out to be inadequate. By drawing attention to mainly the experience of India, the authors conclude that sustainable development would require good policies and effective provision of institutions conducive to good governance.

In his paper on "Governance in Development: A Challenging Partnership", H A Louw develops the theme that a tripartite relationship between Government, business and community, on national, regional and local levels, must form the basis of governance in development. The paper by Louw addresses the topic from a general theoretical perspective and then applies the model to the South African and southern African situation.

Abdul Hamid specifically discusses the case of Bangladesh in his paper on "Good governance and Sustainable Development". He examines how regulatory issues in Bangladesh tend to impinge on the long-term development of that country. His paper deals with the key elements of Bangladesh's regulatory framework including investment controls, exchange controls, quantitative import restrictions, export controls, and industry and agriculture specific regulations. According to Hamid, the normal processes of development in Bangladesh have been stifled by the various and often contradictory regulations by the Bangladesh Government.

The paper by Henry Mutoro, *et al* is a very perceptive study of the political leadership in Kenya as a lesson for other African countries. After the initial growth of the first decade of independence, most African economies faltered and went into decline with some fifteen out of the forty-five sub-Saharan countries recording a negative growth rate in their per capita income in the 1970s. Mutoro and his co-authors argue that stalled development in Africa was *not* to be attributed to traditionally cited factors such as underdeveloped human resources, the disruption that followed the post-colonial period including rapid population growth. The failure of most African countries to record a sustained period of development - according to the authors - "lies largely within the ambit of the kind of political leadership which the Continent has had since independence".

The other paper on Africa is by A Zacarias, who examines the meaning of good governance in the context of the notion of a good State. He argues that the development of the idea of the state in the Western political tradition is based on strong Christian ethics. In the works of Hobbes, Locke, Hegel and Weber the different ideas of the state as a moral force are articulated. Although these thinkers differ on how morality is achieved, they still agree on the fact that the state is not only the highest source of authority but also of all values. Zacarias then goes on to argue that the state in African history lacks a strong ethical basis. The Christian ethics in which the Western State is rooted was alien to African elites, many of whom embraced Marxism. Indeed, Christian ethics is often in competition with religions such as Islam, animism and other local religions. African history records the role of state as a source of power and authority to be obeyed but *not* as a source of moral and ethical values.

Robert Schrire's short but incisive paper discusses the political economy of public policy in South Africa. South Africa's political revolution has now been largely completed but the key challenge is to convert political influence into economic empowerment for the black majority. Schrire explains the economic legacy of *apartheid* and examines the economic policy options available to the ANC-dominated South African government.

Part I of the volume contains three other papers, dealing with specific countries such as China, Thailand and Pakistan. Ren Zhuge and Clem Tisdell examine the case of the Jingpo ethnic minority who live almost entirely in Dehong Prefecture in the south-west of Yunnan province in China. The paper looks at the rural economy of the Jingpo people, and also examines the traditional factors influencing their management of local forests such as their religious beliefs and local means of governance.

In another paper T Kehren and C A Tisdell look at the important role that women play in Thailand in the management of livestock and the use of common property resources, thereby contributing to the development of the economy as a whole. Sustainable development without an active participation of women in economic activity is unlikely to happen in Thailand and elsewhere. There is therefore the urgent need for improvement of the role and status of women in Third World countries.

Samina Yasmeen's paper on Pakistan examines how the partial introduction of Islamic laws in that country in the 1980s targeted women and religious minorities. The laws effectively reduced these two social groups to a status of "lesser citizens" and threatened the process of democratisation in Pakistan. There is the *implicit* suggestion in the paper that the change in the status of women and other religious minorities is a precondition for sustainable development in Pakistan.

In a very interesting paper, Ghosh and Siddique look at the impact of crime and corruption on economic growth in developing countries. The authors examine the complex problem of crime and corruption in the context of the globalisation of the world economy and the increasing impotence of governments to pursue macroeconomic stabilisation policies within their national frontiers. In more recent years, the Hong Kong based Independent Commission Against

Corruption (ICAC), the Berlin-based Transparency International (TI), Interpol, and the World Bank have kindled a new kind of international awareness of how transnational (and multinational) efforts are needed to combat crime and corruption. It is of course arguable whether or not corruption would retard national economic growth. However, Ghosh and Siddique have argued in their paper that certain types of corruption in public life, if it became rampant in a society, would adversely affect the long-term process of economic growth.

Relevant Issues

Part II of the volume contains six different essays which deal with certain relevant issues concerning good governance and development. Talukdar was the former Police Commissioner of Calcutta. In his survey of the crime situation in major cities of India, he has ably shown how an effective police administration has kept a lid on more serious crimes in Calcutta, despite that city's severe problems of overcrowding, of unemployment, and of appalling slums and widespread poverty. Indeed, as compared with Mumbai (Bombay) and Delhi, Calcutta has a much lower crime rate in India. Talukdar's paper contains some very informative and useful statistics.

D K Dutta discusses the trend and structural changes of Australian overseas development assistance, and works out the implications for such changes for the Indian Ocean rim countries. He argues that there has been a declining trend in the Australian ODS/GNP ratio, and that such trend would possibly continue in the coming decade or so. Many of the countries of the Indian Ocean region already face a heavy debt-burden, and are therefore not very attractive for private capital inflow from developed countries. The declining trend in Australia's overseas development assistance is therefore likely to cause more problems for the developing countries of the region in the coming years.

D J J Botha's excellent paper on "Interest Rates and Inflation in South Africa, 1970-1996" examines the *hypothesis* that monetary policy of South Africa had been politically conditioned during almost the past three decades. The main conclusion emerging from the paper is that the South African Reserve Bank did not always act independently of the political influence of successive governments. It is therefore possible to argue, as Sir John Hicks had said, that a country's monetary policy is inevitably rooted in economic reality.

For many Indian Ocean rim countries marine fisheries represent a major source of income and food security. Nokome Bentley and Christine Halais's paper on "The Role of Marine Fisheries in the

Development of the Indian Ocean Rim Countries" points out that, although at the global scale the total marine fisheries catch of the Indian Ocean is relatively small, yet a number of countries in the region have amongst the highest per capita consumption of fish in the world. The sustainable development and management of fisheries resources will be of growing importance to the Indian Ocean region; and Bentley and Halais recommend strategies for governments to achieve such goals.

Pradeep Ray's paper discusses the role of multinational enterprises in India in the context of the liberalisation of the Indian economy since 1991. A large part of his paper deals with the theoretical literature on free market *versus* State intervention. He then examines how the opening up of the Indian telecommunications market to overseas competition has affected the growth of indigenous technology.

Subrata Gupta's paper deals with the question of child labour in India. Gupta recognises that the employment of children is basically an economic problem. However, he argues that children should not be denied the opportunity for their proper development and education. Sustainable economic development presupposes the existence of a labour market in which the workforce is healthy, intelligent and educated. Employment of child labour is therefore incompatible with the long-term development objectives of a country.

Michael Behan's closing address ably summarises his own personal views on the quality and substance of many of the papers presented at the Conference. However, as indicated earlier, many of the papers which were presented at the Conference are not included in the present volume, *either* because they have already been published elsewhere, *or* because of editorial reasons.

CONCLUSION

In presenting this volume to general readers, we are aware of the wide and diverse range of topics covered in the essays included in it. As a result, many of the topics covered such as crime, corruption and good governance offer only a broad *survey* of the fundamental issues involved in sustainable development. Similarly, the case studies involving Africa and Asia do not pretend to cover *in depth* the problems of long-term development of the countries of the Indian Ocean region.

We hope however that the issues raised by the authors, whose essays are included in this volume, will provide food for thought and healthy debates among economists and politicians, who are currently concerned with the nature of good governance and its impact on sustainable development. In the ultimate analysis, it is the efficient management of resources by government, business and the community at large that would determine a society's ability to cope with the complex process of development. Without good governance in a country, the basic pre-requisite for long-term development disappears; and despite all its resources, a country would fail to successfully respond to the challenges of sustainable development both for its present and for its future generations.

2 THE DYNAMIC CONTEXT FOR DEVELOPMENT RESEARCH IN THE INDIAN OCEAN REGION

PAIGE PORTER

OPENING ADDRESS

It is a pleasure to welcome so many visitors to The University of Western Australia and the Centre for Migration and Development Studies (CMDS). The Centre was established in the Department of Economics in 1987 under the leadership of now Emeritus Professor R T Appleyard, and Associate Professors R N Ghosh, R Gabbay and Dr I H vanden Driesen. The current Director is Dr M A B Siddique who joined the group in 1992.

The Centre has been primarily supported by The University, the Western Australian government, and AusAID. Academic teaching has been offered at all levels from undergraduate to doctoral supervision. Its research agenda to date has focused on studies on the global aspects of migration and economic development, immigration to Australia, population in developing countries, India's economic development, Middle East economies, and labour history.

DYNAMIC CHANGE IN THE REGION

In many ways the recent history of the Indian Ocean region can be seen in the research topics which have been pursued here over the past decade. What faces all of you here at this conference now, however, are the major new developments occurring in this region and the dynamic quality of its economic and social activity. Some of these are:

- the historic political changes in South Africa and its future economic development;
- the restructuring of India's economy;
- the continuing strong influence of Middle Eastern countries on energy supplies and prices together with the continued political instability of the region;
- the development and effect of tourism, especially on the island countries;
- the relationship with and interaction between the Indian Ocean rim countries and the "tigers" of Southeast Asia;

- the changing patterns of international trade and the effects of the globalising world economy in the region.

Dramatic changes such as these provide some exciting opportunities and suggest some significant additions to the research agendas of all scholars who would further the study of the Indian Ocean region. New research possibilities include the study of such topics as: changing labour markets; new forms of industrialisation and new pressures on urbanisation; the macroeconomic performance of states; the changing nature of trade and new import-export possibilities; land use issues; the changing role of the state and governance issues; the influence of religious, philosophical and cultural differences in and on international trade; changing and differing organisational and management structures, processes and patterns; the effects of ethnic and language differences; the role of women in the economies of the region; the role of education and the economies; post colonial theories and perspectives; and specific country issues such as the challenges for development in South Africa.

By way of information, the Faculty of Economics and Commerce at this University is attempting to deal with some of these changes in its most basic curriculum as well as its research through the introduction of new majors and degrees at both the undergraduate and postgraduate level. Economics and commerce subjects cannot be adequately taught now without reference to the importance of Australia's geographical position on the Indian Ocean and near Asia, and the growing internationalisation of trade.

GLOBALISATION AND DEBATE

There are, of course, wider issues facing all of us in the kinds of changes highlighted above. While I realise that some economists do not like the term "globalisation", nevertheless, I think the word captures peoples' *perceptions* about a shrinking globe and increasing international economic connections.

What is most notable about globalisation is its economic characterisation. It is not presented as a political concept. We talk about the globalisation of the economy - not the polity. In fact, while the economies of different countries are globalising, thus tying us all together economically, there is little evidence of polities globalising, except on a regional basis under very difficult circumstances (e.g., the European Economic Community). While the United Nations has its moments, it is primarily a voluntary organisation with few sanctions of it own. There is no international government in which political interests can be negotiated. There is no international democracy. There is no international governmental structure to protect citizen rights, or enforce citizen responsibilities. The last two centuries have seen the development, rise and fall of nation states as we know them. If economic imperatives are weakening the "borders" of nation states, it is well to keep in mind that there is no world state with a political process upon which and within which we can deliberate. The point is that we can affect our own governments, but insofar as our own governments no longer control economic aspects of import, we have a limited ability to control those "borderless" activities.

There are a number of significant commentators on the future with fairly negative scenarios offering warnings at this time. Well known economist, Lester Thurow, in his recently published book, *Future of Capitalism* (1996), argues that capitalism has created a global economy but is unable to reconcile it with either social justice or an international order. He sees five great tectonic plates moving which will bring global economic and political earthquakes in the next century. They are: (1) the end of communism; (2) the information revolution; (3) the demographic pressures on the West and Japan; (4) the globalisation of the financial markets; and (5) the decline of United States hegemony.

One of Thurow's central claims is that human resources are now more crucial to a nation's competitiveness and prosperity than natural resources or capital. Thurow argues that the development of human skills has been essential to the economic growth of the twentieth century. He sees both mass and higher education as indispensable public goods. Yet just at the time when the world is facing its worst crises, Thurow argues, the resurgent ideology of *laissez faire* capitalism and the end of the welfare state are coming together to erode the public commitment to education when it is more important than ever. These are controversial views, but they are well worth considering in relation to all of our futures on the Indian Ocean rim.

The idea that the globalisation of markets is making geographic borders redundant through the speed of capital flows and information exchange, and even making nation states obsolete has been advanced by other theorists as well, most recently, *The End of the Nation State* by Kenichi Ohmae (1996). While these claims can be moderated, for example, by pointing out that most world economic activity remains domestic not international, even in the United States, and that the imperialism of Great Britain may have involved as much international economic integration as developing globalisation, there clearly exist significant economic trends that are, at the least, connecting the economies and economic elite in all countries. A major concern must be, however, as noted above, our disenfranchisement at the international level. People are not only consumers, but also citizens, and while it is hard to imagine citizens willingly giving up nation state citizen rights for unfettered consumerism, it could happen by stealth.

Another significant and related trend is the rise of Asian countries and greater participation by them in the international economy. The "miracles" of the tiger economies of Japan, Singapore, Taiwan, South Korea and increasingly Malaysia are well known. While there is no doubt that there is increased economic development and recent economic activity between Asia, the West, and the countries around the Indian Ocean rim, and that it is likely that this new interaction will be significant for all in many ways, it is important to keep a historical perspective. Asia has often been central to world trade and it is only the most recent past with which economic comparisons are typically made. For example, from the 15th to the 18th centuries, international trade and capitalism was centred in Asian countries, particularly, China, India and Islamic countries

THE DIFFICULT ISSUES

It is certainly true that there are also many potentially positive outcomes, well rehearsed publicly, of the increasing internationalisation of economies, most obviously, the likelihood of raising the material standard of living for millions of people, the greater access to different ways of knowing and doing, and the opportunity to learn from others. The down side includes the potential loss of individual unique cultures as international capital brings with it Western culture, and the potential for new forms of imperialism and hegemony to develop, centred around economic elites tied to borderless international capital.

Some of the issues which I think will be particularly difficult to handle include:

Environmental sustainability - How can we ensure this in the rush to development? Political and economic time frames are short and most serious environmental issues have very long time frames. The recent exposure of the enormous ecological mess in eastern Europe and Russia after the collapse of communism is a timely example of what can happen when the environment is ignored.

Indigenous peoples - Virtually all countries have Indigenous populations often tied to traditional ways of living. In many countries internal migration and dislocation are occurring. How can we both nurture and save unique aspects of human culture, yet assist such groups to participate in economic growth and improved material well being?

The changing role of women - Women's increased participation in the paid work force has clearly been tied to the development of capitalism and a focus on individual workers earning a wage on which they could live, as opposed to more traditional family cooperation in accumulating the means to live. Women's participation in public as well as private worlds is related to the growth in the belief in human rights including the doctrine of individual rights. Arguably women's changing role is essential to economic development - but it is disruptive to tradition in many societies. How can we assist in developing the positive aspects of these changes in women's roles with minimum disruption? How can we develop all our human potential?

Social justice - With all the major economic, political and concomitant social change that will occur in the future (whether democracy is embraced in its Western form or other forms of government selected) how do we ensure that all people in a society have equal opportunities and share as equally as possible in the economic rewards? Any society with a significant section of its population in poverty, and another section well off, has potential problems. A classic political science concept that can be used to apply to any proposed reforms is to ask the question who wins and who loses by the proposal? The answer to that question can be a useful guide as to directions to take. One thing is for sure; whatever the political governance system used, there must be adequate modes of participation by all people.

CONCLUSION

The majority attending this conference are academics. Academics are public intellectuals with responsibilities, not only for narrow academic research, but for "thinking our way out" of the significant issues facing our societies. I believe that this is one of our responsibilities to our communities. It is part of our "contract" with society. I hope this conference both helps us to share intellectual commitments and challenges, and helps us to "think our way out" of some of the many issues facing us in an increasingly uncertain world.

REFERENCES

Ohmae, Kenichi, *The End of the Nation State*, Free Press (A division of Simon and Schuster), 1996.

Thurow, Lester C., *The Future of Capitalism*, Sydney: Allen and Unwin, 1996.

3 GOOD GOVERNANCE IN SUSTAINABLE DEVELOPMENT: THE IMPACT OF INSTITUTIONS

K C ROY AND C A TISDELL

INTRODUCTION

The possibilities for good governance depend on institutional structures and the economic resources available for ensuring governance. In some cases centralised governance structures are inefficient. In other cases decentralised structures turn out to be inadequate. In a federal state with a multi-party democracy such as India, the capacity of the federal governance structure to influence the states' governance apparatus is limited when the state administrations are run by political parties not in power at the federal level and since the production and delivery of certain goods and services are controlled by state administrations, conflict is likely to occur when the centre wants to impose its decision on the states. This conflict contributes to ineffectiveness. But the inefficiency may also result from the formulation and application of policies by the central government which is out of touch with the needs of local people and has little knowledge of local environment.

There are numerous cases where the programmes and projects formulated at the top and implemented for people at the bottom did not achieve the desired results.

Roy and Tisdell (1993, 1993a, 1995) in examining the impact of technological change on the rural sector in India, argued that serious deficiencies existed in implementing policies and administering development programmes.

An evaluation of the "food for work" scheme revealed that women accounted for only twenty percent of the beneficiaries (Duvvury 1989). A study of the impact of the Integrated Rural Development Projects (IRDP) by Rath (1985) found that the beneficiaries were mis-classified and that only three percent of the rural poor were able to cross the poverty line. Ben Crow (1992) observes that what the IRDP, first envisaged as a comprehensive strategy for growth with social justice, came to be implemented as the promotion of individual household enterprise because it did not threaten the dominant rural power structure. Thus one can say that the interests that the Indian state represent include those of the dominant rural class. However in Ben Crow's argument the implication is that IRDP at least served the interest of the dominant ruling class but sometimes, the interest of the state may not include the interest of any dominant class. In any case, van Arkadia (1989) argues that the power relations within which states and institutions operate cause them to pursue objectives inconsistent with development.

Decentralised governance structure reduces the need for co-ordination as the centralised structure transfers to lower levels of government those functions which it cannot manage effectively. Chambers (1988) has argued that large centralised and hierarchical organisations such as governments tend to simplify, centralise and standardise. These may be appropriate ways for organising some kinds of activities, but not others.

Decentralisation conventionally has taken three forms – (i) "deconcentration" referring to transferring resources and decision making from headquarters to other branches of central government; (ii) "devolution" referring to devolution of resources and power to autonomous units of government such as municipalities and local governments and (iii) "delegation" meaning delegation of resources and power to organisations outside the regular bureaucratic structures such as public corporations, development agencies or NGO's (World Bank 1983).

"Devolution" and "delegation" if carried out properly, can make development programmes effective. However, decentralisation in developing countries has mostly taken the form of deconcentration. In India, one major act of "devolution" was the creation of *Panchayati Raj* and the transfer of resources and power to these village governments. This does not mean that decentralisation has improved the efficiency of the administration of rural development. In fact, the benefits of such decentralisation have been mostly enjoyed by the dominant power groups of the dominant political party. Moreover local governments suffer from a shortage of technical and administrative skills. Also, genuine decentralisation of resources and power cannot take place in India unless the entire structure of development planning changes. In decentralised power structure, plans are formulated by the rural people at the grass root level and not imposed from above.

Although this form of planning was envisaged by Gandhi to be suitable for India (Roy and Tisdell 1995; Schumacher 1962), it could not have been implemented on a national scale in India because of its inherent limitations.

Decentralisation of power can facilitate empowerment of people. Some writers suggest that local communities should be empowered and that this is likely to result in more sustainable development. Local communities are said to be more knowledgeable about the results of local environmental change. The features of normal bureaucracy which include centralisation of authority, especially financial control and standardisation of rules, recommendations and actions may not facilitate the empowerment of people. Hence, it is felt that the participation of beneficiaries in the formulation, implementation and maintenance of programmes is necessary. The justification of the local community's participation is based on the arguments that (i) local people organise best around the problems they consider most important such as in assessing needs and finding solutions; (ii) local people make rational economic decisions in the context of their own environment and circumstances providing appropriately for the risks associated with the change; and that (iii) local participation also ensures voluntary commitment of resources and local control over the quality and distribution of benefits (Yugandhar and Raju 1992).

On the one hand, centralisation of power in some cases has resulted in destruction of environment, loss of forests etc. as reported for Nepal by Mishra (1982) but on the other, decentralisation has sometimes hastened deforestation and biodiversity loss as in Indian States like Mizoram. Therefore, it would seem that there are advantages and disadvantages of both centralised and decentralised governance structures.

PROPERTY RIGHTS AND ENVIRONMENT

Preservation of the environment, which is the most essential prerequisite to sustainable development, cannot be achieved unless the pressure on forests and other natural resources resulting from their excessive use is eased. But the pressure is unlikely to be eased in the absence of appropriate property rights of local communities. Absence of appropriate property rights is one of the reasons why local communities do not take care of the environment. Appropriate property rights consist of user rights to forests and commons and effective ownership rights to cultivable land. Since the vast majority of the population in Third World countries live in rural areas and since rural women's reliance on renewable resources for providing sustenance to their families is far greater than men's, measures to ensure that rural women enjoy such rights assume crucial importance for good governance. Effective ownership rights to cultivable land by making women more economically independent significantly reduces their need to rely on forests and natural resources and appropriate user rights to forests provide them the incentive to preserve the renewable resources and not to destroy them.

A number of studies (Dasgupta and Maity 1986; Agarwal 1989; Duvvury 1989; Kandiyoti 1992; Roy and Tisdell 1993, 1993a; Agarwal 1994) have commented on the lack of and the need for women's effective ownership rights to land in India. In West Bengal when the control of forests was taken over by the Forest Department, local people were deprived of the user rights to forests. Due to the lack of economic incentive for conservation, tribals specially disadvantaged by changed ownership and user rights and facing possible loss of income from the forests and other villagers have no incentive to protect the renewable resources. Hence, they attempt to exploit the forests before the Forest Department does. The nature of ownership and user rights for tribals and non-tribal villagers in West Bengal and in other states of Eastern India is complex and seems to differ from state to state. But an examination of such rights in the central Himalayan region in Northern India can explain the type of rights enjoyed by the villagers in the past, the reasons for and the consequences of the disappearance of such rights.

Property Rights and Forests in the Central Himalayan Region

Before the onset of commercial forestry in the early twentieth century to meet the demands for railway sleepers and the manufacture of turpentine and resin from *chir* tree, the forests were used and managed by the peasantry. Conservation was achieved by customary limitations on users rather than formal management. However in many oak forests, rules prohibited lopping of leaves in the hot weather and the grass cut by each family was strictly regulated. The penalty for the infringement of these rules included boycott and or exclusion of the offender from the forest.

However, in accordance with the Indian Forest Act of 1878 which empowered the British government to reserve for the state's use all forests not on privately owned land, the government refused to recognise traditional notions of community ownership. Restrictions were imposed on the villagers' use of forests to ensure regeneration of felled trees. Villagers were allotted specific quantities of timber, the number of cattle to be grazed were limited and restrictions were placed on lopping trees for fodder and fuel-wood. The annual practice of burning of the forest floor was banned. Loss of villagers' customary rights to use forests led to massive popular protests and a huge fire in the commercially valuable *chir* forests in 1921. In response to these protests, the government relaxed the restrictions on villagers' access to civil forests. However, in the early 1960s these forests were converted to class I reserved forests and brought under the control of the Forestry Department. The national government in India reintroduced restrictions on these forests again. But with the disempowerment of traditional authority which began in the early 1920s, the villagers' interest in preserving the forest began to decline and forests began to deteriorate.

Since the class II reserved forests were almost exclusively used by the state for large scale commercial exploitation, the hill people's user rights were severely curtailed and their rights of control were lost. These in turn reduced significantly the villagers' incentive to regenerate and conserve forests. The loss of control furthermore, by raising the possibility in the hill people's mind that others might appropriate the forest resources, led to a situation where villagers in violation of the rules exploited the forests for personal gains.

In the next category, there are *Panchayat* forests which mainly consist of oak trees and have been maintained quite well probably because the *Panchayat* which regulates the use of forests is formed by the villagers by electing representatives from amongst themselves with the permission of the Deputy Commissioner.

Even in such forests, lopping of leaves for food in the off-season by women in violation of the rules or theft by women of other villages occurs quite frequently.

Somanathan (1991) observes that the *Panchayat's* administrative style under which decisions regarding the regulation of lopping are taken in closed door meetings by male *Panchayat* members although women feed livestock and do most other agricultural and domestic work is probably in part responsible for them.

On the one hand, although the state took control of the forest land, forest resources were exploited by politicians and bureaucrats in collusion with businessmen for private gains, and on the other hand, the disappearance of community control and restrictions on the user rights of villagers reduced the incentive and ability of them to use forest sustainability in the central Himalayan plains.

Community control was based on the force of social customs and norms which enabled community agreement to be reached on the use of forest resources whereas the fear of social boycott ensured that no one violated it.

A different situation has involved experiment with social forestry in West Bengal which was one of the first states in India to introduce social forestry. This is often undertaken on degraded lands. It has been found that in West Bengal with social forestry, which involves communal management of the forest, productivity or income levels, increase in the villages adopting this and bio-diversity rises.

The social forestry programme in India has three main objectives: (i) to protect the environment; (ii) to satisfy the rising demand for raw materials such as fuel-wood and industrial raw material; and (iii) to raise the level of income, particularly of rural people. The programme has however been criticised on several grounds (Burgess 1992). By referring to the official statistics of Karnataka Government, it has been argued that in South India, the programme has made increasing use of farmland for growing eucalyptus which in turn has meant less land is available for the poor. This in turn means declining output, increasing price and rising malnutrition (Shiva and Bandyopadhyay 1985). However this argument has been strongly refuted with statistical figures by Shyam Sundar (1984). The Forestry Department also rejects the view that farmers were forced to plant eucalyptus and says that a large variety of species were made available to farmers at no cost (Karnataka Forestry Department 1988). However while such criticisms have been made against current social forestry programme in South India, it has also been noted that the area of land used for growing eucalyptus under the programme is very small compared with those used for other agricultural purposes (Shyam Sundar 1984). Furthermore, one cannot dispute the fact that when better lands are used for food crops under green revolution technology, inferior lands should be used for social forestry which by taking pressure off existing forests, produces beneficial effects on the environment. Nadkarni (1989) argues that handing over the power of forest management to the local people would not necessarily solve all the problems and that even when they had free access to the forest, the poor had hardly shown any more concern for the environment than had private commercial interests.

Support from Nadkarni's argument can, to some extent, be found in Russia. It has been claimed that with the demise of the USSR under the weakened power of the central government of the Russian Federation, the conservation in local areas has suffered. Under the communist regime, the USSR maintained by force a system of pristine forested areas on a large scale and local people were not even allowed to use them for excursion. These were protected by force. Now the central government does not have sufficient finances to afford enforcement. Local people are therefore encroaching on these protected areas and in some cases cattle grazing is occurring on them. Because of political changes, pre-existing methods of governance in Russia are disintegrating. Thus it would seem that in some cases, decentralisation will favour environmental conservation for sustainable development; in other cases it will not. It is dangerous to generalise.

Traditional rights do not always promote environmental preservation and sustainable development.

A case in point is in the tribal areas of Northeast India. In this region, population growth has been very rapid and income aspirations are rising (Tisdell, 1995). The traditional form of agriculture in the tribal areas of this region is slash-and-burn and property rights to use land have been devised by tribal groups to support this type of agriculture. This system of rights is very difficult to change.

Given the socio-economic dynamics of the region, intensification and extensification of slash-and-burn agriculture has occurred. As a result, land degradation has accelerated, yields from slash-and-burn (*jhum*) agriculture are declining and considerable biodiversity loss has occurred (Ramakrishnan, 1992, 1995). The length of the *jhum* cycle has now shortened in some cases to 4-5 years and a greater land area is under cultivation and exposed to the elements at any one time. This has accelerated biodiversity loss because the composition of available habitats for species has changed and botanical species requiring other than a few years to re-establish themselves are unable to survive.

As Ramakrishnan (1992) points out *jhum* cycles of 25-30 years are relatively economic as well as in relative harmony with nature. When *jhum* cycles are reduced to 4-5 years, the yield to effort ratio of this type of agriculture becomes very low and this form of agriculture is relatively uneconomic and unsustainable. The need exists to find a settled form of agriculture which is more sustainable, economic and environmentally acceptable.

Although settled forms of conservation agriculture have been developed e.g. alley-cropping with hedgerows, transition to this type of agriculture is difficult (impossible) given traditional land rights. In Mizoram for example, the *Mizos* allocate fallowed land to be brought into cultivation by the village to the villagers by ballot. Individuals have no right to particular pieces of land in perpetuity for all villagers have a right to the balloted land. Private rights in the cultivation of a piece of land only exist for a family as long as the area where it is located is under cultivation by the village.

It has proven very difficult for the Government of Mizoram to modify the system so as to encourage forms of settled agriculture. The Government of Mizoram has through its New Land Use Policy (NLUP) attempted to alienate some land from the tribal system for use by individuals in settled agriculture. Success has been limited, but greatest in the neighbourhood of Aizawl, the capital of Mizoram. However, it should be noted that settled agriculture in this region needs to be of conservation-type rather than conventional if it is to be sustainable. The situation is different as far as allocation of *jhum* lands in Arunachal Pradesh is concerned but land rights are still problematic and an impediment to the introduction of settled agriculture (Roy and Puri, 1995).

If sustainable development is to be achieved in Northeast India, institutional changes and variations in legal practice in relation to land rights will be necessary. This amounts in effect to a change in governance. At the same time, scientific and technical research should be accelerated to develop improved methods of settled agriculture for the region. It should be noted that not all interest groups in Northeast India want a change in land rights. Some are able to exploit the current situation it seems to their own advantage (Roy and Puri, 1995).

THE INTERVENTIONIST STATE AND CORRUPTION

Corruption increases the cost of and reduces the benefits from development programmes to the society. As a result, the gap between the potential and realised achievements continues to widen thereby further undermining the country's chances of achieving sustainable development. Corruption grows in an institutional environment which fosters directly underproductive activities. Since political parties, bureaucracy, law enforcement agency and judiciary are all vital components of the state apparatus, it is important to comment on the theoretical perspective of the role of the state in economic development since the 1950s.

The Keynesian revolution by casting doubts on the ability of the free market to achieve optimal results gave a strong boost to economic planning and the interventionist role of the activist state (Shapiro and Taylor 1992). Keynes' emphasis on domestic economic prosperity as opposed to international concern was extended to support national industrialisation strategies in less developed economies. Support for such strategies also came from the writings of Singer (1950) and Prebisch (1959) which argued that due to the differences in price and income elasticities between LDCs and developed countries, raw material exports of LDCs could not pay for their manufactured imports. Their arguments were extensively used by LDCs to justify the application of Import Substituting Industrialisation (ISI) strategy in development.

However, persistent attacks against state intervention in the market in the form of quantitative restrictions, licenses etc. came from

Bauer (1972, 1984), Buchanan (1980), Bhagwati (1982), Lal (1983), Bardhan (1984) and from many others as well.

Bauer, learning from his experience of Indian development, argued that government failures which manifest themselves in corruption, mismanagement etc. are more important than market failure, and that market imperfections are caused and not cured by government interventions. Hence the state should not interfere with the market mechanism which has the capacity to self-correct. Buchanan specifically raised the issue of economic loss resulting from profit seeking activities of the privileged groups in the presence of the state. Bhagwati consistently argued that under state intervention and a Quantitative Restriction (QR) regime, competition for rents which accrue to the winners of government largesse turns into widespread directly unproductive profit-seeking (DUP) activities such as lobbying, active politics, bribe paying etc. with the result that normal market activity may be replaced by activities seeking government favours. Deepak Lal agrees with Bauer that in an interventionist state the bureaucratic failure may be worse than market failure. Bardhan extends Lal's argument to the Indian case where he finds that the conflicts between bureaucrats and industrialists over appropriation of rents interact with India's traditional rural-urban disparities to perpetuate stagnation. North (1981) suggests that institutional inefficiency creates within the state, political and economic efficiency which transform the state into a vested interest group. For Lal, one of the most ardent neoclassicals of the 1980s, if the free market system cannot operate then the activist state ought to be prevented from being controlled by special interest groups, if necessary, even by a ruthless and undemocratic government. This has the indirect implication that democracy which can foster the growth of vested interest groups is not compatible with growth.

The following two important points seem to emerge from these discussions:

(1) corruption seems to grow within rent seeking activities which thrive under inward oriented development which relies on state intervention and market restriction. Therefore under outward oriented development, market restriction is removed, state intervention disappears along with rent seeking activities and corruption.

(2) The other point is that a ruthless autocratic government will be able to destroy the special interest groups, open up the economy for outward oriented development and eliminate rent seeking activities and corruption.

But neither of these points would be applicable to all the developing economies. For example, to substantiate the first point the reference of East Asian economies is drawn. But in South Korea, state intervention and market restrictions did not completely disappear with the implementation of outward oriented development programmes. Despite corruption and rent seeking during the Import Substituting Industrialisation (ISI) period in both South Korea and Taiwan, the state intervention significantly improved the performance of these economies and made them highly competitive.

On the other hand, the corruption which existed in the Indian economy during the IS period for 34 years from 1956 to 1990 seem to have grown on a massive scale after the opening up of the Indian economy. Therefore, corruption and inefficiency are not always entirely due to rent seeking under a QR regime.

Secondly, a ruthless authoritarian state also consists of individuals who use the state apparatus to achieve the state's development goals. These individuals can easily become corrupt, and can become their own vested interest group, creating a trade-off between economic efficiency and state power as well as extracting rents from the private sector which neoclassical political economy failed to recognise (Shapiro 1988).

One important reason as to why the development economists in the 1950s and 1960s failed to recognise these problems seems to be that they accepted the traditional neoclassical separation of the economic and political spheres (Shapiro and Taylor 1992). In the modern state, the traditional separation between economic, political and even judicial spheres seem to be disappearing. Where this happens, the state can assume the character of a predatory state where the ruler or the government more or less systematically employs its position to extract money or resources from its citizens, without providing very much in return. A purely predatory state does not have any interest in economic policy other than fostering its own welfare by systematically devoting itself to creating and capturing rents of various kinds with the aid of government machinery (Lundahl 1996).

Corruption can be found in almost every polity in many forms. In many African countries, it is virtually impossible to get a government job without paying for it, even if the persons are from the same tribe or clan as those who are in charge of appointment and dismissal (Lundahl 1996). In a predatory state, since corruption originates at the top i.e. President or Prime Minister and other ministers, the magnitude of corruption continues to grow to eventually encompass all bureaucrats and agents of most state apparatus.

Law enforcement agents such as customs and police officials need to be bribed to discharge even their normal duties. Courts pass verdicts in favour of those who pay most. For the school children to pass their examinations, the teachers would have to be bribed. The personnel at state hospitals cater to those who pay them directly. Private sector enterprises factor bribes into their production costs. The presence of a corrupt public sector is in itself an indirect invitation to the private sector to try to secure a proportion of rents being generated by government action (Lundahl 1996).

At every stage of economic activity there seems to exist a principal-agent problem which encourages managers to pursue their own objectives of increasing their benefits even though this reduces the profits of the owners. If the cost of benefits is entirely borne by the owner then the manager has an incentive to increase these benefits substantially. In a predatory state the problem spreads upward in an ascending order from the lowest public official to the head of the state for whom the owner is the society at large.

Thus the existence of such a state produces effects which are extremely negative from the viewpoint of sustainable development.

Law Enforcement and Bureaucrats

People are more likely to commit crime if the likelihood of being caught is low and if a bribe is always the easiest way to eliminate the possibility of being caught. In a corrupt system, the damage to the victims of crime will tend to increase as the laws are enforced more leniently because people will be encouraged to engage in criminal activities. In other words, as the chance of getting caught decreases, more people will be willing to take the chance with the result that the criminal activity and the damage to the crime victims will increase which, in effect, will increase the cost from crime to the society.

When committing crime becomes a norm in a society, it becomes a part of rent seeking activity. There are instances of cases where assets of private individuals have been transferred to the ruler by threats or use of violence or by court decision (Millet 1977).

Inefficient and corrupt law enforcement machinery cannot enforce contractual obligations, uphold and protect property rights and as a result, fail to keep the transaction cost of all economic activities at all levels to the minimum. North (1981) argues that the specification of property rights is the most essential requisite for economic performance, subject to technological change. Referring to the famous Coase Theorem (1937) he observes that clearly defined property rights and zero transaction costs will provide correct incentives to individuals.

Such incentives under free trade will lead to efficient allocation of resources among individuals. However, this cannot happen without an efficient and honest law enforcement machinery. North also admits that changes in the institutional factors and in the theory of the state (which was mentioned earlier in this paper), account for the presence and persistence of inefficient property rights.

Bureaucracy and law enforcement agency are interlinked. Bureaucrats cannot properly implement any government policy if the law enforcement agents are corrupt. Corrupt bureaucracy provides a strong incentive to law enforcement officers to be corrupt as well. A bureaucrat will have a strong tendency to be corrupt if expected income from corrupt practice is significantly higher than the normal salary and perks. Such income should also be high enough to more than offset the cost of likely detection (bribes, job loss etc.).

However in a predatory or semi-predatory state, where the government's only interest is to preserve and further its own vested interest rather than to formulate and apply correct economic policies, the bureaucrats at all levels will be corrupt as public offices are used for granting/selling favours at all levels of the state. In such a situation, the likelihood of the corruption of a bureaucrat being detected is smaller and the costs of avoiding detection and punishment are also smaller. When these happen, the gap between the expected income from corrupt behaviour and the normal salary of a bureaucrat also can be smaller for a bureaucrat to be induced to adopt corrupt practice. Such would be the situation in many Third World countries where the size of the bureaucracy is very large.

However, in recent years some bureaucracies in some countries are embracing institutional change in the process of implementation of development programmes through participatory approaches under which the state bureaucracy joins hands with NGOs which give local people more control over research and development processes (Farrington and Bebbington 1993, 1994; Thrupp, Cabarle and Zazueta 1994). Due to the widely perceived view that since most state agencies are centralised, authoritarian, formalistic and inefficient bureaucracies and are unable to accept and adopt the imaginative change (Thompson 1995; Mouzelis 1994; Wunseh and Olowu 1990; Korten 1980), it is felt that the state bureaucracy, by joining hands with NGOs and local people in the participatory approach, can implement development programmes which are sustainable.

However, experiments in such participatory approaches to development have been confined to a few rural projects in a few countries. Large scale application of such an approach to most development programmes can achieve good results provided, of course, we assume that all institutional preconditions such as the state is developmental, not predatory, the bureaucracy is honest and efficient, law enforcement agents are honest and efficient, the representative rural people who are involved in participatory approaches (as the entire village cannot be involved) have no special/vested interest different from that of the rural community at large and the community at large, bureaucracy and law enforcement agents are not politicised. These are essential components of the institutional framework without which good governance and sustainable development may continue to remain an elusive goal. Unfortunately we cannot make such assumptions for most of the developing economies.

Indian Situation: Some Comments

The Indian state cannot be classified as either a predatory or developmental state. In a predatory state, Lundahl (1996) argues the government action serves to keep the technology stagnant, to hold back the accumulation of physical and human capital, to prevent efficient allocation and use of resources and to distort the income distribution severely by creating a strong concentration in favour of the members of the ruling clique. In India's case, while income distribution may have favoured the wider body of members and supporters of the ruling clique, on other counts, the effects of state action may not have been so negative. On the other hand, although the promotion of general welfare and improvement in the standard of living of people have always been among its objectives, it cannot still be called a developmental state as it has, since the late 1980s, been paralysed by the action of vested interests which have led to the phenomenal growth of corruption and systematic incapacitation of all institutions fundamental to good governance in a developmental state.

Politics dominates daily life as political parties vie with one another for power and plunder of the public purse. High taxes and a complex system of comprehensive controls have produced one of the world's largest and most thriving underground economies accounting for around 50 percent of economic activity. India's economic reform programs appear to have failed to effect the necessary radical institutional reforms. Only reforms which have been politically easy and not threatened the special interests created by the comprehensive control regime have been implemented. The rents continue to accrue to the most powerful interest groups - politicians, bureaucrats, union leaders and members, public sector employees, selected business groups and farmers. All private property rights are still not guaranteed or protected from government encroachment (Kamath 1993). On the state of institutions and corruption, *The Statesman Weekly* (1996) notes that not in the last thirty years since Indira Gandhi set about institutionalising corruption, abusing power, emasculating the bureaucracy and subverting the judiciary, have governments been willing to accept the fundamental postulate of the rule of law. As for the government of Narashimha Rao, it further adds that it has seen brazen attempts to protect corrupt ministers. There has been interference with the due process of law to protect the family/individuals, and the list is endless. There has been subversion of the Central Bureau of Investigation (CBI) to deny investigation of the First Information Report (FIR) in the Bofors case and to refuse to question the Hinduja brothers, Win Chadha and Ottavio Quattrochi despite the knowledge that each of them received money from Bofors into their accounts. The CBI Chief Secretary confessed to the Supreme Court in *Hawala* matter that political interference prevented the Bureau from doing their duty. In the last five years, the other corruptions such as the securities scam, the two sugar scams, the telecom scandal, the cover-up in the *Hawala* case etc. also became intrinsic components of the government (*The Statesman Weekly* 1996). While during Indira and Rajiv Gandhi's Prime Ministership institutions were systematically destroyed, public interest was confused with survival and the distinction between public property and domestic petty cash became blurred, Prime Minister Rao's defence of outrageous corruption and abuse of power and the substitution of one family by another in the process, suggests that everything was being subordinated to tactics not principles, the interests of power not the demands of governance and to the belief that everything was fair in politics and power *(The Statesman Weekly* 1996). Apart from these, corruption was also present in significant measure at the provincial and local administration levels. For example, it is common knowledge that in India a thriving parallel (unofficial) market exists in education. Appointments to the position of teachers at schools, students' places in engineering and medical colleges can be purchased and students wishing to do well in their examination and obtain better results need to be customers in this parallel market for education.

Concluding Remarks

Despite the neoclassical economists' unflinching faith in the capacity of the free market to cure all economic ills of developing countries, free market policies in the absence of good governance do not seem to achieve much success.

Neoclassicists seems to implicitly believe that free market policies will create the appropriate institutions. But if the state systematically destroys the institutions who will force the state to restore the institutions to their rightful status? Neoclassicals perhaps would suggest that people would regulate the behaviour of the state. But when the state assumes the predatory status, what will happen then? Neoclassicals do not seem to find any appropriate answer other than to say that the neoclassical theory had not conceived of a modern theory of state which incorporated all three powers - political, economic and legal, within the state. Although there are corruptions in South Korea and Taiwan, governance in those countries is far superior to that in India. The institutional forces in these two countries were significantly influenced by their intellectual and geographical proximity to Japan which strengthened Confucian cultural values of these societies.

On the other hand, India is not in the geographical and intellectual proximity of such a culture as the Japanese. It is surrounded by countries most of which were parts of an undivided Indian sub-continent. Therefore it is in proximity with parts of its own culture. Thus good economic policies will not achieve sustainable development if they are not implemented properly. But effective implementation of policies depends on good governance. Thus, it can be argued that good governance is just as important as and even more important than good economic policies. However, good governance is crucially dependent on the presence of appropriate institutions. Therefore sound economic policies must be supported by appropriate institutions or effective institutional changes for sustainable growth and development. This analysis also has shown that in some cases, good governance can be achieved by decentralised and participatory approaches but in other cases by centralised governance structure. Hence there is no universal governance structure which is applicable to all situations.

REFERENCES

Agarwal, B. (1989) "Rural Women, Poverty and Natural Resources", *Economic and Political Weekly*, 24(43).

Agarwal, B. (1994) "Gender and Command Over Property: A Critical Gap in Economic Analysis and Policy in South Asia", *World Development*, 22(10).

Bardhan, P.K. (1984) *The Political Economy of Development in India*, Oxford: Basil Blackwell.

Bauer, P.T. (1972) *Dissent on Development*, London: Widenfield and Nicholson.

Bauer, P.T. (1984) *Reality and Rhetoric: Studies in the Economics of Development*, London: Widenfield and Nicholson.

Bhagwati, J.N. (1982) "Directly Unproductive Profit Seeking (DUP) Activities", *Journal of Political Economy*, 90.

Buchanan, J., "Rent Seeking and Profit Seeking", in Buchanan, J.M., Tollison, R.D. and Tullock, G. (eds) (1980) *Toward a Theory of Rent Seeking Society*, College Station, Tx: Texas T&M University Press.

Burgess, M. (1992) "Dangers of Environmental Extremism, Analysis of Debate Over India's Social Forestry Programme", *Economic and Political Weekly*, 27(40).

Chambers, R. (1988) "Bureaucratic Reversals and Local Diversity", *IDS Bulletin*, 19(4).

Clark, C. and Roy K.C. (1996) *Comparing Development Patterns in Asia*, Boulder, Co.: Lynne Rienner.

Crow, B. (1992) "Rural Livelihoods: Action From Above", in Bernstein, H., Crow, B. and Johnson, H. (eds) (1992) *Rural Livelihoods: Crises and Responses*, Milton Keynes: Open University and Oxford University Press.

Dasgupta, S. and Maity, A.K. (1986) *The Rural Energy Crisis, Poverty and Women's Role in Five Indian Villages*, Geneva: ILO.

Duvvury, N. (1989) "Women in Agriculture: A Review of the Indian Agriculture", *Economic and Political Weekly*, 24(43).

Farrington, J. and Bebbington, A.J. "From Research to Innovation: Getting the Most from Interaction with NGOs", in Scoones, I. and Thomson, J. (eds) (1993) *Beyond Farmer First: Rural People's Knowledge*, Agricultural Research and Extension Practice, London: Intermediate Technology Publications.

Farrington, J., Bebbington, A.J., Wellard, K. and Lewis, D.I. (1994) *Reluctant Partners: Non-Governmental Organizations, the State and Sustainable Agricultural Development*, London: Routledge.

Kamath, S.J. (1993) "The Promise and Perils of India's Economic Reforms", *Policy*, Autumn.

Kandiyoti, R., "Women and Rural Development Policies: The Changing Agenda", in Wilber, C.K. and Jameson, K.P. (eds) (1992) *The Political Economy of Development and Underdevelopment*, New York: McGraw-Hill.

Korten, D. (1980) "Community Organisations and Rural Development: A Learning Process Approach", *Public Administration Review*, 40(5).

Lal, D. (1983) *The Poverty of Development Economics*, London: Institute of Economic Affairs.

Lundahl, Mats (1996) "The Economics of Kleptocracy: Some Reflections on Underdevelopment and the Predatory State", in Roy, K.C., Blomqvist, H.C. and Hossain, I. (eds) *Development That Lasts*, New Delhi: New Age International.

Millet, R. (1977) *Guardians of the Dynasty*, Mary Knoll, N.Y., Orbis Books.

Mishra, H.R. (1982) "Balancing Human Needs and Conservation in Nepal's Royal Chitwan National Park", *Ambio*, 11, 246-251.

Mouzelis, N., "The State in Late Development: Historical and Comparative Perspectives", in Booth, D. (ed.) (1994) *Rethinking Social Development: Theory, Research and Practice*, Harlow, U.K.: Longman Scientific and Technical.

Nadkarni, M.V. (1989) *The Political Economy of Forest Use and Management*, New Delhi: Sage Publishers.

North, D. (1981) *Structure and Change in Economic History*, New York: W.W. Norton.

Prebisch, R. (1959) "Commercial Policy in the Underdeveloped Countries", *American Economic Review*, 49.

Ramakrishnan, P.S. (1992) *Shifting Agriculture and Sustainable Development of North-Eastern India*, UNESCO, Paris and Parthenon, Cornforth, U.K.

Ramakrishnan, P.S. (1995) "Sustainable Rural Development with People's Participation in the Asia Context". Pp 421–439 in S.A. Samad, T. Watanabe and S.J. Kim, *People's Initiatives for Sustainable Development: Lessons of Experience*, Asian and Pacific Development Centre, Kuala Lumpur, Malaysia.

Rath, N. (1985) "Garibi Hatao: Can IRDP Do It?" *Economic and Political Weekly*, 20(6).

Roy, K.C. and Tisdell, C.A. (1993a) "Poverty Amongst Females in Rural India: Gender-Based Deprivation and Technological Change", *Economic Studies*, 31(4).

Roy, K.C. and Tisdell, C.A. (1993) "Technological Change, Environment and Poor Women, Specially Tribal Women in India", *Savings and Development*, 17(4).

Roy, K.C. and Tisdell, C.A., "Gandhi's Concept of Development and Nehru's Centralised Planning", in Roy, K.C., Tisdell, C.A. and Sen, R.K. (eds) (1995) *Economic Development and Environment - A Case Study of India*, New Delhi: Oxford University Press (paperback).

Roy, N.C. and Puri, P.K. (1995) "Risk, Land Reform and Agricultural Productivity in Arunachal Pradesh", A paper presented at the International Seminar on Environment, Biodiversity and sustainable Development in North-East India, held 26 and 27 September 1995, North-Eastern Hill University, Mizoram Campus, Aizawl, Mizoram, India.

Schumacher, E.F. (1962) *Roots of Economic Growth*, Varanasi: Gandhian Institute of Studies.

Shapiro, H. (1988) "State Intervention and Industrialization: The Origins of the Brazilian Automobile Industry", PhD Dissertation, New Haven, Conn.: Department of Economics, Yale University.

Shapiro, H. and Taylor, L., "The State and Industrial Strategy", in Wilber, C.K. and Jameson, K.P. (eds) (1992) *The Political Economy of Development and Underdevelopment*, New York: McGraw-Hill.

Shiva, V. and Bandyopadhyay, J. (1985) *Ecological Audit of Eucalyptus Cultivation*, Dehradun: English Book Depot.

Shyam Sundar, S. (1984) "Forest Development and the Eucalyptus Controversy in Karnataka", *Workshop on Eucalyptus Plantation: Papers and Proceedings*, Indian Statistical Institute: Economics Analysis Unit, ISI, Bangalore.

Singer, H. (1950) "The Distribution of Gains Between Investing and Borrowing Countries", *American Economic Review*, 40.

Somanathan, E. (1991) "Deforestation, Property Rights and Incentives in Central Himalayas", *Economic and Political Weekly*, 26(4).

The Statesman Weekly (1996) February 17, April 20, May 11, Calcutta: The Statesman House.

Thomson, J. (1995) "Participatory Approaches in Government Bureaucracies: Facilitating the Process of Institutional Change", *World Development*, 23(9).

Thrupp, L.A., Cabarle, B. and Zaueta, A., "Linking Grass Roots' Actions to Policy-Making for Sustainable Development in Latin America", in Scoones, I. and Thomson, J. (eds) (1994) *Beyond Farmier First: Rural People's Knowledge*, Agricultural Research and Extension Practice, London: Intermediate Technology Publication Ltd.

Tisdell, C.A. (1995) "Biodiversity, Conservation and sustainable Development: Challenges for North-East India in Context", *Working Papers on Conservation and Sustainable Development*, No. 21, Department of Economics, The University of Queensland, Brisbane, 4072.

van Arkadia, B. (1989) "The Role of Institutions in Development", *Proceedings of the World Bank Annual Conference on Development Economics*, Washington DC: The World Bank.

World Bank (1983) World Development Report, New York: Oxford University Press.

Wunseh, J.S. and Olowu, D. (1990) *The Failure of the Centralized State: Institutions and Self-Governance in Africa*, Boulder, Co.: Westview Press.

Yugandhar, B.N. and Raju, B.N. (1992) "Government Delivery Systems for Rural Development - Malady Remedy Analysis", *Economic and Political Weekly*, 27(35).

4 GOVERNANCE IN DEVELOPMENT: A CHALLENGING PARTNERSHIP

H A LOUW

INTRODUCTION

The history of development shows a clear picture of various efforts to come to an understanding of the what, why, how and by whom of development. Over the past decades a continuous effort has been made to come to an understanding of the ultimate solution to the difficult question of the societal welfare.

Such efforts have led to a shift from the so-called growth approach, focusing on man and environment to improve material wealth as priority to a more human centred approach, focusing on human development as priority. This was the result of the disappointing development experience over the past forty years, which led to its peak in the 1980's to the extent that it is called the lost decade. (Loots, 1994:17). The implication of this new orientation demands a fundamental reconsideration of the nature of and priorities in approaching development. It confirms the multi-dimensional nature of development but also change the focus of the primary reason and goal of development. Considering the fact that people are considered as the focus and point of departure of development it is therefore inevitable that a reconsideration of the previous deterministic or top-down approach should take place in favour of a more participative approach where top-down and bottom-up inputs are linked into an integrated approach based on interdependence.

The relationships amongst stakeholders and role-players involved in a situation therefore needs to be reconsidered. On this basis a consideration of governance suitable to promote development can be discussed.

This paper will therefore focus on:

- finding clarity about the concepts involved
- considering the position and roles of role-players involved in development in order to determine the impact thereof on a suitable governance model
- practical implications of governance in development

- an overview of the current situation in SA (South Africa) relating to governance
- SA in the Indian Ocean rim context as part of the international framework of governance

The Concepts of Governance And Development

The changed focus in the 1990's where a distinct role is attributed to "political culture", in terms of which a distinct role is ascribed to people through institutions represents a departure from earlier economic and rationalist orientations. This implies that human nature, choice and preferences become the fundamental point of departure when development is considered.

In terms of the fundamental motivation why development demands attention it can be stated that it is primarily aimed at improving the well-being of people. To achieve this goal, it is necessary that human potential be developed optimally in order to enable people to fulfil their basic calling and satisfy their needs for well-being.

Development should therefore be viewed as an effort to enable people to optimise their potential in order to achieve their desired well-being. It is however realised that although people are recognised as creative and active they still have to survive in a context which represents a reality that forms part of the challenge to and impact on them. Himmelstrand (1994: 17-18) sheds further light on the discussion when he argues that development is a normative concept, but must also be defined on the basis of a scientific understanding of processes of historical change. In considering development it is therefore necessary to consider the fundamental characteristics thereof. Development as structural change can be considered on the basis of six criteria:

- The capability of a given society to, increasingly, use its own resources of land, minerals, and man-power to feed its own people - even in a situation of continuous population growth.
- The, increasing, capability of a country/society to produce or make available to farmers/peasants the basic tools needed in food production, or, in countries with a lack of arable land, the tools in other production necessary for the importation of food.
- The establishment, either through consent or struggle, of a set of shared transaction rules regulating relationships between the main actors involved in economic or other important social activities, that is accepted by the majority as legally and/or morally binding.
- Without indigenous entrepreneurs and labour there is no further development.

- A development of export/import relationships but with a reasonably balanced transaction of this trade so as to avoid too much of "unequal exchange" or exploitation. The growth of a considerable measure of autonomy, self-rule and democracy is required in any given national, or other unit in order for it to qualify as clearly developing or developed.

Development is therefore a multi-dimensional process. From this perspective it is therefore possible to define it as: Development is the achievement of the realistic aspirations by a group, community or society for their own lives or well-being in terms of their basic physical needs as well as their ideals (spiritual or psychological needs) which may imply economic growth, political autonomy and social reconstruction over a broad base as well as cultural change, through the growing competence of the members to manipulate or relate to their situation or environment effectively in a way that will not compromise the opportunity of future generations to also improve their well-being.

Development efforts in the past did not necessarily focus on the wrong aspects, e.g. economic growth. It represents part of the dimensions representing the whole scenario comprising development. It rather refers to the way in which development was approached. The World Bank, for example, took the argument that the medicine itself was not wrong, but that the institutional framework within which structural adjustment was implemented was inappropriate (see Kiely, 1995).

Based on the growing awareness of the failure of efforts based on deterministic and dependency relations manifesting in e.g. using the state for engineering purposes, development discourse has in recent years come to focus on the relationship between democracy and development. It is increasingly argued that "democracy is good for development" to the extent that it may be a causal factor for development (Hyden, 1996: 92). This perspective is reflected in the change towards a focus on the so-called "new-institutionalism" that is largely a voluntarist-perspective but argues that social action is primarily integrative, aimed at going beyond self-interest (Himmelstrand p.315).

Development demands a basis for integration of all relevant aspects or dimensions as well as a relationship amongst its stakeholders that is conducive to the realisation of the aspirations and therefore satisfaction of the needs to improve human well-being.

The World Bank argues that what is needed to achieve development is "good governance". This implies in the words of Linda

Chalker, the British Minister of Overseas development in 1992, : "... accountability and transparency in the decision-making process. It means political pluralism with free and fair elections. It means the rule of law and freedom of expression. It means far less spending on military hardware and war-making and much more on primary schools and healthcare. It means fighting the cancers of graft and nepotism" (Kiely, 1995: 131). The emphasis is therefore on public accountability, pluralism and the rule of law. It implies a move away from a typical top down government approach to a combination thereof with a bottom-up approach in order to implement the principle of interdependence as basic characteristic of good governance.

Governance in essence therefore refers to the relationship amongst the various stakeholders in a development situation. In the case of the current thinking on development it refers to a type of relationship where recognition is given to the position of the human agency or the position of people in development mediated through relevant institutions suitable to facilitate a conducive environment for development.

The Role of the State in Development

Whether or not the state plays a role conducive to development is not predetermined by specific laws, but rather depends on a wide variety of circumstances, like the general societal characteristics, its class structure, level of development, nature and power of bureaucracy, validity of the insights of those who govern and the position and role of the target population.

The assumption underlying much of development thinking relating to the state is that it is a neutral arbiter of disputes, who will inevitably adopt those policies which will be best suited for everyone. Failure to realise the envisioned goals is normally ascribed to inappropriate development theories or incompetent technocrats. The major concern is therefore to evaluate policies in terms of what is appropriate and correct. The primary task of the practitioner is to correct the technical failure of policies.

The ideal and objective image of the state as decision-maker and facilitator of change has however not been accepted in general. This can be explained by various arguments, e.g.

- there are no laws that govern development in a way that allows perfect decisions.
- decisions and ideas do have the potential to influence people in their decisions and behaviour but they must appeal to those involved who have the capacity to change society.

- ideas or decisions are understood on the basis of the interpretations of those involved, which relates to the idea of Anthony Giddens , about the double hermeneutic, which implies the state's interpretations undergo a re-interpretation by its subjects without any guarantee that it will be perceived as correct or desirable.

It is therefore evident that the state should not be seen as the sole and final solution to development needs. This was further argued by the neo-liberals in stating that:

- state interventions in market mechanisms serve the interest of certain lobbies.
- privately run enterprises can do more efficiently most of what is publicly undertaken.
- the state on its own does not have the capacity to finetune the economy which leads to inflation rather than more employment.
- a free-market and for that matter an open society is necessary.

These arguments led to the notion of minimum government as the optimal situation for development. It is evident however that to reduce the state only to a night watchman who should take responsibility for certain functions like internal order, defence, basic education, etc., is in itself also naive. It fails to take note of those cases where state intervention really contributed significantly to development. It also overstates the role of the economy in terms of the nature and pace of social change which brings it very close to the Marxist orientation of economic determinism.

These two viewpoints could be viewed as representing two extreme positions namely the state as source of all wisdom and provision, while on the other side a very limited role is suggested. Recent developments pose interesting further possibilities however.

It is well recognised that not only in the case of development in Western Europe but also in the case of the newly industrialising countries (NIC's) the state played a meaningful role in development. The state has proved to be a catalyst in the development of Asian countries through a strong and interventionist position and role. This role of catalyst in successful development has however not materialised in Africa or Latin America (Hyden, 1996: 102).

It is the structure and functioning of the state which is therefore to be held responsible for both the failures and the relatively few success stories. Booth (1994:127) confirms this argument by stating that, "certain states are better than others at drawing up and implementing development strategies and that it is in fact the actual structure of the state that is the most crucial aspect for understanding why late developers with comparable starting points and resources have performed so unevenly within the world..." The evaluation of the role of the state in different ways and the different expectations can probably largely be ascribed to the various ideas existing about the ideal role the state should play in development, in other words the fact that there are always alternative expectations presented as explanations of failure. Against the background of some of the ideas mentioned above, *Figure 1* illustrates the shifts in ideological perspectives on development:

Figure 1 **Shifts in Ideological Perspectives on Development 1955-90**

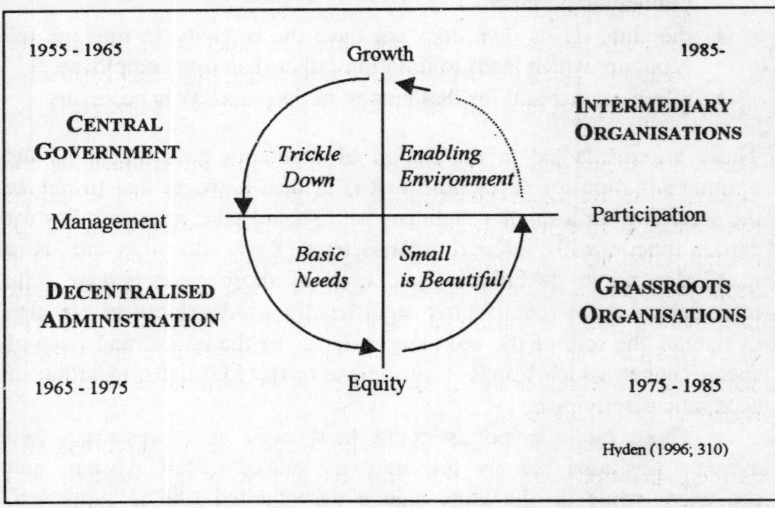

It is therefore evident that the expected role of the state has moved from a centralised top down role, through a more needs based approach and grassroots dominated approach to a stage where the state is put in a new relation to the planned beneficiary through intermediary organizations that functions in an 'enabling environment'. This does not mean that the second last option namely the recognition of the value and necessity of grassroots organizations is neglected. It rather implies that a more effective co-ordination, link and process of empowerment of the groundswell is effected. This point of departure can serve as the basis from which the viewpoint of the World Bank namely that a new institutional framework is necessary for development can be approached.

A possible alternative

Booth (1994:127) argues that: "... the later a country joins the development race, the more it requires guidance from 'above', chiefly from the state or other centralised institutions". The argument is that countries like Norway, Finland, New Zealand and Australia that began their industrialisation relatively late but managed to become more or less part of the so-called developed or First World usually reveals:

- successful agricultural modernisation, resulting not only in increased productivity but also in a certain rural egalitarianism capable of engendering an important home market for industrial goods;
- strong links between the primary and secondary sectors, and more generally the creation of an industrial sector with, sooner or later, its own niche in the world market;
- a state apparatus playing a crucial role in the modernisation of agriculture as well as in its effective link with industry.

In the case of failures the state failed to achieve things like:

- Breaking up traditionally organised big real estates or failed to support resulting smallholders effectively.
- Avoiding the negative effect of failed development initiatives on the state. The more the state fails to develop the more it acquires 'anti-developmental' features. This can serve as stimulus for conflict due to unreasonable expectations and demands on the population. Successful development on the other hand brings balance and realism between state and planned beneficiary. This is the case because successful initiatives create a situation where aspirations and needs can be addressed and self-sufficiency grows amongst the planned beneficiaries.

It is therefore possible to argue that the role of the state should not be seen as a blue-print function which can be implemented universally but rather a case of a sensitive orientation based on the realities of the situation which should guide its role. The effects of the opposite like an unrealistically growing state apparatus that serves as a source to accommodate surplus labour, resources being spent wrongly in a way not relating to the typical development priorities of the moment like on agricultural modernisation, industrialisation, or education when necessary are well known throughout the Third World. Specific examples are Latin America and the Balkan. The explanation for this failure should be sought in the structure and functioning of their states. Due to their late-late character of industrialisation, their only chance to integrate their peripheral economies into the World economy was from above. The state should have intervened flexibly and selectively, in order not to destroy private initiative, but so as to bolster and direct it towards the modernisation of agriculture and the creation of strong linkages between industries and agricultural and mineral resources (Booth, 1994:142).

This implies therefore that these governments were not able to determine the strategic direction necessary within the framework of supply and demand in terms of available opportunity, skills, resources and needs.

Examples of countries where the opposite happened are Taiwan and South Korea. This was as a result of a strong interventionist state approach that kept a close watch over capital (indigenous as well as multinational) but not without strangling private initiative. This implies that in the case of these countries they had success despite state intervention. This indicates that in terms of Third World standards the exceptional structure of the state seems to be the key to the East Asian success story (Kiely, 1995:95). This is therefore a further indication that there is reason to reconsider the view that state intervention should be blamed for failure in development (Lundahl, 1995:1).

It is therefore possible to argue that the key issue for developing countries is not whether to have state intervention or not, but rather effective versus ineffective state intervention (Booth, 1994:144). The argument is therefore not to "roll-back" or minimise the state but rather to introduce measures to aim at a drastic rationalisation and realistic re-positioning of the state's administrative apparatus and a radical change in the relations of domination, so that balanced socio-economic development is no longer systematically sacrificed to politics. This does not mean that any effort of bypassing the state can succeed on the more general and national level.

Against the background of the previous discussion it is therefore possible to conclude that the typical extremes being projected for the role of the state in development namely no or absolute control should not necessarily serve as guideline to try to explain success or failure in development, as discussed earlier. The point of departure should rather be suitable state intervention in terms of the realities of the situation it is serving.

This may refer to a fundamental restructuring of the state apparatus of various less developed countries of which their current arrangements are anti-developmental. It is precisely these state structures which systematically prevent these countries from taking advantage of the developmental opportunities that are existing in the international world of which sub-Saharan Africa represents a great deal.

According to this approach the principles to be considered in positioning the state in the developing country could therefore be considered as:

- positioning and structuring according to the basic supply and demand in terms of resources, skills, demands and needs in the country and internationally. e.g. state capacity has to be monitored and arrangements done accordingly in terms of privatisation of functions etc.
- maintain the strategic direction followed in the interest of development and do not allow any deviation due to other agendas like personal goals or ideologies.
- adapt roles and functions as the development needs of the society changes, which implies a highly sensitive and dynamic state apparatus.

The specific functions of government could however be determined within the following guidelines in order to create a developmental climate and improve governance:

- **The state as provider**
  This includes producing a coherent set of major policies for socio-economic development. It also includes the construction of basic infra-structure, and other functions related to national sovereignty. This is imperative to create an environment conducive for development.
- **The state as facilitator**
  This relates to the implementation of policies and the control of environment for development. The importance of enhancing the indigenous private sector and to allow the emergence of as many initiatives as possible within the constellation of non public organizations. Government as facilitator is the most important component of a developmental state.
- **The state in partnership**
  The state has a responsibility to build a climate of co-operation and trust among the public, private and non-governmental sectors through the development of formal consultation processes, policy forums and joint marketing activities

internationally. From this certain development priorities may include:

- definition of roles of public and private sector in terms of development functions
- develop the potential to move from single centres of decision-making to multiple centres
- promote institutional development for sustainability by developing the capacity to implement policy change through appropriate policies, effective organizations, and the introduction of management techniques and skills
- increasing the accountability of office bureaucrats and clearly defining their roles and responsibilities
- improving the structures and systems of government in terms of the specific role and functions to be fulfilled at a specific stage. (Fitzgerald, et al, 1995: 77-78; Morris, 1995: 424).

ROLE OF SOCIETY IN DEVELOPMENT

It was argued earlier that democracy is important and necessary for development. This implies a specific relationship between state and its people based on ruling, accountability, as well as responsibility.

Normative democratic theory accepts as point of departure, that in a basic sense, the final control over the state and its government and its administrative apparatus should be vested in the citizens of the state.

Two fundamental principles underly this approach, namely:

- majority decisions
- government influenced by the people

This implies that:

- all citizens should be involved in some way in legislative and policy decisions.
- the rulers are accountable to the governed who have the power to get rid of them in a constitutional way.

The implications of accepting democratic principles for governance

Assuming that democracy is good for development, some fundamental implications going hand in hand with it should be considered. This implies that new aspects and role-players are introduced into the debate on governance in development.

Two of the primary concepts forming part of this perspective are, accepting that democracy is good for "social capital" and "civil society". Social capital refers to normative values and beliefs that citizens in their everyday lives share, or according to Tocqueville the "habits of heart and mind". These habits provide the impetus and basis for all sorts of rules. This implies that laws, regulations and development initiatives, etc., will barely be effective if these are not embedded in and reflecting, particular values and norms upheld by groups and communities in a society. Civil society again is considered as the forum in which habits of the heart and mind are being nurtured and developed (Hyden, 1996: 92). It can further be described as all activities which are outside of government structures, e.g. religious, cultural and economic activities, as well as political activities outside of government and state structures including the NGO, CBO structures (Morris, 1996: 427). *Figure 2* illustrates this position.

Figure 2 **Civil Society**

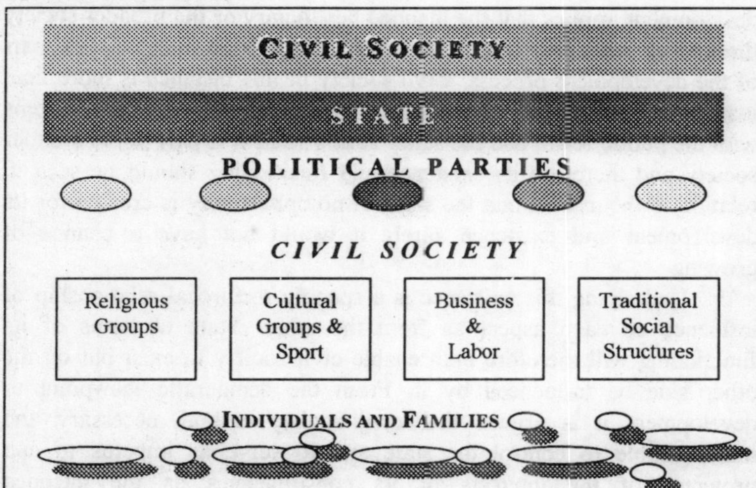

Both social capital and civil society can therefore be seen as analytical categories, independent of democracy. Investment in both is necessary however to achieve democracy and for that matter a basis for development.

Hyden (1996: 92), argues that this approach to development, namely that it should be based on democratic processes, is based on:

- The acceptance that a "top-down" approach to development does not work. This comes after it was accepted for a long time that the state is a rational instrument of controlling and promoting change for development. It is therefore accepted now that development wisdom also lodges in local communities and institutions and not necessarily in state bureaucracies. Concepts like "indigenous knowledge" and "popular participation" are therefore concepts receiving increasing prominence in the development debate.

- The other direction from which this approach stems is the problem of political apathy or lack of organization. Democracy requires organization based on an interest in public affairs.

The nature of the involvement and orientation of stakeholders as the basis of governance in the development process is therefore a determining factor in the possible direction and success of development.

It is therefore possible to argue that the dominant thinking on development implies that the planned beneficiary or the broader society through civil society, based on social capital, is an indispensable part of the development process. Civil society in this instance is more than just society but refers to that part which connects individual citizens with the public realm and the state. In this sense it is part of the broader society and therefore its existence and functioning should be seen in relation to the market and the state. If no opportunity is created for its development and existence surely it would not have a chance of growing.

Underlying this existence is a specific reciprocal relationship of influence on each aspect as from the other. State in terms of its functioning will therefore both enable civil society to exist but on the other side be influenced by it. From the democratic viewpoint to development it is argued that civil society is both necessary and indispensable to control the state and to serve as impetus to and protector of the interests of its constituencies as the intended beneficiaries of development. Civil society however also serves as the mediator of the popular will which prevents it from developing into uncontrolled mass behaviour or tyranny.

Civil society can therefore be seen as the "realm of organised social life", standing between individuals and political institutions of representation. Diamond (in Hyden, 1996: 95), argues that civil society acts to strengthen democracy by:

- containing the power of the state through public scrutiny;
- stimulating political participation by citizens;
- developing such democratic norms as tolerance and compromise;

- creating ways of articulating, aggregating and representing interests outside political parties, especially at the local level;
- mitigating conflict through cross-cutting, or overlapping, interest;
- recruiting and training political leaders;
- questioning and reforming existing democratic institutions and procedures; and
- disseminating information.

Civil society should therefore be considered as the basis on which the partnership between state and planned beneficiary in development is facilitated.

Although the rôle of civil society as a partner in the initiating and governance of development is nowadays accepted as imperative to successful development it should be recognised that in certain countries which had relatively authoritarian governments and did not include civil society effectively positive development results were achieved, for example, South Korea, Chile, Indonesia, etc. Recent arguments however recognise the benefits of participation, openness and freedom for development initiatives, but this is qualified however by the recognition that civil society without a proper political arrangement is in itself not sufficient. This confirms the value of the idea of a partnership in development in which both aspects have a specific role to play as interdependent partners in development.

It is therefore possible to conclude that the implication of accepting a democratic approach to the governance issues is that recognition is given to the necessity to involve all stakeholders in the process of development. This implies that a new basis of relating such parties should be found which should be based on the relationship between state and civil society as link between it and the broad populace. This relationship should constitute the basis for governance in development.

Motivation for affording civil society a partnership position

The most important role civil society has to play in a democracy and in partnerships with the state and its government is the promotion of better government and greater participation by citizens in decision-making. This implies that in terms of governance for development it facilitates the co-ordination and consideration of popular participation which should improve realism and relevance in development. This is the case because:

- Communities often have more commitment to their members than public service agents.
- Communities understand their problems better than service professionals.
- Professionals and bureaucracies deliver services; communities solve problems.
- Institutions and professionals offer service; communities offer 'care'.
- Communities are more flexible and creative than large service bureaucracies.
- Communities enforce standards of behaviour more effectively than bureaucracies or service professionals.
- Communities focus on capacity; service systems focus on deficiencies.

It should be recognised however that in order to benefit from the role of civil society specific arrangements should be in place because its effectiveness depends on proper institutional arrangements, leadership and organization. Such arrangements may differ between situations on the basis of the capacity of the state and the culture, level of development, nature of the development situation etc.

In practical terms this refers to firstly an environment conducive to the existence, development and functioning of civil society namely:

- state apparatus strong enough to create such an environment and maintain it as discussed above.
- policies, procedures and opportunities that may facilitate civil society involvement and impact on governance and therefore development.

Secondly it refers to the environment that should be created on the basis of the partnership between state and civil society to promote an environment conducive for development. This refers to aspects like:

- establishing capacity with the role-players to participate effectively in development opportunities nationally and internationally.
- create opportunities to improve well-being.
- assist with the generation of resources needed.
- creating the necessary legal and policy frameworks to facilitate development initiatives.
- access to information about opportunities.

- creating a culture of tolerance and patience to arrange interaction and ensure commitment and endurance in the development process.
- assisting in determining development priorities and strategies on the basis of the contextual realities of the situation.

The possible contribution of civil society is therefore accepted on condition that the necessary institutional arrangements exist to facilitate it (compare *Figure 2*). This may vary from involvement in forums, representation, community organizations, partnerships in projects, consultation in policy formulation and decisions on initiatives etc. (Elliot, 1994: 59). Through this, governance on development related issues can be democratised and a proper bottom-up and top-down integration established in order to ensure an enabling environment on the one hand but also active involvement towards realistic and effective development on the other.

It should however be accepted that civil society exists in a complex environment which demands involvement on various levels.

Levels of Civil Society

In the development situation it is imperative to consider that the nature of society demands that attention should be focused on the various levels of its societal organization including:

- individuals
- family and other groups
- communities and its organizations
- societies and its organizations on national level
- international relations

Civil society should therefore be viewed on the basis of its capacity to address the reality of each of these aspects. This implies that consideration should be given to the establishment of civil society structures with the capacity to address this reality. The focus should therefore be on making provision for:

- associational structures establishing groups and co-ordinating activities
- community and societal structures based on the social capital of the different situations
- global level based on certain international realities that may contribute to influence international political relations and

impact and also national situations in terms of certain international arrangements (Streeten, 1992: 31).

Criteria for civil society and its development

Considering the role ascribed to civil society it is imperative to ensure that in the establishment of such structures it should have the necessary characteristics to be able to fulfil its role as link between state and planned beneficiary in order to give content to the partnership in democratising the governance process. The following characteristics are crucial:

- autonomy in order to ensure independence from the state
- democratically structured and oriented
- accountability to its constituency
- open recruitment
- the capacity to serve as socialisation agent

Civil society structures should therefore have the capacity to contribute to and function in a democratic governance process by characterising and instituting democratic values.

The critical question however is related to how is it possible to establish a type of civil society with the necessary characteristics to own the capacity to play such a democratising role. The answer to this lies in the acceptance of the following basic assumptions, namely:

- an open environment is necessary for civil society to develop, which implies a specific orientation by the state.
- partnership and networking to facilitate exchange of ideas are imperative for the successful establishment of civil society and the potential thereof to further democratic governance.

This implies active involvement and influence from all parties and not dominance by one in which case the benefit of interacting is lost (*Ibid*, 1992: 31).

- Both too weak and too strong a state can discourage the growth of civil society.
- Civil society should be developed in the sense that it needs the environment and the capacity to become effective. It is therefore a process of empowering it for effective participation in governance.

Position, roles and points of interaction of civil society, the state and business

Considering the partnership between civil society and the state, it is also necessary to look at the role of business or the market, which although it may be part of civil society can also be seen as a specific entity influencing civil society due to the fact that political ideology deciding on capitalism as market orientation may create a specific context in which civil society exists. It is therefore necessary to consider the basis on which this relation and interaction can be planned and implemented. *Figure 3* gives an indication of this relation and interaction.

Figure 3 **Interactions of Civil Society, the State and Business**

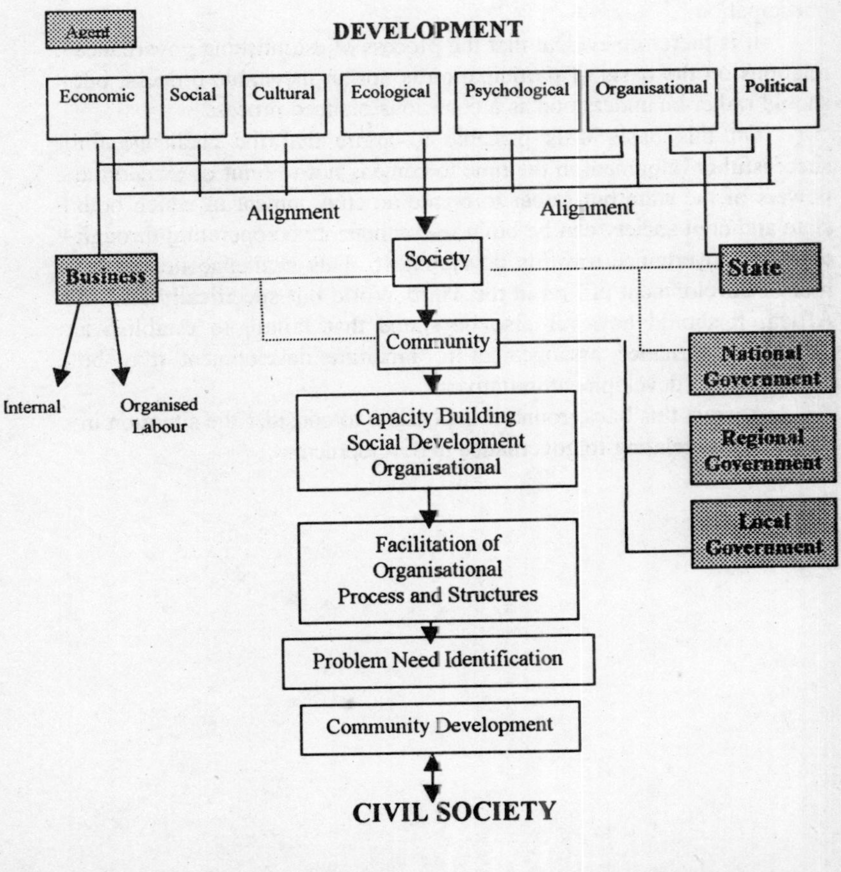

From the model it is clear that the multi-dimensional nature of development inevitably determines a specific logical arrangement in the interaction between the various agents.

Mobilising role-players to fulfil its role
In order to start development initiatives it is imperative that firstly proper alignment exists among the role-players involved and secondly that the partnership is based on co-operation towards development. In order to achieve this, people should be prepared for involvement through understanding and accepting that environment and on that basis included in the process towards development initiatives. The process should depart from planned activities based on valid and reliable information, while people are conscious of their roles and responsibilities and motivated to participate. *Figure 4* illustrates the process of mobilising people towards development through participation.

It is therefore evident that the process of establishing governance relations on the basis of participation is not an inevitable process, but should rather be understood as a conscious planned process.

On this basis it is possible to argue that the challenge for successful development in the time to come is not to limit or extend the powers of the state but rather to create an environment in which both state and civil society can be built as components co-operating through effective governance towards development. This challenge lies at the root of development efforts in the Third World but specifically also in Africa. It should however also be stated that failure to establish a suitable governance arrangement to facilitate development may be detrimental to development initiatives.

Against this background it is possible to consider the situation in South Africa relating to governance in development.

Figure 4 **Process of Community Mobilisation**

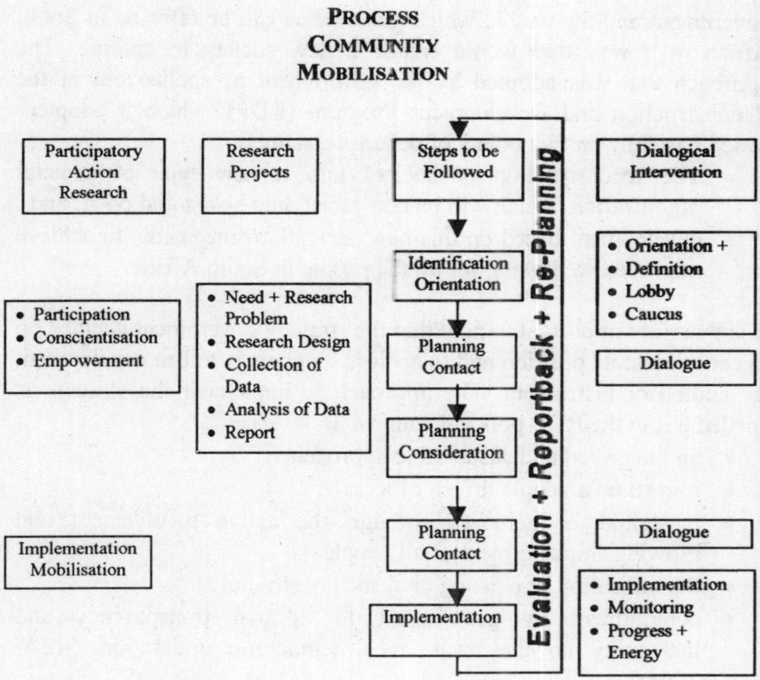

1. Steps to be followed indicate the broad process to be followed.
2. Participatory action research indicate the methodology and method.
3. The Research process id indicated to provide valid and reliable information for explanation and planning.
4. The dialogical intervention process is suggested as method to facilitate the progress.
5. The aspects mentioned under points 2.3 and 4 therefore indicate the methodology and strategy to be followed to give content to each of the steps in process.

GOVERNANCE IN DEVELOPMENT IN SOUTH AFRICA

The political transition in South Africa during 1994 took place in a period when the approach to development internationally had already shifted to an acceptance of the principle of participation, involvement and a focus on the position and role of people in development.

Considering the nature of the political transition in which it was fundamentally influenced by a groundswell amongst the general population a general climate to promote popular involvement was already existing.

This inevitably led to a fundamental re-consideration of the role of government and the way in which governance can be effected in South Africa in a way that would enable a new society to emerge. The approach that was adopted by the government as spelled out in the Reconstruction and Development Program (RDP), which it adopted, rested basically on two points of departure, namely:

- The reconstruction of society into a new type of societal organization, which will be non-racist, non-sexist and open; and
- development based on this new societal arrangements to achieve improved well-being for all the people in South Africa.

It is therefore important to note that the strategy government decided on to consolidate its position and to achieve its goals is to use development as method or instrument. The approach to implement the strategy is spelled out in the RDP policy document as:

- an integrated and sustainable approach
- it must be a people driven process
- it should be achieved through the active involvement and growing empowerment of all people
- the utilisation of existing civil society structures
- commitment by government to optimal transparency and inclusivity on the basis of a democratic orientation (RSA, 1994:5).

Implicit in the approach spelled out is therefore the approach to governance in terms of development. This implies the necessity of co-operation between the state and its government and the broad populace by means of legitimate structures to facilitate it. From this perspective it is possible to take a look at the specific arrangements intended to facilitate this type of governance.

Role-players and relations in governance towards development in South Africa

In terms of the reality in South Africa it is intended to involve all possible stakeholders that can potentially make a contribution to development. This includes:

- the state with its structures

- business which may form part of civil society
- the broader society/community as the broad framework of civil society
- as parts of the tri-partite group envisioned to promote development.

It is acknowledged that the capacity of various stakeholders to contribute varies and therefore an integrated development approach depends on all sources of capacity available.

It is further recognised that national structures on its own do not have the capacity to address the realities of the country on all levels. For this reason the principle of bringing government as close as possible to the people is adopted. The new constitution of SA therefore put it as the responsibility of all tiers of government to take responsibility for development of the population it serves. *Figure 5* illustrates his approach.

Figure 5 **Tiers of the Government of RSA**

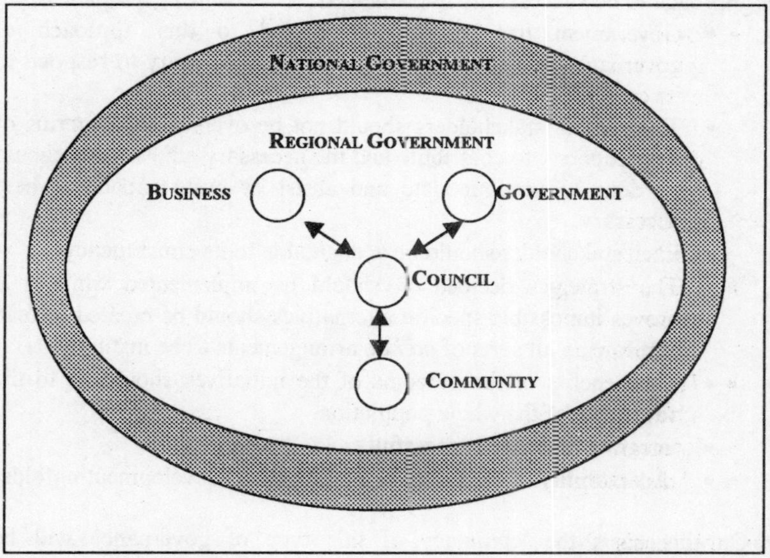

This however presents a unique challenge due to the current situation in South Africa as characterised by large scale poverty and needs in basically all sectors/dimensions of society. Development therefore has to be attempted in a highly unequal environment, relating to almost all aspects, which demands a responsibly balanced approach. This can best be achieved by a participatory approach in a democratic environment facilitating a governance model which can create an enabling environment for development, allowing a focus on all dimensions of development as proposed by the RDP. *Figure 4* above illustrates a possible model that can serve as an explanation of the ideal proposed for approaching development, which may also serve as a guideline for the implementation of the RDP program which is still only a broad policy document.

The model gives an indication of the multi-dimensional nature of development, as well as the possible basis on which interaction can be arranged in order to ensure the involvement of relevant stakeholders in specific issues and also on specific levels.

Governance in this case is based on participation and interaction on various levels of societal reality and authority. This provides the opportunity to establish the necessary capacity and opportunities in a focused way. Although this may sound like a perfect solution to approach the South African situation it is important to acknowledge that there are a number of conditions that have to be met for this approach to be successfully implemented:

- Government has to stay committed to this approach of governance and should have the will and capacity to respond to its context.
- The various stakeholders should not be over-valued in terms of their capacity to contribute and the necessary adjustments should be done to accommodate and assist or build capacity where necessary.
- Each stakeholder should be accountable to its constituency.
- The strategies decided on should be implemented while if it proves impossible specific alternatives should be created instead of allowing all sorts of *ad hoc* arrangements to be instituted.
- The benefits of the outcome of the initiatives should be to the advantage of the whole population.
- Integrate diversity successfully.
- Adaptability of the various role-players as development unfolds.

On this basis the legitimacy of this type of governance will be established which should strengthen it to achieve the development goals envisioned.

The challenge in the South African situation is however further complicated because of the degree of social devastation of black communities. Although the material position of the communities is better than that of their counterparts elsewhere in Africa the disintegration is probably worse. Governance based on participation therefore need to establish an arrangement to establish the necessary integration again to facilitate it. This should however be done on a basis which will:

- constitute a means of empowerment for the economically and politically marginal, in a context of nascent or weak democratic institutions. This empowerment should however be based on who these people are and what their level of development is as a point of departure.
- resist a process where development is depoliticised through:
  - the demobilisation of the popular forces and their inclusion in the local state apparatus
  - the capitulation of NGO's to donor driven agendas and the subsequent financial dependency on them; and
- elaborate a concrete and specific framework of democratic policies that exceeds the predominance of multipartyism.

It is therefore possible to argue that the governance approach in South Africa is based on accommodating the need for participation and involvement, due to the culture of popular involvement existing amongst the majority of the population. This culture is supported by the dominant *ubuntu* culture in Africa at large which departs from the viewpoint that an extended family approach should be followed in approaching challenges.

CONCLUSION

Development initiatives during the past decades failed to deliver the type of results which were expected in many cases. The failure can largely be described as a result of the approach adopted to development in terms of the governance strategy and therefore the ineffective relations amongst role-players and the incapacity to utilise existing potential realistically towards development.

Development is best served by a democratic environment. The governance of development should therefore facilitate such an arrangement. This implies the need for a dynamic and adaptable state and civil society structure in order to ensure that it will have the capacity to change their roles and functions as the supply and demands in terms of development aspects change in the process of development.

The challenge is therefore to ensure that a governance model based on a partnership relationship between stakeholders is established by means of creating an enabling environment thereto which should include the necessary institutional and organizational arrangements.

Although certain countries achieved success through a more authoritarian approach it is significant to note that even in these cases changes are taking place in terms of the relations between state and the market, e.g. in many countries in Southeast Asia.

In Africa, on the other hand, where the type of culture is based on the communal principle a participatory approach from the start is imperative. The way in which it is applied in South Africa is a typical example of such an approach.

The challenge of Africa is however to a large extent that the level of development, including poverty, literacy etc., is so low that it makes it very difficult to involve these people without expecting too much from them. A well planned process is therefore necessary through which governance will facilitate not only participation but also a logical point of departure and capacity building without sacrificing the real content of what forms the basis of societal culture.

References

Booth, D. (ed.) 1994, *Rethinking Social Development*, Malaysia: VVP

Elliot, J.A. 1994, *An introduction to Sustainable Development*, London: Routledge.

Fitzgerald, P. et al. (eds.) 1995, *Managing Sustainable Development in South Africa*, Cape Town: Oxford University.

Himmelstrand, U. et. al. (eds.) 1994, *African Perspectives on Development*, New York: St Martin's Press.

Hyden, G. 1996, "The challenges of analysis and building civil society", *African Insight*, Vol. 26, no. 2, 92-106.

Kiely, R. 1995, *Sociology and development*, London: UCL Press Limited.

Loots, A.E. 1994, "'n Beskouing oor 'n Ontwikkelingsbenadering vir die Negentigerjare", *South African Journal of Economic and Management Sciences*, Summer 1994. Vol. 14 17-26.

Lundahl, M. 1995, "The Economics of Kleptocracy : Some reflections on Underdevelopment and the Predatory State", Paper delivered at the Conference of the IIDS, Helsinki, July.

Morris, P. 1995, "Democracy, governance and partnerships with institutions of civil society and the private sector", *Development Southern Africa*. Vol. 12, no. 3, June. 423-434.

RSA (Republic of South Africa)(1994), White Paper on Reconstruction and Development, Pretoria: Office of the Minister without Portfolio in the Office of the President, September.

Streeten, P. et. al. 1992, "Global Governance for Human Development", *Silver Jubliee Papers 1, 2 & 3* 1966-1991.

5 GOVERNANCE ISSUES AND SUSTAINABLE DEVELOPMENT: A CRITIQUE OF THE REGULATORY MAZE IN BANGLADESH

M A HAMID

INTRODUCTION

Since Independence, Bangladesh has made tremendous progress. Notably, it has almost removed its problem of chronic food deficit by increasing production. Domestic food grains production increased from 11.8 million tons in 1976-77 to 19.5 million tons in 1994-95; it has successfully reduced its population growth rate (from 3 percent to 1.8 percent); it has significantly increased primary enrolments (with overwhelming majority of girls in the latter); it has caused rapid growth of garments exports; and, above all, it has transformed itself from a once-known *international basket case* to a country which has become an *envy* of many developing countries.

But this is just one side of the picture, perhaps, looking at Bangladesh from the wrong end of the telescope. The hard reality is that most people (more than 60 percent) are still living below the poverty line and per capita incomes are increasing only very slowly. In other words, the development efforts have not become sustainable, to say the least.

Why is it so? It is indeed possible to identify a host of factors responsible for this state of the economy. But for a heavily aid-dependent country like Bangladesh, let us see what the donors have to say: "The Bank's experience has shown that the programs and projects it helps finance may be technically sound, but fail to deliver anticipated results for reasons connected to the quality of government action. Legal reforms, however urgent, may come to naught if the new laws are not enforced consistently or there are severe delays in implementation. Efforts to develop privatised production and market-led growth may not succeed unless investors face clear rules and institutions that reduce uncertainty about future government action" (WB 1992 : 2).

In other words, the basic issue is one of governance, that is, management of a country's affairs. In effect there is now world-wide evidence that there exists a significant and positive correlation between *good governance*[1] and *sustainable development*[2]. A particularly worrisome feature, which undermines good governance in Bangladesh is that there are excessive rules, regulations, licensing requirements and so forth and that these are surely impeding the functioning of markets and encouraging rent-seeking. The Government of Bangladesh (GOB) is not unaware of this phenomenon of the economy. As it says: "While regulation is a natural corollary to a market-oriented system, the current regulatory regime tends to have a stifling effect on economic performance through its pervasive and vague nature and adds to the 'cost of doing business'" (GOB 1995 : 66). Among the measures undertaken by the GOB, one very important one is "the review of the existing regulatory framework in order to make it transparent, accessible, affordable and non-discriminatory" (*Ibid*, P-67). The present study is an attempt to help the GOB in realising this pious hope.

The overall objective of the paper is to make an appraisal of the rules and regulations used by the development agencies and those used by the government bureaucrats in arriving at a decision. The specific objectives are:

- to identify the basic issues of governance in the regulatory maze;
- to determine the social costs of the perverse rules and regulations;
- to find out the basic characteristics of a good regulatory regime; and
- to suggest some reform measures.

The paper is prepared primarily on the basis of the materials obtained from secondary sources, the most important one being the World Bank study in 1996. These are, however, supplemented and updated by interviewing a cross section of the executives connected with various development agencies and representatives of the business community (including some foreign investors).

---

1 The term *good governance* is used in the paper in a very limited sense, close to what the World Bank says: it is "the manner in which power is exercised in the management of a country's economic and social resources for development (WB 1992:3). For an excellent discussion on this terminology see J. Bertenstein (1994) and M. M. Khan (1995).

2 *Sustainable Development* is defined as: "to meet the needs of present generations without compromising the ability of future generations to meet their own needs" (WECD 1987).

GOVERNANCE ISSUES

"Ill made legal shoes pinches the citizen's foot". Keeping in view this Chinese proverb, we begin with the identification of governance issues with reference to the rules and regulations used by the development agencies and those used by the bureaucrats in making decisions in Bangladesh.

Regulations Used by Development Agencies

Like many other countries, the development agencies in Bangladesh use innumerable rules and regulations; what distinguishes it from other countries (mostly those of East Asian economies like South Korea, Malaysia and Singapore) is that many of them are not only unnecessary but also perverse in nature and ultimately lead to lengthy and unwarranted decisions. What follows is an attempt to identify the basic governance issues of the regulatory regime in Bangladesh as followed by the development agencies like the Board of Investment (BOI), the Bangladesh Export Processing Zones Authority (BEPZA) and the Export Promotion Bureau (EPB).

(*i*) *Unnecessary*

Many regulations are unnecessary and create botheration for private industrialists and ordinary citizens. One good example relates to the import of reconditioned/second hand machinery worth over Taka 0.2 million ($4,750). According to the current Import Policy, private investors are required to produce a certificate from an international surveyor to the effect that it has a working life of at least 10 years. The logic of this provision is that it would guard against imports of junks and flight of capital. But the question remains: who would ensure this? Is it not the importers who can better judge the usefulness of this kind of imports?. Again, in Bangladesh, before connecting a gas line for an industry, the gas company requires the *original title deed*. This is also unnecessary. The gas company can at best demand (as in many countries) the name and address of the applicant and a deposit.

(ii) *Vague/Open-ended*

Some regulations are characterised as vague or open-ended. For illustration we mention one SRO (Statutory Regulation Order) of the GOB i.e., "private sector petroleum imports are allowed only with authorisation from *government* upon fulfilment of *other* legal rules and regulations". The undefined terms as shown in italics make room for the concerned personnel to interpret them in any way they like leading to ultimately side-payments and delays in decision making (see also the next section). Similar case can be seen from an Import Policy Order of 1993-95 i.e., "*old, job-lot, stock-lot* goods and *prime quality* billets are banned". The terms printed in italics beget the same comments as above.

(iii) *Contradictory*

The 1991 Industrial Policy allows private investment in all but five sectors. At the same time, it requires the promotional agencies to ensure against over-saturation even in the free sectors. Accordingly, as gathered through personal communication, some agencies(e.g., the BOI) is advising some financial institutions not to finance such industries as edible oil refining and electric fans. Similar cases can be seen in case of high tariff on polythene bags and restriction of some pharmaceutical products. These types of restrictions not only contradict the very spirit of promoting privatisation but also opens the opportunity of rent-seeking activities. Such controls are treated as *reinstatement in disguise of the Old Discouraged List of Industries, which have already been scrapped in order to remove controls on private investment.*[1]

(iv) Fractional

Several examples can be cited to show that many regulations are fractional in nature. "Taka, the nation's currency, is convertible for international payments in current account" (BOI 1995:25). This provision of convertibility has been made largely meaningless because *Taka* has not been put on a free float against other currencies and in effect it is not convertible except under clearly defined circumstances. Moreover, in this case the Bangladeshi firms and foreign firms have not been treated equally. Despite the government's stated export-oriented stance and recent liberalising changes a few controls have still remained. These include controls on the exports and imports of samples for exports and an export ban for a number of goods on trade reasons. These fractional deregulatory changes tend to negate the whole spirit of trade liberalisation of the government.

(v) Excessive

Excessive rules, regulations and licensing requirements are another pointer of poor governance in Bangladesh. To illustrate this aspect of

---

[1] For a good discussion on the impact of changes in industrial policies and infrastructure facilities on foreign direct investment see Hamid and Islam (1996).

regulatory framework, we can refer to the garments industry, which is now regarded as the leading sector of Bangladesh. A new investor of the garments sector is presently required to obtain over a dozen major licenses and clearances. These relate to (among others) import trade control, export trade control, textiles registration, and rules regarding factory construction. The issue becomes more burdensome when the annual renewal requirement is taken into account. Understandably, the process requires very long time and involves side-payments (see also the next section).

(vi) Non-transparent enforcement

In Bangladesh, regulations are exclusively administered by under-paid low level officials. Anyone seeking to undertake private commercial activity is forced to obtain help and assistance from these numerous petty bureaucrats who use every opportunity to ostensibly monitor compliance. Truly speaking, they take full advantage of the non-transparent process to extract rents.

(vii) Defective process of making regulations

All regulations emanate from laws in Bangladesh. The regulatory agency has the responsibility for developing and drafting supportive rules and regulations. One important criticism of this drafting process is that it tends to be tilted in favour of the regulator and generally does not consider the views of those people likely to be affected by the regulations.

Regulations Used by Bureaucrats

In Bangladesh, the government officials are guided by various rules and regulations for arriving at a decision. The most important ones are Rules of Business & the Secretariat Instructions. Undoubtedly, these rules have many good features, but on the whole, they are ineffective. The basic governance issues in these rules may be stated thus.

(i) Outdated

One obvious governance issue is that most of these rules are outdated. Truly speaking, these rules represent conglomeration of the erstwhile provincial rules, the Bengal Service Rules of the British period - renamed as the East Pakistan Service Rules and now the Bangladesh Service Rules - and the Central Government rules. Amendments and additions are compiled in Establishment Manuals, but there remains considerable confusion about the applicability and procedures of different rules.

(ii) Complicated

Many rules are complicated and written so confusingly that it is simply not possible to understand the message by one reading. To illustrate the case we borrow one example as produced in one GOB Report (1989: 63):

> *"...Subject to the provisions of Chapter VII, a Government servant who is appointed to officiate in a post shall not draw pay higher than his substantive pay in respect of a permanent post, other than a tenure post, unless the officiating appointment involves the assumption of duties and responsibilities of greater importance than those attaching to the post, other than a tenure post, on which he holds a lien, or would hold a lien had it not been suspended. For the purpose of this rule, the officiating appointment shall not be deemed to involve the assumption of duties and responsibilities of greater importance if the post to which it is made on the same scale of pay as the permanent post, other than a tenure post on a scale of pay identical therewith".*

(iii) Ineffective

Many of the rules governing the behaviour of the bureaucrats in Bangladesh are ineffective and can delay decision-making. Sir Richard Tottenham commented as early as in 1945 on these Rules and Instructions by saying that " the disadvantages of the system could be summed up in two phrases - excessive noting and file shifting, the combined effect of which is delay and inefficiency" (GOB 1989, fn 6, P.62).

(iv) Reliance on control rather than performance:

The rules and regulations as followed by the government bureaucrats are made in such a way that there is excessive reliance on control rather than on performance. Naturally, the bureaucrats always try to justify their decisions on the basis of their rules; quality of outcomes has no value at all.

(v) No monitoring system

Effective monitoring system is an essential pre-requisite of good governance. Unfortunately, this is totally absent in the implementation process. There exists no system of checking whether or not files are disposed of in time.

(vi) No mistake (please!)

In Bangladesh, the bureaucrats may be penalised for taking initiatives and making quick, but sometimes bad, decisions; there is no system of punishing anybody for delayed decisions. In effect, all the incentives in government are in the direction of not making mistakes!

(vii) Excessive approvals

Excessive approvals, even for trivial matters, are a rule rather than exception in Bangladesh. One ridiculous example is the need for second-ranking officials to have permission from the Prime Minister for overseas travel to attend seminars or workshops.

SOME SOCIAL COSTS OF THE PERVERSE RULES AND REGULATION

The regulatory maze as discussed above has serious adverse implications for private sector development. On the one hand, it causes business uncertainty and risk, and, on the other, it generates delays in implementation of development projects and adds to transaction costs for the private sector. This section is devoted to an analysis of the effects of the perverse rules and regulations as prevailing in Bangladesh. These costs are assessed both in terms of time and in terms of money. Two situations are distinguished viz., utility services and setting up of a garment factory.[1]

Utility Services

Table 1 exhibits the necessary information on the four types of utility services namely electricity, gas, water and telephone Of these services, electricity connection is the most difficult one to obtain. If it is required on an emergency basis, say for one week, the unofficial fee may go up to Taka 150 thousand ($3,750) for high-tension line and Taka 20,000 for low-tension line.[2] The official cost for getting a gas connection is Taka 3,000 and the waiting time is three months. However, if one is required to have this connection urgently, then one is required to spend some Taka 40,000. Similar costs are involved in water connection. Since cellular telephone is available in the Dhaka City, one can acquire it very easily, but the capital cost and running cost become very high when compared with normal telephones. This service is from the private sector. If one wants to get the service from the government agency on an urgent basis, this costs Taka 70,000; the official

---

1 The data used in this section are adapted from the World Bank (1996).

2 In October 1996 the exchange rate was: $1 = Taka 42 (approx.).

procedure is also very lengthy: one may have to wait for a period of up to 12 years!

Table 1 **Perverse Effects of Regulatory Regime in Bangladesh**
(The Case of Utility Services)

Services Required	Hidden Costs in Terms of	
	Taka (dollar)	Time
Electricity: (i) High-tension line (ii) Low-tension line	 100,000 - 150,000 (2,500 - 3,750) 10,000 - 20,000 (250 - 375)	 Urgent (within a week) Urgent (within a week)
Gas: (i) Official (ii) Urgent	 3,000 (75) 40,000 (1,000)	 3 months Within a week
Water: (i) Official (ii) Urgent	 1,500 - 2,000 (38 - 50)* 14,000 - 20,000 (350 - 500)	 3-4 months Within a week
Telephone: (i) Official (ii) Urgent	 10,000 (250)* 50,000 - 70,000 (1,250 - 1,750)	 3 - 4 months

N.B. * indicates the information collected by the author himself from the Rajshahi Office

Source: The World Bank (1996), P.81, Box 5.3.

Trade Licences

The procedure for obtaining various types of trade licences is also very lengthy and unofficially very costly too. For illustration, we may cite the case of a garments factory as shown in *Table 2*.

Table 2 **Perverse Effects of Regulatory Regime in Bangladesh**
(The Case of Garments Factory)

Services Required:	Hidden Costs in Terms of	
	Taka (dollar)	Time
Trade License: (I) Official (ii) Urgent	 Small amount* 5,000 - 8,000 (125 - 200)	 One year Within a week
Factory construction license (i) For authority approval (ii) Clearance by the Chief Inspector of Factories (iii) Factory license	 40,000 (500) 5,000 - 8,000 (125 - 200) 5,000 (125)	 Official time is one month, but in practice much longer time
Total Costs: (i) Official (ii) Side-payments	 91,640 (2,291) 310,640 (7,763)	 For comments see text

Source: As in *Table 1*.

It is found that for a trade license required for setting up a garment factory on emergency basis, the unofficial cost varies from Taka 5 to 8 thousand. It is possible to get the license without side-payments, but in that event the industrialists in question will have to wait for a very long time (say, a year). For factory construction license, the investor needs clearance/license from three authorities. For formal approval, the fee (unofficial) is Taka 40,000; for clearance by the Chief Inspector of factories up to Taka 8,000 and for factory license Taka 5,000.

In *Table 2*, an attempt is made to estimate the total official and unofficial costs for the establishment of a Garments Factory within a normal time period. It is shown that this comes to Taka 91,640 ($2,291) as official and Taka 310,640 ($7,763) as unofficial costs. This unofficial cost is found to be 340 percent higher than the official costs. To this, if one adds the annual renewal fee, the percentage shoots up to 712.

It may be of interest to add that in order to find their way through the regulatory maze, the investors very often cannot but approach to facilitator, locally known as *dalals*. These *dalals* can be seen loitering around in each and every office where people go for collecting various services. Actually monies as detailed above are expended mostly through these *dalals*. The *dalals* also are sometimes to get their things done by another type of institution popularly called *mastans*. It is known that the share of the total speed-money is higher for *mastans* than that of *dalals*.

CHARACTERISTICS OF GOOD REGULATORY REGIME

The following are some of the basic characteristics of a good regulatory regime:

(i) Simplicity

Regulations should be simple, unambiguous and non-controversial so that they can be effectively monitored even by the under paid low-level government officials.

(ii) Structured

Structured regulations should be preferred to conduct regulations. The former needs to be applied only occasionally and the latter would become administratively more difficult and would require continuous monitoring.

(iii) Decentralisation

This is a very essential component of good governance. This component would not only ensure the regulations more accountable but also enable the regulators to make comparisons between different alternatives.

(iv) Simulative

Regulations should not be rigid but simulative. People should not be afraid of following the rules and regulations in their day-to-day life.

(v) Cost-effective

When making regulatory proposals, it would be of crucial importance to identify and, where possible, quantify all the costs and benefits. Existing regulations should be subjected to similar cost-benefit assessment.

(vi) Public consultation

Before implementation, all rules and regulations will need to be discussed with the citizens. This would, among others, ensure accountability.

SOME OVERHAULING MEASURES

"Good piano won't play bad music". The governance issues as identified in connection with the regulatory framework in Bangladesh, cannot possibly be redressed by simply omitting or rewriting or revising the perverse rules and regulations. For a sustainable development, it would be necessary to take some overhauling measures as suggested below.

Making Rules and Regulations

Firstly, a comprehensive deregulation programme will have to be initiated. This can be accomplished by establishing Deregulation Commission consisting of government officials, private sector specialists and technical experts. This Commission, among others, would use process technical reviews including cost-benefit analysis. The first priority would be the review of regulations that affect day-to-day life of ordinary citizens.

Secondly, in order to keep track of regulations, a clearing house in the Ministry of Law will have to be created. As a first step, this office should prepare a comprehensive documentation, which incorporates in one place all the laws and regulations. This should be supplemented and updated every month.

Thirdly, with few exceptions for emergency situations and criminal matters, no rule should be promulgated without public hearing. This would help ensure transparency and accountability in the rule making process.

Fourthly, a regulatory system for utilities and monopoly sectors will need to be established. This should encourage the private sector entry into these areas and heighten competition.

Expediting the decision-making process

For enhancing the speed and quality of decision-making, radical changes are needed both in the *process* and in the *behavioural* aspects of the regulatory regime.

Firstly, both the rules of Business and the Secretariat Instructions will have to be updated and streamlined. Importantly, the current structures of inherited provincial and central government rules need to be integrated.

Secondly, documentation centres in each agency will have to be established as early as possible. These centres should provide access to all relevant printed regulations, and, if possible, provide access to updated computerised information.

Thirdly, financial power of the heads of the agencies will have to be enhanced for the day-to-day expenditure as well as procurement of civil goods and services. This will certainly help reduce the delay incurred due to permission from the ministries.

Fourthly, the number of decisions requiring Prime Minister's approval should be reduced. This approval should relate to only those which are essential for the functioning of the government.

Fifthly, it is suggested that the Cabinet Committee on procurement be eliminated and instead establish a permanent secretary level inter-ministerial committee to take the responsibility for procurement which exceeds the authority of line ministry secretaries.

Sixthly, staff dealing with development programmes in the area of procurement in each ministry should be trained so that they can become more proficient in preparing bidding documents and more conversant with the results and procedures.

Lastly, Standing Evaluation Committee in each Ministry with appropriate technical experts should be established so that quick decisions are taken and minor deviations from specification and fewer cases are sent back for rebidding.

SUMMARY AND CONCLUSION

The review of the rules and regulations as used by the development agencies for private sector development as well as by government bureaucrats for the decision-making process has revealed that the regulatory regime in Bangladesh entangles in a number of governance issues i.e., the regulations are not only unnecessary but also vague, contradictory, fractional, excessive and defective in character. The rules as followed by the bureaucrats are, in most cases, outdated, complicated, ineffective and provides no scope for monitoring, transparency, and, above all, accountability. The social costs of these perverse regulations are very severe. These cause delays in the implementation of the development projects and add huge transaction costs to the private sector.

The paper makes a number of recommendations styled as 'overhauling measures'. Among others, it is suggested that a Deregulation Commission and a Clearing House be established as soon as situations permit. These bodies would, respectively, effectuate the technical reviews and prepare a comprehensive documentation of the existing rules and regulations. For expediting the government's decision making process, a number of suggestions have been made with respect to both process changes and behavioural changes.

As a concluding remark it may of importance to point out that the 21st century is knocking at the door. Bangladesh must enter the century with clean slate. In a fiercely competitive global market, a quantum leap in efficiency, and in good governance, is urgently needed if it wishes to accelerate and sustain growth and thereby improve the living conditions of the toiling masses.

REFERENCES

Bertenstein, J. (1994), *Overcoming Fuzzy Governance in Bangladesh: Policy Implementation in Least Developed Countries.* The University Press Limited.

Board of Investment (BOI)(1995), *Guide to Investment in Bangladesh.* Prime Minister's Office, Government of Bangladesh (GOB), Dhaka, Bangladesh.

Government of Bangladesh (1989), *Public Administration Efficiency Study*, Vol. 2, Ministry of Establishment.

________(1995), *Bangladesh Economic Review.* Ministry of Finance, June.

Hamid, M. A. and Saiful Islam (1996). "Promoting Regional Economic Co-operation in Foreign Direct Investment Policies and Related Institution Building Among Asian and Specific Development Countries: Bangladesh Case Studies", A Report prepared for the ESCAP/DRPAD, Bangkok.

Khan, M. M. (1995), "Governance in Bangladesh", *Journal of Administration and Diplomacy.* Vol. 3, Nos. 1 & 2.

The World Bank (WB), (1992), *Governance and Development*, Washington, D.C.

________(1996), *Bangladesh: Government That Works - Reforming the Public Sector*, University Press Limited, Dhaka.

The World Commission on Environment and Development (WCED), (1987), *Our Common Future.* Oxford University Press Limited, Dhaka. (Also known as Brundtland Report.

6 POLITICAL LEADERSHIP AND THE CRISIS OF DEVELOPMENT IN AFRICA: LESSONS FROM KENYA

HENRY MUTORO, LUDEKI CHWEYA & WANJALA NASONG'O

INTRODUCTION

There is a causal relationship between political leadership and economic development. There is evidence that the deterioration of economic conditions in Africa since independence is owed to poor management of public economic affairs by the incumbent state leadership. This argument implies that whereas the continent may not be very well endowed with natural resources, this may not be held solely responsible for the existing economic woes. Whatever resources exist are capable of generating economic development, indeed economic breakthrough, if they are harnessed and utilised efficiently. Conversely, a country may be endowed with enormous natural and human resources, but may remain characterised by poverty and economic backwardness if it is not endowed with visionary, dedicated and rational political leadership capable of appropriating such resources for the purpose of national development and for the prosperity of the citizens.

It is noteworthy, for instance, that whereas Africa has continued to experience economic decline in recent decades, some Third World countries elsewhere which were previously in the same economic situation have experienced relatively high economic growth rates leading to the emergence of the so-called Newly Industrialised Countries in the case of South-East Asia. This discrepancy raises one important question: Why does Africa find it difficult to achieve economic development whereas similar Third World countries are succeeding? The contention of this paper is that Africa faces special structural and associated problems which have not been tackled effectively. These problems lie largely within the ambit of governance, specifically the quality of political leadership which the continent has had since independence.

The paper, therefore, attempts to demonstrate the relationship between political leadership and economic development. In doing so illustrations are drawn from post-independence Kenyan experience. However, examples from other parts of Africa and the developing regions in general will be incorporated where necessary.

THE STATE OF ECONOMIC DEVELOPMENT IN AFRICA

African economies recorded considerable growth as well as development during the first roughly one decade of independence, that is between 1961 and 1971. Thereafter, the continent entered a period of stagnation stretching up to about 1980. But from 1980 onward outright decline has been the hallmark of the continent's economy [World Bank, 1989:2]. Since about the mid 1970s, Africa has been, and continues to be, notorious for poverty, famine, deprivation, hopelessness and, what is more, civil strife. In fact, 21 of the world's poorest countries are in Africa. This unpleasant economic scenario has been depicted by three important players in the arena of African economic development: the World Bank which is a leading donor agency, African Governments themselves under the auspices of the Organization of African Unity (OAU), the United Nations (especially, the Economic Commission for Africa) and, of course, scholars. All have declared Africa to be in a state of economic crisis.

Economic development is often measured at two levels: macro- and micro-level. Macro-level indicators include Gross National Product (GNP), Gross Domestic Product (GDP), per capita incomes, and the balance of payments situation. Whereas macro-level factors are important so far as they attempt to summarise the performance of the entire economy (whether national or regional), they fall short of indicating the real situation as it affects the daily life of individuals and communities. This is why the micro-level indicators, or what are at times described as social indicators become more meaningful. Among these indicators are: satisfaction of basic needs - food, housing, and clothing as well as access to fundamental social services, notably education, health care and social security. Micro-level factors are sometimes given the single term: standard of living, which may range from "very low" to "very high". It may be appropriate, therefore, to describe Africa's economic development on the basis of both macro- and micro-level factors. In doing this it is recognised that substantial variation exists among the individual African countries. Nevertheless, average figures validly used represent the continent-wide situation.

GNP per capita rose at an average annual rate of about 1.2 per cent (2.9 if Nigeria is included), but stagnated at an average of -0.1 (0.1 if Nigeria is included) between 1973-1980. Thereafter, GNP per capita recorded an annual rate of decline of -1.2 per cent (-2.8 when Nigeria is included). In South Asia GNP grew at a higher rate of 1.5 per cent between 1960-1970 remaining the same between 1970-1979. In developed countries the rate of growth was recorded at 4.1 per cent in 1960-1970 and 2.5 per cent between 1970-1980.

Per capita GDP grew at a rate of 2.0 per cent between 1961-1973, stagnated at about -0.1 per cent between 1973-1980, and in the period after

1980 growth rate declined at an annual rate of -2.6 per cent. In South Asia per capita GDP grew at a rate of 1.2 per cent between 1961-1973, 2.0 per cent between 1973-1980 and 2.8 per cent between 1980-1987. During the same period, Africa's balance of payments deficit was a humble US$1.5 billion, but rose to US$8 billion in 1980. The rate of Africa's external indebtedness rose from US$6 billion in 1970 to US$32 billion by 1979 and US$105 billion by 1987. In fact, by the mid-1980s, African countries had become unable to meet their loan obligations and were calling for either debt cancellation or rescheduling (World Bank, 1989).

At the micro-economic level, the situation has not been much different. On acquisition of independence in the early 1960s, the new independent governments in Africa launched themselves into a fervent search for development strategies that would ensure rapid economic growth and development so that all the people of the continent are free from poverty, want, and deprivation. With specific reference to the Kenyan situation for instance, its first development plan was largely aimed at accelerating economic growth coupled with greater and more modern use of the country's natural, physical and human resources for purposes of involving all nationals in productive activity through socio-economic structural transformation. The basic objective was to attain greater distribution of economic benefits as manifested by reduction in poverty levels, ignorance, unemployment, disease, an inequality.

In spite of these seemingly well-thought out and carefully articulated development plans however, available evidence indicate that there has been a steady decline in living standards as well as agricultural production over the years. Agricultural output, for instance, has grown by less than 1.5 per cent per annum on average since 1970, a growth rate that is less than that of the population. This has led to widespread food shortages that were an exceptional phenomenon in the 1960s. In fact, according to World Bank figures, about one quarter of sub-Saharan Africa's population (more than 100 million people) face chronic food insecurity. Accordingly, the African continent has had increasingly to rely on external food supplies, both imports and relief hand-outs, to feed its people. Little wonder, therefore, that some scholars have referred to Africa as a continent on the brink of disaster.

Furthermore, whereas such social services as education and health care were given priority in the post-independence development strategies, they have not in recent decades, received the same emphasis; neither have they been given sufficient attention. To be sure, public expenditure has been devoted to other priorities. The resultant effect has been increasing shortage of basic drugs and medical equipment in hospitals leading to an increasing number of deaths from curable diseases such as malaria. Lack of a constant

two out of every three Africans are still without safe water yet universal access to clean water is acknowledged as a prerequisite for better health. The incidence of mortality rate serves to illustrate this health problem better. For most of sub-Saharan Africathe infant mortality rate ranges between 100 and 170 for every 1,000 live births compared with only 33 in the case of Sri Lanka, for instance. In many countries of this region, deaths of children under the age of five represent close to half the number of total deaths; in the poorest of these countries such as Burkina Faso, Ethiopia, Mali, and Niger, only 70 to 77 per cent of children live to the age of five (World Bank, 1989). With regard to education, though there has been a remarkable expansion in school enrolment over the decades, this has more often been attained at the expense of the quality of education; even more worrying is the fact that overall emphasis has been placed on expansion of university education without due regard to the characteristics of the job market. This has resulted into over-production of university graduates who cannot find jobs.

Generally therefore, the standards of living in sub-Saharan Africaare very low by any set of criteria and the problem of development remains as gigantic as ever even on the most optimistic assumptions. The paradox of this situation is that much capital and other related development resources have been channelled towards development financing including vast amounts of foreign aid capital; yet as C.Fundaga [1974] observes, 'There is probably more hunger and starvation in Africa today than before the continent was swamped with donor agencies'. It is glaringly apparent therefore that the purposes of raising the living standards of the majority of the people of sub-Saharan Africa have not been served by the kind of development programmes that have been initiated by the governments of the region. The consequence of this conjecture is that the majority of the people of the continent continue to live in abject poverty, with very low levels of literacy, and lack of accessibility to the basic social services such as housing, health, and education. Hence whereas the rest of the world is moving forward by most of the normally accepted indicators of socio-economic progress, Africa is moving backwards. Taking cognisance of the fact that thirty-five or so years since independence, Africa has moved from food self-sufficiency and plunged into widespread hunger, L. Timberlake [1991], argues that Africa is dying because of its ill-planned, ill-advised attempt to modernise itself, it has cut itself into pieces. He contends that cities, which are citadels of governments, have been torn from the countryside and development projects have been directed towards filling the cities with hotels, factories, cars, universities, and associated monuments of glory, all of which have been paid for by milking the seven out of ten Africans who live on the land by taking much from them in terms of labour and produce and giving back little in terms of money and support. Indeed, on this score, one Senegalese peasant farmer once lamented:

> *Twenty years on [since independence] we've come to realise what independence really meant. It was just for the towns. One of these days we'll be asking Dakar for a reckoning, you'll see [Timberlake; 1991:40].*

Timberlake posits that in these policies of lopsided approaches to development programmes with regard to rural areas vis-à-vis the urban centres, Africa has been 'advised' and financed by Western governments and aid agencies. This approach has succeeded in creating 'modern' cities surrounded by shanties, hotels full of Western development 'experts', factories either idle or producing goods few can buy, universities churning out graduates who can't find jobs, and expensive cars full of civil servants, businessmen, soldiers, and policemen, while the rest of the masses survive below the poverty line. Against this background, one Western observer noted thus: "It is hard to look at black Africa without feeling that something has gone terribly wrong. It is not just the spectacle of suffering that troubles us. It is the sense that we - we of America and the West who thought we knew how to help these people - did not know well enough ... our advice has been deeply flawed" [Timberlake, 1991:2-3]. It was against this background of ever deteriorating standards of living coupled with dim economic prospects that by fall of 1979, African governors of the World Bank wrote a memo to the Bank's President expressing alarm at the dim economic prospects for the nations of sub-Saharan Africa and impressing upon the Bank to prepare a special paper on the economic problems of these countries and an appropriate programme for their remedy. The Bank has subsequently issued a number of Reports detailing the region's economic maladies as well as outlining their possible causes and probable solutions. In the same vein, the fact of Africa's development crisis was never lost on the continent's political leadership which, in recognition of the ever deepening economic quagmire into which Africa was continuously sinking, held a number of conventions culminating in the Monrovia Declaration of 1979, which was a precursor to the Lagos Plan of Action [LPA] of 1980. The basic objective of the LPA was to promote the economic development of the peoples and nations of Africa, and to promote progressive integration over great regional areas with a view to setting up an African economic community by the turn of the 21st century. The ultimate end was to attain industrialisation between 1980 and the year 2000.

Conventional Explanations for Africa's Development Crisis

The problem of development in Africa has attracted a wide range of explanations some of which vary from one development agency to another. About five of these explanations may be identified here. (1) Global economic recession, especially as caused by the oil crisis of the early 1970s and 1980s. The effect of Africa manifested itself in terms of inflation and low investment rate, etc. This factor is often cited by African governments individually or jointly under the auspices of the OAU. (2) Unfavourable terms of international trade which resulted in the balance of payments deficits and depressed levels of foreign exchange earnings. The OAU as well as the World Bank share in this view. (3) Poor natural resource endowment as evidenced by the high incidence of drought as well as widespread deserts and rapid desertification. African Governments as well as World Bank share in this view. (4) High rate of population growth which has disturbed the balance between human needs and resource availability. (5) Limited economic assistance from the developed world. (6) Poor management of public affairs, especially in utilising public resources.

A close examination of each of these factors reveals that none is a cause of Africa's economic crisis. In fact, they are only either consequences of the crisis or its manifestations. For each of these factors that are said to be responsible for Africa's economic woes it is possible to pose the question: What causes it? or How did it come about? If these factors are only the effects or manifestations of the crisis, then the causal factors remain to be identified. The rest of this paper argues that the principal cause of Africa's development crisis is the kind of political leadership the continent has enjoyed since independence.

Political Leadership as a Causal Variable

The attainment of political independence in Africa in the early 1860s brought a new kind of leadership into power - into government. Judged from their pronouncements and their statements of intent, these new political leaders were very enthusiastic about the developmental needs of their respective countries. 'Economic development' and 'nation-building' became the catch-words for most of these new political elites. With regard to Kenya for instance, the leadership promised to embark on development programmes geared towards eradicating hunger and malnutrition, illiteracy and ignorance, as well as poverty and deprivation. In fact, these goals constituted the campaign platform of the victorious political party, the Kenya African National Union (KANU). They were subsequently enshrined in the first national development plan covering the period 1963-1970 and elaborated upon in the celebrated Government Sessional Paper

No. 10 of 1965 on "African Socialism and its Application to Planning in Kenya". Moreover, the struggle for independence had been motivated chiefly by the promise or anticipation of socio-economic transformation of the society upon *Uhuru*. More than three decades on, however, the development promises and declarations that were made at independence remain largely unfulfilled and most, if not all, of Africa's political leadership stand indicted for this eventuality.

The first point to observe is that whereas development remained an important pursuit of goal of the post-independence governments, it did not continue to be or remain the only one. Rather, it was soon to be pursued simultaneously with a new goal; the goal of consolidating the power base of the new political elite. This particular goal had not been envisaged during the nationalist struggle as well as during the transition period. This, in itself, may not have been a problem. What posed a problem, however, was the conflict between the two goals and the outright propensity of the new governments to assign greater importance and urgency to the latter goal. The first hurdle in the pursuit of development was therefore one of goal substitution or displacement.

The first task of the Kenyatta government soon after independence was to neutralise Opposition politics and political pluralism in general. To achieve this, it was important, first, to disband Opposition parties and, possibly, to absorb their membership into KANU, and second, to establish an authoritarian system of governance that would suppress any political dissent. In fact, this remained the main pre-occupation of the KANU leadership in both the Kenyatta and Moi era. These two were therefore era that were characterised by government political manoeuvre, manipulation, and sheer intrigue, that absorbed all governmental energies and resources.

The independence constitution had created in Kenya competitive politics characterised especially by Opposition political parties, namely the Kenya African Democratic Union (KADU) and the Akamaba Party (APP) as Paul Ngei had formed it as a bait for gaining recognition in KANU which he did. But after independence, KADU remained the only major problem in KANU's effort to consolidate power. It had to be dealt with. First of all, KADU had to be disbanded. This objective was achieved within one year from the date of independence when Ronald Ngala announced to Parliament that :

> *...in the interests of Kenya, I have full mandate to declare today that the official opposition is dissolved and KADU joins the government under the leadership of Mzee Jomo Kenyatta... We intend to face the national issue with one purpose [Gertzel, 1974:110].*

Through a systematic undermining of constitutional provisions therefore, KANU managed to arm-twist KADU into disbanding itself and crossing over to the Government side in parliament. This merger however engendered a bitter ideological polarisation within KANU between the radicals (socialists) and the conservatives (capitalists). The power struggle between the two ideological cleavages culminated into the March 11-13, 1966 Limuru KANU Delegates Conference which succeeded in effectively marginalising the KANU left-wing from the centre of power before they could make any impact on both the country's domestic and foreign policy. The conservatives under Jomo Kenyatta hence entrenched themselves as the men in charge of the country's political destiny [see Gertzel, 1974]. The struggle for political power did not end here. The marginalised and therefore embittered political leaders led by Oginga Odinga and Bildad Kaggia, among others, resigned from KANU and formed the Kenya People's Union (KPU). Quite a number of backbenchers in parliament crossed the floor and joined the new opposition party prompting the government to rush to parliament a constitutional amendment requiring those who defected to resign their seats and go back to the electorate. This culminated in the now famous 'Little General Election' of 1966 which brought to the House most of those who had crossed over to the opposition. The final show-down between these two political groups came in 1969 during Kenyatta's visit to Nyanza province. On this occasion, a verbal exchange ensued between Kenyatta and Odinga followed by a riot by Odinga's supporters which prompted the police to shoot a number of civilians. Thereafter, Odinga was put under house arrest, the KPU was proscribed and, for the rest of Jomo Kenyatta's reign, Kenya remained a *de facto* one party political system. Indeed, Kenyatta had committed himself to a "no Opposition" political system when he had declared on the occasion of KADU's "self dissolution" that: "...the opposition for opposition's sake has died *for ever and ever, Amen*" [*Ibid*:110; Italics ours].

The rise of Arap Moi to power upon Kenyatta's death in August 1978 represented, of course, a change of personality, but the system of rule was marked by continuity. Indeed, Moi himself had declared during his inauguration that he would follow Kenyatta's *Nyayo* (footsteps). When it came to dealing with political Opposition, the approach was therefore the same one, namely, suppression. Of course, the forces of Opposition that had been sent underground during the Kenyatta era resurfaced soon after his demise. This was partly because of the hope that the source of authoritarianism was no more and partly because of the widespread belief at the time of the transition that the new President was weaker than his predecessor. However, both views were to be proved wrong. An attempt by George Anyona and others to form an Opposition political party in May

1982 was dealt with quite decisively. First of all, their application was rejected by the Registrar of Societies. This was followed by a constitutional amendment that transformed Kenya into a *de jure* single party state and a systematic arrest and detention of political opponents and dissenters. These measures succeeded only in forestalling any formal challenge to Moi's Presidency. But it did not make any guarantees about the future, especially in view of the attempted *coup d' etat* in August 1982. Such future guarantees had to be made through the use of more civil methods, notably, self popularisation and establishment of ethno-political alliances. This is what preoccupied Moi's Presidency after the premature General Elections of 1983. It is also what preoccupied Kenyatta between the conclusion of the Opposition party problem in 1969 and the President's death in 1978.

With regard to self popularisation, it must be pointed out that Kenyatta was less of a populist than Moi. The first President did not do much to endear himself to the citizens except, perhaps for marketing himself as a fearless freedom fighter and a *Mzee* (Old man) deserving of respect and adoration. This, together with his high oratorical ability may have earned him the status of a charismatic leader. This is the extent to which Kenyatta adopted civil and legitimate methods of staying in office. By and large, however, Kenyatta employed intimidation and ruthlessness to keep political opponents and dissenters at bay. The long chain of political assassinations during the First Republic (particularly of Tom Mboya - 1969, Pio-Gama-Pinto-1965, Ronald Ngala-1973, Kung'u Karumba, and J.M. Kariuki - 1975) as well as the long list of political detainees - all succeeded in humbling Opposition.

On the other hand, Moi was more of a populist leader who preferred to use persuasion as a first instance approach, but turned uncivil as the last resort. Although this may mean that the two leaders had basically the same approach to governance the apparently minor difference of attaching a higher premium to populism and tremendous repercussions upon economic development placed Moi on a different footing.

Ethno-political coalition formation was a method applied by both Kenyatta and Moi. Kenyatta relied heavily on his Kikuyu community as a nucleus of his power. Subsequently in the early 1970s, this power base was expanded so as to include the Kikuyu related communities, notably, Embu and Meru with the establishment of the Gikuyu Embu Meru Association (GEMA). GEMA was essentially a lobby group. Nonetheless, even within GEMA, Kenyatta had to contend with cleavages and antagonisms within its ranks. These cleavages emanated from claims that the regime was biased in favour of the Kikuyu from Kiambu (President's home district) to the disadvantage of the rest of the GEMA community. These claims were authenticated by the fact that the inner core of the Kenyatta regime was composed of Kiambu personalities, notably Mbiyu Koinange (Minister of State in the President's Office), Njoroge Mungai (Minister for Defence), Charles Njonjo (Attorney General), Ben Gethi (Police Commissioner), Ignatius Nderi (Director of Intelligence), among others. The much publicised talk to the effect that the "Presidential motorcade will never cross the Chania River", meaning the Presidency will never leave Kiambu further accentuated the cleavage in GEMA. Matters came to a hilt in March 1975 following the murder of J.M. Kariuki, the Member of Parliament for the then Nyandarua North Constituency (beyond the Chania) and a leading spokesman for the poor among the Kikuyu and ostensibly among all Kenyans, who advocated for equitable distribution of national resources, arguing that the policies adopted by the Kenyatta government would lead to the creation of "ten millionaires and ten million beggars". J.M. Kariuki's assassination engendered a lot of disaffection against the government even by Kenyatta's own Kikuyu community so much so that it necessitated the administration of an oath to help blind these people and rally them behind Kenyatta.

Towards the end of Kenyatta's era, the President had to grapple with a somewhat different ethno-political puzzle, this time it was a confrontation between the Kikuyu (read the inner core), on one hand, and the pro-Moi's 'candidacy' as Kenyatta's successor on the other. Under the aegis of the Change the Constitution Movement, the former group wished a Kikuyu to succeed Kenyatta, and thus safeguard their economic and political interests. According to the Constitution, however, the Vice President was the heir apparent. Thus the Kikuyu sought to amend the Constitution in order to forestall Moi's rise to power upon Kenyatta's death that had become quite imminent. This political saga placed Kenyatta in a dilemma: he had to choose between support for his Kikuyu allies and Moi, his loyal Vice President. Eventually, Kenyatta settled for the latter.

Impact of Authoritarian Governance on Development

Authoritarianism has far-reaching implications for the whole idea of development. Because of the fact that such governments wield power absolutely, they go about the business of governing in a manner that is neither accountable to the general public nor to the legislature. The *raison d'etre* for such governments is self-preservation. The pursuit of this goal has had adverse consequences for the whole essence of economic development. More specifically, it undermined the expected role of political leadership to (1) develop and utilise appropriately human resources, and (2) mobilise and utilise financial resources efficiently. Economic development is therefore contingent upon these two factors. It may be useful to articulate each of these factors.

Development and Utilisation of Human Resources

In the first place, allocation of positions in the public service by such a government is never based on a system of merit but purely on the economy of affection, with primordial sentiments being the overriding factor rather than ability to do the job at hand. It is against this background that, as already pointed out, most of the plum jobs in the public service during Kenyatta's regime went to his fellow Kikuyu tribesmen. This state of affairs elicited a lot of impassioned indignation in Parliament with one Member claiming that tribalism originated from Kiambu (the president's home district), as all major jobs were dished out to people from this district. Challenged to substantiate, he named the then Attorney-General, Commissioner of Police, Controller of State House, and the Administrative Secretary of the National Assembly [Gertzel et al, 1972:44]. Another MP went further to observe that three quarters of all District Commissioners were Kikuyu and that the same applied to District Officers "...the number of Kikuyu DOs is greater than (that of) all other tribes put together" [*Ibid*, :43]. This situation has continued unabated under the Moi regime. In any case, on assuming the presidency, Moi vowed to follow in Kenyatta's footsteps and true to type, now Kenyatta's Kikuyu beneficiaries of state largesse have been replaced by Moi's own Kalenjin people, with the result that many unqualified people find themselves appointed as District Commissioners, and therefore chairmen of District Development Committees under the strategy of District Focus For Rural Development put in force in the mid-1980s. The negative impact on development of such appointments cannot be belaboured.

This appointment of people on the basis of ethnicity, regionalism, and political loyalty undermines professionalism and promotes corruption as those who are so appointed owe their loyalty to their political godfathers and not the offices they hold or the people they are supposed to serve. The incidence of outright corruption among such top governmental leaders has greatly contributed to the economic malaise that has bedevilled the continent of Africa over time. In fact, the contention by the World Bank to the effect that one of the casual determinants of Africa's development crisis is declining (foreign) investment [World Bank, 1989:25] can be seen in terms of the corrupt nature of the investment climate manifested in political as well as bureaucratic rent-seeking and subtle kick-back demands. It is instructive that a Kenyan Cabinet minister recently observed that demands for kick-backs on government contracts had escalated from the hitherto 10 per cent to 40 per cent! This kind of corruption adds an incalculable hazard to usual bureaucratic red tape which dismays and frustrates investors, both local and foreign who find that the unofficial cost of starting an enterprise is too great for it to be profitable. Additionally, the entrepreneur who acquiesces to corruption and bribes to get a government contract, charges the bribe to public funds in the final analysis. Hence corruption, a consequence of authoritarian governance and its lopsided modes of utilisation of the human resources, is a major hindrance to economic development as it engenders inefficiency, waste of public resources, and discouragement of foreign investment.

It is against this background that Adedeji Adebayo, long time Executive Secretary of the United Nations Economic Commission for Africa (UN-ECA) argues, from experience, that the African continent cannot hope for sustained economic development until its people achieve good governance. He asserts, "What we confront in Africa is primarily a political crisis albeit with devastating economic consequences" [*Sunday Nation*, September 15,1996:7]. Only good governance will create the requisite conditions for utilisation of the human resources on the basis of merit rather than on the basis of affection which fosters the incidence of corruption.

Utilisation of Financial Resources

Financial resources are the wherewithal for stimulating development. Since the advent of the money economy, funds have become the key determinant of access to labour, land and materials. The universality of its value and its "liquid" characteristic signifies that whoever gains access to money gains access to development and prosperity. In short, the concept of resources could justifiably be considered to be synonymous with the concept of money. It is of little wonder, then, that politics is defined in terms of competition for resources: who gets what, when, and how much.

Resources are often considered to be scarce; to be less than wants. Nearly all Third World governments have employed this maxim as a scapegoat for their failure to meet the development expectations of the citizens. Whereas resources may be truly scarce, it may be necessary to establish whether against the few resources that are available there is a proportionate measure of development being achieved. In Kenya, there is a discrepancy between the amount of financial resources that are available to the government and the degree of attainment of the goals of development. This discrepancy is a direct effect of a *de facto* governmental policy of misallocation and of public funds; a policy whose implementation is facilitated by the no longer functional system of governmental accountability.

Evidence of misallocation and misappropriation of public funds as a *de facto* governmental policy abound. But the more authentic of this evidence is that which is presented in the annual reports of the Controller and Auditor General. Every financial year, these reports tell the same old story about public financial mismanagement. In fact, they are a running commentary of *inter alia*, irregular tendering, operation of unauthorised bank accounts, payments made for work not done or for supplies not delivered, inflation of costs, unrecorded expenditures and, non repayment of government-borrowed loans by key government or party officials and supporters. Through these methods, the public loses colossal amounts of money, money that could have fuelled the engine of development some extra miles. For example, in his report in 1988, the Auditor General reported that government had lost Ksh 420 million due to irregular tender awards, appointments, and variation orders for the construction of Kasarani sports facilities; in 1989, he reported that Government Ministries had left the Paymaster General's accounts some Ksh. 3 billion the poorer in overdrawn unauthorised borrowing [*Sunday Nation*, August 18, 1996:7].

One of the most interesting facts about misuse of public funds such as outlined above is the reluctance and in some instances outright refusal of the government to impeach public officials implicated in of public funds. Witness, for example, the failure of the Attorney General to prosecute public officials implicated in the Goldenberg scandal in which the state is reported to have lost Ksh. 13 billion through official conspiracy. When the Law Society of Kenya (LSK) stepped in to undertake private prosecution of the suspected officials, the Attorney General took legal action to stop the proceedings.

Besides misappropriation of public funds, utilisation of public financial resources suffers greatly from governmental misallocation. Economic development is a technical process that requires economically rational decision-making if the desired goals should be maximised. This means that as much as practicable, financial resources should be allocated on the basis of objective economic criteria. But such neat arrangement of things presupposes the existence of a working democratic culture in which any departures from this arrangement are counteracted sufficiently by opposition groups who are always prepared to constitute an alternative government. It follows that in a failed democracy such as the Kenyan one, public financial resources are often allocated in accordance with the political expediency of the day while the collective socio-economic needs and imperatives in the society receive only secondary consideration. In the end public funds are allocated, first, to socio-economically irrational and wasteful projects and programmes and, second, to non-priority areas and regions.

Evidence abounds to socio-economically wasteful development projects and programmes, but which are perceived to be of tremendous political benefit. The establishment of a third international airport in Eldoret town whose construction commenced without the project going through international tendering procedures, and the construction of the Turkwel Gorge Hydro-electric Power generating complex which cost hundreds of millions of Kenya shillings, are cases in point. The Eldoret airport is considered to be an economically unviable project given the fact that the existing two similar airports in Mombasa and Nairobi are already operating below capacity. On the other hand, the Turkwel Gorge Project was built in an arid locality on a seasonal river such that it has not been able to satisfy the country's energy needs. However, the two projects are poised to satisfy the political goal of establishing modern physical and institutional infrastructure in the President's political stronghold of Rift Valley. In fact, during Presidents Moi's tenure, concerted efforts have been made to develop Eldoret town into a city. Such institutions as a second national university, the third branch of the Central Bank, military barracks, among others, have been established here.

Allocation of resources on economically irrational criterion is manifested also in the tendency to make more favourable allocations to groups and regions that belong to the political coalition of the incumbent regime and less favourable allocations or outright deprivations for regions and communities that are perceived to be critics or opponents of the incumbent regime. During Kenyatta's era, the Central Province and members of the Kikuyu community in general were considered to receive more favourable allocation while the Luoland is said to have received the least allocations [Nasong'o: 1996]. During Moi's era, on the other hand, the pattern of allocation changed in favour of the Rift Valley and the Kalenjin people more generally while the least favoured remains to be Luoland.

The establishment of multi-party system of government at the turn of the 1990s promised, *inter alia*, the restoration of governmental accountability to the public. Indeed, this is one of the cardinal pillars of democratic government. In the case of Kenya, however, the democratic benefit of governmental accountability was not realised. The outcome of the 1992 general elections had afforded the KANU government numerical superiority in the National Assembly with the consequence that the Opposition side emerges as a humble minority in the event of a vote aimed at censuring improper financial decisions and actions on the part of the government. Given this kind of scenario, misallocation of resources by the government persists. For instance, in the Auditor General's Report for the 1994-95 Financial year, it was revealed that a net total of ksh. 26 billion was not reflected in official financial accounts [*Sunday Nation*, August, 18,1996:7].

Responsibility for monitoring and checking utilisation of public funds by the government is bestowed more specifically in two organs of the National Assembly, namely the Public Accounts Committee (PAC) and the Public Investments Committee (PIC). Whereas these committees are chaired by Opposition Members of Parliament, their efficacy is inhibited by reliance on the officials of the government they are expected to control for records, information, oral evidence, and permission to visit public premises and installations in order to ascertain purported construction works or purchased supplies and equipment. For example, in July 1996, PAC wrote an open letter to the President requesting him to direct the Commissioner for Lands to surrender important records which he had declined to do. A few of these filed were subsequently submitted to the Committee. But, permission to verify public works at the Changamwe Military Barracks was denied. So was the request to compel certain public officials to present evidence before the Committee.

In short, the established Parliamentary machinery for controlling use of public funds by the government is not effective under the present multi-party politics as much as it was not during the preceding single party era. The covert persistence of authoritarianism on the part of the incumbent government has ensured that to the furthest extent possible, KANU MPs vote in favour of the government and against the Opposition in any motion that pits the two sides against each other, notwithstanding the substantive importance or validity of the matter at hand. Whatever gains of effectiveness which PAC and PIC has gained since the advent of the multi-party system is under severe threat from the government. For example, the KANU government has proposed that membership as well as chairmanship of Parliamentary committees should reflect the numerical size of a Party's representation in the National Assembly. Presently, these committees are chaired by the Official Leader of the Opposition and their numerical composition favours Opposition MPs. Therefore, if the proposed changes should be effected, the substantive impact will be to have the financial activities of the KANU government checked and monitored by its own persons. This in turn, will spell adverse repercussions on the principle of mutual checks and balances.

CONCLUSION

Sub-Sahara African countries have remained in a state of economic crisis throughout the last almost three decades of independence. The persistence of poverty and deprivation on the continent may be attributed to the failure of policy makers and academics alike to recognise the root cause of the problem. Conventional wisdom has suggested scarcity of resources and environmental hostility to be leading causes of the crisis of development.

However, empirical evidence as adduced in this paper suggests that despite the prevalence of resource scarcity and a hazardous environment, higher measures of development in Africa and Kenya in particular, are possible if there is in place more visionary and accountable governments. Thus, the development crisis in Kenya and in Sub-Saharan Africa in general is a crisis of political leadership.

REFERENCES

Fundaga, C. (1974) "The Economics of Foreign Aid" in Baghwati, C. *Aid and Dependency,* Penguin Books.

Gertzel, C. (1974), *The Politics of Independent Kenya,* Nairobi: Heinemann Educational Books.

Gertzel, C. *et.al.* (eds) (1972), *Politics and Government in Kenya*. Nairobi: East African Publishing House.

Nasong'o, S.W. (1996), "Nationalism and State Integrity in Kenya", A Paper presented at the African Association of Political Science (Kenya Chapter) Seminar on "Democracy and the Constitutional Process in Kenya", Nairobi: April 26, 1996.

Organisation of African Unity, (1982), *Lagos Plan of Action for the Economic Development of Africa 1980-2000,* Geneva: International Institute for Labour Studies.

Sunday Nation, September 15, 1996.

Timberlake, L. (1991), *African in Crisis: The Causes, the Cures of Environmental Bankruptcy,* London: Earthscan Publications.

World Bank, (1981), *Accelerated Development in Sub-Saharan Africa: An Agenda For Action,* Washington.

__________ ,(1989), *Sub-Saharan Africa: From Crisis to Sustainable Growth,* Washington.

7 AFRICAN GOOD GOVERNANCE: REVISITED

AGOSTINHO ZACARIAS

INTRODUCTION

The idea of good governance implies the notion of the good state. Throughout generations, philosophers, statesmen and other thinkers, informed by practical experience, have tried to produce an account of the state that can best provide an ameliorated quality of life, reduce conflict, and secure harmony among people. However, the accounts of the state produced do not seem to enjoy much consensus around the world. The international society has yet to agree on the account of a good state and on the role of the rest of the community in situations where qualifying criteria for a good state are not fulfilled.

This paper examines the nature of the African states, that is to say, those that resulted from the process of de-colonisation. It argues that good governance without a good state is impossible, since good governance is premised on understanding of the needs of, and a sense of justice for, the people, things which under the present international system are to be granted by a legitimate state. However, legitimate states are yet to be created in Africa. The paper further argues that although in the Western political thought, there may be a disagreement on how morality is achieved in society, in the works of Hobbes, Locke, Hegel and Weber, there is agreement that the state is a moral realm. The state is a source of all values and authority conferred by strong Christian ethics which it rests upon. African states are a place for competition between Christian, Muslim and local religions which inspire different practices, priorities, agendas and ethics. The paper further argues that the nature of colonisation that Africa was subjected to has not allowed the assimilation of basic concepts underpinning modern political and economic thought. The Western agenda for good governance is thus doomed to failure because it takes an ethnocentric view of legitimacy, human rights, and democracy. This ethnocentricity has tended to create more problems than it solves, and to jeopardise the stability of newly created states. Good governance is a medium if not a long term goal that needs to be achieved by strengthening civil society.

IDEAS OF THE STATE IN WESTERN SOCIETIES

The development of the idea of the state in the Western political tradition has always been motivated by the search for the optimal account of the state, the ethical space that would best serve the needs of its citizens. It is in the works of philosophers such as Hobbes, Locke, Hegel, and Weber that the different ideas of the state as a moral entity are best articulated.

For Thomas Hobbes, morality without the state was impossible, because obligations could not be maintained in unlegalised social conditions. He held, in his work *Leviathan* (1651), that no recognisable social order could exist without the state. This has led people to assume that the mere existence of the state is sufficient to guarantee the moral realm, legitimising the struggle of different communities to create their own state. However, Hobbes had his own idea of the good state and the ways to achieve it. The good state, for him, would be attained through a social contract between the citizens and the *Leviathan* (the supreme sovereign)[1]. The members of the political community should give their original freedom to a Leviathan who would make laws to regulate relations among citizens, monitor breaches of the law, and eventually punish the guilty. So Hobbes's good state would be one that had a coherent government and a legally and indisputable administrative system. For Hobbes the principle of good governance rested upon the efficient way in which the Leviathan made use of his authority to make laws, mitigate conflict among citizens, and punish lawbreakers in the way he believed right. In Hobbes's account of the good state, citizens would have certain rights, such as the right to judge whether the supreme sovereign was maintaining public order. However, their judgement could never imply putting into jeopardy the existing order, since the Leviathan, as absolute sovereign, symbolised the summation of individual freedoms. For Hobbes, political agendas other than those coming from the Leviathan were not welcomed, because the disruption of order entailed moral risk.

Hobbes's contemporary John Locke, in his *Two Treatises of Government* (first published in 1690), argued that a natural order preceded the existence of the state. Families, corporations, judgements, and punishments were there before the state existed. His was a pluralistic society in which the state existed to manage and mitigate the diversity of requirements coming from different individuals and groups. In other words, as Navari puts it, "the state was founded to deal only with the inconvenience which is brought about by a variety of social

---

[1] See, Thomas Hobbes, ***the Leviathan***, (London: Penguin Classics, 1976).

impulses"[1]. Thus in the Lockian account, a good state would be one which is responsive rather than one with self-government. Good governance in his mind would be the attempt to create an order similar to the present liberal democracy, in which the state would merely facilitate the interaction between individuals and the various groups in a society, rather than defining rules and providing leadership in the political sphere. Thus, the primary ethical feature in this account is not a coherent government but a reactive political process which merely performs a responsive function to individual and group requirements. A government that took initiatives would be practising bad governance, by interfering with a naturally generated process that reflects the will of the citizens. To practise good governance, it would have to wait until it was asked by the members of the society to facilitate.

Writing in the mid nineteenth century, G.W.F. Hegel held a third view. For him, the Lockian concept of a pre-state society did not exist at all. Pre-state societies were particularistic in their nature. They were bound by cultural traditions, beliefs, and norms extensive only to those societies. However, it was not until the state was created that the ultimate ethical test was passed, when the conditions of corporate existence transcended the cultural boundaries of particular societies and the potential selfishness of mere need and want. Hegel argued that whereas it was in particular cultural groups that the potential ethical community could be forged, it was in establishing the legal order of the state that people showed their willingness to make sacrifices for the community they belonged to.[2] Therefore, a state assumes a moral purpose of wanting a greater good for that particular community. Thus, for Hegel, a good state is only attainable within a nation state, in which the community coincides with the boundaries of the state. Good governance, for him, would be the process of serving the collective will of a particular community, regardless of the ways this community is internally structured.

Another thinker, Max Weber, argued that science was the only moral basis that can provide a sound political action, since science was the only legitimate basis for knowledge. He argued against the idea that the Hegelian community could provide for the rational reasons of the state. For him a good state would be one that took the form of a rational, knowing, technocratically oriented bureaucracy which served the state-purpose, the purpose of a collective organisation of multiple

---

1 Quoted in Iaian Hmpsher-Monk, *A History of Modern Political Thought, Major Political Thinkers From Hobbes to Marx*, (Oxford: Blackwell,1992), pp.73-107.

2 *Ibid.* pp.413-465.

needs and requirements, comprehended rationally[1]. All the pre-Weberian states serve pre-articulated prejudices, such as religion or other cultural and particular politics. For Weber, the only good state would only be the Weberian state. Thus, he saw good governance as the ability to undertake rational, scientifically grounded political action and to create institutions that would be equally scientifically grounded. Thus, the Weberian account of the state excludes states founded on religious principles, such as the Zionist state or the Islamic state including those with doubtful scientific foundations lacking means to put the bureaucratic machine in operation. Many states around the world, especially those created in the 1950s and 1960s, would hardly correspond to the Weberian account of the state.

Despite the apparent differences of the Western philosophers on how the good state is achieved, the Western state lies on strong Judaic-Christian ethics. Its laws, traditions are deeply rooted in Christianity. Historians tell us that Mediaeval society was criss-crossed with overlapping groups and conflicting loyalties and rules. The only loyalty that transcended particular communities was to the Church. For example, in *Respublica Christiana*, Christianity and Citizenship were inseparable. All authority was derived from God. Christian education and learning was part of civil education. The Church was considered the highest authority. As Vincent put it "the Church was not only higher and more important than civil authority but to an extent incorporated in it"[2]. This marriage between Christianity and statehood became the main vehicle through which the state came to gain such ethical grounding. The debate between Western philosophers helped to shape the nature of states that look so stable today in the Western world. Inspired by thinkers mentioned above and by other scholarly work, Europeans went through various processes of war, trial and error, and intellectual debate culminating in the present modern state which is regarded most people's political predicaments and social conditions.

The fact that the European debate over the ideas of the state responded to the main socio-political demands of the European public and were deeply rooted in their heritage meant that they could be easily assimilated and appropriated by them and passed on to younger generations, as traditions. This has created a sense of stability even

---

1 See, Max Weber, "Politics as a Vocation" in H. H. Gerth and C. Wright Mills (eds), ***From Max Weber: Essays in Sociology.*** (London: Routledge,1993), pp.77-128.

2 See, Andrew Vincent, ***Theories of the State,*** (Oxford: Blackwell, 1987), p.15.

when these states tended towards secularisation. Christian traditions brought about a sense of self-containment, responsibility, and preparedness to protect traditions and values regarded as crucial, when these were threatened by new ideas These traditions became part of European culture and European history.

THE AFRICAN STATES

The development of African statehood, did not, however, follow the same path. Indeed, African states are in a disadvantaged position compared with European states. They did not have the chance to choose whether they should develop in the direction of Hobbes, Locke, Hegel, or Weber. African states were not a part of the society that created the international system. Their place and fate in the international system had been decided long before their existence as independent units. When they emerged, a well-established society of states, with established rules, regulations, and power distribution,- the Western International System- was already in place[1]. The principle of sovereignty that African states have inherited was not sufficient to accord them the rational choice of a model of the state and a form of government most suited to their social conditions. Since they were created by international law, the idea of adjusting to the status and rules of the international society in which they operated took precedence over the idea of organising their political space in the best possible way.

There is yet another disadvantage which would make the task of catching up difficult. African states are successors of colonial states which had been established to fulfil functional purposes, often in disregard of ethics. These states were bureaucratically designed and repressive in character. They were discriminatory and exploitative in nature and they hardly regarded native Africans as citizens. The violent character and exploitative nature of these states could not be reconciled with Christian ethics. They were seen by most Africans as alien structures, whose primary concern was to assure the domination of natives rather than their common good

There is a need to consider yet another factor Not all the people who came to power at the day of independence had been influenced by Christianity. Some were Muslims, others were atheists. Others were also strongly influenced by local religions such as Totemism and Animism. This implies that they had different conceptions and outlooks

---

1 See, Hedley Bull and Adam Watson (eds), *The Expansion of International Society*, (Oxford: Oxford University Press, 1985).

of the idea of the state. Some regarded it as a source of authority, others regarded it as a source of the long waited accumulation of wealth, while others expected the state to become the source of the common good. Thus, in African state-making, Christian ethics found itself in competition with other values such as Islam and other local religions. For example, the Islamic conception of statehood are different from those of the West. The state, in Islam, is not regarded as a territorial unit, but a community of people bonded by the same religion, *umma.* Unlike the notion of the Western state, the concept of *dar al Islam,*[1] is not a territorial based concept, but a people's based concept. Regardless of where they are, if people profess Islam they are part of the Muslim nation and state.[2] Islam would also respect the sovereignty of the all merciful and all-powerful and all-compassionate God-Allah whose laws were revealed to his prophet, Mohammed. This implies that political authority in Islam is interlinked with the religion, only a religious leader would be legitimate to occupy a public office. However, this notion of statehood, is in direct contradiction with principles informing the Western state wherein sovereignty is conferred by man-made laws and rules, and these are adjusted or amended on a basis of a dialectical process debating what is believed to be beneficial to the entire society.

Animist and Totemism practices are also often in contradiction with Muslim and Christian ethics. They emphasise ancestry, family and individual relations with Gods.[3] Ethical community is best achieved within the family or within the family of ancestors. The gods or the totems of the family explain the relationships between families and their ancestors or individuals and their ancestors. They explain what is wrong with nature, with friends, with sources of authority or colleagues at work. Harmony in much larger groupings is achieved by extending this kinship. Family is the centre and provides the foundations for the state. This implies that from the animist point of view, the state will be seen as bonding different families in relations of harmony and not by contractual relations.

Moreover, it is noteworthy that at independence, Africa inherited high illiteracy rates. The only people who have had access to education are those who filled the vacancies left by the colonisers in central

1 *Dar al Islam* is an area of peace and harmony inhabited by the faithful, which in time would encompass the entire planet.

2 See for example, Muhammad Fazl-Ur-Rahman Ansari, *The Qur'anic foundations and the structure of Muslim Society*, Vol.II, (Karachi: Zubair Printing Press), pp. 344-349.

3 See, Anthony Giddens, *Sociolog,y* (London: Polity Press, 1989), p.459.

government. Thus, African states became an array of clusters of African elites occupying public offices in the capitals of new states. The notion of the state boiled down to what these elities thought it should be and what they were capable of doing. This implies that the state in Africa, far from being a moral realm, a place of consensus, the synthesis of common good, from the outset it has been a place of conflict between competing ethical values and elite interests.

Although secularism represented a compromise between these different ethical perspectives shaped by different cultures and religions, secularism did not rest upon common traditions. It made African states to look like any other European state viewed from outside, but their home conditions were different[1]. They came from different traditions and heritage, Elites did not conform to the idea of homogeneous political units upon which most states are premised. Citizens of African states had various allegiances at the sub-national level. State structures that Africans had inherited were alien and different from the way their political culture and organisation was shaped during colonisation.

The final thing to consider is that the processes of self-determination that led to the formation of African states were more exogenous than endogenous. The pressures of granting self-determination in post-1945, did not allow for the transformation of a colonial state into an instrument serving the common good. Independence meant replacing a white government and a foreign flag, by a black or coloured government and national flag, but no substantial transformation on the nature of structure was attained. National self-determination was needed because it would avoid war amongst the Great Powers but its implications for the new states were underestimated. States lacked a financial base, know-how, human resources and skilled labour to maintain their independence and compete with other states in the international arena. These new states lacked strong economic and political base to manage societal conflict and interests of various groups. Thus they lacked foundations for good-governance.

CHALLENGES TO GOOD STATEHOOD

The process of building a good state has not proved to be simple, and it has often met with opposition both within the state and outside its boundaries. Internal opposition groups often claim fairer distribution of the scarce resources, while external agents insist on specific policy

---

[1] See for example Caroline Thomas, *The New States, Sovereignty and Intervention*, (Harvester Wheatsheaf and Lynne Rienner, 1985).

agendas which in many instances are not what home governments feel to be the highest priority or the correct course of action. Thus, African governments are left with the only opportunity to negotiate their survival through the search for an optimal balance between pleasing the domestic constituencies and the external actors rather than adopting measures leading to the common good of their peoples. There is constant interference by Western governments, Bretton Woods institutions and NGO's bringing external policy agendas in the domestic environment of Africa thus limiting choices. African governments are now burdened with multiple policy agendas given to them as strings attached to aid, or through a genuine will to help. Today, a minister of finance of one of these states, before adopting a particular fiscal policy, rushes to make sure that the policy he adopts does not harm IMF or the World Bank policies. A minister of law and order, before submitting a tough piece of legislation to the parliament or suggesting imposing the state of emergency, rushes to see whether this legislation will displease states A, B, or C, who provide aid to his country under the democratisation programme. When he/she formulates a land reform policy, the minister of planning and development thinks about whether it will upset certain foreign governments upon which his country is dependent for aid and not to what extent his policies are beneficial to his fellow nationals. The minister of agriculture cannot take any measures that may upset NGOs active in the countryside, since this may also be reflected in the aid budget the country will receive in the following year.

This interference has often resulted in weakening governments' authority, inspired polarisation and fragmentation rather than national unity, that is, the consolidation of existing states into coherent political units. Despite all the weaknesses of African states and inconsistencies of their governments, the post-colonial state in Africa is still being presented as the only way to win international recognition and support, the only way for Africans to have a say in international affairs. However, this implies that their design is no longer aimed at suiting the interests of their peoples, but those of the prevailing international order. The weak economic basis of the African states increased their vulnerability to external manipulation. They are unable to control the multitude of agents operating in their political space, and their chances to become good states have been further undermined by project designs of contradictory nature or by an obsession to establish a particular order.

Indeed, the situation suggests the existence of divergent political projects right from the outset, that is, when African states achieved their independence. Judging from the principles enshrined in the OAU charter, African states were chiefly concerned with the process of nation-building, keeping together communities that had very little in common other than inhabiting the same territorial state and being colonised by the same power. The countries of the West, to which the present international system is owed to were more concerned with preventing the newly formed states from challenging the status quo. The difficulty in reconciling the priorities for maintaining the international system with those of the different communities in Africa is one factor responsible for undermining the process of building good or stable states. For example, the West's agenda on good governance, democracy and human rights are placed high. It is noteworthy that democracy is often used as a euphemism for liberal democracy. However, Africa has found Western conceptions of democracy different from its conceptions and priorities on human rights agenda irrelevant to their domestic arena. What scholars and politicians have not found is a yardstick of what constitute a model of the good state and principles and a formula - similar to the Newtonian formula in Physics to be followed in order to create a good state.

DEMOCRACY IN CRISIS?

The theme that democracy can lead to international stability is found in Kant. It was re-asserted by Wilson in his liberal internationalism agenda which led him to advocate national self-determination as the basis for international order. This line of argument was recently stressed by Doyle in his assertion that stable democracies do not fight;[1] hence the West's insistence that this should constitute the basis of international order. However it was already clear for John Stuart Mill that democracy could not always be trusted. It could produce the wrong results. He argued that it was likely to be subverted by strong groups in a given country[2]. Indeed, winning multiparty elections is not always the best option and the best criterion for assessing how democratic a certain state is or according legitimacy to a particular government. Other factors than its legitimacy can get a government elected, such as intimidation, fraud, or gerrymandering. Recent developments in Algeria and elsewhere in the continent have proved Mill right and have created more confusion as to what type of democracy could be an indication of good governance. Multiparty democracy, which is regarded by Western

---

1 Michael Doyle, "Liberalism and World Politics", *American Political Science Review*, Vol.80:4, 1986, pp.151-69

2 John Stuart Mill, *Representative Government*, London, Penguin, 1976, Chap.16

states as more legitimate, since it allows free political competition and the opportunity to choose a government on the basis of its merits; or on the popularity of the policies it purports to implement,[1]has led the Islamic fundamentalist movement *Front Islamique du Salut* (FIS) to win the 1992 elections. However, the FIS was not allowed to take power and top echelons of the military formed a government. This government, though largely contested internally, is strongly supported abroad, particularly by Western governments, because it is perceived as strengthening the status quo.

In Angola, attempts at establishing multiparty democracy have led to the post-Bicesse Civil war which had to be resolved through power sharing or consociation arrangements which had little to do with multiparty free competition. Indeed events in Angola led the West to adopt a revisionist version of democracy: "Competition, yes! — but the winner cannot take all." This version of democracy "the winner cannot take all" informed the post-1992 peace negotiations in Angola that led the signature of Lusaka Protocol, it was offered as a source of stability for Mozambique, and it was adopted as a guiding principle for the 1994 South African elections. Yet, this principle was rejected by the Mozambican government and it was rendered unworkable by the South African National Party. Despite grumbles in certain quarters, the West has found Museveni's "democracy without parties" a major spur for economic development in Uganda.

What the above examples show is the inconsistency of the West in agreeing to abide by one set of rules; the difficulty in finding an answer as to which type of democracy and which political formula can lead to political stability. This situation raises the question whether the concept of legitimacy can be externally imposed or be exported to other societies; whether good-governance can be judged from a country's democratic record, and whatever the standards of measurement may be.

In most African countries the basis of legitimacy is kinship and seniority. In rural societies legitimacy is accorded to elder members of a certain lineage rather than to someone else who might have better education or a fancy political program.[2] The family that has lived longest in a certain place can have more legitimacy than any politician promising to introduce an ambitious programme. The legitimate leader is more likely to be the one who could win over a stranger to become a

---

1 See "Taking into account good-government" *Technical Note 10, Government and Institutions Department*, (Overseas Development Administration London, October, 1993).

2 See, Christian Geffray, *La cause des Arms au Mozambiqu,e* (Paris : Karthala, 1991).

member of the family than the one who promises to observe the prescribed development policy strictly. Kinship is accorded a high value and plays a very important role in binding the society together. Where real kinship is non-existent, the tendency is to replace it with an artificial kinship.[1] The idea of kinship constitutes the basis of identity for rural societies in Africa and is a core value taken into account by the law-making institutions. This suggests that if liberal internationalism does not respect these realities it will cut across important cultural traditions and values in a way that further weakens the sources of authority, thus undermining good-governance.

The difficulty in reconciling the priorities of African communities with those of the international system has also made African governments insecure. African governments see themselves as having to perform miracles in very short time that they are elected to government. Given the amount of resources available and the endemic problems African states face most governments have found good-governance- the task of building a good state-, to be an impossible task. This situation has tended to reinforce the view of the state as vehicle for accumulation of wealth. Members of African governments are generally from poor background, while their countries do not possesses important business that can absorb ex-government members and accord them the level of privileges they had when they were members of government. This has tended to reinforce corruption in the most cyclical manner. The honest remain honest while outside the government. His/her honesty ceases the day he/she ascends to power. What this situation raises is the question whether the recommended agenda for good governance is dealing with concepts that can be universally applicable? The answer to this question is no, which suggests that we are to come up with a theory that need to look to the question of governance in its historical context.

HUMAN RIGHTS AND GOOD GOVERNANCE

In the context of good governance, the human rights discourse has tended to emphasise the process of government rather than the content of policies. However, in the agenda of good governance, human rights is about the process of government as well as the content of policies. Focusing on the process of government inevitably leads to the situation in which a hierarchy of rights is established, most often using the least convincing criterion.

---

1 See details in *Mozambique Street Children*, Study Prepared for UNICEF, 1989.

When President Carter came to power in 1977, in expression of the Administration's commitment to Wilsonian "idealism" accorded human rights high place in his government agenda. Africans, and most of the Third World, were led to believe that the US, was finally going to address most of their problems, such as famine, disease, i.e. the rights of subsistence. But the US came to support only civil and political rights. The idea that economic rights, and in particular the rights of subsistence should also be placed high in the agenda of the great powers, has been resisted since the 1970's and this resistance was reiterated in the 1993 World Conference on Human Rights in Vienna.[1] None the less, the idea that civil and political rights are more important than economic and cultural rights is questionable, particularly when one thinks that the notion of human rights, when reduced to its least significant form, means the right to life. The ensuing question, then, becomes whether political and civil rights are more crucial guarantors of the right to life than economic, social, and cultural rights. The difference on which rights are the most fundamental has become a gap between the North and South and is difficult to bridge. Africa and the Third World have argued that the insistence of the West in placing high, in the debate on good governance, civil and political rights, establishes a hierarchy strongly influenced by cultural priorities and interests of the promoters of the agenda. This insistence is less convincing to Africa, and is yet another factor undermining good-governance.

The other level of debate about human rights pertains to the question who should do what in the case of these rights not being observed by governments. In other words, what are the rights and obligations of outsiders when human rights are violated in a given state? Should the rest of the international community intervene or take action against this government, and which are the rights that will help to formulate the criterion for intervention? Should political and civil rights have precedence over social, cultural, and economic rights? Shall the rest of the community sanction or work towards the replacement of this government? These questions do not seem to have easy answers. The idea that the United States considers flogging in Mozambique (before 1988) or in Singapore a violation of human rights, while it retains capital punishment at home, has not helped to clarify this issue. Instead, it has allowed the human rights debate to be seen in terms of

---

1 See, *Democracy and Human Rights: Where America Stands* speech delivered by the US Foreign Secretary, Warren Christopher, at the World Conference on Human Rights in 1993.

power relations. Only weak states, those that are economically over-dependent, would agree to a *quid-pro-quo* for economic aid, to implement this agenda. The Singapore government, for example, would say that tough laws and tough punishment help to create a safe environment and deter criminals, while soft laws do not discourage criminal activity. Governments such as Mozambique, are most likely to agree with Singapore, because since the relaxation of law, liberalisation of markets, the roll back of the state, imposed by the necessity to create economic efficiency, has resulted in criminality climbing high. Now, donor countries threaten to cut aid if security in the country is not improved. However, by no means should this be taken to mean that governments should ignore civil and political rights from their good-governance agenda. What it says is that if the idea of rights is a social construct accorded by recognition of certain values by a particular society, it is to be expected that values of other societies that have not been assimilated by any particular society will be rejected.[13] Therefore, the good-governance agenda should recognise the specific conditions of societies.

The other question which the human rights debate has not solved pertains to the hierarchy of claimants of human rights: it is the question of whether the rights of an individual should take precedence over the rights of a group or nation, and who determines priorities.[1] Can a number of states, or a supranational institution, find an objective criterion which would enable this hierarchy to be established determine who should intervene in the case of a violation and what to do?

The challenge is whether the criterion for allowing the rest of the international community to intervene or take action against a government can escape the scrutiny of cultural relativism and be as objective as possible, so as to allow all members of the present international community to intervene in other states' affairs on an equal footing, wherever human rights are violated. This would help us to regard the question of human rights as a collective duty and responsibility rather than as an instrument allowing the powerful to impose their political objectives.

However, these normative questions cannot be resolved without addressing the question of universal fundamental rights. The question of universal human rights raises, in turn, the question of institutions, since it is not sufficient to assert that universal rights exist and

---

1 Se, R. J. Vincent and Peter Wilson " Beyond Intervention" in Ian Forbes and Mark Hoffman (eds), *Political Theory, International Relations and Ethics of Intervention*, (London: MacMillan, 1993), pp 122-130.

everyone needs to uphold them. Institutions responsible for organising, promoting, and giving practical significance to these rights are necessary. These institutions would have to dissociate themselves from the national interest agendas of their individual countries and have as their constituency the citizens of the whole world.

The enquiry made by critical international theory into the question of the obligations and rights of outsiders in cases where human rights are violated by the government of a particular state recognises the present difficulty in defining these obligations and rights as inherent in the state system, because it is bound by the principle of sovereignty and territorial integrity which discriminates between outsiders and insiders. Yet the state has increasingly been called into question as a form of organising political life. This has taken Hoffman to suggest, instead, the expansion of political communities to the point where there will be no distinction between outsiders and insiders in a given political space. Hoffman argues that this would both avoid the dangers of cultural imperialism and embrace cosmopolitanism, which self-consciously acknowledges the possibility of multiple identities.[1]

This proposition leaves us with a very important question: where should we start and how should we proceed in the event of an agreement on adopting international citizenship? Shall we start by granting economic rights to the new states so as to bring them up to the standards of the developed world, and then proceed with the cultural homogenisation of societies? Or shall we start by educating societies in the idea of the cosmopolis and then proceed to grant them equal economic rights so as to improve their living standards? Will the new identities be strong and attractive enough to detach everyone from their original identities in such a way that they would feel part of the world society[2] and placed at the core of it? Or would they continue to be on the fringes, as most people feel now in the present arrangement of systems and states?

These considerations suggest that the section of the good governance agenda dealing with the question of human rights should seek to ensure that the content of policies undertaken by a particular government are beneficial to the majority of its people, rather than concentrating on the process of government.

---

1 See, Mark Hoffman, "Agency, Identity and Intervention" in Forbes and Hoffman, *op. cit.*, pp. 194-20.

2 The term "World society" is used here in the sense of a global society in which there is a certain degree of homogenisation.

WHERE DO WE GO FROM HERE?

Because the problems of African states are endemic, and because the West has spent large amount of resources in trying to fix them without results, in the 1990s, the West has tended to treat the continent with carrot-and-stick approach. Aid conditionally is the most evident example. However, in many instances, foreign policy agendas of the Western states have tended to push African governments to adopt certain policies, often without noticing whether there is a capacity to guarantee continuity of these policies.

When these policies are devised it is assumed that:

- states and societies in Africa have to be shaped on the Western model;
- the policies devised will work in these states because they worked elsewhere;
- the target states have the necessary conditions, and that it is in their interest to implement these policies.

The evidence has, however, demonstrated that Africa has a different cultural, political and economic environment, particularly, from that of Europe. Unlike Asia, Africa has not invested much in education, and training especially of technocrats in the last 30 years. Because of their diminished importance in the global strategic interests African states have not attracted the support of big powers such the US or Japan, i.e. they have not been given conditions and enough time to mature. Foreign policy agendas and the advice coming from outside has failed to recognise these particular conditions, and has often responded with intolerance.

To shape African states on the Western model, which is a pre-condition to access good-governance from the Western view point, will require altering the cultural foundations on which these states rest upon. This task is only attainable in the medium, if not in the long term. It will require large investments in education, to guarantee that the state is run by technocrats, or by individuals with deep seated Western state culture. As things stand, at present, the action of governing elites collides with that of the majority that have not been permeated by Western state traditions. The governing elites, cannot take initiatives that are unpopular at home and abroad. However, what is popular at home is often unpopular abroad. They are thus fragile, and powerless. While their political power is internally determined their economic power is externally determined. This has reduced their ability to attain good governance. However, the development of statehood in Europe shows that authority and discipline are asserted if there is unity between economic and political power. In his fascinating work Charles Tilly has demonstrated that European states began as instruments of subjugation and as protection rackets, in a symbiotic relationship between those who held instruments of violence and the merchants[1]. To do their business without risking their lives and robberies, merchants bought protection from those who had instruments of violence. Those who had the instruments of violence could increase their power, and their quality of governance due to the economic benefits they received from merchants.[2] Tilly's insight tells us that it will be difficult to achieve good governance if there is no marriage between economic and political power. Economic power is crucial and provides incentives for better political organisation while good political organisation results in economic and other material benefits. It is in the marriage of these two powers that lay the foundations of good statehood. This implies that good governance in Africa can only be achieved with economic empowerment of the civil service. Provision of good salaries and housing and other incentives can make the task of governing worthwhile.

Economic empowerment of the civil service is not by itself sufficient to attain good governance. There is a necessity of establishing conditions in which it will be possible to check and control the excesses of governing elites. This can be achieved by strengthening the various elements that comprise the civil society.

The question of strengthening civil society however, raises the question of who is going to do it and how? This issue has aroused controversy, since states are concerned with the question of protecting their sovereignty.

Governments, the population at large and the donor community, all have responsibilities in strengthening civil society and they should see this to be to their advantage. Governments can only be stable if they are trusted by the people who elected them and if their domestic environment is not characterised by pervasive conflict. The responsibility lies in creating a legal framework and encouraging organisation which will help to strengthen the country, economically, socially and politically. Without encouragement or an adequate legal framework, the population will find it hard to organise and this may

---

1 See, Charles Tilly, "War Making and State-Making as Organized Crime", in Peter, B. Evans, Dietrich Rueschmeyer, and Theda Skocpol (eds), *Bringing the State Back In,* (London: Cambridge University Press, 1985), pp.169-191.

2 *Ibid.*, pp 175-184.

invite interference from the outside. The population at large is the ultimate beneficiary of a strong civil society. The population is the one that knows its preoccupations and interests which can be achieved through the organisation. Finally, it is to the advantage of the donor community to strengthen civil society, because they are likely to spend less and avoid conflict with African governments. However, this will require from them different approaches. Instead of pushing policies through they should support local initiatives and be patient when these are not forthcoming. The donor community can also help create regional networks by supporting networking projects and programs and links between regional organisations and overseas.

CONCLUSION

Good governance, in the Western conception, is a medium if not long term project in Africa. States are not equipped to undertake good governance in Western terms. African states lack appropriate human resources, financial resources to , at least, maintain in state machinery, the few qualified people available in their countries. They are struggling to create a common culture that can provide an ethical grounding to the state. States in Africa have been a place of competition between different ethical values, to change this and providing a common culture needs time to develop indigenous dynamics, which can bring into conflation Western principles with local culture and sensitivities. Donors need to be more understanding of the environment in which they operate.

8 Corruption and Growth: A Study of Corruption Types

R N Ghosh and M A B Siddique

Introduction

For over three decades now, serious scholars have been examining the impact of corruption on economic growth. In the literature going as far back as 1963, Olson argued that rapid economic growth would tend to undermine good political institutions and create instability. In other words, Olson was looking at the negative correlation between good institutions and economic growth, and sought to explain crime and corruption as an outcome of a process of rapid economic growth, in which *expectations* of the masses to improve their material standards outstripped the ability of the political, judicial, bureaucratic and economic institutions of a society to deliver the goods. For example, during a festive season if the expectation of a community is that people should travel out of metropolitan areas to have a holiday in the country-side, the transport system involving roadways, railways and the air-network may not be able to cope with the rush, creating a situation where the more desperate people would try to bribe their way out by offering monetary incentives to, say, railway booking clerks for receiving preferential treatment. In other words, whenever the demand for a particular good or service exceeds its supply, there would be a potential for both crime and corruption. Economic scarcities tend to promote corruption; and crime and corruption are virtually the two sides of the same coin.

Mancur Olson's argument was further developed by other writers in the 1960s to put forward the view that corruption, instead of creating potential institutional instability, would actually improve efficiency and might indeed *raise* economic growth. For example, Nathaniel Leff (1964) and Samuel Huntington (1968) argued that the effect of corruption on economic growth was likely to be positive. First the "bribe money" offered to bureaucrats might "speed up" and reduce red-tape and delays in important decision-making processes. For example, an investor, who faces a government regulation that an application for an industrial licence must be lodged at least six months in advance, could possibly bypass the system by bribing the bureaucrats to make a much quicker decision. In this case, however, corruption would work to facilitate growth in the countries where bureaucratic regulations are too complex and cumbersome.

In another situation where the level of red-tape is not too cumbersome, corruption might still have a beneficial effect on economic growth if it would induce the bribe-takers to work harder than they would normally do. For example, if an official takes bribe to work an additional hour to make an important decision for, say, a potential investor such corruption should promote economic growth. Bribery, then, is seen as an incentive to work harder, as in an "overaward" system.

By the late 1970s the contrary view was gaining currency *viz.* that corruption would tend to lower economic growth. For example, Susan Rose-Ackerman (1978) was arguing that it would not be easy to limit corruption to areas in which it might be economically desirable. Once corruption begins to spread like a cancerous cell, it would eat into even healthy areas of the society and destroy any change towards - to borrow Pitman's (1993) term "civicness" i.e., civilised existence. For example, if corruption were to encourage officials to overlook enforcements of the quality control of drugs, its effect would not be beneficial for economic growth and 'civicness'.

The studies conducted by Leff and Huntington have been severely criticised by several writers in more recent years. Paolo Mauro (1995) pointed out that government officials might artificially create delays in order to receive the speed money (bribe). In this sense, corrupt practices, which might avoid delay for an individual, would actually increase the red tape for the economy as a whole. The same problem would also occur where bribes were used a piece rate compensation. Officials would artificially lower their output rate when bribes were not received, thereby creating a direct relationship between output and bribery.

Following Becker and Stigler (1974), a number of studies have been made to examine the perverse effect of corruption in public life on economic development. The Gould and Amaro-Reyes (1993), United Nations (1989), and Klitgaard (1988), studies conclude that corruption slows down development. The structure of government institutions and of the political process are very important determinants of the level of corruption. Shleifer and Vishny (1993) argue that weak governments that do not control their agencies experience very high corruption levels. Moreover, the illegality of corruption and the need for secrecy would make it much more distortionary and costly than its "sister activity", taxation. It might explain why in many developing countries with weak governments, the level of corruption is high, thereby retarding the rate of economic growth.

THE WORLD BANK ON GOOD GOVERNMENT

The World Bank monograph on *Governance and Development* (1992) was a turning point in the debates concerning the effects of corrupt governments on economic growth. The World Bank argued that good governance was an essential complement to sound economic policies. Efficient and accountable management by the public sector and a predictable and transparent policy framework are critical to the efficiency of markets and governments, and hence to economic development.

In general, it is possible to advance the proposition that in a liberal economic system, based on the principles of free market, economic freedom and competition, the scope for corruption in public life to distort economic processes is more limited than in a highly regulated and controlled economy based on excessive governmental intervention. However, "even in societies that are highly market-oriented only governments can provide two sorts of public goods: rules to make markets work efficiently and corrective interventions where there are market failures. With respect to rules, without the institutions and supportive framework of the state to create and enforce the rules, to establish law and order, and to ensure property rights, production and investment will be deterred and development hindered". (The World Bank, 1992).

To prevent market failure, the state has to provide services such as education, health and essential infrastructure, so that the private sector is not deterred by the high costs of such services. Direct government investment in areas of market failure is not always a good solution to the problem. Historically, in many developing countries the public sector undertakings failed to operate efficiently. As a result, they did not yield adequate returns on capital, and led to misallocation of resources.

A free market is an *artefact*. Players in the market such as producers and consumers have to follow the rules of the market, as otherwise there would be market failures. (Robbins, 1952). The role of a good government is to set the rules of the market in a transparent manner and to enforce the rules on producers as well as on consumers. The ideal market is of course a perfect market. In real life, deviations from the perfect market structure occur regularly. Monopolies and oligopolies tend to emerge. The role of the government is to act as a watchdog to prevent such deviations.

The World Bank recognises that there cannot be a prescriptive set of rules to ensure good governance. Each country is at a different level of political, economic and social development reflecting a wide array of historical, geographic, and cultural factors. Some countries, for example, Singapore have developed highly successful policies in creating the institutions and rules that promote broadly based economic development. Some other countries, on the other hand, are still under severe political, institutional and other constraints on government performance.

Although it is therefore not easy to offer a simple definition of good governance, it is possible to argue that corruption among government officials would destroy the fundamental basis of good governance. Some of the symptoms of poor governance - according to the World Bank - are:

- Failure to make a clear separation between what is public and what is private, hence, a tendency to divert public resources for private gain.
- Failure to establish a predictable framework of law and government behaviour conducive to development, or arbitrariness in the application of rules and laws.
- Excessive rules, regulations, licensing requirements, and so forth, which impede the functioning of markets and encourage rent-seeking.
- Priorities inconsistent with development, resulting in a misallocation of resources.
- Excessively narrowly based or nontransparent decision making.

In other words, accountability, transparency in decision-making and the rule of law are three fundamental pillars of good governance, and are needed to stamp out, or at least reduce corruption at all levels of government. (Brautigam, 1991).

International Corruption: A Global Concern

A new aspect of the corruption issue is its recent trend towards internationalisation. Over the past two decades the problem of international corruption has been attracting a growing interest among government officials, business executives and academics.

In drawing our attention to the problem of international corruption, three agencies have played a major part in recent years:

1. Independent Commission Against Corruption (ICAC),

2. International Criminal Police Organisation (ICPO), or Interpol, and
3. Transparency International (TI).

1. Independent Commission Against Corruption (ICAC)

ICAC originated in 1974 as a low enforcement agency with a mandate to remedy the then widespread corruption in Hong Kong. It has developed ongoing relationships with foreign law enforcement agencies and has achieved some success in international corruption investigations. The first formal International Anti-Corruption Conference was hosted by the ICAC in Washington D.C. in 1983. Since then similar conferences have been held regularly on a bi-annual basis, and the latest one was held in Beijing in October, 1995.

After reviewing all of the papers presented at the Beijing Conference, McCormack (1996) reported that international corruption could be classified into two broad types:

(i) **Transnational Corruption**: involving conspiracies of officials of two or more nations and/or more transnational corporations or organised crime groups.

(ii) **Intra-national Corruption:** involving conspiracies of officials of a single nation and one or more transnational corporations or organised crime groups.

The principal actors in the international corruption rings are:

- corrupt government officials at every level of government - national, regional, or local;
- private sector corporate officers who offer financial incentives or other rewards to receive favoured treatment in business transactions; and
- members of organised crime groups interested in competing in both the legitimate markets and in organised criminal activities such as money laundering, drug dealing, hijacking, piracy, smuggling and even terrorism.

The rise of international corruption has led to a situation in which national governments, acting on their own find it almost impossible to stamp out corruption without transnational efforts. The inability of a country with a common land border with another country, particularly one that has hostile political relations with the other, makes it very difficult to stop international corruption across borders, and calls for urgent international co-operation.

2. International Criminal Police Organisation (ICPO)

The current President of (ICPO), Interpol, Bjorn Eriksson, who presented his written views at the Beijing Conference, underscored the danger of the growing transnational nature of crime and corruption and the role of Interpol in combating it.

Focusing on the transition of organised crime from illicit enterprises to legitimate businesses, Eriksson described the investment of the proceeds of crime into the world market. Criminal enterprises buy into legitimate business as a means of laundering their illegal profits. They do so in a professional way, hiring lawyers and bankers to assist them. They present a threat to the legitimate international market and tend to corrupt politicians.

Interpol exists to facilitate the co-operation of the criminal police forces of more than 125 countries in their fight against international crime. The aims of the organisation are to promote the widest possible mutual assistance between all the criminal police authorities of the affiliated nations within the limits of the laws existing in those countries and in the spirit of the (United Nations) 'Universal Declaration of Human Rights'.

Interpol's principal target is the international criminals, who are of three main types: those who operate in more than one country, such as smugglers, dealing mainly in gold and narcotics and other illicit drugs; criminals who do not travel at all but whose crimes affect other countries - for example, a counterfeiter of foreign bank notes; and a criminal who commits a crime in one country and flees to another.

Interpol has its headquarters in Lyon, France; and it keeps an extensive record of international criminals. In its confidential circulars to member nations Interpol keeps them informed about the activities of international criminals, and sometimes asks that a particular criminal be detained in order that extradition proceedings can be started.

3. Transparency International (TI)

TI is a Berlin-based watchdog organisation. It was established in May 1993 by Peter Eigen, a former World Bank director. TI's focus is on corruption relating to international business transactions, and it has now established national TI Chapters in several countries, including Australia.

Transparency International does not play an investigative role in corruption management. Its main role is to create a national consensus to control corruption by uniting business leaders, politicians and academics from different countries around a common purpose: curbing corruption that has a stunting effect on development.

TI has collaborated with Johnn Graf Lambsdorff of the University of Goettingen in preparing an index to measure the levels of corruption in different counties. This index is regularly updated on an annual basis, and the latest index was released early this year (1996).

The corruption index does not seek to measure the actual level of corruption in a country. It is rather a *subjective* measure of the perception by business of the prevalence of corruption in a particular country.

The 1995 TI Corruption Perception Index ranked New Zealand as the least corrupt country, followed by Denmark, Singapore, Finland, Canada, Sweden and Australia. The Index put Indonesia as the most corrupt country. Only slightly less corrupt than Indonesia were China, Pakistan, Venezuela, Brazil, Philippines and India.

THE BUSINESS INTERNATIONAL INDEX

The Business International (BI), now incorporated into *The Economist Intelligence Unit* produces indices proxying for corruption and various other institutional variables. BI is a private firm and it sells these indices typically to banks, other financial agencies, multinational companies and other international investors. It has its network or correspondents and analysts based in the countries covered. Assessment reports submitted by correspondents are further investigated in order to ensure accuracy, uniformity, comparability and consistency of the results. The BI indices are regarded as highly reliable and the BI clients are prepared to pay substantial sums in order to obtain them.

The BI indices reflect the *subjective* opinions of BI's correspondents. The advantage of such indices is that they can capture the investors' *perception* of risks involved in investing in a country. The disadvantage is of course that the indices are not based on objective and quantifiable measures of corruption and inefficiencies.

In the main, the BI index is based on a number of variables proxying for institutional efficiency and the levels of corruption. Some of the variables used by BI are as follows:

(1) Political Change – institutional : The possibility that the institutional framework will be changed within the forecast period by election or other means.

(2) Political Stability – social: relates to the conduct of political activity and the degree to which the orderly political process tends to disintegrate or become violent.

(3) Probability of Opposition Group Take-over during the forecast period.

(4) Stability of Labour: refers to the degree of risks involved in manufacturing and other business activity due to strikes and other industrial disruption by labour.
(5) Political, economic and commercial relations with neighbouring countries, which may affect companies doing business in the country.
(6) Terrorism: The degree to which individuals and business are subject to acts of terrorism.
(7) Legal System, Judiciary: Efficiency and integrity of the legal environment as it affects business.
(8) Bureaucracy and Red Tape: Integrity of the bureaucracy; and the regulatory environment foreign firms must face when seeking approvals and permits.
(9) Corruption: the degree to which business transactions involve corruption or questionable payments.

(1) to (6) variables do not *per se* relate to corruption and graft, but more directly refer to institutional efficiencies. The variables (7) to (9), on the other hand, directly relate to the integrity of the legal system and the bureaucracy and the additional transaction costs due to corruption in doing business in the country.

Mauro (1995) noticed that all BI variables are positively and significantly correlated. For example, be noticed that the simple correlation between the corruption and red tape indices is to 0.79.

Mauro's finding that all categories of country risk tend to move together in the same direction is an interesting result that cannot be reached unambiguously, *a priori*. But this multcollinearity makes it difficult to say which of the several institutional factors is crucial for investment and growth. Mauro (1995) therefore follows the procedure of combining groups of variables into composite indices.

In this study (1995), Mauro observed a significant negative association between corruption and investment, as well as growth, both in a statistical and in an economic sense, and he then concluded that corruption would tend to lower both investment and economic growth rates. On the investment side, Mauro predicted that "a one standard deviation increase (an improvement) in corruption index is associated with an increase in the investment rate by 2.9 per cent of GDP". On the growth side, Mauro predicted that a one standard deviation improvement in the bureaucratic efficiency (corruption) index is associated with a 1.3 percentage point increase in the annual growth rate of GDP per capita.

CORRUPTION AND GROWTH

Despite the findings in the current literature (for example, Klitgaard, 1988: World Bank, 1992; Shleifer and Vishny, 1993; Mauro, 1995; Busse, Ishikawa, Mitra, et al., 1996) that corruption tends to lower investment, particularly foreign investment, and economic growth, empirical findings do not always collaborate the results.

For example, TI index (1995) put Malaysia, China, Thailand and Indonesia in the categories of some of the most corrupt countries. And yet the actual economic performance of all these countries were well above the *average* in the first half of the 1990s.

Similarly, although in 1980 BI reported Thailand to be the most corrupt country, yet its economic performance has been relatively good. Korea has been developing very fast, in spite of the fact that the BI reported Korea to have relatively inefficient institutions.

An explanation for the above anomaly in results must therefore be sought elsewhere, mainly on the basis of *a priori* reasoning.

First, the typology of corruption could hold the key to our understanding of the impact of corruption on economic growth. *Second*, we have to look for other factors, apart from corruption, which might influence business decisions and investments.

Corruption either can be all pervasive in the sense that it affects all levels of political decision-making, the legal system and the bureaucracy *or* it can be localised in small segments of an economy.

An all pervasive corruption, when it becomes virtually a way of life in a society, creates great uncertainties for business and makes it shy away from investment, For example, if an investor did not know the integrity of the legal system to uphold claims to property rights, nor the integrity of the political system to have access to profit, nor the integrity of the police and the bureaucrats to ensure freedom of operation of business, he would certainly have serious worries about making a *positive* investment decision. If, on the other hand, by bribing the corrupt bureaucrats, the investigator knew that he (or she) could establish the business, and then did not have to worry about dishonest policemen, politicians, lawyers and accountants, he would then be better able to calculate the additional transaction costs due to corruption, and plan whether or not to go ahead with positive investment decisions.

For example, as Shleifer and Vishny (1993) noted, in some countries such as Korea and Russia under the Communist, while corruption was rampant, the person paying the bribe was assured that he would get the government good that he was paying for, and did nor need to pay further bribes in the future. In yet other countries, such as many African countries, India and post-Communist Russia, numerous bureaucrats need to be bribed to get a government permit, and bribing one did not guarantee that some other bureaucrat or even the first one did not demand another bribe. In this latter type of situation, in which different ministries, agencies, para-statal bodies, the army and the police do *not collude* but set, independently of one another, the levels of their own bribes, the basic structure of monopolistic corruption would not apply. Therefore, a *potential* investor would not be able to establish in advance the cost of setting up business.

Ethnolinguistic fractionalisation of a society tends to be associated with non-collusive bribe setting, as bureaucrats may favour members of their own group. More homogeneous societies such as Japan and Korea are likely to come closer to joint bribe maximisation, which is a less harmful type of corruption in terms of its effects on investment and economic growth. Using what is now known as ethnolinguistic fractionalisation (ELF) index, Mauro (1995) observed a negative and significant correlation between institutional efficiency and ethnolinguistic fractionalisation. In his calculations, countries, such as Angola, Bangladesh, India, Kenya, South Africa and Zaire are among the most ethnolinguistically fragmented countries. Therefore, corruption of government officials in all these countries has a more deleterious effect on investment and growth than in relatively more homogeneous countries such as Egypt, Haiti, Hong Kong, Ireland, Japan, Korea, Norway and Portugal.

The type of corruption would also depend upon the purpose for which it is given. When a bribe is given to cut short the red tape to get approval of a project more quickly than it would otherwise be possible, corruption would fall into one category *viz* to speed up a normal process. But if a bribe is given to stop a rival from getting a permit, the purpose of corruption is to induce an official to do something that should *not* be done. This latter type of corruption would surely create great uncertainties in the investment environment, thereby reducing the potential economic growth rate.

Becker and Stigler (1994) developed the principal-agent model of corruption, and recommended a wide range of policies from efficiency wages to indoctrination (Klitgaard, 1988) to combat corruption. Where there is a wide gap between an *expected* standard of living and the *realistic* standard achievable through real market wages, there would be room for corruption to flourish. To resolve the problem efforts should of course be made to raise wages as far as practicable.

But in the longer term, efforts are needed to lower *expectations* to more *realistic* levels.

Then, there is the question of what ultimately happens after a person, or a group of persons have given the bribe money. The after-effects of corruption may vary. For example, Indonesia is reported to be a very corrupt country, where the Suharto family have reportedly amassed billions of dollars by setting up business in the key sectors controlled by the State. The Suhartos family members have expanded into telecommunications, petroleum, mining, gas, power, broadcasting, media, satellites and agribusiness.

But corruption in Indonesia is different in its impact on the overall economy, as compared with corruption in the Philippines under the late Ferdinard Marcos. The Philippine's first family spent its ill-gotten fortunes in buying luxury apartments in New York, or opening secret bank accounts in Switzerland. By contrast, the Suhartos were investing largely in Indonesian assets, such as roads, telecommunications and power plants. Such after-effects of the Indonesian type of corruption are likely to be less harmful on the economy than the Marcos type corruption.

In making investment decisions, *potential* investors, especially those from overseas, will of course take into account the risks of investing in a country that is reputed to be corrupt. However, there are other inputs also in that decision-making process such as labour costs, proximity to markets, availability of infrastructure such as roadways, railways and telecommunications, energy costs and other allied costs of setting up a business. Corruption cost is an additional, albeit uncertain, cost, but the relative objective cost advantage of a country may completely swamp off the uncertainty due to corruption there, and could still persuade investors to invest in that otherwise corrupt country. Whilst it is possible that corruption itself might discourage investment, when the prevalence of corruption is seen in *perspective* with the general economic climate in a country, investment decisions are made in a very complex manner.

Conclusion

There is no simple way to assess the impact of corruption on investment and economic growth. The existing literature on the subject does not give a definitive answer, though the weight of current opinion seems to be that corruption tends to slow down growth.

In a statement, issued on 22 October, 1996, Johann Graf Lambsdorff of Göttingen University was reported to have said: "The more liberal a country, the fewer opportunities for corruption. Hence the direction of reform is obvious: liberalise" (*Corruption & Economic Freedom,* Internet, 22 October, 1996).

Policies that enhance efficiency and policies that reduce corruption tend to largely overlap. Corruption in the private sector can be significantly reduced by governmental efforts to enhance competition in the market. The troublesome instances of corruption arise at the interface of the public and the private sector. If this is so, then a clear demarcation of the boundary between the two sectors is essential. As Arthur Lewis (1995) pointed out a long time ago: "The list of government functions ... is even wider in the less developed than in the more developed economies ... On the other hand, the governments of the less developed countries are at the same time less capable of taking on a wide range of functions than are the governments of the more developed. Their administrations tend to be more corrupt and less efficient, and a smaller part of the national income can be spared for government activity. ... In fact, one cannot usefully consider in an abstract way what functions a government ought to exercise without taking into account the capabilities of the government in question. It is very easy to overload the governments of less developed economies, and it is quite clear that it is better for them to combine themselves to what they can manage than for them to take on an excessive range". (Lewis.1995:382, quoted by Lambsdorff).

Policy implications from Lewis' statement are sufficiently clear. If government is bad and corrupt, there is a strong case for a greater private sector role. Where government is efficient, a larger government role may be justified. But Adam Smith pointed out more than 200 years ago that the integrity and honesty of all government officials must be suspect, and that therefore a small government was by far the best solution for corruption in public life.

REFERENCES

Becker, Gary S., and George J. Stiglar, 1974, "Law Enforcement, Malfeasance, and the Compensation of Enforcers," *Journal of Legal Studies,* 1974, pp. 1-19.

Brautigam, Deborah (1991), *Governance and Economy: A Review,* The World Bank's Policy Research Working Papers, WPS 815.

Busse, Lawrence, Noboru Ishikawa, et.al., "The Perception of Corruption: A Market Discipline Approach", http://userwww.service.e…tyavero/ip/project2.btml (29.09.96).

Frischtak, Leila L., *Governance Capacity and Economic Reform in Developing Countries,* World Bank Technical Paper Number 254, World Bank, Washington D.C., 1994.

Gould, David J. and Jose A. Amaro-Reyes, *The Effects of Corruption on Administrative Performance,* World Bank Staff Working Paper No., 580, The World Bank, Washington D.C. 1983.

Huntington, Samuel P., *Political Order in Changing Societies,* Yale University Press, New Haven, CT, 1968.

Klitgaard, Robert, *Controlling Corruption,* University of California Press, Berkley, C.A., 1988.

Lambsdorff, Johann Graf, "Corruption and Economic Freedom", received on Internet on 22.10.96.

Leff, Nathaniel, "Economic Development through Bureaucratic Corruption," *American Behavioural Scientist, 1964, pp. 8-14.*

Lewis, Arthur, *Theory of Economic Growth,* Richard D. Irwin, 1995, p. 382.

Mauro, Paolo, "Corruption and Growth", *The Quarterly Journal of Economics,* 1995, pp. 681-712.

McCormack, Dr Robert J., "International Corruption, A Global Concern", http:/www.acsp.uic.edu/oicj/pubs/CJ1/120413.htm (29.09.96).

Olson, Mancur, "Rapid Growth as a Destabilising Force", *Journal of Economic History, 1963, pp 529-552.*

Putman, Robert D., *Making Democracy Work: Civic Traditions in Modern Italy,* Princeton University Press, Princeton, N.J., 1993.

Robbins, L., *Theory of Economic Policy in English Classical Political Economy,* Macmillan Co., 1952.

Rose-Ackerman, Susan, "The Economics of Corruption", *Journal of Public Economics,* 1975, pp. 187-203.

Rose-Ackerman, Susan, *Corruption: A Study of Political Economy,* Academic Press, New York, 1978.

Schleifer, Andrei, and Robert W. Vishny, "Corruption", Cambridge, Mass, 1993, pp. 599-617.

Stiglar, George J., "A Theory of Oligopoly", *Journal of Political Economy, 1964, pp.44-61.*

United Nations, *Corruption in Government,* New York, United Nations, 1989.

World Bank *Governance and Development,* The World Bank, Washington D.C., 1992.

World Bank, Governance: *The World Bank's Experience,* The World Bank, Washington D.C. 1994.

9 THE POLITICAL ECONOMY OF PUBLIC POLICY

ROBERT SCHRIRE

The progressive exclusions of black people from the South African polity from 1910 inevitably produced a political reaction which emphasised the attainment of political rights and political equality. If the De Klerk reforms are carried to their logical conclusions, the narrow issue of political rights at least partially will be resolved. A compromise political framework will emerge which will probably embody non-racial egalitarianism within a decentralised consociational institutional system. Although this will not be acceptable to all South African political groupings, it will probably enjoy majority support.

The legacy of apartheid - its impact both on racial stratification and on racially-based socio-economic inequalities-consequently will take centre stage in the political debate. To some degree this has already happened and the South African public currently is being overwhelmed by conferences, workshops, party documents, and seminars devoted to the issue of redistribution, restructuring and development.

There is, however, no longer a genuine 'economic debate'. With the demise of Marxist states such as the Soviet Union and East Germany, there is today a growing and near-universal acceptance of the broad parameters for economic growth and the elimination of poverty. Effective markets, appropriate educational systems, public policies which encourage entrepreneurship and individual incentives, and relatively limited but effective government are now considered essential elements of an efficient economy.

This growing consensus does not remove economics from the public arena. Indeed, in every major capitalist state, from the United States to Germany, to Japan, economic issues dominate the political agenda. The debate there has moved, however, away from basic principles to secondary issues such as spending priorities, interest rates, taxation and international trade.

In South Africa, most members of the population have been excluded, at least in part, from both the political debate and the economic system. While the almost universal trend in the advanced societies after 1948 was towards some form of welfare state, deracialisation, civil liberties, and Political equality, South Africa was moving in a diametrically different direction and the country debated narrow issues of 'race' policy to the almost total exclusion of economic and other considerations.

Time has caught up with South Africa. For both political and moral reasons issues of distribution and equality will be in the forefront of the future debate. There is nevertheless a danger that South Africans will ignore the experiences of other countries over the last forty years.

Redistribution has been defined as 'a process whereby command over goods and services is transferred from one group of persons to another without the *quid pro quo* of exchange'.[1] This definition has the advantage of stressing the dynamic nature of distribution as a process rather than a one-off event. It also narrows the topic to state policy in that it excludes the changes in command over goods and services brought about through the market system. For example, income is redistributed, often on a very substantial scale, through market-related changes in competition, interest rates, fluctuations in the level of prices, and changes in the comparative value of currencies. Indeed, it is probably true that market forces are the most important determinant of both income distribution and changes which take place over time.[2]

This paper, however, has a policy orientation. Policy must reflect not only a technocratic consensus (if any) but also a political agreement - the reasons for the focus on state public policy and economic power groups in this book. Policy advocates, therefore, must be essentially pragmatic and ask such questions as:

- What can the state do to change the pattern of distribution?
- What policies are feasible within a relevant time-frame?
- What policies are politically viable?

Students of redistribution frequently make a distinction between wealth, income, and opportunities. The stock of wealth of a nation is made up of assets such as land, capital, and human skills. The flow of income, which is in large part derived from the distribution of wealth, includes income from work, dividends, interest and royalties. Opportunities, which need to be broadly defined, include the distribution of

1 D. Collard 1980, 'Limits to Redistribution: An Overview', in D. Collard et al. (eds.), *Income Distribution: The Limits to Redistribution*, Bristol: Scientechnica.

2 For an economically-orientated analysis of South Africa the reader is referred to I. Abedian and B. Standish (eds.) 1992, *Economic Growth in South Africa*, Cape Town: OUP.

educational opportunities and the allocation of jobs in the private and public sectors.

The regulation of remuneration through the following policies:[1]

- the regulation of remuneration and pricing;
- extraction and reallocation of income derived from existing productive arrangements (fiscal policy for example);
- direct state production or involvement in finance, marketing, and so on.

The specific policy instruments at the disposal of government include:

- *Taxation*. The tax system is an important instrument for redistribution in that it can be used to extract more resources from the wealthy than from the poor. Direct taxes may be levied not only on income but also on wealth, capital gains, land, and capital transfers. However, its impact is limited by its negative influence on growth as manifested by emigration, capital exports, the emergence of a 'black' economy, and tax avoidance.
- *State expenditure*. This is perhaps the most effective tool in government's armoury. Government can target certain groups for special benefits and in general control considerable resources. The demands for special treatment are overwhelming, however, and a rapid and dramatic increase in state expenditure not supported by economic growth is usually a recipe for macro-imbalances in the price level, interest rates, and the balance of payments
- *State supported industrial action*. Governments may seek to influence the distribution of resources through policies such as minimum wages, employment quotas, or, more profoundly, by creating and sanctioning systems of workers' participation in management. These policies are limited by basic economic constraints such as the need to remain competitive and the impact on capital and investments.
- *Nationalisation/confiscation*. In an interdependent and capital-scarce world, this is a policy, option which is almost universally recognised to be non-viable.

The historical experiences of redistributive policies indicate several harsh realities. Firstly, the ability of the state to change distribution

---

1 This formulation closely follows the description in W. Ascher 1984, *Scheming for the Poor*, Cambridge Mass: Harvard University Press, pp 45, 46.

significantly is more limited than was formerly believed. In general, state power seems to have declined relative to private power, perhaps as a consequence of modern communications and the erosion of state sovereignty. Secondly, patterns of distribution remain remarkably stable and seem to change very slowly, irrespective of the goals of the state. Where distributions have changed significantly and rapidly, it has been the result of revolutions and confiscations which have also reduced overall levels of income and wealth quite substantially.

In general, redistributive policies will only succeed if the economic and political barriers to change can be neutralised. These include the power of the 'haves' to resist redistribution and the economic constraints on change such as the balance of payments factors, budgetary realities, and bureaucratic bottle-necks. Policies of redistribution also contain significant dangers: benefits may get into the hands not of the targeted groups but of the relatively advantaged; redistribution may produce unintended consequences such as a loss of future increases in output of goods and services; the power of state officials may increase significantly at the cost of honest administration; and civil liberties may be harmed.

Nevertheless, redistribution may hold important advantages. A public perception that the state is concerned with the welfare of the least advantaged may reduce political tension; a reduction in gross inequalities may legitimise the political economy and improve its moral foundations; future economic growth may improve as a result of a decrease in the loss of human talent which results from widespread poverty.

What are the probable economic demands which will face a transformed South Africa? Within the population the following groups can be distinguished, each with its own demands:

- black workers who are already in employment in the formal sector, taking white incomes as their reference point, will demand higher incomes, improved benefits, and job security;
- those who are unemployed or subsist in the informal sector will demand work in the formal sector;
- peasants will demand a redistribution of land and will justify this by the present land inequalities and the historical roots of dispossession;
- the presently disadvantaged will demand improved pensions, housing, education, and health facilities;
- the poor will demand a safety net of social services and financial assistance which will include unemployment compensation, food schemes, and pensions.

The emergent black elites will demand:

- employment and rapid promotions in the state bureaucracy and parastatals at the higher levels;
- a change in the nature of South Africa's 'racial capitalism' to make the commanding heights of the economy more racially equal. This will include a demand for share-holding in the major conglomerates and for greater public sector support for black enterprises.

These issues will dominate future politics. Although it is not the purpose of this paper to debate the options and limits of change in these areas, it is important to provide a foundation for the debate. Placing the South African realities in the context of global experiences, a broad technocratic consensus could probably be reached around the following propositions:

- Despite popular mythology, South Africa is not a wealthy country. At best, South Africa is a middle-income developing state. According to the World Bank report of 1990,[1] income per capita was \$2,290 in South Africa, \$19,840 in the USA, and \$21,020 in Japan. South Africa's life expectancy of 61 years was exceeded not only by developed societies such as the United Kingdom (75 years) and Japan (70 years), but also by poorer countries such as Sri Lanka (71 years), Zimbabwe (63 years), and Egypt (63 years). Indeed, genuine poverty is widespread; it has been estimated that about 17.5 million people in South Africa, constituting 47 per cent of the population, live in households with incomes below the minimum income level of R695 per month at 1990 prices. In addition, South Africa's economic growth rates are significantly lower than many other states of the world, and overall levels of poverty are probably increasing rather than decreasing.
- In terms of the distribution of both income and wealth, South Africa is one of the most unequal societies on the globe and may even be the most unequal. In addition, this inequality largely coincides with race, whites being the most affluent and Africans the most impoverished. As McGrath summarised the situation, 'In per capita terms for 1980, white incomes were respectively 12.9, 3.9, and 5.3 times greater than African, Indian and

---

[1] World Bank 1990, *World Development Report 1990*. New York: OUP.

coloured incomes'.[1] Quite clearly, these inequalities could only continue as long as blacks were politically disenfranchised. If reform entails the extension of political rights to those at present excluded, it must also mean a concerted programme by the state authorities to reduce these economic inequalities. A non-racial polity superimposed upon the existing economic inequalities will simply not be politically viable. It would be an invitation to disaster.

- Economic sovereignty has become a myth and international factors will be of decisive importance in determining South Africa's economic destiny. As Ronald Bethlehem, has said '80% of the performance of the South African economy is determined not endogenously (internally), but exogenously (externally)'.[2] A major factor behind South Africa's economic decline since the late 1970s has been the impact of the global economy: commodity prices, including gold and base metals, have declined in real terms on international markets; foreign investment has largely dried up; sanctions and disinvestment have increased in scope and effectiveness; and South Africa, as a consequence, has become a capital exporter. Until South Africa can once again become a capital importer through international loans and foreign investment, redistributive issues will simply not be amenable to policy actions.
- Economic growth is the most important element of any redistributive strategy. This is not to argue that growth is the only economic value which should be pursued, or that growth alone is sufficient to reduce inequalities. However, redistributive issues cannot even be tackled unless the economy grows at a significant annual rate. Failing this, all that can be redistributed is poverty and misery. As Anthony Crosland, a leading socialist thinker, argued more that two decades ago: 'I do not of course mean that rapid growth will automatically produce a transfer of resources of the kind we want; whether it does or not will depend on the social and political values of the country concerned. But I do assert dogmatically that in a democracy low or zero growth wholly excludes the possibility. For any substantial transfer then involves not only a relative but an absolute decline in real

---

1 R. Schrire (ed.) 1990, *Critical Choices for South Africa: An Agenda for the 1990s*, Cape Town: OUP, p. 94.

2 T. Bethlehem 1991, "The global economy: Structural change", paper delivered at the South African Institute of International Affairs Seminar, Johannesburg, 10 Sept., and published as an occasional paper by the Institute.

incomes of the better-off of the population . . . and this they will frustrate.'[1]

- An exclusive reliance upon the free market system to reduce inequalities is neither economically possible nor politically feasible. If one were free to design a South African system *ab initio*, one would allocate the factors of production, including knowledge and capabilities, on a random basis and thus enable free markets to operate with both efficiency and justice. However, given the skewed distribution of resources and the use to which state power has been used in the past to benefit whites, free markets and limited state intervention would probably increase inequalities in many areas. For example, if all legislation which limited the right of any individual to purchase land was removed, it is probable that much of the land presently controlled by black Africans, especially in the homelands, would be purchased by whites. This would certainly increase the already high level of inequality in land ownership. Politically, too, an exclusive reliance upon the market would not be viable because many South Africans, perhaps even a majority, rightly or wrongly view markets with suspicion and would not accept any 'trickle-down' approach which is inherent in an exclusive market-orientation.
- An exclusive reliance upon state action to reduce inequalities is neither economically feasible nor politically desirable. Apart from a shrinking circle of neo-Stalinists, this proposition is widely accepted. As one expert explained:

  > *Markets do a better job than governments, from the standpoint of both allocative (or static) efficiency (namely, realising a higher ratio between outputs or product, on the one hand, and inputs or costs, on the other) and dynamic efficiency (namely, sustaining a higher rate of economic growth over time)* [2]

In the political sphere empirical experience has confirmed the insight that the concentration of political and economic power in one set of institutions makes government accountability and a democratic culture extremely unlikely.

---

1 Quoted in D. Collard et al. (eds.) 1980, *Income Distribution: The Limits to Redistribution*, Bristol: Scientechnica, p. 186.

2 C. Wolf 1988, *Markets or Governments*, Cambridge, Mass: M.I.T. Press, p. 153.

- The very definition of the 'redistributive' problem is political and normative. Although there is a near consensus on the unsustainable nature of the inequalities in the South African economy, there is no consensus on how the issue should be defined. Some would define 'redistribution' as the elimination of poverty, others as increasing economic growth, while many would define the issue as one of justice and even retribution for past injustices. Clearly the definition of the issue determines to a great extent the policy instruments and options which will be chosen. If poverty is viewed as the major element, then presumably growth would be a favoured option. Alternatively, if the emphasis is on the historical roots of inequality, then the actual income and wealth gap between the various communities becomes of paramount importance. Groups in South Africa will define the problem largely in terms of their own interests: business will tend to favour growth strategies, organised labour will tend to advocate more explicitly redistributive policies, while politicians will seek to reward their constituencies.
- There is an intrinsic conflict between economic and political rationality. The dismal science of economics must grapple with restraints and limits. In the South African context, as will be discussed later, choices are severely constrained. In the political sphere, however, the rational political actor will seek to build a constituency by mobilising grievances and promising rewards to key voting blocs. Given the poverty of most South Africans and the built-in structural inequities, an effective strategy would be to mobilise the majority 'have-nots' against the minority 'haves'. A campaign built upon themes such as 'land for the landless', 'jobs for the unemployed', 'higher incomes for the workers', 'soak the rich', and 'expropriate the capitalists' would evoke powerful support from many groups. A rational politician facing an election campaign will always be more concerned with the short term rather than the long term, with promises rather than delivery, and with benefits rather than costs. Rational economics, by contrast, leads to diametrically opposite calculations - a concern with the long term and with real possibilities and costs. A conflict between political behaviour and economic realities is inherent in all political systems. It is how this conflict is managed that is critical.
- There are no quick-fix or big-bang solutions to the issue of economic justice. None of the dramatic solutions which often have been advocated are applicable to contemporary realities.

Nationalisation is neither economically effective nor politically feasible. The ability of the state to extract vast new resources from the economy is limited by the already high tax rates on most economic groups, the mobility of capital, and the fragility of innovation. Similarly the introduction of a 'free market' would not produce a rapid or sustainable economic miracle.

- In the short term, the prospects for meaningful redistribution are limited. In the longer term, the instruments exist to substantially reduce unemployment and poverty and reduce, at least to some extent, the glaring racially-based inequities. However, it is probable that even in the medium and longer terms, colour and class will broadly coincide. While the economic position of blacks may improve, and many blacks may even become important and powerful economic players, whites will continue to be the most affluent segment of the population and black Africans the poorest.

Indeed it is an historical tragedy that the beneficiaries of *apartheid* are the only economic actors in South Africa with the economic resources and expertise necessary to get the country moving again. It is, alas, in the interests of the least advantaged in society that the most advantaged continue to prosper. Redistribution mechanisms do exist, however, to reduce the level of these inequalities. A multidimensional strategy would include the following aims:

- To reduce population growth through a mix of public education, the provision of birth control devices, and a liberal abortion policy.
- To improve the quality of the workforce through in-house training, improved management (including greater worker participation), and the provision of nutrition and health services.
- To increase growth rates through creating incentives for domestic and foreign investment, improved technology, and adequate primary, secondary, and adult education.
- To increase equity through policies of affirmative action, through broadening the racial base of land and capital ownership, and through re-orientating public expenditure and tax policies towards greater equity options.
- To create a realistic safety net for the poor, through policies such as school feeding schemes, the provision of water, electricity, housing, and unemployment benefits.

POLITICAL REALITIES

As noted earlier, the so-called 'economic debate' is, in fact, a political debate. Public policy is rarely, if ever, based exclusively upon technocratic expenditure and theoretical knowledge. In all societies economic policy is formulated by political elites within a political context. Objectives such as getting re-elected, rewarding allies, and punishing opponents are often more important in shaping policy than 'neutral' economic objectives such as macroeconomic stability or economic efficiency.

Few, if any, governments are totally committed to redistributive policies. Political leaders have many goals including securing their own interest, increasing employment levels, price stability, success in the global market place, and macroeconomic stability. Redistribution is at best simply one of many policy goals. It is inevitable that leaders must choose between conflicting goals in a context constrained by both political and economic factors. Redistribution interests will often get lost in the political struggles over public policies.

This leads to a key reality: the success of redistribution will not be determined by carefully designed intellectual arguments or the good intentions of the government. The most important factor will be the ability or inability of the poor to use the ammunition of progressive ideas in a political struggle where the outcome will be determined by political power rather than normative imperatives.

The historical record is decidedly unpromising. In almost all societies the poor, even if a majority, tend to be politically marginalised. It is the non-poor who are best placed, by virtue of their skills and institutional positions, to shape redistributive policies in ways which favour their interest. Policies such as land reform and affirmative action have generally favoured those who already have something - for example, the middle class and small landowners -rather than the proletariat or peasant.

In the South African context, where it is not the most poorly paid workers in the formal sector who are the true 'have-nots' but the millions who are unemployed or barely survive in the subsistence sector, a real danger exists that public policies will benefit the relative 'haves' and ignore the 'have-nots'. At present it is the relatively-privileged unionised workers who are likely to have influence over wage rates rather than the unemployed who would benefit from lower wage rates. Similarly it is the emerging black middle class that is in a position to benefit from policies of affirmative action and public health and educational expenditures rather than the poorest of the poor.

Political elites benefit themselves and their supporters from the coffers of the state. One of the sad lessons of the recent past was the recognition that the levels of corruption were very similar in both right-and-left-wing autocracies. Irrespective of the self-description of the ruling elites, it was not the peasants or workers who prospered but the rulers. Good intentions, no matter how sincere, are never by themselves sufficient to produce good policies. And bad politics will inevitably lead to bad economics.

As the old South Africa draws to an end, the great political debate over redistribution begins. In the new South Africa, the economic issues will not only be debated but will become, for the first time, the lifeblood of the politics and policies of the day. The configuration of intellectual and political forces in the policy arena will determine whether political power, economic rationality, or some synthesis of the two dominates public policy. The consequences of the policy struggle will be profound for all South Africans.

Irrespective of the talents and preferences of any South African government the short-term constraints on redistribution are overwhelming. A zone for political opportunism will exist which will enable political entrepreneurs to mobilise support around utopian promises which cannot be met.

For many reasons, including widespread illiteracy, the lack of a democratic tradition, and the passions evoked by racism and exploitation, South Africa does not enjoy a legitimate paradigm which embodies the accepted beliefs about the society. The politics of unreason, which represents the demonstrably wrong interpretation of South African realities, is not automatically destined to be defeated by the politics of reason, which represents the demonstrably accurate facts about South Africa. No analyst of any competence and integrity can argue any longer that drastic redistribution could rapidly provide all South Africans with a decent set of life chances. Similarly, all the quick fixes - nationalisation, massive state expenditures, and state control - are clearly unworkable. However, these ideas could provide powerful ammunition to the proponents of the politics of unreason.

Earlier I indicated the intrinsic conflict between political and economic rationality. For policy to be effective, it must be both politically feasible and economically rational. A very real trade-off will exist between economics and politics. Thus while an optimum economic strategy with an emphasis on markets and growth will not be politically viable, the optimum political strategy of rewarding members of the majority constituency will be enormously costly. It will therefore be vital to trade off political and economic factors to create a viable political strategy with the least cost for economic efficiency and growth.

Therefore, cold analysis will not by itself destroy the politics of opportunism. And given South Africa's tortuous history, the scope for unreason is immense. What is clearly needed is a forum to both establish the parameters of the possible and to create a political foundation of support for the economics of reason. A 'Grant Accord', representing important and credible elements from the labour movement, the business community, agriculture, and the state, is a *sine qua non* for a viable politics of reason.

At the same time it is vital for government to launch a massive and dramatic 'War against Poverty' campaign to convince all South Africans of the importance it attaches to issues of human welfare and suffering. Even though this 'war' may be as much rhetorical as action oriented, the symbolism of such a campaign will be of vital importance. After all, if expectations cannot be met fully under any policy framework, it is important for those who remain disadvantaged to perceive that this has not been the result of indifference or ineptitude. And a wide range of limited but effective micro-policies could create a generalised perception of action and progress.

Government Instruments in Economic Policy

Manipulation of current balance of expenditure
Manipulation of overall balance of expenditure
Government investment subsidies and capital transfers to enterprises
Transfers to households
Government stock changes
Current purchases of goods and services
Wages and salaries
Transfers in the rest of the world
Direct taxes on household incomes
Direct taxes on enterprise incomes
Indirect taxes on internal transactions
Customs duties
Social security contributions
Taxes on property
Succession duties
Transfers from the rest of the world
Lending abroad
Lending to household and enterprises
Borrowing from abroad
Borrowing from households and enterprises

Open-market operations in short-term securities
Other open-market operations in existing debt
Bank rate
Legal imposition of maximum rates
Government guarantees of loans
Reserve ratio's, etc.
Quantitative stops on advances
Approval of individual loans
Other directives, recommendations, and persuasion
Control of local authorities and nationalised enterprise borrowing
Control of private companies' borrowing by new issues
Control of hire-purchase transactions
Control of other financial institutions
Deviations
Revaluations
Control of private imports
State import trading
Control of private exports
Exchange control
Control of immigration
Price controls of goods and services
Rent control
Dividend control
Control of wages
Control of investment
Raw material allocation
Control of operations
Regulation of conditions of work
Control of exploitation of natural resources
Rationing of consumer goods
Quality controls and standards
Changes in the system of transfer to households
Changes in the system of subsidies to enterprises
Changes in the tax system
Changes in the credit system
Changes in the system of direct control
Agricultural land reforms
Changes in the conditions of competition
Changes increasing labour's influence on management
Changes in the extent of public ownership of industry
Creation of national institutions
Creation of international institutions

10 Land-Use Issues and the Sustainable Development of the Jingpo Communities of Yunnan, China: Impacts of Governance, Institutions and Culture on Resource Management

Ren Zhuge and Clem Tisdell

Introduction

Since 1950, the major forest resources of China have been controlled and managed by governments at various levels. National, local, and household interests all converge on forest resources which are often a source of conflict but which have the potential to be managed so as to benefit rural households and communities with access to them. When the "Household Responsibility System" of agricultural land allocation and the "Two Mountains System" of non-agricultural land allocation were introduced in 1982, there were clear differences between these two different categories of land. Since 1982, farmers and villages have been given rights to use most of the collective forestlands. But this has not been so far in the state forestland. The traditional management of state forests takes no account of local communities. Hunting, cutting and gathering by villagers in the state forests is illegal. For this reason, native people are often roughly treated by the managers and officials of state forests for engaging in these activities in state forests. Consequently, local communities obtain no benefits from state forests and the phenomenon of the "rich forests, poor people" mentioned in many current publications would continue to exist in these areas. In actual fact, forest resources have been handed down from generation to generation for over a thousand of years by the local people through the powerful impacts of traditional governance, institutions and culture on resource management before any modern administrative interference was involved.

This paper reviews the management and use of natural resources by local communities of the Jingpo ethnic group in the Dehong Prefecture and focuses on land-use issues and sustainable development of the Jingpo communities based on local forest resources and local management. The objectives are: understanding the current problems of local development in Jingpo communities and diagnosing the weaknesses of local community development and providing some suggestions for sustainable development of the Jingpo communities. Information has been drawn from a field survey undertaken during 1994 - 1995 using methods of RRA (Rural Rapid Appraisal) and PRA (Participatory Rural Appraisal).

CHARACTERISTICS OF DEHONG PREFECTURE AND JINGPO COMMUNITIES

Yunnan's westernmost spur of land, known as the Dehong Prefecture, juts into Myanmar. The prefecture is located between 97°31'-90° 43' of longitude east and 23°50'-25°20' of latitude north. It has a common boundary with Myanmar and the Baoshan Prefecture. The prefecture has jurisdiction over two cities and four counties and its total area is 11,526 km^2. The Dayinjiang River, Longchuanjiang River and the Ruilijiang River form the upper reaches of the Irrawaddy River. The average annual temperature is 19.4°C and the annual rainfall on an average comes to 1,659 mm. This region contains the terminal of Gaoligong mountain range. It has a hot and rainy season from May to October and a dry sunny season for the rest of the year. The landforms of the prefecture face the southwest wind that carries a lot of warm and wet air masses from the Indian Ocean. The altitude of the prefecture varies from 210 - 2,595 metres above sea level and the topography is quite varied. Because of its warm and damp climate, rich tropical forests and mountain subtropical evergreen forests are common. Rubber, coffee, tung trees, mango, betelnut, guava, pomelo, jackfruit and papaya can grow well in this area. The main grain crops are upland rice and maize. Vegetables, beans, melons, spices and some medicinal herbs are usually intercropped with the main crops.

Dehong has a total population of 960,000 people, of which the different minority people account for 51.76%. Among the minority groups, the Jingpo and Dai are the most important ethnic groups, accounting for 12.34% and 32.01% respectively of the population of the prefecture. The Dehong Dai are considered by many Chinese to be even more handsome and refined than their brethren in Xishuangbanna. Other minorities of over 1,000 people in Dehong are the Achang, Lishu, De-Ang, Bai, Hui, and the Yi (Wu, 1994). Although over the half of the local population in this prefecture consists of minority people, the majority Han people and superior minority Dai people mainly live in the urban and lowland areas. The Jingpo people account for the overwhelming majority of the local ethnic groups in the uplands of Dehong.

A population of 118,000 Jingpo people live in the subtropical mountainous areas of Dehong prefecture at heights of 1,500 to 2,000 metres above sea level. They account for 95% of total Jingpo population of China. The Jingpo minority villages, scattered in the mountainous areas, keep traditional modes of production and practice slash-and-burn agriculture.

In the Jingpo areas, only about 11% of the land is arable. About 80% of forestland and grazing land produce 30% of general income. *Figure 1* shows the sources of income in some close communities (six townships) of the Jingpo people.

Figure 1 **Sources of Rural Income in Six Communities (townships) of the Jingpo**

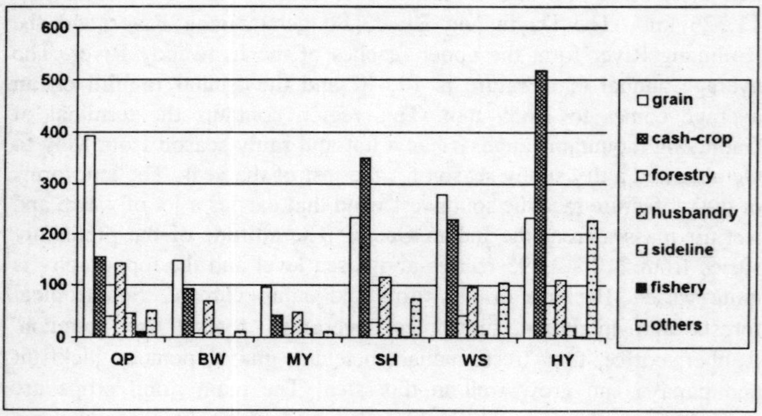

Scale: 1 = 10,000 yuan (100 USD = 820 yuan)
Townships: QP = Qingping, BW = Bangwa, MY = Mengyue, SH = Saihao, WS = Wangshuzi, HY = Huyu
Data from the *Year Book of the Dehong Prefecture 1994*

The income in these townships is greatest from grain and cash crops other than grain. Animal husbandry is the next most important source of income. Forestry and sideline activities are significant sources of income in some townships. The item *sideline* in the figure is the income from selling sideline products such as bean curd, farm tools, rattanware, bamboo work and other non-agricultural products. The item *others* in the figure refers to non-agricultural income from sources such as local industry, commerce, transportation and so on. The fishery in most townships is almost negligible.

Traditional Factors Influencing Management of Local Forest Resources

In major Jingpo areas, the primitive public ownership system continued until the end of 1950s. Under this system, forests, arable land and grazing land all belonged to the local Jingpo communities. "Shanguang" was the title of the chieftain of a Jingpo community and the title was inherited. A Shanguang usually ruled several villages and controlled a vast tract of forests. He had privileges to occupy and sell the fertile farmland belonging to the community, but the other people had no rights to do so without permission. Immigration of outside people must be approved by the Shanguang first. In the beginning of a busy farming season, local people had to give one-day voluntary labour to their Shanguang. Together with the elders in the community, the heads of villages and the leaders of religious affairs, Shanguang decided which tract of forestlands could be slashed and burnt for cultivation this year, how the lands would be allocated to each household and he settled land disputes between villages or village people. After 1958, the Shanguang system was phased out. Vast areas of virgin forests were taken over by the state and the other small pieces of forests near the villages and farmlands shifted to community. However, up to now, the community management of forestlands is still important in Jingpo society.

Living on their land for several centuries, the Jingpo people accumulated a lot of knowledge and developed many skills for their production and life support. They are careful in the management and use of forest resources in this area. Their religious beliefs and their local means of governance perfectly reflect the feelings of the local people for the forests.

Effects of Religious Beliefs

Jingpo people believe that "all things on earth have spirits". They worship almost all natural things such as forests, trees, animals, mountains, rivers, etc. They think that the spirits of their ancestors reside in the big trees and in the forests near by the entrances of villages. These trees or forests can bless and protect the village and bring good weather for its crops. For this reason, the Jingpo keep the trees and forests holy and inviolable and hold grand ceremonies twice a year to offer a sacrifice to trees or forests. In accordance with the roles of the forests, Jingpo people used to distinguish between and manage three kinds of forests. Holy forestshouse the ghosts of their ancestors, so that no tree and shrub in these forests can be destroyed. Village people believe if anyone offends the ghosts in the forest, he/she will become seriously ill or the whole village will suffer disaster, therefore, it is strictly forbidden to cut these forests, hunt in them, graze stock in them and even relieve oneself in them. Around the village is the landscape forest. It is forbidden to cut trees in this forest without the permission of village leaders. Watershed forests protect the water supply of the village for living and farming. Besides the protection of these three kinds of forests, the Jingpo people also believe the ghosts or spirits like to stay in the mountain valleys and ravines. So they do not cut forests in these areas.

Unfortunately, their religious tradition has been eroded since the end of the 1950s, and was especially undermined in the era of the "Cultural Revolution". Today the new generation in some villages does not take the old rules and regulations seriously. As a result, many forests around these villages have been damaged. Remaining protected forests are mostly in the remote areas where the local customs are little affected by the outside world.

Powers to Make Decisions

With the collapse of the Shanguang system in Jingpo areas, a village council accepted by the local government replaced it. The village council took over the management of the natural resources of village. The village council were selected by the local people or appointed by a special team on behalf of local government. They make decisions to protect forests and to arrange slash-and-burn cultivation. They may decide where the villagers can get their timber and firewood. Usually, the elders and wizards in a village influence such decisions. In fact, a respected elder or wizard sometimes has more rights to speak for the affairs of the village than the leaders of the village council. A village council is always willing to listen attentively to the suggestions of the traditional village leaders; consequently, traditional or religious rules influence the management of natural resources.

Local Regulations and Rules

Because all the natural resources are public property in the traditional system of ownership in Jingpo areas, some rules for management of natural resources are widely accepted through common practice. Usually the community regulations and rules are developed by several consultative meetings of local community leaders. They are respected by all villagers after a ceremony of swearing an oath accompanied with a blood sacrifice. Representatives from villages in the community participate in the ceremony. The local laws usually refer to various affairs of the local community such as the code of conduct of village people, the management of productive actions, protection of forests and landscapes. In the local laws, regulations for protecting forest resources are quite detailed. For example, the local law preserved in Mangben village provides the following words: " ... any tree cannot be cut down during the period of closing hillsides to facilitate afforestation; it is forbidden to fell watershed forest, landscape forest and the trees by the entrances to village; the holy trees near the village cannot be touched roughly; trees for timber cannot be cut without approval of village leaders...". The final rules and regulations will be announced in a mass rally and implemented under mutual supervision.

Violations of the rules result in serious punishment. In the past, the special punishments such as cutting off fingers or limbs have been given to those violating protected trees and forests and even the extreme penalty could be taken in the case of destroying holy trees and forests. Although the extreme penalty has ceased in recent decades, special punishments are still retained in some remote areas. More civilised measures of punishment such as payment of indemnities, voluntary labour for the community or provision of an apologetic dinner to the whole village have become more common. From the local rules of Bengling village, the amount of indemnity is listed in detail: "one yuan (RMB) for cutting a small tree; five yuan for a middle tree; ten yuan for big one; fifteen yuan for a tree by a stream ..."

VALUABLE INDIGENOUS KNOWLEDGE ABOUT LOCAL FOREST RESOURCES

The indigenous knowledge about their local forest resources is handed down from generation to generation. This kind of knowledge is based on experiences from daily life. Therefore, it may be more useful and suitable to the local conditions. To collect and analyse these sorts of information may help us find some solutions for the paradox of socio-economic development and environmental protection. The Jingpo possess much knowledge about the use of local forest resources.

Timber

There are various native well-known tree species for higher timber quality. *Dalbergia fusca, Schima wallichii, Morus macroura, Dipterocarpus turbinatus, D. gracilis, Shorea assamica, Betula alnoides var. pyrifolia, Cinnamomum glanduliferum, Phoebe lanceolata, Lindera megapphylla, Litsea monopetala, Photinia beckii,*

Michelia sp., Lithocarpus eremiticus, Alangium kurzii, Carallia brachiata, Syzygium tetragonum are all used as popular building materials in local communities. Some of them produce very hard wood and have found commercial use recently.

Fuelwoods

Fuelwood is the most important type of rural energy. In the mountain areas the fire pan is a symbol of life. The mountain ethnic people, including the Jingpo people, have the traditional custom of making a fire in a pan set in the middle of the bridal chamber on their wedding day. From then on the fire should be kept burning until the death of the couple. The Jingpo have the experience to select wood with good and durable burning qualities and with few showers of sparks for safety. Naturally, they know of the best fuelwoods in their location. The local best fuelwood is considered to be the wood of Lithocarpus spp., especially the species *Lithocarpus mannii.* Besides, *Hyptianthera stricta, Dalbergia burmanica, Broussonetia papyrifera* etc. are also good native fuelwoods.

Bamboo

Bamboo is a very special kind of plant. It grows quickly and can be easily cultivated around buildings and corners of the field. In the Jingpo areas, bamboo has a wide range of uses such as for building materials, fences, containers, mats, stools and so on. Bamboo shoots are considered to be a traditional tasty food. They are processed for export and a unique species of nymph living in the culm of bamboo is a local food delicacy. More than ten local bamboo species are used: *Bambusa burmanica, Bambusa pallida, Cephalostachyum virgatum, Cephalostachyum pergracile, Chimonobambusa yunnanensis, Dendrocalamus semiscandens, Dendrocalamus membranaceus, Dendrocalamus patellaris, Dendrocalamus giganteus* and *Pseudostachyum polymorphum* are distributed widely in these areas.

Wild Vegetables

Almost all nationalities in upland Yunnan utilise native vegetable plants. According to the survey in several local markets, vegetables marketed involve many kinds of trees, shrubs, herbs and vines. The edible parts of plants consist of roots, stems, leaves, shoots, flowers, fruits and seeds. *Callipteris esculenta, Houttuynia cordata, Solanum nigrum var. photeinocarpum, Tupidanthus calyptratus, Monochoria vaginalis, Dickinsia hydrocotyloides, Ehretia corylifolia, Oenanthe javanica* and *Crateva unilocularis* are all welcome vegetables in local communities. Some of these have been introduced to home gardens for commercial cultivation.

Wild Fruits

The common wild fruits in the markets of Jingpo areas are *Calamus viminalis* (rattan palm), *Elaeocarpus decipiens* (ebony heart), *Rubus spp.*(raspberry), *Baccaurea ramiflora* (rambai), *Canarium strictum* (canarytree), *Nephelium chryseum* (rambutan), *Syzygium forrestii* (rose apple) and so on. Industries processing wild fruit juices are rapidly increasing in the other areas of the province and often benefit the local rural communities. This kind of forest resource provides an opportunity for the development of Jingpo community.

Forage

One of the major sources of local income is from raising livestock. Almost all households without exception have several head of cattle. Many families have a few goats or pigs as well. Usually the cattle and goats are not fenced, but roam freely in forests or grasslands. Pigs are fed forage from wild areas and forests. *Impatiens arguta, Rumex nepalensis, Melampyrum roseum, Enseta glaucum, Pilea martinii, Lecanthus peduncularis, Gynura segetum, Commelina bengalensis, Amischotolype hispida* and *Elscholtzia rugulosa* are commonly used for forage in Jingpo community. *Enseta glaucum* is even planted in garden and its stems are seen as a good kind of forage.

Medicinal Herbs

Many medicinal herbs occur in this region. There are over 1,000 species of medicinal herbs commonly used in the area. Some herbs are found to be effective cures for local epidemic diseases. For example, the leaves of *Lysimachia christinae* and the roots of *Gomphostemma lucidum* are good for treating the most common disease - malaria; the flowers of *Buddleja officinalis* can be used for curing hepatitis; and the fruit of *Symplocos cochinchinensis* has a curative effect on mumps.

Specially Used Plants

Polygala arillata and *Vitex simplicifolia* are two local kinds of common hedge shrubs; *Engelhardtia spicata, Sambucus williamsii* and *Quercus acutissima* are useful for green manure in paddy fields; it means the season of slash and burn is coming when *Symplocos paniculata* and one kind of *Rhododendron* is in full bloom; it is the proper time for buckwheat planting when pear and peach are in full bloom; before red bayberry matures, upland rice should be sown;

Arenga pinnata and one kind of cogongrass are used as the roof materials for thatched cottages; the wizard of a village uses a leaf of *Curculigo orchioides* or a piece of culm of *Pseudostachyum polymorphum* as tools for divination; *Anthoxanthum hookeri*, a fragrant grass, is a unique gift for a girl friend; *Carex alta* is a valuable material for the weaving of mats.

KEY PROBLEMS CONFRONTING SUSTAINABLE DEVELOPMENT OF THE JINGPO COMMUNITIES

The new idea of sustainable development originated from the United Nations Stockholm Conference in 1972, but prevailed throughout the world nearly twenty years later. Although there are now several concepts of sustainable development and some new concepts are evolving (Cf. Tisdell, 1994), many argue for the development of "sustainable" economies in order to deal with issues of growth, economic and community development, and environmental protection. The emphasis of sustainable growth and natural resource development will help the Jingpo communities use natural resources more prudently and sensitively than in the past and ensure their continued survival.

The sustainable development of the Jingpo communities is confronted with various hindrances, but the following factors can to be regarded as most urgent issues.

Evaluation of Slash-and-Burn Cultivation in Practice

The Jingpo people have been the Dehong prefecture as a significant ethnic minority engaging in slash-and-burn cultivation for about six centuries. According to the legends of the Jingpo, their ancestors migrated from the eastern edge of the Tibetan plateau along the Hengduanshan mountain range to their present location. The Jingpo people were described prior this in the historical records in the Sui and Tang Dynasties (A.D. 581-907) as a minority living in mountains and hunting for their livelihoods (Yin, 1993). Slash-and-burn agriculture is a primitive method of cultivation. Trees and shrubs in forest are cut down and left to dry in the sun for nearly two months, and then burnt to prepare the land for cultivation. Slash-and-burn agriculture can be divided into two types, i.e., one year cultivation and cultivation for several years, usually for two or three years, before fallowing. The latter type of slash-and-burn agriculture is popular in Xishuangbanna. The Jingpo cultivate their land for only one year and then shift to another woodland for their cultivation. The used land is left uncultivated for several years until the new generation of trees and shrubs cover it. The duration of fallow of land after cultivation used to be a dozen of years in this region, but it has been gradually curtailed to 7-8 years because of increased population density and loss of forested land for cultivation.

In the slash-and-burn cultivation system of the Jingpo people, upland rice is the main crop. Many crops such as wheat, corn, millet, buckwheat and sorghum, garden pea, broad bean, soy bean, kidney bean, cucumber, bitter cucumber, loofah, pumpkin, white gourd, eggplant, chilli, tomato, cabbage, oil-seed rape, radish, garlic, ginger, coriander, shallot, chive, fennel, mint etc. are intercropped with upland rice. The Jingpo people sometimes adopt a mixed cultivation system of upland rice and alder trees (*Alnus nepalensis*) to enable faster rehabilitation of forests after cultivation and provide some small timber for their use.

Slash-and-burn agriculture depends on full forest resources and strict land-use rotation. In a Jingpo community, usually a village, land resources for the cycle of slash-and-burn cultivation are divided into twelve parts, called "Yingwang". One "Yingwang" and sometimes a few small pieces of forestland will be slashed and burnt for cultivation in a village each year. Every household occupies a plot of land in the "Yingwang" just sufficient for its food production. After cultivation for a year a Yingwang is left for 11 years before it is cultivated again. Increasing population in some regions has produced a shortage of land resources. In some Jingpo communities, the duration of the fallow has to be reduced to 7-8 years. Village people can borrow or hire lands from their friends, or relatives in neighbouring villages if they really need more farming lands for grain production.

Every family slashes its own allocated forestland in January or February and can take useful logs and fuelwood from the land. Usually in the latter of April, the strong and experienced young persons in the village set fire to the slashed field. The whole action is fully discussed and elaborately organised under the direction of village elders and leaders beforehand. A firebreak of about three metres in breadth will be set up in advance. Who is to start the fire, where and when, how to withdraw safely, and how to put out the fire to save the forests outside the slashed area will be considered before the burning begins.

Slash-and-burn cultivation in the Jingpo areas is a typical rotation system. In the early times when there were richer forests and a sparse population, this cultivation system yielded the following benefits to local communities and ecosystem:

- many trees and shrubs can survive and flourish quickly after cropping stops;

- fewer weeds and pests harm crops after burning so that it saves cost and labour;
- less soil is eroded because of the till-less agriculture;
- higher productivity can be expected in this land because plant ash fertilizer and nutrient build up in the soil;
- some special seeds of plants can sprout and grow well after burning; and
- some herbivorous animals like to roam and seek food in the cultivated land.

This productive system has been greatly changed since the rapid reduction of forestland and expansion of local population. Slash-and-burn cultivation is becoming less economic and hence a new system should be developed to substitute for the old one. However, good aspects of the system should be retained. Furthermore, the farming culture included in this system such as sacrificial rites for slash-and-burn, sowing and harvest should be studied as well.

Transformation of Land Ownership System and Tenure Conflicts

In the early 1950s, except in a few minority ethnic areas, almost all lands, minerals and forests in China were nationalized. Through the legislative process, land and forest tenures were divided into two types: state ownership and local collective ownership. Before 1950, most agricultural lands and forests of Yunnan belonged to landlords, ethnic chieftains and local tyrants. Only a few forests such as the Yipinglang Salt-well region, the Gejiu Tin Mining Enterprise and a few forest experimental stations were under the control of the Yunnan provincial government. After the establishment of the People's Republic of China, three types of changes in rights to land were implemented in Yunnan: i.e. 1) the People's government took over the state lands and forests of the old government; 2) virgin soil and forests, and private forests with an unbroken area of over 500 mu (about 33.3 hectares) were nationalised; and 3) small, broken scattered lands and forests of landlords were allocated to local communities or individual peasants (Zhao *et al.*, 1993).

Up to the period when the "Household Responsibility System" for agricultural land allocation and the "Two Mountains System for non-agricultural land were introduced in 1982, most village lands or community lands were allocated to each land-based household according to contracts which spelt out their rights and responsibilities as well as how profit after harvest would be shared between the farmer and the collective. Only small areas of land were set aside under collective ownership and management with the revenue from harvested timber often being set aside for community expenses such as the village school or the maintenance of infrastructure such as roads, bridges and irrigation canals. In fact, while most farmers had a legal certificate guaranteeing their usufruct of land, very few farmers have a contract document specifying the content and limits of the farmer's obligations to the collective. That caused severe conflicts and deforestration. Because of legal uncertainty, unstable policies and an increasingly urgent need for agricultural land for feeding an expanding population, almost half of the forests in Yunnan were destroyed after the late 1950s.

State forest and collective forests form the basic components for forest resource management in China, and these two types of ownership have functioned over the vast areas of China since 1950s. Collective land is the traditional place for the production and life of village people. In this land, local people have rights for self-determination. For example, they can determine which piece of forest should be slashed and burnt for cultivation, which piece of forest should be protected as a water source forest, and they can work out some local regulations and rules for the management and use of village forest resources. Collective forests belong to the local communities. The term "collective" contains the administrative villages and the individual natural villages. On this basis, collective forests are the common estates of community members. However, local governmental departments, for example, the local forest station also have some powers to control this type of forests. The commercial felling in this kind of forests requires a license from the local forestry bureau.

In order to prevent the further deforestation, readjustment of land and forest tenures had to be initiated by the countrywide political authorities. In the Jingpo areas, the task was completed with a solution of some protracted land conflicts in 1983, but the survey and planning of a nature reserve in Dehong Prefecture introduced a series of new problems. The Tongbiguan Nature Reserve is a provincial protected area located in the Jingpo region. It has resulted in sharp conflicts between local villages and local administrative authorities since its establishment in 1986. There are 13 villages in the reserve and a large quantity of village forests and croplands were transferred to the protected reserve. In 1988, the provincial government approved a resolution for removing the local people to other areas and allocated a sum for resettlement, but owing to the shortage of funds, the plan failed. The local people raised a higher claim than the government could meet and simultaneously the conflicts between villages to use forested land and the reserve became increasingly intense. Finally in 1993, the provincial government agreed to transfer the usufruct of 4,000 hectares of forestland to local communities. The new boundaries for the reserve were drawn up in 1995, but the conflicts are still occurring because the Jingpo have insufficient arable land and forestland for slash-and-burn agriculture.

Local governments have attempted to control the depletion of forest resources, especially in the past decade. Many official coercive measures for forest protection caused frequent conflict between governments and local people. Although governments have a very strong power to punish the activities of felling trees unlawfully, it has been ineffective in preventing increasing deforestation. For example, according to the statistics of the Prefectural Office of Natural Protection, 402 cases of deforestation occurred in the period January - August in 1994 in the state forests of Dehong Prefecture. This number increased by 175.5% compared to 1993. The destroyed areas and the losses of forest value are 9 and 22 times of those in the same period of 1993 respectively. Of course, the rapidly rising price of timber encourages the trend to deforestation.

Adequate land and forest tenures are at the core of community development in the Jingpo areas. The development of the Jingpo community should stress the conscious participation of local people in the use of such resources. Clearer property rights in land and forest resources and rights to manage these will motivate local communities and villagers to take better care of these resources. The present policy of land leasing gives a good beginning for reducing conflicts. According to the new land policy of the "Transfer for Four Types of Wastes on Lease", the wastelands, barren mountains, flood lands, and unused water resources whether state-owned or belonging to the collective will be shifted to individual households on lease. That can at least address the land claims of local people partly. Even in the above mentioned protected area, there were about 4,500 hectares of forestland destroyed in 1970s. Now it still remains barren. Local people would like to cultivate the land, but without explicit permission from higher authorities, local administrative officials hesitate to allow it. According to the new land policy, the barren mountains could be managed by local people on lease. But they can only plant trees and shrubs. Furthermore, where a tenant fails to do this the land will be taken back and transferred to other people.

Techniques and Markets for Cash Crops

Dehong Prefecture has a good climate for many crops. Sugar cane is one of the most important cash crops and its area of cultivation is only second to that of grain in the Jingpo areas. Tea plantations and rubber tree plantations are often listed in importance after sugar cane. Fruit trees, rape, tobacco, coffee, pepper, and amomum are also significant cash crops. Actually in some richer townships, the cash crops surpass income from grain production and provide the largest sources of income (see *Figure 1*, Saihao and Huyu townships). Local major sources of income from forestry include bamboo shoots, seeds of tung trees, walnuts and palm fibre besides timber products. Other local non-timber forest products are chestnut, edible fungi, lac, tea-oil, Chinese prickly ash, and anise.

Technique is the most important limiting factor for the production of cash crops. For example, the per hectare yield of sugar cane in the Dehong Prefecture in 1993 was 55.6 tons, but Fujiang and Guangdong provinces with similar climate have an average per year yield of 69 tons and 66 tons respectively. The output of tea plantation in this prefecture in 1993 was only 494.5 kg per hectare, distinctly lower than the state average yield of 660 kg per hectare (Li, 1993). Major reasons are the following:

- available skilled personnel mainly work in the institutions of governments, research institutes and state-run farms
- lack of technical services at the basic level
- lack of an effective technical extension system
- low educational level of local communities

Another factor affecting the production of cash crops in Dehong Prefecture is China's international commercial policy. Due to limited tropical areas in China, China's outputs of tropical cash crops are insufficient to meet its domestic consumption. It therefore imports tropical products. But a problem rose after the government eased controls on exports and imports in 1980s. The price of products from tropical crops started to fluctuate. For example, during 1987 and 1988 the prices of sugar and rubber were up to the 3 times the state fixed prices because of reduced imports. Stimulated by the market, the growers of sugarcane and rubber extended the areas of cropping in the next year. Simultaneously, the central government eased import restrictions and the local governments and subordinate departments were given more authority to import. In the following year, large amounts of sugar and rubber were imported. Consequently purchase of domestic sugar and rubber fell to very low levels so that in some areas sugarcane remained unharvested and the crude rubber went bad on farms. The results affected the Jingpo communities in the Dehong Prefecture. Other tropical crops in the prefecture such as coffee, shellac, amomum and pepper faced a similar situation.

Poverty in the Jingpo Communities

The incomes in major Jingpo townships from agriculture, forestry, husbandry and sidelines are listed in the following table with reference to the population, arable land, average income and grain production per capita per year. There are three townships where average per capita income is below the poverty line of 530 yuan net income per capita. These townships contain 33,558 people make up about 60% of the total population of these seven Jingpo townships. Actually in the Jingpo communities, the incidence of poverty is higher than for the Han, Dai and the De-An people who are living together with the Jingpo.

Table 1. **Population and Economic Situation of Major Jingpo Communities**

Township	Population	Jingpo %	Arable Land (mu)	Total Income (Million yuan)	Total Grain Production (Million kg)	Per Capita Net Income (Yuan)	Per Capita Grain (kg)
Quinping	13266	55.9	27800	8.3394	6.2345	402	485
Bangwa	7023	89.4	15328	3.4315	2.5303	429	373
Menguye	3057	83.9	8448	2.2820	1.2074	637	414
Saiho	7663	68.9	23329	8.2046	3.3825	759	458
Wangshuzi	13269	48.5	24722	7.6379	3..9403	399	306
Huyu	6130	40.0	20415	11.7777	3.2508	1006	560

1 hectare = 15 mu , 100 USD = 820 yuan

The average food per capita includes staple food and non-staple food or coarse cereals

Data from the *Year Book of the Dehong Prefecture 1994*

According to current views, the major causes of impoverishment in the Jingpo areas are the subsistence type society, low educational levels, poorly developed economic system and drug addiction. The concrete reasons are described as follow:

- As mentioned above, the development of the Jingpo communities was basically in the period of primitive commune before 1950s. The major means of production belonged to the community. However, the new relations of production were forming and the Shanguan was becoming the owner of lands and forests at that time. Although this ownership system was gradually stopped by the end of 1950s, the level of productivity and the mentality of non-commodity exchange have changed little since then. Consequently, the slash-and-burn agriculture with extensive cultivation remains the Jingpo's main means of survival and can only meet their lowest level of economic needs.

- Based on the survey of educational departments of Yunnan Province, the illiteracy rate of minority population in poor mountainous areas is up to 40% and the percentage of children not attending to school in 7-11 old group is nearly 30% (Shen, 1992). In the Jingpo areas, many small villages are scattered in the remote mountainous districts. The children from remote villages spend one or two, even more hours in walking to school. The situation has not been improved because of the insufficient investment in education and the shortage of teachers in these areas.
- The less developed society and low educational level result in the existence of poor economic base for the Jingpo. In fact, the characteristics of the Jingpo economic system is still simple, isolated and natural though change has occurred since 1980s. Generally speaking, the life of the Jingpo people almost completely relies on the endowment of nature and they are self-sufficient. The major items in the local markets are natural products such as mushrooms, wild vegetables, wild fruits and wild animal meat. Even in the remote areas, local people are still ashamed to sell their own products. The appearance of the towns and township enterprises are the new things in the Jingpo areas. The isolated mountainous environment and lack of believe in commodification prevents the development of the local economy.
- Drug addiction is currently a serious local social problem that worsens the local living conditions. Lots of the Jingpo villages are close to the well-known drug base of the Golden Triangle Region. Since the middle 1980s, the prefecture has been one of the major passageways for drug smuggling. Consequently, the local people suffered not a little from drug taking. Some statistical data indicate the serious situation in Jingpo villages. During 1992-1993, Luliang administrative village had 103 drug addicts and 5 died; in 1990, Huyu township has 335 drug addicts, of which 274 were the Jingpo, and 9 died. A small village of only about 200 people, Banyang Jingpo village, has had 11 drug addicts dying in past decade. Recently, the local government has introduced strict measures to force the drug addicts into give up the drug. For example, Longba township uses a special wood coop to keep drug addicts in. The wood of

Schima wallichii makes drug addicts excruciating itchy when they touch it. Finally after a few months, it was said that all drug addicts gave up the drug. That is a cruel and miserable story, but local communities are always dealing with this kind of problem and go to extremes to punish the victims of drugs because many social issues are related to the drug addiction. For instance, theft was unknown in Jingpo society, but it prevails in the present decade.

STRATEGIES OF SUSTAINABLE DEVELOPMENT IN THE JINGPO COMMUNITIES

Poverty and environmental deterioration seem to be twin brothers. None can control the excessive exploitation of natural resources by a mass of poor people facing starvation. Due to the deep influences of traditional culture and farming techniques, rapid change in the Jingpo communities is almost impossible. Gradual advance might, however, be made by means of some currently proven effective approaches for sustainable development in rural areas based on the local realities. For this reason, social forestry is a useful tool for sustainable mountain development.

Social forestry or community forestry is a practice referring to a broad range of tree- or forest-related activities which rural land owners undertake to provide wood products for their own use and to generate local incomes. Its definition can be traced back to the 8th World Forestry Conference held at Jakarta in 1978. At that time, "Forests for People" became the theme of the conference and social forestry or community forestry was defined as:

> *any situation that intimately involves local people in a forestry activity. It embraces a spectrum of situations ranging from woodlots in areas which are short of wood and other forest products for local needs, through to the growing of trees at the farm level to provide cash crops and the processing of forest products at the household, artisan or small industry level to generate income, to the activities of forest dwelling communities. It excludes large-scale industrial forestry and any other form of forestry that contributes to community development solely through employment and wages, but it does include activities of forest industry enterprises and public forest services which encourage and assist forestry activities at the community level. The activities so encompassed are potentially compatible with all types of land ownership. While it thus provides only a partial view of the impact of the way in which forestry and the goods and services of forestry directly affect the lives of rural people (FAO, 1978).*

In the literature, social forestry is used interchangeably with the terms rural forestry, farm forestry, community forestry, forestry for people, forestry for local community development, rural development forestry and community woodlots etc., the differences being purely semantic and definition of most of these terms is fuzzy. The relationship between them and what occurs in practice are often not clear (Arnold, 1987; Winterbottom and Hazlewood, 1987).

The old saying "those living on a mountain live off the mountain" reflects the fact that the core of mountainous community development is the rational exploitation of mountain. To develop mountainous region one must focus on sustainable forest management and use and rehabilitate a forest ecological environment. Agroforestry, a major technique of social forestry, can be introduced as one of alternatives to local slash-and-burn agriculture and it can be connected with the traditional governance, institutions, culture and indigenous knowledge of the Jingpo people.

Unlike the mountainous Han people who have been practising terraced agriculture for centuries, the Jingpo people are used to practising slash-and-burn cultivation based on rich tropical and subtropical climate conditions and old institutions. In past decades, in order to prevent the shrinking of forests, local governments attempted to forbid the slash-and-burn cultivation, but it failed because they could not found a proper solution for the supply of the subsistence needs of the local people. Although some experts, today, suggest that the Jingpo adopt terraced agricultural techniques as an alternative to the slash-and-burn cultivation system, most believe that the adoption of some indigenous knowledge such as the establishment of permanent plantations originating from local practices is more likely to meet the demands of the mountainous communities because their daily subsistence relies very much on forestlands for fuelwood, fodder, grazing, and for generating cash income (Lu, 1995; He, 1995). Recent surveys conducted in the nearby Baoshan Prefecture has shown that there are 5 patterns, 10 subpatterns and 27 types of agroforestry plantation models which prevail the mountainous areas of the Prefecture (Guo, 1993). Many of these models also exist in the Jingpo areas according to our field work. For example, the type of *Alnus nepalensis* + upland rice intercropping can produce food, small timber, fuelwood and green manure to meet the demands of the Jingpo communities. It maintains as a "sustainable" production cycle by the regular rotation of the crops and trees and the nitrogen-fixing capabilities of *Alnus nepalensis* trees (Cf. Zhuge & Tisdell, 1996). Tea plantations commonly established in this region have also proven to be a practical alternative to slash-and-burn agriculture. In addition, the development of ecotourism, animal husbandry, small processing industries, especially those based on the local natural resources, provision of employment opportunities in management of nature reserves and service industry can play an important role in altering the traditional productive system as well (Cf. Tisdell, 1995).

Participation of local communities and role of government is another important subject in social forestry. Early in June 1992, the Earth Summit on the global environment and development declared the first global statement on forests in human history. In this historical document, the following policies were aired:

> *Governments, in full partnership with indigenous people and their communities should, where appropriate:*
>
> *Develop or strengthen national arrangements to consult with indigenous people and their communities with a view to reflecting their needs and incorporating their values and traditional and other knowledge and practices in national policies and programmes in the field of natural resource management and conservation and other development programmes affecting them;*
>
> *Cooperate at the regional level, where appropriate, to address common indigenous issues with a view to recognising and strengthening their participation in sustainable development (UNCED, 1993, p228).*
>
> *Launching or improving opportunities for participation of all people, including youth, women, indigenous people and local communities, in the formulation, development and implementation of forest-related programmes and other activities, taking due account of the local needs and cultural values (Ibid., p92).*

According to the statement, local people have a right to take part in activities which concern local community development. Their "participation" is not only limited to participation in investigation, planning, designing, management, monitoring and evaluation, but also includes sharing of the benefits. The real participation of local communities should reflect the principles of equity and equality. In reforming land ownership systems and in the solution of tenure conflicts, government should listen attentively to the views of local people and simultaneously government should provide some guiding opinions for reducing biases in the traditional culture. For example, the various reform types of land tenure or usufruct are currently the major sources of tenure conflicts in this region. Local governments are more willing to transfer power to the local leader teams, usually village councils of local communities than before. These local leader teams take charge of the concrete tasks involving in land allocation. But a new question may come up. Since the issue of gender is so frequently neglected in the Jingpo communities, some women may lose their living conditions because they have no inheritance of land and this will produce a negative impact on the sustainable development of local communities. Therefore, a side-by-side approach, i.e., combining the knowledge of both government and local people rather than either a top-down approach or a bottom-up approach, is necessary to improve the participation of local communities and the decision making of government under the rational way (Tisdell, 1995).

Otherwise, the development of social forestry in local communities should also combine with the superiority of local natural resources and geography. For example, the Dehong Prefecture is contiguous to Myanmar with a boundary line of 503.8 km and has many trading ports and passages Since the prefecture started to open its border ports to the world in July 1990, cross-border trade has developed quickly. According to the statistics, the total sum of import and export through local border ports in this prefecture were to 20,150 million yuan (about 2,400 million USD) in 1993, 17.3 per cent higher than 1992 and the sum of export is 1.6 times that of import. Furthermore, cross-border tourism becomes more and more attractive to countrymen and foreigners that promote the vitality of social forestry projects such as ecotourism projects based on natural resources and environment and the growth of local tertiary industry. The total income from tourism in this prefecture in 1993 reached 30 million yuan, nearly to be double that of last year (Wu,1994). Cross-border trade and tourism indeed have increased the incomes of the Jingpo communities and introduced the idea of commodity exchange that may contribute to the economic development of local communities. The full potential of cross-border trade and tourism in the Jingpo areas still remains to be exploited. For example, the booming tourism attractions of folk villages organised by local minority people in Xishuangbanna can also be introduced to the Jingpo areas. However, cross-border trade and tourism have successfully attracted outside investment and techniques, and formed numerous local markets for the exchange of local non-timber products that could generate a steady income for local people. Local Jingpo communities such as those in Huyu, Saihao and Tongbiguan townships were initially lifted out of poverty by means of the development of tertiary industry and cross-border trade.

Concluding Comments

The Jingpo communities in Yunnan experienced much change in forms of governance and in property rights regimes in the second half of the 20th century. The Jingpos' traditional forms of governance and poverty rights were altered by the Chinese communist government after it came to power, although vestiges of the pre-existing system remained with only little effective modifications being possible in remote areas. Furthermore, the Jingpo continued many of their traditional ways of life. For example, they continued to engage in slash-and-burn agriculture, showed little interest in commercial exchange and persisted with a subsistence life-style based on their established customs and use of traditional production techniques. However, with rising population and changing income aspirations, their way of life has become increasingly unsustainable and poverty among the Jingpo has become widespread.

To some extent the economic position of the Jingpo was made more difficult by the transfer of much of their communal land to state control by the widespread creation of state forests and reserves after 1949, a process accelerated later by the Cultural Revolution. This change meant the availability of smaller land areas for legal communal use by the Jingpo. Consequently, they often illegally used state property (state forests and reserves) which now were treated more like open-access resources. Despite such changes, the culture of the Jingpo seemed to survive.

With the commencement of China's economic reforms in 1978, a new economic system began to develop for the Jingpo, not instantaneously but with a lag. With China's economic reforms, new forms of governance and poverty rights as well as new methods and wider scope for exchange and choice of production techniques began to emerge.

Features of the new system are greater creation of *de facto* private property rights (signalled by the introduction of Household Responsibility System and the Two Mountains System increased use of market systems, greater freedom of movement, greater state consultation with local communities with increasing use of side-by-side governance. In addition, China's opening up to the outside world has exposed local communities such as the Jingpo to international market forces. Being on the border with Myanmar they are in a position to gain from increased cross-border trade. At the same time however, such trade and increasing involvement in the market system exposes them to market risks such as fluctuating prices for their produce and may necessitate economic restructuring of village activities. Old customs and traditions may lose their social and economic relevance and new forces of social tension and disintegration may be unleashed, evidence to some extent by the incidence of drug addiction amongst the Jingpo.

It seems that little can be done to shield minority and tribal groups from the forces of social and economic change, except in some cases to moderate the pace of change to allow their social system to co-evolve without undue strain and to develop techniques and methods to help them cope with transition to a new socio-economic system. In this respect, the best aspects and techniques of the Jingpo people need to be re-examined. For instance, it seems that slash-and-burn agriculture is becoming less and less viable. An alternative is to develop settled forms of agroforestry and communal forestry of a sustainable nature tailored to the experience and needs of the Jingpo. Such systems can involve a combination of private property and communal property. With economic change it is also possible that an increasing number of the Jingpo will have to seek non-agricultural occupations and education can play an important role in preparation for these. There is little doubt that a change in Jingpo society is inevitable, as it is for many tribal and minority groups throughout Asia and on the Indian Ocean rim. The big question is how can these societies best manage social and economic change which usually involves variations in governance and in property rights. It is a pipe dream to believe that the socio-economic situation of such communities can remain frozen in time. Even if it could be, it is far from obvious that such sustainability would be desirable.

REFERENCES

Arnold, J.E.M. 1987: Community forestry. *Ambio* 6: 122-128.

Booz, P.R. 1987: *Yunnan: Southwest China's Little-Known Land of Eternal Spring*, Chicago, Passport Books, p52.

Food and Agriculture Organization (FAO) 1978: Forestry for local community development. Rome: FAO Forestry Paper 7.

Guo, Huijun. 1993: *Agroforestry Systems In Baoshan, Yunnan, Southwest China*. Yunnan University Press, Kunming.1.

He, Peikun. 1995: Primary analysis of slash-and-burn in Yunnan. In He, P.K.: *Social Forestry - Research And Exploration*, Yunnan Science and Technology Press, Kunming, pp118-122.

Li, Liangsheng. 1993: *A Study On The Exploitation Of Tropic Resources In Southwest Part Of Yunnan Province*, Yunnan People's Press, Kunming

Lu, Rongsen. 1995: Rehabilitation of degraded lands in mountain ecosystems: a technical report of plantation establishment in Nepal. In Pei, S.J (ed.): *Rehabilitation Of Degraded Lands In Mountain Ecosystems Of The Hindu Kush-Himalayan Region*, published by ICIMOD, Kathmandu, pp85-106.

Shen, Kangda. 1992: Social and economic factors of impoverishment and analysis of its structure. In Guo, L.X. & D.M. He (eds.): *Poverty- A Problem Challenging Human Beings*, Chinese Science & Technology Press, Beijing, pp45-64.

Tisdell, C.A. 1994: Sustainability and sustainable development: are these concepts a help or a hindrance to economics? *Economic Analysis & Policy* 24(2): 133-150.

Tisdell, C.A. 1995: Issues in biodiversity conservation including the role of local communities. *Environment Conservation* 22(3): 216-228.

United Nations Conference on Environment and Development (UNCED). 1993: Agenda 21: Programme of Action for Sustainable Development, the United Nations Conference on Environment and Development, 3-14 June 1992, Rio de Janeiro, Brazil. Published by the United Nations Department of Public Information.

Winterbottom, R. and P.T. Hazlewood. 1987: Agroforestry and sustainable development: making the connection. *Ambio* 16: 100-110.

Wu, Zhixiang (ed). 1994: *Annual Book Of The Dehong Prefecture*. Dehong Nationality Press, Mangshi. .

Yin, Shaoting. 1993: *A Farming Culture Born Out Of Forests: Swiddening In Yunnan, China*, Yunnan People's Press, Kunming.2..

Zhao, Junchen *et al*. 1993: *Social Forestry In Yunnan*, Yunnan Science and Technology Press, Kunming.

Zhuge, Ren & Clem Tisdell. 1996: Developing community-based forestry in the uplands of Yunnan: dictates of environment and socio-economics. In Tisdell, C.A and Chai, J.C.(ed.): *China's Economic Growth And Transition: Including Regional, Environmental, Technological And Other Dimensions*. Department of Economics, The University of Queensland, Brisbane, 4072 (forthcoming).

11 Women and Common Property Resources in the Management and Health of Livestock in Thai Villages

Tatjana Kehren and Clem Tisdell

Introduction

Livestock industries in Thailand have experienced considerable changes during the past decades, and the management of livestock as well as the use of common resources are crucial factors in their future development. Women play a significant, but undervalued role in animal husbandry and their impact on the health of livestock as well as their potential contribution to an improvement of the present state needs to be considered. Both village bovines and poultry utilise common property resources to a considerable extent which has implications for the productivity and healthiness of village livestock.

An Overview of Livestock Industries in Thailand

Traditionally, the livestock sector in Thailand has been, as in most of South-East Asia, complementary to the subsistence economy, with pigs and poultry being raised for village consumption, and cattle and buffaloes mainly being used for draught purposes. Livestock industries are important in Thailand and make a significant contribution to food production. Thai farms are small due to the high man-land ratio, and crop production on the farm can neither generate sufficient income to satisfy farming families, nor provide full time employment for family members. Thus, livestock production on a small farm usually plays a complementary, yet significant role to crop production. Livestock utilize by-products from crop production, generate income and diversify employment opportunities for the family. In particular, the importance of the pig, poultry and cattle industries in Thailand seems to have increased in recent years, whereas buffaloes play a relatively minor role, especially as a source of draught power, since animal drawn ploughs have progressively been replaced by tractors.

Under existing farming systems in Thailand, 60 per cent of farmers are still small farmers living in rural areas of whom almost 90 per cent are self employed. These small farm households whose living standard is mostly at the subsistence level frequently operate an integrated farming system, consisting of field crops, horticulture, fishery and livestock. Livestock, however, are most important to these farmers, including buffaloes, cattle, pigs and poultry, and - to a lesser extent and mainly in the s outh of Thailand where Islam is important - goats and sheep. The varying importance of these animals is explained by their differing income to the farmers, with dairy cows supplying one of the highest returns, and buffaloes yielding the lowest annual income. Among farm operations, land is relatively evenly distributed, with average land holdings of 5.6 ha (35 rais). However, there are still a number of small farmers who own less than 1.6 hectares of land, and some are landless.

The Pig Industry

Throughout the 1960s and 1970s, pig crossbreds were raised in backyards of small farms for consumption and generation of supplementary income. While pigs generated the largest share of value added in the Thai livestock sector in 1975, the development of pig production had been remarkably slow up to the 1980s (Murphy, Tisdell and Kehren 1996). The virtual stagnation of the industry in the past was - to a large degree - due to a considerable degree of government intervention, which discouraged private investment in the pig industry. In addition, the market price of pigs and feed costs were quite unstable. Over the last decade, commercial pig farms have increased significantly, particularly in Eastern and Central regions of the country, due to a rapid increase in urban demand for pork. A recent estimate is that 80 per cent of pig production in Thailand is undertaken by commercial enterprises (Sheehan 1993). Today, a small number of live pigs and frozen piglets are exported to Hong Kong and Singapore.

Until the mid-1980s, small middlemen (often the agents of large wholesalers) collected the required supply of pigs by travelling from village to village, delivering them to the often illegally working slaughterhouses (Murphy, Tisdell and Kehren 1996). In recent times, however, with the development of commercial pig raising farms in provinces around Bangkok as a consequence of a rapid increase in urban demand for pork, the role of small middlemen has diminished. Supported by a small number of feed mill companies providing piglets, animal feeds, drugs, veterinary services and farm management expertise to contracted pig producers, and through improved conditions of slaughterhouses, Thailand's exports of pork increased markedly towards the end of the 1980s.

Thailand has the potential for significant expansion of pigmeat exports (Harrison and Tisdell 1995), but foot-and-mouth disease

(FMD) is still a major problem in the country, which leads to enormous losses of profits. Although high mortality rates for FMD outbreaks are rare amongst adult livestock, they can reach up to 90 per cent, in particular among piglets in high density populations (Donaldson 1994).The periodic shortage of some vaccines when disease outbreaks occur and inadequate treatments present additional serious problems.

FMD led to imports of pigs (from Malaysia) to Thailand in the early 1990s because of enormous damage to local pig farms, particularly in the country's South, and a resulting shortage of pigs. (Anon 1991). In addition, strongly fluctuating pig and feed prices - partly a consequence of frequent government intervention and changing policies - also have a constraining impact on the growth of the Thai pig industry. In 1993, economic losses in the Thai pig industry were at a record high, due to an oversupply of pigs and consequently low prices. If substantial improvements could be made with respect to the eradication of foot-and-mouth disease in the pig industry in Thailand, there would be many opportunities to increase the country's pig export market.

The Poultry Industry

The Thai poultry industry consists of ducks, broilers and laying hens. Ducks only play a minor role and their value of exports (to Hong Kong, Japan, Germany and Singapore) has been relatively insignificant. Similar to the pig industry, the principal area for broiler production is the Central Plains region where more than 35% of broilers are raised. The largest chicken raising provinces are Chacheongsao, Chon Buri and Nakhon Pathom. While the commercial poultry industry in Thailand has grown significantly, large numbers of poultry are still raised by village households. In general, the number of poultry in each household is quite low, the most common number being between 3 and 10, according to a survey in Northern Thailand. Poultry is generally used by village householders to provide either food (meat and eggs) or supplementary income.

Chicken farms in Thailand can be classified into three types (Murphy and Tisdell 1995):

First, there are the backyard farms where chickens are raised on a small scale for consumption and supplementary income purposes. Ten years ago, virtually all growers (approx. 99.5%) were backyard growers, though they produced only about a third of production. Nowadays, they account for less than one quarter of production, due to the expansion of commercial production.

Independent commercial growers are the second group of producers who often engage in contract farming with smaller growers. However, their numbers are likely to decline in the future because of their inability to benefit from the economies of size associated with the larger contract growers.

The third group of producers, the contract growers, mainly started to develop since the late 1970s. The Charoen Pokphand Company introduced wage and price guarantee contracts in 1976 and since then, contracts between chicken growers and hatcheries or feed companies became widespread.

Prior to the 1970s, there were few attempts to encourage growth in the poultry industry. In 1946, modern production methods were introduced and in 1956, the importation of high yielding stock commenced. Even by the early 1970s, most farmers raised only a small number of indigenous chickens for their own consumption, and hardly any poultry was exported. Yet, a few large private firms began to contribute to a significant expansion of the poultry industry, with the Charoen Pokphand Company commencing to export chickens to Japan in 1973. Modern chicken processing companies developed which established their own slaughterhouses and adopted modern marketing strategies. Nowadays, Thailand is one of the world's largest chicken producing countries in terms of broilers produced, and one of the largest exporters to Japan.

A distinctive characteristic of the Thai poultry industry is that it is dominated by a relatively small number of multinational companies. It is estimated that about 80 per cent of the broiler sector is controlled by 10 to 12 companies, including for instance the Charoen Pokphand Group, General Foods and Sun Valley (Anon 1996). This oligopolistic market structure is not necessarily beneficial to everyone, however, and creates public concern about possible exploitation of small farmers or even monopolisation of the market.

Thailand has been a major exporter of poultry meats, but in the past few years, the country's broiler exports experienced a decline by about 5-10 per cent. China has become Thailand's major competitor for exports of chicken to its principal export market, Japan. Thailand's competitive edge is starting to diminish with rising wages and therefore higher labour costs. Shortages of livestock feedstuff also contribute to the decreasing competitiveness of Thailand's poultry industry. The country's large supply of agricultural and fishery products is becoming scarcer, and the quality is relatively low. Moreover, feed costs in Thailand and China seem to be similar, yet they are well above the costs in Brazil and the US. Thus, the present situation for Thai broiler producers does not appear to be very auspicious.

The Dairy Industry

Indian settlers commenced dairying operations in Thailand in the 1950s. Their activities were centred around Ayutthaya[1], with Bangkok being the major market for their milk. Today, the Central Zone is still the primary region for dairying activities, due to its rich agricultural land and the almost continual availability of cattle feed throughout the year (Rao 1990). At present, the main dairy cow raising areas are Chiang Mai, Nakorn Pathom, Ratchaburi and Saraburi (Office of Agricultural Economics 1992).

Extensive dairy development in Thailand began with the establishment of a joint venture between the Thai and Danish governments in the early 1960s, the Thai Danish Farm and Training Centre (TDDF) at Muak-Lek [2] (Pichet 1991). A few years later in 1968, another joint venture, the Thai-German Dairy Training and Processing Plant, was founded in Chiang Mai until it was taken over by the Department of Livestock Development in 1977. During the 1970s, the popularity of milk as a beverage continued to rise considerably as a result of increased advertising in the mass media. In addition, manufacturers strongly promoted milk powder as a substitute for mother's milk and now milk powder represents - in terms of value - a significant proportion of Thailand's milk imports (Chinwala and Umrod 1993).

Due to factors such as strong government support and increased economic growth in Thailand, local milk production has expanded rapidly since the 1980s. An estimate of the total raw milk output in 1995 is about 300,000 litres per day. In 1982, Thailand had 13,700 cows producing 27,240 tonnes of milk. By 1991, the amount of milk had risen to 178,000 tonnes, with domestic herd sizes also displaying similar growth - to over 70,000 cows (ADC 1993). This growth of the Thai dairy industry has been due to a rapidly growing economy and population, changes in consumers' lifestyle and buying patterns, active promotion of milk products by the Thai government and a range of customs duties.

However, the supply of milk in Thailand is still insufficient for the rapidly increasing domestic demand in recent years. Despite

---

1 This is the ancient Thai capital, located about 80 kilometres north of Bangkok.

2 Muak-Lek is located in the province of Saraburi, about 250 kilometres northwest of Bangkok.

considerable growth in production and herd numbers, the average herd size in Thailand is only about 6 cows (compared with 104 for Australian farms), with relatively low average yields of around 9-10 litres (per cow) a day (ADC 1993 / Watkin and Sukpituksakul 1992). Apart from low productivity, infertility is also a common problem of dairy cows in the country. It is believed that deficiency of minerals is one of the nutritional constraints limiting the cow's reproductivity (Vijchulata 1995). Since the extent of mineral deficiencies and their influence on the fertility of lactating cows in Thailand is still largely unknown, further research is needed.

Around 60 per cent of Thailand's drinking milk is sourced from local production. Since the early 1980s, Thai imports of milk products increased considerably. The consumption of milk in Thailand exceeds domestic production by far. Local cattle does not produce much milk and due to financial constraints, small farmers are unable to purchase improved breeds of dairy cows or obtain a bank loan. In support of the domestic dairy production, the Thai government has attempted to improve this situation by providing active support to small farmers who cannot afford the initial investment in a dairy cow. The Department of Livestock Development offers small loans as well as technical advice, milk collection and veterinary services as financial support to small farmers (Thummabood and Morathop 1993).

A number of other factors also hinder the development of the Thai dairy industry. Marketing of dairy products is difficult for small farmers because of high milk collection and transport costs (from farms to milk processing plants) and poorly developed refrigerated distribution systems. The majority of dairy farm sites in Thailand are widely scattered which makes evaluation, collection and transportation of milk difficult (Chinwala and Umrod 1993). Moreover, there is a shortage of milk collection centres and milk delivery trucks which causes irregular quality and immense losses of raw milk. All these factors result in high expenses of disease prevention and treatment, as well as of extension work.

A low level of local dairy management skills and a lack of adaptability of imported dairy breeds to Thailand's tropical climate also constitute serious problems for small scale livestock producers. In addition, inadequate feed supplies and high production costs (particularly of meal concentrate) are amongst the most serious problems for small farm households. Improvements in feeding and nutrition are crucial for higher production levels of milk in Thailand.

The high cost of high quality energy [1] and protein ingredients [2] for dairy cattle influences the level of imports required, and thereby the cost of production for Thai farmers, with protein being the most expensive ingredient (Wanapat and Devendra 1992

Meal concentrate clearly constitutes the highest cost to the farmer, amounting to almost 60 per cent (Wanapat and Devendra 1992, Watkin and Sukpituksakul 1992). Concentrates are widely used by milk producers in Thailand because of the low availability of forage and roughage.

Limited access of farmers to pastures leads to overgrazing and low levels of milk production. Sometimes, small farmers even hire trucks in order to collect green forage outside the village, up to 100 km away from their homes. Due to limitations of pasture as a source of feed, the use of concentrates and other feeds, including rice straw, pineapple waste and whole sugarcane, is of importance. An unpublished study by Wanapat and Sommart (Wanapat and Devendra 1992) of 30 farmers in the Northeast of Thailand using locally available feed resources, including cassava chip [3], rice bran, dried cassava leaf, broken rice and cotton seed meal, in order to reduce their production costs by formulating their own concentrates, found a decrease in cost by 1-2 Baht/kg, compared with the production costs of commercial concentrate. This suggests the use of locally available feed resources through the cooperation of farmers (and an improvement in production techniques) as a possible future alternative for improved feeding and nutrition of dairy cows in Thailand.

All of the above mentioned factors still limit the productivity of the small scale dairy producers in Thailand. An improvement in these conditions is necessary in order to achieve substantial growth in Thai milk production and exports.

THE ROLE OF WOMEN IN THE VILLAGE LIVESTOCK ECONOMY

Women comprise close to half the population of Thailand and have made a substantial contribution to the household and national economies. In the past, women in the agricultural sector used to play a very important role in household income production. In fact, under the absolute monarchy, men had to leave their farms for extended periods of time to perform various services for the ruling class. Thus, the

---

1 Including, for example, maize and cassava.

2 Soyabean meal, groundnut cake and fish meal, for instance.

3 Cassava chips are reported to increase milk production and decrease the cost of feeding in Holstein Friesian cows (Wanapat and Devendra 1992).

women who were left behind were forced to manage the farms, including all the buying and selling activities that were required (Chotipimai 1995). Even though females shared economic responsibilities with males, women were generally responsible for managing household finances and had an important role in trading and marketing activities as well as managing agricultural production, they had little real economic power in the family.

Changes in the economic structure and within the Thai society took place as a consequence of industrialisation, commercialisation and the promotion of economic growth in Thailand. In 1991, Thai women constituted 47% of the workforce, the highest percentage in Asia (Chotipimai 1995). Despite this high proportion of females in the labour force, however, the majority of women are employed as unskilled workers in low paid agricultural or industrial work. Women are concentrated in the lowest income brackets in all industries (Chotipimai 1995, Rao 1990). In fact, 'unpaid family worker' is the only employment category in which the number of women is greater than the number of men, as can be seen from (Chotipimai 1995).

With respect to Thai women's contribution to farm work, controversial figures exist. In a survey of 135 farm households in Northern Thailand in late 1994 (ACIAR 1994), the proportion of males constituted approx. 55% and women accounted for approx. 45%. This survey indicates that males comprised significantly more of the workforce (64%) than females (36%,) and those having the main responsibility for caring for the animals were predominantly male. According to the survey results, a greater proportion of family members participated in working with crops (54%) than were involved in stock work (44%). While women and men participated roughly equally in working with crops (45% females to 55% males), significantly more males participated in stock work than females. However, in analysing these figures, it needs to be considered that about 90% of the respondents were males, which is likely to produce biased results, and that the average household size of the survey was 4.3 people, which is a smaller number than the national average (of 6 family members).

In another survey, conducted in 17 provinces and comprising 200 small farm households, similar percentages were found with respect to workforce percentages. About 70% of the farm work was reported to be done by men, and 30% by women. It was also found that more than half the work done by men involved stock work (Thummabood and Morathop 1993). However, it also has to be considered that the family size in this survey was larger than average

(7 people). Yet, both surveys indicate that Thai women contribute around a third of the work on the farms.

However, it is not true that women contribute only a third to the farm work. *Table 1* indicates that Thai women are highly represented in the agriculture sector, the sector where lower wages generally apply. As can be seen, Thai women are highly represented in agricultural and farm work, contributing at least half of the work to farm management as well as small scale animal raising. It is true that rural women appear to increasingly leave the agricultural sector to find work in urban areas. During 1960-1990, the labour force participation rate in the agricultural sector decreased from around 80% to around 60%. The participation of women in the agricultural sector decreased from almost 88% to about 57% during the same time period (Chotipimai 1995).

There are, of course, several reasons for the migration of people from rural to urban industrial areas. One of the main arguments is that it is a consequence of the neglect of rural areas in the government's industrialisation strategy, as people are migrating to urban areas in the hope of finding employment. It has also been argued that the exclusion of Thai women from agricultural development programmes has been an additional factor contributing to women leaving the agricultural sector.

Table 1 **Percentage of Thai Women's Participation in Agricultural Development (1985)**

Activities	Organization	Women Participation (%)
Rice cultivation	Dept. Of Agri. Extension	50
Field crop cultivation	DOAE	50
Horticulture	DOAE	50
Vegetable/orchard growing	DOAE	100
Sericulture	DOAE	100
Beekeeping	DOAE	20
Soil improvement	DOAE	10
Plant protection	DOAE	30
Farm management	DOAE	70
Post harvest: harvesting	DOAE	50
Storing, food processing	DOAE	90
Small scale animal raising	Dept. Of Animal Husbandry	50
Small scale aqua-culture	Dept. Of Fishery	90
Co-operatives	Dept. Of Co-operatives	50
Home food preservation	DOAE	100
Home food processing	DOAE	100
Compost	DOAE	100

Source: Sheehan (1993), p.23

While the agricultural sector has experienced a decline in its proportion of the Thai labour force, labour force participation has increased rapidly in the commerce, manufacturing and service sectors, including female workers. However, the figures in *Table 1* are percentages, and despite the decline of women's participation in agricultural work, it is very likely that their farm work activities have not changed and are still the same today. In most developing countries, women are to a large extent involved in agricultural activities and make up the majority of subsistence farmers (Roy, Blomqvist and Tisdell 1996).

Even though more women than men left the agricultural sector to work in the commerce, manufacturing or service sector, this does not mean that a much greater proportion of women are now in higher positions. First of all, the agricultural sector still provides the vast majority of employment compared with all other sectors which means that the proportion of employment in other industries is still rather low. Some Thai women now hold senior positions in business and academia, and women are well represented in higher education (Sheehan 1993). However, the percentage of women in politics, in particular occupying provincial or national government positions, is still much lower than that of men, as *Table 2* displays.

Moreover, while now many jobs are at least in theory open for women, in practice, it is still difficult for women to hold leadership positions in local communities because of strong traditional values (Chotipimai 1995). Thai women who leave the agricultural sector to work in urban areas have limited employment opportunities and can frequently only work in low wage industries, due to their lack of skills and education. While young men from poor families are encouraged to continue studying following their compulsory education, girls have to start working (Chotipimai 1995). In many cases, sisters have to work to send their brothers to school or university as well as being responsible for their families.

Table 2 **Employment by Gender in Thailand at Various Government Levels in 1993**

	Total Number	Percentage Female	Percentage Male
National Government			
Members of Parliament	360	4.2	95.8
Senators	270	2.6	97.4
Cabinet Members	48	2.0	98.0
Secretary to Ministers	14	0	100.0
Judges	1,534	12.3	87.6
Attorney	1,574	9.2	90.8
Civil Servant Executives			
Permanent Secretary	13	0	100.0
Director-General	134	8.9	91.1
Deputy Director-General	336	5.6	94.4
Provincial Government			
Provincial Governors	73	1.4	98.6
District Officers	779	0	100.0
Deputy District Officers	4,674	0.3	99.7
Elected Government			
Provincial Council Members	2,046	4.9	95.1
Municipality Council Members	2,112	6.0	94.0
Sub-District Heads	6,669	1.0	99.0
Village Heads	60,554	1.2	98.8

Source: Chotipimai (1995), p.32

The result is an illiteracy rate of Thai women that has been more than double that of Thai men since the 1930s. While there has been a significant decline in illiteracy for both women and men over the past 40-50 years, the rate of illiterate women in proportion to men seems to have grown since the 1960s (Sheehan 1993).

However, there seems to have been improvements in more recent times. According to Thummabood and Morathop (1993) from the Department of Livestock Development in Thailand, training courses in animal husbandry are held for Thai farmers by district livestock extension officers (under the supervision of the Department of

Livestock Development), addressing issues such as animal nutrition and the prevention, management and control of disease. After these training courses, the farmers are provided with high quality forage seed for the improvement of their pastures. At present, women represent only about 20-30 % of the people trained. Yet, interestingly livestock extension officers have recognised that it would be more beneficial if more women could participate in these training courses and spread livestock technologies, for two reasons. Firstly, women seem to be more effective at applying the knowledge they gained from these courses, as they practice more than men. Sometimes, men ignore the new technologies and do not apply them. Secondly, women seem to believe women more than men, probably for cultural reasons. In this regard, it is even more important that considerably more women receive training for effective instruction and dissemination of livestock technologies and disease control.

As in many developing countries, women are the most underprivileged group in Thailand and suffer the extremes of poverty (Patanapongsa 1992). Even though they contribute - in addition to all the household chores - at least as much as men to the farm management and animal husbandry, their participation is never acknowledged and they do not have a say in any economic affairs of the family. This might be related to the fact that Thailand is a patriarchal society and the male is seen as the head of the household (Sheehan 1993). The husband should love, respect, care and work for his wife and family, whereas his wife should obey him, defer to him and look after him and the children. Even if the wife is in a higher professional position, these convictions still hold true.

The lack of power over economic affairs is a crucial factor for rural women in Thailand which hinders an improvement in their conditions and status. The successful establishment of the Muak-Lek Dairy Project in the province of Saraburi in Central Thailand (Rao 1990) proves that Thai women can make a great contribution to an increase in rural families' income and to sustainable development through participation in the Thai agricultural industry, if they are given access to credit. Since it is unusual for Thai women to have an opportunity to participate in the agricultural industry, the project is very significant. It has channeled government resources and secured commercial bank financing to make women the key participants in a relatively new and growing agricultural sector in Thailand, and it has had a major impact on women's income, status, and access to financial resources.

COMMON PROPERTY RESOURCES

Private property rights in Thailand have evolved gradually in response to the increased benefits of defining property rights in land, induced by the commercialisation of agriculture (Feder and Feeny 1991). When land was abundant and labour scarce, property rights in labour were often defined with much greater precision than property rights in land. In the early nineteenth century, slaves rather than land served as collateral in financial markets. With increased exports of rice, land value in Thailand appreciated and land disputes became endemic.

In 1892, a major comprehensive new law on land rights was enacted, but the lack of adequate surveys and record-keeping prevented an end to the disputes. It created nine types of land and provisions were made for transferable title deeds that could be used as collateral (Thomson, Feeny and Oakerson 1992). A formal system of land titling was established in 1901, followed by surveys of the commercialised areas in the Central Plains region. The present system regarding land rights in Thailand is based on the 1954 legislation, which is a compromise between the traditional practice of allowing citizens to bring unoccupied forest land under cultivation as private property and the requirements of the land titling system. However, in many areas outside the Central Plains region, the degree of documentation of land rights is insufficient to be used legally as collateral on loans, which means that farmers in these areas have restricted access to credit.

Keeping animals in a safe and hygienic environment is a prerequisite for their health and growth. With respect to poultry raised in villages, the conditions vary. In some countries, they share the house of the owners and might be regarded as companion animals. Only in a few places in developing countries are good housing and supplementary feed provided for animals. Usually, poultry have very primitive housing, or no housing at all, and their conditions are almost those of feral animals.

The situation is similar in Thailand. Village livestock and poultry are raised in traditional ways in Thailand (Khajarern and Khajarern 1989). Some pigs and poultry are kept under the house at night, but often only a small percentage of animals (11%). During the day, most (if not all) of the poultry are free roaming. Many farmers raise chickens as stray chickens, i.e. let them find their own food, sleep under trees or scattered within the house (Patanapongsa 1992). Usually, the small amount of care bestowed upon the birds, such as table scraps or limited amounts of grain each morning, is given by the women of the household.

Only very few households raise chicken for sale. In most countries, the village chicken is considered a gourmet meat and thus the price paid is considerably higher than for a similar sized commercial chicken. However, the production yield from these flocks is very low, hardly exceeding 3 birds per month. Production is too unreliable and villagers are reluctant to commit any investment of their limited resources. Therefore, they regard these scavenging chickens as a "natural low grade crop that offers a very desirable meat on occasions." (Cumming 1992, p.21).

Considering the poor feeding, the unhygienic conditions and the lack of disease and vaccination control in Thai villages, it is not surprising that diseases can occur and spread easily. Little attention is paid to maintaining the health of flocks which, being in the field, can mix and thereby spread diseases easily. The major disease affecting village chickens around the world is Newcastle disease, which generally appears in the most severe form, often killing 100% of the birds (Cumming 1992). Outbreaks are often associated with a change of season, particularly the start of the wet season (Martin 1992). The recommended vaccination and deworming programmes as well as other veterinary services are not strictly followed by small farmers.

In trials with oral Newcastle disease vaccination in Thailand, some observations have been made (Jackson 1992). Particularly during the rice-growing seasons, birds needed to be confined overnight prior to feeding in the morning, or fed immediately on leaving the roost at dawn. Birds irregularly and reluctantly returned from their scavenging to receive the feed vaccine. Many of the birds also appeared semi-feral in their behaviour, and the impact of the stress associated with catching, transport and confinement is as yet unknown.

While women in Thailand take care of pigs and poultry, ruminants are looked after by the elderly or children on farms. Buffaloes and cattle are usually kept under the house at night and are mainly fed with crop residues and native grasses from village communal lands. In order to collect water for the bovines, farmers frequently have to leave their village. The conditions of these animals are greatly affected by environmental conditions, particularly rainfall, as feed shortages occur between February and August, and feed supplements are rare. According to a survey of 135 farm households in Northern Thailand (ACIAR 1994), the most important problems for cattle and buffaloes were FMD (39%), leg injuries (14.3%), not enough food (8.3%) and weight loss (7.1%).

In the dry season, these animals graze on the harvested paddy fields, whereas in the wet season (which is the crop growing season), they graze along roadsides, on edges of cultivated plots, and in the forests and mountains. The type of grazing can be broadly categorised as either public or private with the seasonal (Murphy and Tisdell 1955). Public (communal) grazing is particularly evident in the wet season when Thai livestock owners mostly graze their stock in the forests and mountains.

The nature of grazing is regarded as an important factor in the degree of infection and spread of FMD in village stock. As Donaldson (1994) noted, seasonal variations in animal husbandry can markedly influence the spread of FMD in a herd and its severity. Stocking density and increased contact through communal grazing are significant factors in the spread of FMD. The seasonal pattern of FMD outbreaks in Africa, for instance, have been explained by Rweyemamu (1970 in Donaldson 1994) as a consequence of climate and increased animal contact. During the wet season in Africa, animals are dispersed due to the prevalence of water holes. Consequently, there is little opportunity for the dissemination of the FMD virus. By contrast, in the dry season, animals congregate at the limited number of waterholes and hence, there is increased contact between livestock and of livestock with wildlife. Therefore, a greater opportunity exists for the spread of infection. While communal grazing and interaction of herds is most common in Africa during the dry season, in Thailand it is most common in the wet season. The latter is the case in Thailand because at that time, rice fields are under cultivation and unavailable for grazing. According to a survey of 135 farm households in Northern Thailand, a very high percentage of public grazing (41.5%) in Thailand's wet season takes place in the forests, as can be seen from *Tables 3* and *4*.

Table 3 - **Private Grazing**

Season		At Home	Rice Field	Orchard Garden	Total
Cool	No*	0 22.	85.0	5.0	112
	%	16.3	63.0	3.7	83
Hot	No*	19.0	101.0	3.0	123
	%	14.1	74.8	2.2	91.1
Wet	No*	33.0	11.0	14.0	58
	%	24.4	8.1	10.4	42.9

* Number of village families reporting

Source: Based on ACIAR (1994)

Table 4 - **Public Grazing**

		Public pasture	**Forest**	**Mountain**	**Near water**	**Roads**	**Total**
Cool	No*	2	12	6	0	3	23
	%	1.5	8.9	4.4	0	2.2	17
Hot	No*	0	7	1	4	0	12
	%	0	5.2	0.7	3.0	0	8.9
Wet	No*	5	56	13	0	3	77
	%	3.7	41.5	9.6	0	2.2	57

* Number of village families reporting
Source: Based on ACIAR (1994)

Dairy cattle are mostly managed under stall feeding systems, the milking cows being kept in the milking barn almost all the time. Dry cows and heifers are tied under trees (or other shady areas), whereas calves are confined together in small cages close to or in milking barns.

Most of the dairy cows are fed with roughages that are harvested from along the roadside and from waste areas which are often far away. If these areas are too far away from their farms, small farmers have to hire trucks to collect the grasses. Some of the farmers will travel as far as 100 kilometres. According to a survey of households throughout Thailand (Thummabood and Morathop 1993), small farmers collect 68 per cent of green and dry fodder for cattle and buffaloes from communal lands. Almost five hours per day are needed to take animals to and from public grazing areas, and farmers spent around four hours every day to cut and carry fodder from these fields.

Watkin and Sukpituksakul (1992) suggest an adjustment in dairy farmers' feeding strategies in order to optimise the use of pasture, the cheapest source of feed available. With a wet season of 6-7 months and a dry season of 5-6 months, there is not sufficient pasture for milk production for about half a year. Yet, most farmers in Thailand are undergrazing their pastures during the wet season and overgrazing them during the dry season by letting their cows calve throughout the year, which is not in accordance with pasture growth and supply. Thus, an adjustment of letting dairy cows calve at the beginning of the wet season and maintaining only non-lactating cows during the dry season is a possible change in farmers' strategies for an improvement in pasture growth.

CONCLUSION

The importance of livestock industries for small farmers in Thailand and the use of common property resources in their development has increased in recent years, as some of these industries - in particular pigs and poultry - have experienced growing competition from the commercial sector. Despite a rapid development of the Thai dairy industry since the 1980s, small farmers are still faced with a number of difficulties which limit their productivity.

Women do play a significant role in the management of livestock as well as in other farm activities. While there has been some progress with respect to women's status in Thailand and their access to various professions in recent years, the significant contribution of women's work on farms in rural areas is still denied. The Muak-Lek Dairy Project has shown that women in rural areas could contribute even more in terms of earning additional income, provided they are given the opportunity and have access to credit. For a healthier and sustainable development of the livestock industry in Thailand, more resources need to be directed towards the training of rural women regarding animal husbandry, as well as towards an improvement in their access to credit.

REFERENCES

Anon (1991) "Thailand to Import Pigs from Malaysia", *Pigs*, Vol. 7 (6), Nov./Dec. 1991, p.5.

Anon (1996) "Developments in Southeast Asia", *Poultry International*,Vol.35 (3), March 1996, pp.18-23.

Australian Centre for International Agricultural Research (ACIAR) (1994) *Thai-Australian Animal Health Project Cross Sectional Village Survey*, Bangkok.

Australian Dairy Corporation (ADC) (1993) *Thailand*, Dairy Market Briefings, ADC, Victoria.

Chinwala, A. and S. Umrod (1993) "Thailand", pp. 355-372 in *Dairy Farming in Asia*, Report of an APO Study Meeting, 26 July - 6 August 1988, Tokyo, Asian Productivity Organization, Tokyo.

Chotipimai, C. (1995) *A Review of National Planning in Thailand From a Gender Aware Perspective*, Master Thesis, Department of Anthropology and Sociology, The University of Queensland, Brisbane.

Cumming, R.B. (1992) "Village Chicken Production: Problems and Potential", pp.21-24 in P.B. Spradbrow (ed.) *Newcastle Disease in Village Chickens*, Proceedings of an International Workshop held in Kuala Lumpur, Malaysia, 6-10 October 1991, ACIAR Proceedings No. 39, Canberra.

Department of Foreign Affairs and Trade (1994) *Thailand May 1995*, Country Economic Brief, Canberra.

Donaldson, A.I. (1994) "Epidemiology of Foot-and-Mouth Disease: the Current Situation and New Perspectives", pp.9-15 in Copland, J.W., Gleeson, L.J. and C. Chamnanpood (eds.) *Diagnosis and Epidemiology of Foot-and-Mouth Disease in Southeast Asia*, Proceedings of an International Workshop held in Lampang, Thailand, 6-9 September 1993, ACIAR Proceedings No.51, Canberra.

Feder, G. (1987) "Land Ownership Security and Farm Productivity: Evidence from Thailand", *The Journal of Development Studies*, Vol.24 (1), October 1987, pp. 16-30.

Feder, G. And D. Feeny (1991) "Land Tenure and Property Rights: Theory and Implications for Development Policy", *The World Bank Economic Review*, Vol.5 (1), pp.135-153.

Harrison, S. And C.A. Tisdell (1995) "The Role of Animal Health Programs in Economic Development", Research Papers and Reports in Animal Health Economics, No. 7, The University of Queensland, Brisbane.

Jackson, A.R.B. (1992) "Observations on Some Difficulties Encountered in Trials with Oral Newcastle Disease Vaccination", pp.15-17 in P.B. Spradbrow (ed.) *Newcastle Disease in Village Chickens*, Proceedings of an International Workshop held in Kuala Lumpur, Malaysia, 6-10 October 1991, ACIAR Proceedings No.39, Canberra.

Khajarern, S. And J.M. Khajarern (1989) "Patterns of Use of Livestock in Thai Villages: Present and Future", *Proceedings of the International Seminar on Animal Health and Production Services for Village Livestock (I.S.A.H.)*, pp. 26-31, Department of Animal Sciences, Khon Kaen University, August 2-9, Khon Kaen.

Martin, P.A. (1992) "The Epidemiology of Newcastle Disease in Village Chickens", pp.40-45 in P.B. Spradbrow (ed.) *Newcastle Disease in Village Chickens*, Proceedings of an International Workshop held in Kuala Lumpur, 6-10 October 1991, ACIAR Proceedings No.39, Canberra.

Murphy, T. And C.A. Tisdell (1995) "Overview of Pigs and Poultry: Specific Livestock Industries, Livestock Diseases and Policies in Thailand", *Research Papers and Reports in Animal Health Economics*, No.10, The University of Queensland, Brisbane.

Murphy, T., Tisdell, C.A. and T. Kehren (1996) "The Pig and Poultry Industries in Thailand: Development, Trade and Commerce", forthcoming in *Sasin Journal of Management*, Bangkok.

Office of Agricultural Economics (1992) *Agriculture in Thailand*, A Commemoration Edition on the Occasion of the Centennial Anniversary, Ministry of Agriculture and Cooperatives, Bangkok.

Patanapongsa, N. (1992) "Small Farmers in a Watershed Development Programme", pp.260-271 in *Technology Transfer for Small Farmers in Asia*, Report of an APO Study Meeting, 10-19 December 1990, New Delhi, Asian Productivity Organization, Tokyo.

Pichet, S. (1991) "The Development of Dairy Farming in Thailand" in Speedy, A. and R. Sansoucy (eds.) (1991) *Feeding Dairy Cows in the Tropics*, Proceedings of the FAO Expert Consultation held in Bangkok, 7-11 July 1989, FAO Animal Production and Health Paper No. 86, FAO, Rome.

Rae, A.N. (1992) "Interaction Between Livestock and Feeds Policies: Evidence from Southeast Asia", *Agricultural Economics*, Vol.7, pp.25-37.

Rao, A. (1990) *The Muek-Lek Women's Dairy Project in Thailand*, Seeds No.12, New York.

Roy, K.C., Blomqvist, H.C. and C.A. Tisdell (1996) "Economic Development and Women: An Overview of Issues", pp.1-24 in Roy, K.C., Tisdell, C.A. and H.C. Blomqvist (eds.) *Economic Development and Women in the World Community*, Praeger, Westport.

Sheehan, B. (1993) *Thailand - An Introduction to Thailand, Its People, Trade and Business Activity*, 2nd ed., The Australia-Thailand Business Council, Melbourne.

Spradbrow, P.B. (1987) "Newcastle Disease - An Overview" , pp.11-18 in J.W. Copland (ed.) *Newcastle Disease in Poultry*, Australian Centre for International Agricultural Research, Canberra.

Thomson, J.T., Feeny, D. And R.J. Oakerson (1992) "Institutional Dynamics: The Evolution and Dissolution of Common-Property Resource Management", pp. 129-160 in D.W. Bromley (ed.) *Making the Commons Work*, ICS Press, San Francisco.

Thummabood, S. And S. Morathop (1993) *Livestock as a Component of Rural Development of Thailand*, Department of Livestock Development, Thailand.

Vijchulata, P. (1995) "Blood Plasma Minerals and Fertility of Dairy Cows in Central Thailand", *Asian-Australasian Journal of Animal Sciences*, Vol.8 (3), June 1995, pp.263-265.

Wanapat, M. and C. Devendra (1992) "Feeding and Nutrition of Dairy Cattle and Buffalo in Asia", pp.177-194 in Bunyavejchewin, P., Sangdid, S. And K. Hangsanet (eds.) *Sustainable Animal Production*, Proceedings of the Sixth AAAP Animal Science Congress Vol. II, The Animal Husbandry Association of Thailand, c/o Department of Animal Science, Kasetsart University, Bangkok.

Watkin, B.R. and P. Sukpituksakul (1992) "The Place of Improved Pastures for Economic Milk Production in Thailand", pp.195-205 in Bunyavejchewin, P., Sangdid, S. And K. Hangsanet (eds.) *Sustainable Animal Production*, Proceedings of the Sixth AAAP Animal Science Congress Vol. II, The Animal Husbandry Association of Thailand, c/o Department of Animal Science, Kasetsart University, Bangkok.

12 Islamisation and Democratisation in Pakistan: Implications for Women and Religious Minorities

Samina Yasmeen

The notion of citizenship has come under increased scrutiny in the 1990s. What is meant by citizenship? Who is a citizen? What are the rights and responsibilities of citizens and what spheres do they operate in? These and other similar questions are being asked and answered by analysts the world over.[1] Against the backdrop of the end of the Cold War, emergence of different forms of democracies in Eastern Europe and religious revivalism in different parts of the world, the linkages between citizenship, democratisation and religion is also emerging as an area of concern. This paper attempts to explore these linkages with reference to the situation in Pakistan. To this end, it begins by outlining the assumptions about the notion of citizenship which form the matrix within which the analysis is undertaken. Then it focuses on the context of Islamisation in Pakistan initiated in the late 1970s, and the extent to which it affected women and religious minorities as citizens. The last part analyses if the process of democratisation has changed the position of these two groups in the country.

Citizenship: A Multi dimensional and Evolutionary Concept

Citizenship is more than the mere political act of voting and/or participating in the political organs of the state. As elaborated in T.H. Marshall's famous work entitled *Citizenship and Social Class,* citizenship finds expression in civil, political, and social spheres[2]. But

---

1 See, for example, Michael Hill and Lian Kwen Fee, *The Politics of Nation Building and Citizenship in Singapore*, (New York: Routledge, 1995); and David Prior, John Stewart and Kieron Walsh, *Citizenship: Rights, Community and Participation*, (London: Pitman Publishing, 1995).

2 T.H.Marshall, *Citizenship and Social Class, and Other Essays*, (Cambridge: Cambridge University Press, 1950); see also, Martin Bulmer and Anthony M. Rees (eds.), *Citizenship Today: The Contemporary Relevance of T.H.Marshall*, (London: University College London Press, 1996).

the concept is even wider in scope than suggested by him.[1] The idea of citizenship includes an emotional and psychological aspect; the sense of belonging and the feeling that the citizen is not just part of a system but is acknowledged and respected in this system. The psychological dimension also involves a feeling that a citizen can express ideas and explore one's individuality without fear or concern of being denied this right. It involves a written and/or unwritten claim to human equality in economic, political, social and psychological arenas.

The claims to equality notwithstanding, not all citizens are equal. The relationship between the individual, the society and the state can be structured in a manner that creates classes of citizens. Some citizens are more equal than others. At the same time, other citizens can be reduced to the status of 'lesser citizens' by rendering them unable to operate freely and openly in spheres of their choice. Effectively, therefore, the philosophical notion of equality coexists with a visible or invisible inequality and hierarchy of citizens which is often either encouraged or sanctioned by the state.

The notions of citizenship and the right and responsibilities of citizens, however, are not static. Instead they are evolutionary concepts which change with a change in the nature of a state, regime and/or society. The evolution is not necessarily linear and can be cyclical in nature. A change in regime, for example, can set in motion societal processes that lead to a redefinition of rights and responsibilities of citizens. The pressures thus created, in turn, can force the state to either question or condone the redefinition of what and who is a citizen. At the same time, the state can also introduce change in a society's attitudes which facilitate a further redefinition of the concept of citizenship. The manner in which Islamisation and the return to democracy have determined the status of women and religious minorities in Pakistan is a vivid example of this non-linear evolution.

ISLAMISATION IN PAKISTAN: THE CONTEXT

Since its independence in August 1947, Islam has occupied a central place in Pakistan's mass consciousness. That the movement for its creation was triggered and spurred on by the need for Muslims to find a separate state has not been an issue. Nonetheless, the question of the relationship between Islam and state has attracted opposing views. On one end of the spectrum have been the 'modernists' who led the independence movement and subsequently propagated the idea of a secular state while accepting the centrality of Islam in the Pakistani

---

1 Hill and Fee, *op.cit.*, pp.27-35

society. This separation of the state and societal religious values effectively translated into a notion of a Pakistani state for Muslims but not an Islamic state. The corollary to this view was the notion of equality of citizens irrespective of their gender, race or religion. On the other end of the spectrum have been the 'traditionalists' who were initially opposed to the creation of Pakistan on the grounds that the concept of an Islamic *Ummah* (nation) was not bound by or could be restricted to artificially created boundaries. Since Pakistan's independence, however, these traditionalists have argued for and viewed the relationship between the state and Islam as non-negotiable. Pakistan is seen as having been created for Muslims and, therefore, by implication and necessity accorded an Islamic identity. Pakistan is not merely seen as a *state for Muslims* but as an *Islamic state*. For the traditionalists, not only does sovereignty lie with Allah but the *Sharia* provides the only source of knowledge for mediating the relations between individuals and the Pakistani state. While such a view does not necessarily entail inequality of citizens, their patriarchal and narrow Islamic interpretations of *Sharia* do open the way for creating hierarchies of citizens based on their gender, race and religion.[1]

In this struggle of opposing notions of the Pakistani state, modernists held sway for nearly two-thirds of the country's existence. Pakistan's first Governor-General, Mohammad Ali Jinnah, categorically stated that Pakistan was a state for Muslims but one where followers of other religions could also be sure of their equal rights as citizens.[2] That such claims were supported by actions was obvious from the fact that the first meeting of the National Assembly of the nascent state was chaired by a non-Muslim, Mr Mandal. Soon, Mr Mandal, a Hindu, was inducted into the country's first cabinet as the Law Minister. At the same time Pakistan's first Foreign Minister was chosen from the Ahmediyya community— a heretic sect in Islam whose founder claimed prophethood thus questioning the basic foundations of the religion which is based on the belief that Prophet Mohammad is the last messenger of God. The dominance of the modernists continued as the military took over the reins of the country. The Chief Martial Law Administrator and later the President of Pakistan, Ayub Khan, stressed the modern and secular character of the state by allowing a number of Ahmadis to rise to the top echelons of government. In the late 1960s

---

1 Ishtiaq Ahmed, *The Concept of An Islamic State*, (New York: St Martinis Press, 1987).

2 G.W.Choudhury (ed.), *Documents and Speeches on the Constitution of Pakistan*, (Dacca: 1967), pp.21-22

and the 1970s, the mantle of modernism was taken over by Zulfiqar Ali Bhutto. The 1973 Constitution of Pakistan, which was unanimously passed during Z.A. Bhutto's rule therefore, clearly articulated the principle of equality of its citizens irrespective of their gender and/or religion.[1]

The modernists, it is important to note, maintained their relative preponderance in Pakistan by carefully negotiating and incorporating some of the ideas presented by the traditionalists into the construction of Pakistani statehood. The Second Draft Constitution of 1952, for instance, introduced the idea of a board of Ulema who 'would examine if any Pakistani law was repugnant to Quran and Sunnah'.[2] Similarly, while adhering to the notion of a state for Muslims, Ayub Khan was amenable to declaring Pakistan an Islamic Republic in the 1962 constitution. His successor, General Yahya Khan, also indirectly supported the main Islamic party, Jamaat-i-Islami during the 1970 general elections. More importantly, during the mid-1960s, Z.A. Bhutto introduced the discourse of Islamic Socialism in Pakistan. By claiming to bring alive the real socialist spirit of Islam through the Pakistan People's Party (PPP), he acknowledged the need to incorporate some of the ideas presented by the traditionalists in a modern form.

While this trend continued during Bhutto's rule (1971-1977), the early 70s marked the beginning of the traditionalists' moves to assert their ideas. Against the background of Pakistan's defeat in the 1971 Indo-Pakistan War, emergence of an educated middle class and quick social mobility resulting from mass migration of labour force into the Middle East, Islamic political parties began identifying 'fertile grounds' for their ideas. Educational institutions, especially colleges and universities, provided such a venue with student wings of Islamic parties emerging as major contenders for power. Islam came to occupy a special position in the political discourse in these institutions. It was, however, not until the 1977 elections that Islam emerged at the centre of national political discourse. The Pakistan National Alliance (PNA) which consisted of anti-Bhutto parties including the Jamaat-i-Islami, argued for introducing *Nizam-i-Mustafa* (The system of Prophet Mohammad) and, by implication, projected the PPP as a less-Islamic

---

1 *The Constitution of the Islamic Republic of Pakistan*, As modified upto 27th July 1994, (Islamabad: National Assembly of Pakistan, January 1997), Articles 25 and 26.

2 Hamza Alavi, *Pakistan and Islam: Ethnicity and Ideology*, in Fred Halliday and Hamza Alavi (eds.), *State and Ideology in the Middle East and Pakistan*, (London: McMillan, 1988), pp.106-107.

regime. The rigging in the 1977 elections which denied the PNA direct access to power paradoxically strengthened their position.

The traditionalists gained preponderance in Pakistan as a result of the military coup in July 1977. General Zia-ul-Haq had initially seized power for 90 days with the declared promise of holding elections. Soon he shelved these promises and planned to rule Pakistan indefinitely. To legitimise this shift and balance the appeal of the PPP, General Zia forged a *de facto* alliance with conservative elements in the country. The traditionalists were the main beneficiaries of this change. Maulana Mawdudi of the *Jamaat-i-Islami* (Islamic party), who had emerged as the main opponent of Bhutto during the 1977 elections, was courted by the military regime. For the first time in the country's history, his ideas were given prominence by the government controlled media.[1] References to the need for Islamising Pakistan became frequent with General Zia often taking the lead in the process. The traditionalists, however, demanded more than mere pronouncements. If they were to provide the necessary political legitimacy to a military regime, they expected *real moves* towards establishing an Islamic state in Pakistan. To appease the traditionalists, therefore, Zia embarked on a policy of tokenism; Islam was introduced in the country but only in a piecemeal fashion. The emphasis was on symbolic changes that gave the impression of a state-sponsored move towards Islamisation rather than on implementing the real spirit of Islam.

ISLAMISATION, WOMEN AND RELIGIOUS MINORITIES

At a general level, Zia's tokenism found expression in the introduction of Islamic banking in Pakistan, establishing a Federal Shariat Court and identifying the Parliament as the *Majlis-e-Shura* (Advisory Council). The military regime also tinkered with the penal code; previously accepted punishments for robbery and prohibition of alcohol were dressed into Islamic garb to appease the traditionalists. Specifically, however, Zia's Islamisation process targeted weaker elements in the society; women and religious minorities.

The military had traditionally been the harbinger of modernity in Pakistan. It had introduced laws that protected weaker elements in the society. Ayub Khan, for instance, had introduced the Family Law ordinance in 1961 which regulated marriage, divorces, and controlled

---

1 Seyyed Vali Reza Nasr, *Mawdudi & The Making of Islamic Revivalism,* (Oxford: Oxford University Press, 1996), pp.41-46.

polygamy.[1] In marked contrast to this trend, General Zia reverted to a conservative and traditional interpretation of Islam. The notion of *purdah* supported by Mawdudi was propagated in terms of *chador aur chardevari* (veil and the sanctity of home). Women were increasingly reminded of their role as nurturers within the confines of home - the private sphere - with the explicit and implicit admission that the public sphere was to be left to men only. To stress the need for such segregation, women appearing on national television were ordered to cover their heads and behave modestly. In line with the principles supported by the *Jamaat-i-Islami*, schemes were floated for separate women's educational institutions, including women's universities.

This symbolism was paralleled by changes in the legal system with serious ramifications for women.[2] In February 1979, the Hudood Ordinance (plural of Hadd (Limit) refers to punishment for the offences for which limits have been defined in the Quran and Hadith. Rubya Mehdi, The Islamization of the Law in Pakistan), was promulgated which dealt with crimes of 'theft, drunkenness, adultery, rape and bearing false witness'. The clauses dealing with adultery (*Zina*) and rape (*Zina-bil-jibr*) were apparently introduced to tackle with the problem of moral decay. The manner in which they were introduced, however, contained the possibility of their exploitation for abuse, and not protection, of women. *Zina*, according to the Ordinance, was classified as a crime against the state and not the husband as was the case in the penal code inherited from the British system. Specifically, in line with the Islamic principles, it required four witnesses who could testify that *Zina* had taken place. Based on the testimony of these witnesses, the ordinance provided for maximum punishment under *hadd* of stoning to death for married people and 100 lashes for unmarried individuals. In cases where four witnesses were not available, the ordinance provided for the lesser punishment under *tazir* consisting of 'imprisonment for up to 10 years, and flogging of up to 30 strips and/or a fine'.

In 1980, the Council of Islamic Ideology (CII) drafted a law dealing with *Qisas*, or retribution for harm done, and *diyat*, blood money in lieu of a murder or bodily harm. The draft bill, which was

---

1 Khawar Mumtaz and Farida Shaheed, *Women of Pakistan: Two Steps Forward, One Step Back?*, (Lahore, Vanguard Books, 1987), pp.57-61.

2 The following discussion of the legal changes draws heavily upon: Khawar Mumtaz and Farida Shaheed, *op.cit.,*, chapter 7; and Anita M. Weiss, "The Consequences of State Policies for Women in Pakistan", in Myron Weiner and Ali Banuazizi (eds.), *The Politics of Social Transformation in Afghanistan, Iran and Pakistan*, (New York: Syracuse University Press, 1994), pp. 412-444.

passed by the *Majlis-i-Shura* in August 1984, relegated women to a secondary status; it provided for blood money equivalent to the value of 30.63 kg of silver for a man and half that amount for a woman murdered. The provision was defended on grounds that while men are the breadwinners, women remain dependent on men. The clauses related to *Qisas* also discriminated against women. They required two male witnesses for a murder to be proven. By excluding women, they provided for situations where testimony of women could go unnoticed. Two years later, in April 1982, the CII proposed a new Law of Evidence. Designed to replace the Evidence Act of 1872, this law originally aimed at literally halving the value of testimony by women. It argued that two women witnesses equalled one man! Faced with opposition from women's organizations, the draft law was modified and made applicable to financial cases only. For other cases, determining the value of a single woman's testimony was left to the concerned judge.

Together, the symbolic and legal changes reduced women to the status of 'lesser citizens' in Pakistan. They were not only denied the protection of the state but the door was opened to increasing their exploitation. The Hudood Ordinance, for instance, failed to distinguish between rape and adultery by setting similar requirements for witnesses. The witnesses had to be male and needed to have witnessed the act of *Zina* or *Zina-bil-Jibr*. Not only did the provision regarding gender of the witnesses denied women the right to accuse rapists of rape, but by implying that a child born out of a wedlock was a proof of a crime committed, it put women in an unwinnable position. Even if they were raped, bearing a child as a result of the rape could be considered *their* crime against the state while the rapists could walk freely for want of four witnesses. The problem with the ordinance further stemmed from its failure to establish clear linkages with previous laws of the country. For example, it did not clearly distinguish between *Zina*, which is a sexual relationship outside a marriage, from the failure to report a second marriage. In a patriarchal system, where women are equated with the notion of *Izzat* (honour), these loopholes were easily exploited by interested parties. Often men accused their divorced women who chose to remarry of committing *Zina* and led them to being imprisoned until the case was dismissed by the courts. On other occasions, rape went unpunished while the victim was punished because she gave birth to a child as a result of the rape.

Religious minorities became the other major target of the symbolic Islamisation in Pakistan. According to the 1981 census, 2.8 million non-Muslims constituted 3.3% of Pakistan's total population.

Of these, Christians and Hindus formed the two major groups accounting for nearly 89% of the total non-Muslim population. Ahmadis, who were declared non-Muslim by virtue of a decision by the Parliament in 1974, formed the next biggest group with 104,244 members. Most of these communities had settled in Punjab and Sindh.[1] The 1973 Constitution of Pakistan granted them equal rights as citizens. Although the Fourth Amendment to the Constitution introduced special seats for religious minorities and women, it did not deny them the right to participate politically in the system on equal footing. Soon after coming to power, General Zia-ul-Haq ended this equality. In September 1978 he introduced an amendment to the electoral system which was later embodied in the 1973 Constitution (Articles 51 and 106). By virtue of this amendment, separate electorates were created for non-Muslims in National and provincial assemblies. Not only could non-Muslims not vote for Muslim candidates, but they also had to elect their own representatives from across the country and/or the provinces. For this purpose, Christians and Hindus were given four seats each in the National Assembly, while Sikhs, Buddhists and Parsi communities and other non-Muslims were given one seat. Ahmadis were given one seat as well. At provincial level, the minorities were allocated 23 seats with Sindh and Punjab accounting for 17 of the seats.

The change in the electoral system was prompted by a need to please the traditional elements in Pakistan. Mawdudi's notion of citizenship in an Islamic state, for instance, had included a dichotomy between Muslims and *Zimmis* (protected subjects).[2] An interest in reducing the chances of progressive groups, especially the PPP, to win support of religious minorities, provided the other incentive. Interestingly, it was also supported by some non-Muslim Pakistanis, such as Julius Salik, as well.[3] The net result of the change was an alteration in the rights of non-Muslim Pakistanis as citizens. While the Constitution invoked principles of equality irrespective of gender, race and religion, the amendment relegated non-Muslims to the status of lesser citizens. No longer could they operate in political space as equals.

The process of Islamisation resulted in other legal changes which also restricted the psychological space for non-Muslims as Pakistani

---

1 *Report on The General Elections 1988*, Vol. I, Election Commission of Pakistan, pp.205-207.

2 Nasr, *op.cit.*, pp.99-102.

3 Personal interview with a leader of a religious minority group, 1 July 1996.

citizens. Blasphemy laws were added to Pakistan's penal code which was amended to make defiling of Holy Quran punishable with life imprisonment (295-B), of the name of the Holy Prophet with death (295-C) and of any other personage revered in Islam with three years imprisonment (298-A).[1] Equally discriminatory was the promulgation of Ordinance No.20 which barred Ahmadis from calling their places of worship mosques, reciting *Azaan* (call for prayers), and directly or indirectly passing themselves as Muslims or referring to their religion as Islam. Given that Ahmadis had consistently identified themselves as Muslims and viewed themselves as a sect of Islam, rather than a religious minority, the ordinance directly targeted their sense of identity and made it difficult for them to practice their religion.

The legal injunctions affecting women and religious minorities came under heavy criticism from domestic human rights groups and women's organisations. Internationally, Amnesty International, United Nations and the US Congress urged General Zia to end the discrimination of the weaker groups of Pakistani society.[2] The pressures were faced and absorbed by a regime which was confident of its usefulness to the West. Aware of the American need to rely on Pakistan as a front-line state against the Soviet incursions into Afghanistan, General Zia studiously avoided giving in to the pressure. Combining Islamization and military dictatorship, therefore, General Zia was directly and indirectly able to maintain a hierarchy of citizens in Pakistan until his death in August 1988. To what extent his death, and the introduction of democracy rectify this categorisation of Pakistani citizens? The answer to this question necessitates an understanding of the societal implications of Zia's policy of Islamization and an appreciation of the context in which democratisation in Pakistan has proceeded since late 1988.

DEMOCRATISATION AND SOCIETAL ISLAM

The state sponsored Islamisation triggered a societal change in Pakistan. Until Zia's use of Islam for political purposes, religion was considered a personal rather than a state issue. The attitude was partly due to the influence of sufi tradition in South Asia which survived despite the presence of more orthodox approaches to Islam. Once the military regime deployed governmental resources, especially the

---

1 *State of Human Rights in 1995*, (Lahore: Human Rights Commission of Pakistan), pp.104-105.

2 Mohammad Waseem, *Politics and the State in Pakistan*, (Islamabad: National Institute of Historical and Cultural Research, 1994), pp.379-86.

government controlled print and electronic media, the relative balance changed. Pakistani people were regularly exposed to the traditional interpretation of Islam, as well as the notion of Pakistan as an Islamic state. This gradually altered the dominant notions of identity. While in the past, Islam was primarily used to distinguish Pakistani Muslims from Indian Hindus(!), the general public now began to use Islam to construct their national/domestic identity. People came to be identified in terms of good and bad, practising and non-practising Muslims. Just as Islam had moved to the centre stage of political reality, it also came to occupy a special position in the social discourse and construction of social identities.

The process was aided by the Zia regime's policies on education. Within the context of privatisation of education and support for privately funded institutions, the military regime embarked on a process of supporting religious educational institutions, *deni madrissas*. The number of these institutions increased exponentially from 868 in 1975 to more than 1644 during Zia's rule. Not only were these schools allowed to receive financial assistance from foreign sources, the government also met approximately 36% of their costs through the Zakat Fund. The policy was not restricted to any one religious denomination. Instead followers of all schools and views, such as *Deobandis*, *Brelvis*, *Ahle-Hadith* and *Ahle-Tasih*, received such assistance. By the 1990s, the number of such religious educational institutions had reached 2512 in Punjab alone with a total number of 218,939 resident and non-resident students.[1]

The cumulative effect of these policies has been the creation of groups of educated citizens who subscribe to different, and often contradictory, interpretations of Islam. The state sponsored Islamisation of the 1980s, in other words, has led to a situation where Islam dominates social discourse.

Parallel to this trend has been the introduction of controlled democracy in Pakistan. The process started in 1985 when General Zia, in quid pro quo to lifting martial law, secured an amendment to the 1973 constitution by the Parliament elected on non-party basis in 1985. Known as the Eighth Amendment, the change in the constitution altered the balance of power between the President and the Prime Minister. While the Prime Minister was elected by the National Assembly and retained executive powers, the President acquired the right to nominate the Prime Minister and dismiss him if he deemed it appropriate. The

---

1 Tanveer Kureshi, "Madariss fanning sectarian hatred", *The Friday Times*, 22-28 February 1996, pp.6-7

President acquired the powers to appoint judges of the Supreme Court and the High Courts, provincial Governors, chiefs of the army and other senior bureaucrats. Most importantly, the article 58-2(b) of the constitution inserted via the Eighth Amendment gave the president the discretionary power to dissolve national assembly if considered that the federation was not functioning appropriately. These alterations to the constitutions effectively changed the nature of Pakistan's political system; instead of being a parliamentary system, it came to include elements of Presidential system as well.

Given that General Zia was both the President and the Chief of Army Staff (COAS), the Eighth Amendment resulted in a dyarchy, with the balance of power favouring General Zia against the Prime Minister, Junejo. That this anomaly was fraught with dangers for the country's political stability became apparent as General Zia summarily dismissed Junejo's government in May 1988 due to personal differences. Three months later when Zia was killed in a plane crash in August 1988, the situation changed, albeit slightly. The November 1988 elections were held on party-basis and Benazir Bhutto became the first democratically elected Prime Minister. The structural inequalities in the political system, however, persisted. The dyarchy of 1985-88 was replaced by a troika consisting of the President, the COAS and the Prime Minister. With the military and the President holding most of the actual and real power, Benazir Bhutto was forced to focus on managing this triangular relationship as a prerequisite for her political survival. The pervasiveness of corruption in the society, government and political circles, as well as personal and institutional interests of the President and the military, however, made management of the troika difficult for Bhutto and her government was dismissed by the President in August 1990. Nawaz Sharif's rise to power in 1990 did not change the situation. Instead, the trend set in 1985 continued resulting in nine governments in as many years!

The political instability, massive corruption and the imbalance between Presidential and Prime Ministerial powers, which have been the hallmark of Pakistani political system from 1988 to 1997, have contributed to each government's failure to address pressing social and political problems. Interested in ensuring their political survival, these governments have shied away from tackling issues that are either too divisive or risky. Questioning the implications of Zia's Islamisation policies falls in the second category of too risky a business. Given that Islam has come to occupy a special place in social discourse, and traditionalists have been able to mobilize masses in the name of Islam (evidenced in the case of demonstration against Salman Rushdie in

1990), no government has attempted to seriously alter the hierarchy of citizenship created by General Zia. Instead, they have resorted to a policy of tokenism aimed at placating critical elements in the society.

The policies pursued by Benazir Bhutto during her two terms as the Prime Minister (1988-90 and 1993-96) are a vivid example of such tokenism. During her first term, she upgraded the Women's Division established by General Zia to the status of a Ministry. She also established a Women's Bank operated by women only.[1] During her second term, she introduced the idea of police stations managed by women only. The initiative was taken on the grounds that often women intending to complain avoided visiting police stations for fear of more harassment by male police. Similarly, the idea of lady health visitors was introduced with the avowed belief in increasing women's ability to earn income and disseminate knowledge about health issues to other women. At the same time, the government controlled electronic media, especially television, was used to alter the commonly held images of women's role in private and public spheres. Beyond these symbolic and token gesture, however, no *real* progress was made to improve the condition of women in Pakistan. So obvious was the need to restrict oneself to tokenism that the issue of reviving reserved seats for women (introduced in 1973 and lapsed in 1990) became a hostage to political wrangling. Instead of unilaterally declaring that the PPP would issue tickets to more women in the next elections, Bhutto's government insisted on tackling the issue on a bilateral platform with the Pakistan Muslim League.[2] The record of Nawaz Sharif's first term as the Prime Minister was equally flawed. Instead of attempting to repeal the legal changes introduced during Zia's period, his government got the *Sharia* Bill passed which indirectly strengthened the hands of the traditionalists in the country.

The state's inability to protect its citizens and correct imbalances in the status of different members of the system has had serious repercussions for women and religious minorities in the 1990s. The society has generally tended to translate and evaluate issues in terms of good and bad practices, and attempted to find *Islamic answers* to even previously accepted practices with negative connotations for women. The question of *halala* (remarrying the ex-wife after her marriage to someone else) raised in January 1996 as a result of a judgement of the Sindh High Court is a case in point. In this decision, the judge condemned the practice of *halala* and of divorcing a woman by three

---

1 Weiss, *op.cit.*, pp.438-444

2 Personal interview with a member of the Bhutto government, August 1996.

simultaneous pronouncements of *talaq* (divorce). Soon afterwards Ulema differed on the notion of *halala*.[1] The controversy raised doubts about the divorces resulting from simultaneous pronouncements and/or the remarriages of divorced women. The controversy surrounding Saima Waheed's (a Pakistani woman) marriage of her own choice and her father's opposition on grounds of the right of the *wali* (guardian) in a marriage is another example of the negative implications of unreflected references to and rigid interpretations of Islamic principle. That the country was divided on the merits of the case until it was settled by judiciary is an example of how the piecemeal Islamisation has affected women's rights in the country.

Apart from the general notions of a woman's role, justified on erroneous notions of Islam, Zia's policy of Islamisation has continued to have negative impact on women. The abuse of the *Hudood* ordinance, which was obvious during the military regime, has continued in the 1990s. According to the Human Rights Commission of Pakistan, for instance, of the more than a thousand women jailed in 1995, a majority were imprisoned under this ordinance.[2] The increased recourse to these laws is obvious from the fact that recently men from middle and upper middle class have also come to use the *Hudood* ordinance to take revenge on their divorced wives. The frequency of dowry deaths, a phenomenon where brides are accidentally killed if they do not bring enough dowry, has also been on the rise.

The implications of the interplay between Islamisation and controlled democratisation have been equally, if not more, devastating for religious minorities. The policy of separate electorates for non-Muslims has introduced a *de facto* apartheid in Pakistan in which the inequality of citizens is condoned and supported. While this inequality was less obvious during the Zia regime, it has become apparent during the 1990s when frequent elections have been held in Pakistan. The boundaries of the electorate are determined by the state boundaries in case of the National Assembly, and the provincial boundaries for provincial assemblies. Such a delimitation imposes severe pressures on those willing to represent their respective communities. A Christian candidate for the National Assembly, for instance, has to canvass across the country, whereas a candidate for the Punjab Assembly needs to do the same across the province. Not only is the cost prohibitive for

1 Khaled Ahmed, " 'Halala', anyone?", *The Friday Times*, 8-14 February 1996, p.9

2 *State of Human Rights in 1995*, (Lahore: Human Rights Commission of Pakistan), p.141. The other major cause of women's imprisonment was illegal immigration.

the candidates but it also adds to the overall expenditures incurred by the Election Commission.[1] More importantly, such a policy limits the rights of non-Muslim citizens in securing appropriate representation at national and provincial levels. If faced with any problem, the non-Muslim citizens cannot approach their Muslim members of the Parliament as they do not play a part in electing these representatives. The problem becomes significant when the religious minorities are harassed on religious grounds and denied access to jobs.[2] To put it differently, the system of separate electorates not only restricts the political space but also constricts the economic and social space for Pakistan's religious minorities.

The Islamisation started during the Zia regime and its societal implications in the 1990s also restricts the psychological space available to non-Muslim Pakistani citizens. With the possibility of being accused of blasphemy in the background, religious minorities find themselves under a constant threat of undue victimization. Not that such threat does not exist for Muslim Pakistanis as well, but non-Muslims have been suffering more than their Muslim counterparts from the effects of the blasphemy laws of the Zia regime. The internationally publicized case of Salamat Masih (1993-95),[3] in which a 13 year old boy was accused alongside two other Christians of blaspheming, is an example of the negativity created by these laws. As the High Court heard the case and released the accused, religious parties and groups announced prizes for those who would kill Salamat and Rahmat Masih!

THE FUTURE FOR *LESSER* CITIZENS

Faced with the continuation of their secondary status as citizens, a number of women and members of the religious minority groups have established organizations aimed at rectifying the situation.[4] The moves, however, are unlikely to bear results without an active role played by the state. The February 1997 elections which resulted in an unprecedented victory by the Pakistan Muslim League led by Nawaz

---

1 Personal interview with a leader of a religious minority community, July 1996; see also, Khaled Ahmed, "Unbearable irony of separate electorates", *The Friday Times*, 14-20 March 1996, p.9

2 C.M.Naim, "The Second Tyranny of Religious Minorities", *South Asia Bulletin,* Vol.XIV, No.2, 1994, pp.104-105.

3 *State of Human Rights in 1995*, (Lahore: Human Rights Commission of Pakistan),pp.104-107; *State of Human Rights in 1993*, (Lahore: Human Rights Commission of Pakistan), pp.40-43

4 Najma Babar, "Ready for Action: Minorities", *The Herald, Election Special 1993*, pp.42-44

Sharif may make it possible. Having repealed parts of the Eighth Amendment dealing with Presidential powers on 1 April 1997, the new regime needs to shelve the other discriminatory laws that were introduced by General Zia and made sacrosanct through the Eighth Amendment. Without such a bold action, which is bound to irk the traditionalists, women and religious minorities will remain lesser citizens in Pakistan.

Part II

Some Relevant Issues

13 THE CRIME SCENARIO AND THE LAW AND ORDER SITUATION IN MAJOR CITIES IN INDIA

T K TALUKDAR

Calcutta like any other Indian city faces serious law and order problems. The unplanned growth of the city, unchecked influx of migrants, disparity of income distribution and lack of employment opportunities in the city have all contributed to social unrest. The divergent political parties in quest of extending their political base are ever eager to exploit discontent and deprivations and launch political movements often not hesitating to resort to violence in the streets. Unscrupulous politicians often exploit the sentiments of minority communities for their selfish purposes. There are also protagonists of radical and revolutionary ideologies who believe in the forcible overthrow of a democratically constituted government by resorting to terrorist activities. It is, therefore, quite amazing that Calcutta has been generally successful in maintaining law and order, despite inter-union rivalries in industries, conflicts and clashes between political parties, student unrest, and attempts to create communal tensions. It is of course true that the existence of a democratic set-up takes much of the steam out of such movements by allowing it to grow to a certain level. Furthermore, the responsible attitude of the ruling parties and the alertness and efficiency of the city police administration have also so far proved to be effective for the maintenance of peace and internal order in the city.

The economic growth of a city largely depends on a social order offering stability and a peaceful atmosphere. Calcutta stands out as being one of the most peaceful metropolitan cities in India in spite of having the second highest population and all kinds of problems surrounding it. The city has the problems of a continuous influx of population, a huge number of slum dwellers, presence of different ethnic and religious groups, inadequate civic amenities and an acute unemployment problem. The British probably visualized all these future problems of the capital city of Calcutta way back in the nineteenth century. In 1856 shortly after some drastic changes were brought about in the police set-up in London, the same Commissionerate system with almost the same Police Act was introduced in the Presidency towns of Calcutta, Mumbai and Madras. The system envisages the supremacy of the Commissioner of Police who is vested with necessary magisterial powers and functions. Even 50 years after India's Independence the system has not changed significantly. Realising the advantage of this system, more and more cities in India have now adopted the police system prevailing in Calcutta. At present there are 23 large and medium metropolitan cities in India which have been brought under the purview of this system. The basic structure made by the British definitely stood the test of time. The police administration has faced new challenges and new problems ever since and the track records are quite satisfactory by any standard. This does not mean that there is no room for further change or improvement. In fact, the basic structure may not be able to bear the burden of new modes of crime unless structural changes are brought about and more resources are placed at the disposal of the City Police Administration.

The prevailing criminal justice system in India is not conducive to efficient Policing while dealing with crime and criminals. The detection and prevention of crime is handicapped by complex formalities and longdrawn processes of trial, reluctance of the witness to give evidence, repeated appeals by the accused persons and liberal grant of bails by the judiciary. Moreover, there is a huge backlog of criminal cases awaiting trial. All these factors tend to encourage the criminals to carry on undeterred. In order to ensure that the police can take effective action against crime and criminals, the entire criminal justice system needs to be thoroughly revamped, as otherwise the police would be compelled by circumstances to have recourse to strong-arm methods on the diehard criminals. And, of course, any strong action by the policy would upset many groups like the human rights activists.

The present world-wide social revolution has ushered in an era of metamorphosis in the society. Continuous growth of population, awakening of the masses, and development of modern information and communications technology have led to an urban environment marked by all-round modernisation. Whilst urbanisation leads to all kind of changes in the pattern of population distribution, its work habits, housing, leisure pursuits, industrialisation, employment opportunity, it also provides opportunities for crime with reduced risk for detection. It also means greater complexities of life and more impersonal relationships.

India is predominantly a rural country with 74.3 per cent of its population living in the rural areas. Of the total urban population i.e. 217.18 million as per the 1991 Census, nearly one-third live in 23 metropolitan cities having one million or more population. The proportion of the population of these metropolitan cities to the national population is 8.7 per cent. The newly emerging urban and industrial areas are fast becoming the breeding ground of crime, as the cities are prone to a higher incidence of crime compared to rural areas. Slums in the cities are the breeding ground for criminals. Excessive overcrowding creates appalling living conditions, which violate minimum standards of health, hygiene and decency. The slum dwellers have their own way of life with their unique subculture regulated by its own norms and values.

India, still, has one of the lowest crime-rates in the world owing to its closeknit social fabric and also religious factors. Available data indicate that Canada, with crime rate of 1273.5 per one million of population in 1991, topped the list of the most crime prone society, followed by England where the crime rate was 1040.3. In Asia, Japan had the crime rate of 145 per million of population in 1991, while in India the crime rate was 59.43 per million. There had been a decline of 3.5 per cent of the total cases under the Indian Penal Code at the national level in 1993 over 1992.

So far as the metropolitan cities of India are concerned, a substantial decline of 10.3 per cent cases under Indian Penal Code was noticed in 1993 over the previous year. Mumbai recorded the highest number of cases under the Indian Penal Code in 1993 with its share of 15.3 per cent in the total cases of the metropolitan cities, while Delhi and Bangalore had their share of 14.5 per cent and 11.3 per cent cases respectively in 1993. As against these figures, Calcutta had its share of only 5.2 per cent. A comparative crime chart appended herewith contains details related to 22 Metropolitan cities of India.

The city of Calcutta, when viewed from the standpoint of its population complex, is like India in a miniature. Its massive population growth over the past few decades has made this vast metropolis the second most populous city in the country. The city had to bear the burden of millions of refugees who migrated to India after the partition of Bengal in 1947. Even today, Calcutta continues to receive thousands of migrants from the rest of the country, and also from neighbouring countries such as Bangladesh, Nepal and Bhutan. The unchecked and unplanned growth of population in the city not only increases the number of slum dwellers but also threatens the basic structure of the city in various ways. A survey of basic civic amenities in slums revealed that each latrine is used by 40 to 50 people in a day and each source of water, like a tubewell or a tap, by 35 to 40 people. The usual living space for a family of five is 10 to 12 square metres. A series of welfare schemes have been taken up with national and international funding, but several factors prevent any marked improvement in slum conditions. The facilities provided are over-used and seldom maintained properly. The slum dwellers are unable to increase their income significantly over the years and new groups pour in to join the queue of the people without confirmed occupation. A large proportion of the slum dwellers become criminals in order to earn their livelihood. Apart from the traditional property crime, they also indulge in organised crime rackets such as drug peddling, *satta* (gambling), sale of illicit liquors etc. Normally they are lured into such illegal trade by crime syndicates who exploit the poverty of these slum dwellers.

Calcutta also has a sizeable population of pavement-dwellers. It may be as high as 5 per cent of the population of the city. The pavement-dwellers consist of entire families seeking a new life in the city. These pavement dwellers come from the poorest group in rural areas, with about 68 per cent from West Bengal and the rest from other States. They migrate to Calcutta because they think they can somehow find a living in the city, but most of them have no special skills by which they can earn their livelihood. Physical labour is their only asset. Their chief occupations are those of daily wage labourers, domestic servants, sweepers, transport workers like rickshaw and handcart pullers. India's biggest slums are in Mumbai, followed by other big cities like Calcutta.

Among India's big metropolitan cities, Calcutta has by far the worst system of roads. Only 6.5 per cent of Calcutta's city area has roads, as compared with Mumbais' 16 per cent, and Delhi's 23 per cent. The focus of road congestion in Calcutta is the central business district area in BBD and Chowringhee.

Apart from roadways, Calcutta is also served by both a suburban railway network and the tube railway system. But the railways cannot cope with the volume of traffic because of the shortage of rolling stocks.

The transportation problem in Calcutta is accentuated because the city is cut off by the River Hooghly from most of India and therefore long distance traffic must cross the river to reach Calcutta. Besides the old Rabindra Setu (commonly known as the Howrah Bridge), there are two other bridges - one is the newly constructed Vidyasagar Setu (the second Hooghly Bridge) and the old Vivekananda Bridge at Bally. Still those bridges are not sufficient to cope with the heavy goods traffic coming from the rest of the country. The approach roads, except for the newly constructed Vidyasagar Setu, are woefully inadequate. Calcutta has other traffic problems which are somewhat unique. There is a range of slow traffic such as handcarts, hand-drawn rickshaws and animal drawn carts. There are about 6,000 licensed rickshaws and more than 18,000 licensed handcarts. But unlicensed rickshaws and handcarts far outnumber those which are registered. There is an acute shortage of parking space in Calcutta and hence cars are habitually parked in the streets. Over and above, Calcutta is uniquely receptive towards small tradesmen on its pavements and on the carriageway itself. There are said to be about 100,000 street hawkers. Their stalls tend to cluster around road junctions, obstructing pedestrians and slowing down the traffic to an average speed of about 10 km per hour.

Management of traffic systems in Calcutta is, no doubt, a very critical and difficult task and this task is increasingly getting complex with the further growth of traffic -- both vehicular and pedestrian. Lay-out of the city is such that most movements are concentrated in the central business district area or at some specific locations. It may be mentioned in this context that at present the city has about a million registered vehicles including two-wheelers. However, recently a number of steps have been taken to regulate traffic in the city. Installation of automatic signals, restriction of pedestrian movements in some intersections and introduction of one-way traffic systems are a few of them. Very recently the State Government has taken a firm decision to remove the hawkers from the city's main thoroughfares and replace the hand-pulled rickshaws and handcarts by introducing auto-rickshaws and small delivery vans.

Calcutta is known for all sorts of petty and violent crimes. Apart from the conventional crimes involving pick-pocketing and other petty property crimes, theft of automobiles and their accessories, hijacking of taxis, theft of two-wheelers, violent and petty crime by domestic servants, theft of telephone cables, extortion, pilferage from Port/ Dock area, varieties of white collar and syndicate crimes like cheating, criminal breach of trust, bank fraud, defalcation and forgery, soccer vandalism, trafficking in women, boot legging, different forms of gambling, sale of obscene literature, exhibition and sale of obscene films, video and audio cassette piracy are increasingly becoming more common. Side-by-side with these offences there has also emerged a generation of desperados. Some of them, being armed with sharp cutting weapons and/or indigenously produced firearms, move about in hijacked taxis/cars and commit violent crimes like dacoity or robbery and victimise pedestrians, businessmen travelling in taxis, while some others commit dacoity or robbery at factories, godowns, commercial establishments and residential flats. Other forms of crime like forcible collection of subscription on various pretexts, deception of the persons in search of flats and unauthorised construction of buildings are gradually adding up to the city's crime situation. Moreover, interparty clashes and group clashes of the anti-socials over some vested economic interests at times deteriorate the city's law and order situation. Fortunately, drug-trafficking is still not a serious problem in Calcutta. In spite of a lot of constraints, the city police with its limited manpower and resources have been able to contain the activities of the anti-social elements and thereby maintain the law and order situation in the city.

Over the past few decades, the Indian society has become more and more divided between rich and poor. Some inequalities encourage crimes and criminals. Moreover, some rich people, with ulterior motives, seek to win the politicians and the upper echelon of the bureaucracy to their side by virtue of their moneypower. Such attempts by the rich tend to encourage corruption among politicians and bureaucrats. Moreover, the political parties, in order to reach their goal during the elections, take assistance of the musclepower. Such a practice by the politicians eventually leads to the criminalisation of politics and adds to the suffering of the common people. Money laundering, evasion of tax, manipulation of Customs procedures and rampant smuggling generate undeclared income depriving the national exchequer of its legitimate revenues. The huge undeclared income known as blackmoney builds up a parallel economy which is controlled by the so-called Mafias. A sizeable portion of this money is generally invested in organised crimes, procurement of illicit arms and explosives, and making contacts with criminals in other countries. Politicians and bureaucrats are easily lured into the traps of such criminals.

The organised crime has always been a world-wide phenomenon. It is also becoming increasingly sophisticated. Besides its traditional spheres of activity which included extortion, seeking protection money, kidnapping, boot legging, gambling, prostitution and smuggling, it has now added narco-terrorism, gun running, money laundering etc. White collar crimes and other economic offences are likely to occupy the centre stage in the days to come. Apart from making the lives of the citizens insecure, organised crime drains out billions of rupees from the Indian economy by its illegal activities. The main purpose of organised crime is to amass wealth which is used for corrupting the administrative machinery, specially the law enforcement agencies, in order to carry on and enhance illegal activities as well as secure power.

In the context of organised crime in India, the city of Mumbai has become a focal point. Some of the gangs have become so powerful that some of India's hostile neighbours have started using them for destabilising India's economy and political system. Evidence of such foreign intervention has been mounting in Mumbai and Delhi. The situation of Delhi is also not comfortable. Although in Calcutta we do not have any such organised criminal gangs that operate either in foreign countries or in Mumbai or Delhi, we do have organised crimes in the shape of gambling, illicit business in real estates, crimes such as unauthorised construction of multistoried buildings, collection of funds by some non-banking financial institutions, money laundering etc. The Bowbazar Bomb Blast case in Calcutta (March 1992) was the outcome of the organised crime. With the arrest of the prime accused, in the Bowbazar case, the Calcutta Police were able to clamp down on gambling by organised groups. Stern actions against the non-banking institutions by police also played an important role in preventing collection of illicit funds which eventually ruin the savings of the poor and middle class people, particularly in rural areas.

In the present criminal justice system in India, the police, the judiciary and the prison authority, have generally failed to check organised crimes in the society. Basically the laws of the land tend to favour the accused. Jails are also hardly a deterrent to a criminal. The active members of the criminal gangs including their bosses, money collectors, liaison workers, and ancillary workers, and conspirators operating inside the country while international connections usually escape the clutches of law for want of adequate provisions in the criminal law. The main hurdle in taking effective action against the gangsters residing and operating from abroad is that, except for Nepal, India does not have an Extradition Treaty with UAE and other Gulf countries. India also does not have any other agreement or arrangement with these countries for mutual assistance in investigation and prosecution of crime and other related matters. There is also no clear provision in the Criminal Procedure Code in India for confiscation of property, acquired or held by an absconding accused in other countries. The law enforcing authorities of these countries, where most of the criminals reside, are reluctant to take any action on the orders or requests issued by Indian courts on the ground that these are not in consonance with the law in their country. In order to counteract the menace of organised crime in India, a national level workshop was organised in Mumbai in January (1996). As expected, the focus was on the Mumbai scenario followed by a close look at Delhi. The consensus was to set-up a Special Task Force which will take care of technical and legal issues as well as inter-agencies co-ordination. It was felt that the most immediate task was to enact a special legislation having stringent provisions for dealing effectively with the organised crime.

Prevention and detection of crime and maintenance of order is the primary duty of the police. As a total crime free society is a utopia, we should aim at controlling crime by reducing its causes as far as practicable. There is a need for change in the attitude of the police particularly in urban areas with regard to social services to the community as a whole. Public support to the police is most essential in law and order matters. Public co-operation would be more forthcoming if the corrupt and inefficient image of the police could be removed from the public mind. To achieve this the first and foremost necessity is to bring about changes for the eradication of traditional police vices. Better talents, improved training facilities, more amenities etc. are the basic requirements to ensure effective implementation of various social defence programmes. Efficient police leadership is also essential for boosting the morale of the police today. Existing Police Acts and criminal laws should be more realistic and needs based. Laws on procedure and evidence should also be simplified by avoiding provisions for observance of unnecessary legal ceremonies which only add to inordinate delay in dispensation of speedy justice. Thorough re-orientation of the outlook and attitude of the judiciary, lawyers, prison authorities and the police is the crying need for improvement in the existing mode and manner of administration of criminal justice.

Population and incidence of crimes under Indian Penal Code indifferent Metropolitan cities in India during 1994

City	Population NDPS (in millions)	Murder	Dacoltv	Burglary	Theft	Rape
Ahmedabad	3.52	101	17	868	4554	20
Bangalore	4.48	213	90	2547	8965	61
Bhopal	1.21	51	2	634	1402	62
Mumbai	13.91	354	113	2707	13484	150
Calcutta	11.51	77	35	174	4897	36
Coimbatore	1.15	23	0	230	778	1
Delhi	9.21	396	11	1442	12654	252
Hyderabad	4.90	99	7	1327	3243	49
Indore	1.19	89	2	745	2499	29
Jaipur	1.67	63	4	771	2489	22
Kochin	1.28	25	4	227	262	7
Lucknow	1.88	177	32	994	3096	33
Ludhiana	1.18	40	0	112	155	11
Madras	5.73.	94	4	453	2829	14
Madural	1.13	26	4	171	977	4
Nagpur	1.76	87	8	864	2648	46
Patna	1.15	224	63	471	1763	25
Pune	2.73	92	15	839	2035	52
Surat	1.71	93	17	456	1683	10
Vadodara	1.24	35	7	364	1305	13
Varanasi	1.10	NA	NA	NA	NA	NA
Vishakhapatnam	1.20	24	3	347	1094	21

NA: Indicates not available.

14 Trend and Structural Changes of Australian Development Assistance: Some Implications for the Indian Ocean Rim Countries

D K Dutta

Introduction

Official development assistance (ODA)[1] consists of net disbursements of loans and grants made on concessional financial terms by all bilateral official agencies and multilateral sources. Its basic objective is to promote economic development and welfare, mainly of the developing countries. During the recent years, due to the ongoing phenomenon of *globalisation*, countries are becoming increasingly active participants in global markets. But there are the smaller and poorer countries in different regions of the world which have failed not only to actively participate in global markets, but also to attract private investment. This issue is discussed in a brief policy statement entitled *Development Partnerships in the New Global Context* made by the members of the Development Assistance Committee (DAC) of the Organisation for Economic Co-operation and Development (OECD) on 3-4 May 1995. This statement recognises the following:

> *Private investment flows are mainly attracted by the most dynamic countries and sectors of the developing world, and private donations are directed primarily to immediate humanitarian needs. Official development assistance remains vital for many key investments in developing countries, especially the poorer countries.*[2]

---

1 Two major sources of ODA are the Development Assistance Committee (DAC) member countries under the *Organisation for Economic Cooperation and Development* (OECD) system and the *Organisation of Petroleum Exporting Countries* (OPEC). Multilateral financial institutions, including the International Monetary Fund (IMF), the World Bank, and the three regional development banks in Asia, Africa and Latin America, have also been important sources of assistance, although primarily in the form of loans, both concessional and nonconcessional.

2 *Development Co-operation: 1995 Report*, OECD, p. 19.

As a DAC member country, Australia has been involved in the ODA program. She has her own bilateral aid programs, although in a limited scale except in the Asia-Pacific region. Due to recent changes on both economic and political levels in various regions, time has now come to think about restructuring her development assistance program, particularly its bilateral aid component, and therefore to bring it in line not only with her foreign policy, humanitarian and commercial interests, but also with various DAC policy statements made in recent years.

CURRENT AND FUTURE TRENDS IN ODA PROGRAM

As a result of various political and economic changes in many parts of the world over the past decade or so, a number of major revisions[1] of the ODA program have already been made and some are under way.

Firstly, since the mid eighties, the form and terms of official financial assistance have become differentiated, reflecting the diverse situations and prospects facing different groups of developing countries. For instance, there has been a significant increase in disbursements from multilateral institutions associated with the European Community over the past few years, in part reflecting larger assistance to Central and Eastern Europe. The recent continuing shift by both multilateral and bilateral creditors toward highly concessional financing for low-income countries is also noteworthy. For example, the share of bilateral ODA channeled to low-income countries increased to 60 percent in 1992, compared with 52 percent in 1989 and 45 percent in 1985[2].

Secondly, the total ODA disbursed annually by the DAC member countries fell sharply in 1993, from $60.8 billion to $55.9 billion, bringing the ODA/GNP ratio down to 0.30 per cent from the ratio which was steadily maintained (between 0.32 and 0.34 per cent) over almost two decades (1973-92)[3]. The situation has been marginally eased in 1994 when 8 of the 21 DAC member countries reported declines (in real terms), compared to 16 in 1993 (see *Table 1*).

---

1 During the period from 1989 to 1993, a few countries have been added to the list of ODA recipients: Albania (1989); the Black Communities of South Africa (1991); Kazakhstan, Kyrgyzstan (now the Kyrgyz Republic), Tajikistan, Turkmenistan and Uzbekistan (1992); Armenia, Georgia and Azerbaijan (1993); and Eritrea (formerly part of Ethiopia) (1993). Over the same period, the following country and territories have been removed from the ODA recipient list: Portugal (1991); French Guiana, Guadeloupe, Martinique, Reunion and St Pierre and Miquelon (1992) (*Development Co-operation: Report 1994*, OECD, p.118).

2 *Official Financing for Developing Countries*, IMF, April, 1994, p 35.

3 *Development Co-operation: 1994 Report*, OECD, p. 2.

Although most DAC member countries argue that the decline has not been disproportionate when compared to other government programs, their recent concern for 'aid effectiveness and development results', especially since the end of the Cold War, is easy to understand. They would like to treat the ODA as an instrument for the emerging paradigm of sustainable development "as an integrated process of political and economic stability, good governance, popular participation, investing in people, reliance on market forces, concern for the environment, and a vigorous private sector." The trend (during 1987-1994) and projections (in 2005 and 2010) of the ODA/GNP ratio for eight selected OECD member countries (including Australia) are shown in the following *Table 1*.

Table 1: **ODA/GNP ratio for selected OECD members: Trend and forecast**

	1987	1988	1989	1990	1991	1992	1993	1994	2005	2010
Australia	0.34	0.46	0.38	0.34	0.38	0.37	0.35	0.35	0.29	0.26
Canada	0.47	0.50	0.44	0.44	0.45	0.46	0.45	0.43	0.39	0.35
France	0.60	0.72	0.78	0.79	0.62	0.63	0.63	0.64	0.55	0.49
Germany	0.39	0.39	0.41	0.42	0.41	0.39	0.37	0.34	0.36	0.27
Japan	0.31	0.32	0.31	0.31	0.32	0.30	0.26	0.29	0.21	0.20
New Zealand	0.26	0.27	0.22	0.23	0.25	0.26	0.25	0.24	0.24	0.22
United Kingdom	0.28	0.32	0.31	0.27	0.32	0.31	0.31	0.31	0.35	0.35
United States	0.20	0.21	0.15	0.21	0.20	0.20	0.15	0.15	0.12	0.08

Source: Table 1 in *Appendix.*

It is to be noted that the trend projections of ODA/GNP for the years of 2005 and 2010 in *Table 1* are made on the assumption that the instituted economic policies, and the political as well as the economic stability of the recent past, are maintained in both donor and recipient countries during the coming decade or so. According to the trend projections for 2005 and 2010, all the selected countries, except the United Kingdom, will have a somewhat lower ODA/GNP ratio. In the case of the United Kingdom, the big increase in the ODA/GNP ratio from 0.27 in 1990 to 0.32 in 1991, and then its maintaining at the level of 0.31 for the following three successive years, are the reasons why the projected figure turns out to be higher than the actual ODA/GNP ratios of the recent past. If this projected ratio for the United Kingdom is realised, then that ratio will exceed that of Australia in the very near future. *Table 1* also shows that, during the coming decade, France, Canada and Germany will maintain a higher ratio than that of Australia, and that, in turn, Australia will maintain a higher ratio than that of New Zealand, Japan and the United States. There are also some tendencies in the case of three pairs of countries to converge to different common values of the ODA/GNP ratio in the foreseeable future. For example, there is a possibility for such convergence between Australia and Germany sometimes before 2005, between New Zealand and Japan around 2005, and between Canada and the United Kingdom in 2010.

Thirdly, official creditors and donors have increasingly linked the availability of new financing to countries' policy environments and performance under structural adjustment programs. An important development was the agreement on 15 February 1992, among the OECD Consensus participants, to amend the guidelines on tied-aid credits to " *better-off developing countries*."[1] The new rules limit the use of tied-aid for projects in those countries and thus reinforce the trend away from concessional financing for commercially attractive projects which could otherwise be financed by export credits and private financing. In fact, private flows to developing countries increased from 53 percent of total net resource flows in 1992 to 56 percent (US$ 93.9 billion) in 1993, and net flows of export credits grew strongly in 1993 to US$5 billion (3 percent of total flows)[2].

If we look at the selected OECD member countries as shown in *Table 2* below, one could easily see that during the recent past there has been an upward trend in long term private flows (at market terms) from these countries (except Japan during 1992-93 and Germany during 1991-92) to developing countries and multilateral organisations.

Table 2: **Private flows of financial resources from the selected OECD member countries to developing countries and multilateral organisations (US$ million)**

Country	1990	1991	1992	1993	1994	2005 (forecast)	2010 (forecast)
Australia	442	-3499	2694	874	800	6878	9422
Canada	219	606	864	2273	2583	9623	12820
France	-2287	-1918	1701	2455	3837	22365	30675
Germany	4374	3578	18	5712	12602	29424	38719
Japan	4690	10788	1547	618	11807	11173	13205
U.K.	2934	1527	5328	5290	6687	19003	24637
U.S.A.	-2356	7599	17666	45405	46330	198660	266249

Source: *Development Co-operation Report 1994*, OECD, Tables 13-19.
Development Co-operation Report 1995, OECD, Tables 14-20.

1 *Official Financing for Developing Countries*, IMF, April, 1994, pp. 40-41.

2 *Australia's Overseas Aid Program 1995-96, 1995-96 Budget Related Paper No. 2*, Canberra, pp. 4-5.

The composition of private flows to developing countries has, however, become more diversified. *Foreign direct investment* (FDI), which is driven primarily by longer-term and structural factors, has increased for the majority of developing countries in 1993 (see *Table 2* in Appendix). Total FDI to developing countries rose 17 percent in 1994 over the previous period, even as portfolio flows fell[1].

Fourthly, the continuing increase in private flows to developing countries is, however, by-passing s. An expansion of FDI in sub-Saharan Africa in 1993 was insufficient to offset a substantial decline in total *official development finance* (ODF) flows[2]. ODF flows to this region fell by 12 percent to just under $20 billion in 1993, most of it being attributable to a fall in bilateral and multilateral concessional flows[3].

Australia and Her Major Development Assistance Partners

If one looks at the allocation of Australian ODA over the past 25 years, one could easily see that Papua New Guinea and Indonesia respectively continue to be the largest and the second largest recipients of Australian aid. Among the other major recipients are the South Pacific region and countries in South Asia, South-East Asia and North Asia. As is evident from *Table 3*, only a few African countries, such as Egypt, Mozambique, Tanzania and Kenya, could sometimes be identified as major recipients of the Australian ODA over the past 25 years.

According to the announcement made in 1995 by the former Federal Minister for Development Cooperation and Pacific Island Affairs, the Australian aid program was supposed to have increased to $1563.2 million in 1995-96[4]. This was an increase in real terms of about 1.8 percent or $28 million over the expected expenditure in 1994-95. Consequently, Australia's ODA/GNP ratio was expected to be 0.33 in 1995-96, which was still less than that of 0.34 maintained during the previous two years, 1993-94 and 1994-95[5]. It is also

---

1 *Global Economic Prospect and the Developing Countries: 1995*, World Bank, 1995, p. 13.

2 *Official Development Finance* (ODF) flows includes ODA (both bilateral & multilateral) and other official flows for development purposes (including refinancing loans) which have too low a grant element in terms of a commitment (interest rate, maturity and grace period).

3 *Australia's Overseas Aid Program 1995-96, 1995-96 Budget Related Paper No. 2*, Canberra, p. 5.

4 *Ibid.*, p. v.

5 *Ibid.*, Table 2, p. 18.

noteworthy that the trend in ODA (even inclusive of the student subsidy incorporated in ODA since 1983-84) has fallen far behind that in GDP in Australia since the mid eighties[1].

Table 3: **Major recipients of and their shares (%) in gross disbursements of total Australian ODA**

1970-71		1980-81		1992-93		1993-94	
PNG	66.9	PNG	42.9	PNG	23.6	PNG	22.4
Indonesia	8.2	Indonesia	7.0	Indonesia	8.3	Indonesia	8.8
India	2.2	Bangladesh	3.0	China	4.3	China	5.7
Thailand	2.0	Philippines	1.9	Philippines	3.3	Philippines	3.1
Malaysia	1.6	Pakistan	1.8	Thailand	2.8	Thailand	2.7
Vietnam	1.5	Fiji	1.7	Malaysia	2.3	Vietnam	2.6
Pakistan	0.8	Myanmar	1.6	Fiji	2.0	Malaysia	2.2
Laos	0.6	Thailand	1.3	India	1.5	Bangladesh	1.6
Cambodia	0.6	Egypt	1.3	Vietnam	1.4	Fiji	1.5
Sri Lanka	0.6	Malaysia	1.2	Mozambique	1.1	Cambodia	1.1
Fiji	0.5	Sri Lanka	1.0	Laos	1.1	India	1.1
Myanmar	0.4	Tanzania	1.0	Vanuatu	1.0	Mozambique	1.0
Nepal	0.4	Solomon Is.	0.9	Solomon Is.	1.0	Laos	1.0
Singapore	0.3	Tonga	0.7	W. Samoa	1.0	Solomon Is.	1.0
Bangladesh	0.3	Kenya	0.6	Bangladesh	0.9	Vanuatu	1.0

Source: *Development Co-operation Report 1994*, OECD, Table 45, p. H16.
Development Co-operation Report 1995, OECD, Table 42, p. A69.

The statistics over five years (1989/90 to 1993/94) shows (see *Table 3*) that about one-third of Australia's total ODA (at 1993/94 constant prices) goes currently to Papua New Guinea (24%) and the South Pacific region (9%) together. During the same period, the South-East Asian region has received approximately 21% to 25.5% and the North Asian region from 3% to 6% of the Australian ODA, having an increasing trend in both the regions. On the other hand, amounts allocated to the regions of both South Asia, including the Indian Ocean island states, (from 8.37% to 5.42%) and sub-Saharan Africa (from 8.22% to 6.09%) have shown a declining trend, even though Australia has very limited development assistance programs in these parts of Asia and Africa.

STRUCTURAL CHANGES OF AUSTRALIAN DEVELOPMENT ASSISTANCE

Although Australia's development assistance program could be traced back to its beginnings in the pre-war years in Papua New Guinea, it was the *Colombo Plan* in 1950 that got Australia involved in making wider response to the development needs of other countries in its region. However, during the sixties and the seventies, 'there were only marginal changes in the geographic distribution of Australia's bilateral

1 *Ibid.*, Diagram 3, p. 14.

aid program, with South East Asia gradually gaining importance at the expense of South Asia.'[1] In order to get some specific idea of the motivations behind Australian development assistance, one can go back to the Jackson Committee (*Committee to Review the Australian Overseas Aid Program*, 1984) which argued that Australia gives aid principally for humanitarian reasons, as well as to achieve commercial and strategic objectives. The *Report* also stressed that a higher proportion of Australian aid should be allocated to countries in South East Asia and the South Pacific. As Gounder (1994) rightly remarks, there is statistical evidence to indicate that the regional focus of Australia's bilateral aid program advocated by the Jackson Report has been implemented by the Australian government[2]. For such diverse interests, Australia has, in fact, been very much committed in the past to a rigorous approach to the provision of assistance to the South Pacific region, and, as a result, she is the largest bilateral donor to this region. As we have already mentioned the DAC member countries as a group have been increasingly linking the ODA as an instrument for the emerging paradigm of *sustainable development*[3]. Australia therefore needs to think about restructuring her development assistance program in the same line as well.

From the forecast presented in *Table 1* above, one can see a declining trend in the Australian ODA/GNP ratio in the coming decade. The projected values of this ratio for other selected countries (except the United Kingdom) are in line with those of Australia. For a lower rate of growth in GNP, the declining trend in the ODA/GNP ratio of a specific country will mean that either its ODA disbursement needs to be cut or its growth rate will need to be lower than that of its GNP. For example, Japan has already cut her ODA by 10.6 per cent in 1996 compared to the previous period[4]. A similar trend seems highly likely in Australia under the new Coalition Government, which has already taken steps to abolish *the Development Import Finance Facility* (DIFF) scheme. It is noteworthy that this scheme has an allocation of

---

1 *Australia's International Aid Program: 1990-92*, AIDAB, 1992, p. 8.

2 Gounder (1994, footnote 2, p. 110)

3 According to a widely accepted definition of *sustainable development* as proffered by The World Commission on Environment and Development (*Our Common Future*, 1987), it is 'a process in which the exploitation of resources, the direction of investment, and the orientation of technological development and institutional change meet the needs of the present generation without compromising the ability of future generations to meet their own needs.'

4 Croll's Press Clips , *Daily Commercial news*, 1 February 1996.

A$123 million in the next year.[1] Because of the recent surge in private flows (including direct investment, bank lending and equity purchases) mainly to the better-off developing countries, the pressure on the need for development assistance has become less acute. This however does not mean that this need will disappear altogether in the foreseeable future. A need for such assistance will certainly exist in the developing countries with heavy debt burdens and/or with stagnant economies, which are generally found to be unattractive to private investors.

As a guide for future disbursement of Australian ODA to the selected recipient countries, one may look at *Table 4* and *Table 5* given below. As *Table 4* shows, Thailand and Fiji have attained both high real GDP per capita based on purchasing power parities[2] (PPP) and a high Human Development Index[3] (HDI). Termination of Australian aid to Thailand in the very near future before 2005, and to Fiji in 2010 (as forecast in *Table 5*), is therefore justified at least from the economic point of view. Regarding the forecast figures of ODA (as % of total Australian ODA) for Papua New Guinea and other South Pacific countries, all show declining trends except that for Kiribati, which has an increasing trend and therefore a higher forecast value. But sharp declines in Australian ODA from its actual figure in 1993/94 to its forecast in 2004/5 for Papua New Guinea (from 24.03 to 10.30), Tonga (from 0.76 to 0.43) and Solomon Islands (from 0.99 to 0.68) are to be taken with caution, especially for policy purposes. This is due to Australia's long-term commitment to sustainable development in the Pacific region which has limited resources at its command and fluctuating growth rates in both total GDP and GDP per capita.

It is also to be noted that Australia is facing some degree of competition for the ODA to the Asia-Pacific regions, not only from Japan but also from some of the newly industrialising countries like Taiwan and South Korea. For instance, during the last year Taiwan had expressed her willingness for donating $US1 billion to a fund for developing nations in order to bid for a seat in the United Nations[4]. It is

---

1. *The Sydney Morning Herald*, Editorial, 24 February, 1996.
2. The purchasing power parities (PPP) is defined as the number of units of a country's currency required to buy the same amounts of goods and services in the domestic market as one dollar would buy in the United States (*World Development Report 1995*, World Bank, 1995, p. 243).
3. Human Development Index (HDI) is a composite measure of human development containing indicators representing three equally weighted dimensions of human development - longevity (life expectancy at birth), knowledge (adult literacy and mean years of schooling), and income (purchasing power parity dollars per capita).
4. *The Sydney Morning Herald*, June 27, 1995.

also reported that the Government of PNG has recognised Taiwan politically in return for short-term financial assistance and will consider a move to full diplomatic recognition in return for a major foreign exchange rescue package[1]. On another occasion, the Prime Ministers of both Vanuatu and Indonesia agreed to open diplomatic relations and to exchange visits between officials and business people from both countries[2]. Similarly the Cook Islands will, according to a statement made by the Cook Islands High Commissioner in Wellington last year, soon seek membership of the United Nations. If successful in the near future, the Cook Islands then could be able to plot its future without any more direct involvement from New Zealand.[3] This might have some spillover effect on Australia, in the sense that Australia might be approached by the Cook Islands for more development assistance. Similarly, in the future Vanuatu may seek foreign assistance more from Indonesia than from Australia.

Over the past two years or so, the United States has been making some attempts at restructuring its aid program. Because of the economic successes in many of the East and South-East Asian countries, the Clinton Administration has already taken the decision to slowly turn the region away from aid and towards trade and investment for its future prosperity. Recently, the United States also seems to have taken some steps towards strengthening ties with Europe, starting with greater cooperation to aid the poorer nations in this region, and by removing trade barriers - possibly leading to a free trade area encompassing North America and Europe.

For sometime now Japan has been proposing to use the Asia-Pacific Economic Co-operation (APEC) forum as a vehicle for mobilising aid to the region's less-developed countries. Although the United States has shown little enthusiasm for the Japanese proposal, Australia might find it useful (in the spirit of APEC) to reconsider her ODA to Indonesia - the second highest recipient after PNG, and surpassing the total Australian ODA given to the South Pacific region as a whole over the past two years. Not only that, aid to Indonesia also shows an increasing trend from 8.35% of Australia's total ODA in 1989/90 to 9.26% in 1993/94 (*Table 3*). This increasing trend, when translated into forecasts, shows that in both 2004/5 and 2009/10 Indonesia will remain the second largest recipient of Australian aid (*Table 5*). According to the forecast, China, not Papua New Guinea, is

---

1 *Ibid.*, May 31, 1995.

2 *Ibid.*, July 4, 1995.

3 *Ibid.*

going to be the largest recipient of Australian aid in both 2004/5 and 2009/10.

Table 4: **Recent trends in development indicators for selected ODA recipient countries**

Country	World Bank classification* 1995	People In absolute poverty (%) 1980-90	Average annual growth rate in GNP per capita 1980-92	Average annual rate of inflation (%) 1980-92	Average growth rate in exports as % of GDP 1980-91	National conservation strategy [year/in preparation (IP)]	Real GDP per capita (PPP$) 1992	HDI rank (H) High (M) Medium (L) Low 1995
Bangladesh	LI	78	1.8	9.1	0.7	1987	1,230	146(L)
Burma (Myanmar)	LI	35		14.8			751	132(L)
Cambodia	LI						1,250	153(L)
China	LI	9	7.6	6.5	9.6	1990	1,950	111(M)
Fiji	LMI		0.3	5.6	5.5	IP	5,410	46(H)
India	LI	40	3.1	8.5	4.9	IP	1,230	134(L)
Indonesia	LI	25	4.0	8.4	-2.1	IP	2,950	104(M)
Kiribati	LMI		2.0	5.4	-0.1			
Laos	LI						1,760	138(L)
Mongolia	LI						2,389	110(M)
Mozambique	LI	59	-3.6	38.0			380	167(L)
Nepal	LI	60	2.0	9.2		1987	1,170	151(L)
Pakistan	LI	28	3.1	7.1	2.7	1991	2,890	128(L)
PNG	LMI		0.0	5.1	-1.2		2,410	126(M)
Philippines	LMI	54	-1.0	14.1	1.4	IP	2,550	100(M)
Solomon Is	LMI		3.3	12.1	4.4		2,616	125(M)
Sri Lanka	LI	39	2.6	11.0	2.4	1988	2,850	97(M)
Thailand	LMI	30	6.0	4.2	4.2	IP	5,950	58(H)
Tonga	LMI		13.4		1.3			
Vanuatu	LMI			5.3			1,956	119(M)
Vietnam	LI					1985	1,010	120(M)
W. Samoa	LMI			11.2			1,869	102(M)
Zimbabwe	LI		-0.9	14.4		1987	1,970	121(M)

*Note: LI = Low Income, LMI = Lower Middle Income, UMI = Upper Middle Income, and HI = High Income.

Sources: Various issues of *World Development Report*, World Bank; *Human Development Report*, UNDP; *Statistical Yearbook for Asia and Pacific*, UN; and *World Resources*, World Resources Institute.

Table 5: **Trend in Australian ODA for selected recipient countries**

	Percentage of Total Australia ODA				Forecast* % of Australian ODA	
Country	**1990/91**	**1991/92**	**1992/93**	**1993/94**	**2004/5**	**2009/10**
Bangladesh	1.66	2.02	1.20	1.76	-2.08	-3.63
Burma (Myanmar)	0.08	0.07	0.02	0.05	-0.73	-1.06
Cambodia	0.66	1.19	1.39	1.68	4.52	5.82
China	3.19	4.44	5.48	6.15	14.09	17.75
Fiji	1.80	2.19	1.73	1.66	0.53	0.00
India	3.03	1.73	1.36	1.12	-3.72	-5.90
Indonesia	8.56	8.69	9.21	9.26	12.03	13.26
Kiribati	0.31	0.39	0.39	0.50	0.62	0.70
Laos	0.67	0.92	1.18	1.21	2.93	3.69
Mongolia	0.00	0.03	0.05	0.06	0.23	0.31
Mozambique	0.94	1.14	1.26	1.18	1.76	2.01
Nepal	0.25	0.27	0.65	0.42	1.26	1.60
Pakistan	0.48	0.63	0.43	0.58	-0.29	-0.63
Papua New Guinea	26.41	25.18	24.07	24.03	10.30	4.38
Philippines	3.98	3.55	3.83	3.56	5.79	6.66
Solomon Islands	1.01	1.10	1.02	0.99	0.68	0.54
South Africa (Black communities)	0.00	0.00	0.47	0.06	0.86	1.15
Sri Lanka	0.49	0.54	0.63	0.72	1.43	1.77
Thailand	3.06	2.89	2.91	2.69	-0.42	-1.78
Tonga	0.85	0.86	0.79	0.76	0.43	0.27
Vanuatu	1.11	0.99	0.99	1.15	1.14	1.17
Vietnam	0.80	0.96	2.25	3.51	9.00	11.77
Western Samoa	0.98	1.18	0.86	0.85	0.77	0.70
Zimbabwe	0.54	1.01	0.74	0.34	-1.02	-1.70

*Negative values of forecast for any specific country may be read as the termination of aid prior to the year of 2005, unless the recipient country changes to be a donor one.

Source: *Table 3* in Appendix.

Unlike the economies of Indonesia, Malaysia, Thailand, China, etc. in North and South-East Asia, which are becoming self-sustaining, during the coming decade other Asian economies such as the Philippines, Cambodia, Vietnam, Mongolia, Laos, etc. will continue to receive ODA in increasing amounts not only from Australia but also from other developed nations, such as Japan and the United States. For instance, in spite of a plea by Ms Aung San Suu Kyi, the leader of the

National League for Democracy, to wait for real progress in human rights and democracy in military-ruled Burma (Myanmar), the Japanese Government is poised to resume billions of dollars worth of government aid, trade and private investment to this country. In the case of Australian aid to Burma (Myanmar), only a small percentage (ranging between 0.02 and 0.08) of her total ODA had been disbursed, with a declining trend over the past few years. As a result, its forecast figure becomes a negative one i.e., termination of Australian aid looks like going to take place earlier than in 2004/5. The reason for this forecast apparently seems to be more political than economic.

As a follow-up of an Australian Government sponsored International Forum on the Indian Ocean Region which took place in Perth on June 11-13, 1995, some degree of momentum has been generated, at least in terms of exploring the possibility for establishing a regional institution along the lines of the APEC. Because the Indian Ocean region contains a disparate set of countries at different levels of socio-economic development, this possibility may be a remote one. Whatever the outcome in some foreseeable future, it seems likely that this region will attract aid from the developed regions especially because of its high poverty incidence. On the basis of current trend, it can easily be shown that not only the countries of these regions will very likely have HDI values less than the average HDI value for all the developing countries in the coming decade, but also most of these countries will have Low Income (LI) status in the next decade. Although, over the recent past, there has been an upward trend in Australia's flow of very limited ODA to a few countries like Nepal, Sri Lanka, Mozambique, etc.(*Table 5*), its overall trend in the regions of South Asia, Indian Ocean Island States, Indian Ocean sub-Saharan Africa, and Other Sub Saharan Africa is a declining one[1]. This is reflected in the negative forecasts for Australian ODA to the countries like Bangladesh, India, Pakistan, Zimbabwe, etc. (*Table 5*).

---

1 As *Table 3* shows, Australia's limited ODA as a percent of her total ODA has declined from 7.52% to 4.95% in South Asia, from 0.85% to 0.47% in Indian Ocean Island States, from 2.19% to 2.02% in Indian Ocean Sub-Saharan Africa, and from 6.03% to 4.06% in Other Sub-Saharan Africa over the past five years.

Conclusion

Against the background of current 'emphasis on the human and the global dimensions of sustainable development,' the need for official development assistance is vital for many key investments particularly in poorer developing countries. In the process of preparing the new *Development Partnerships* statement, the DAC member countries as a group recognise that 'development partners should try to help *countries* improve their capacity to participate in the global economy and should try to help *people* improve their capacity to overcome poverty and be able to participate fully in their societies.'[1] It is also expected that the developing country partners, both governments at different levels as well as various non-governmental organisations, should genuinely assume responsibility in 'helping the poor people develop greater capacity to do things for themselves' irrespective of their religious faith, political belief, cultural tradition, etc. It is yet to be seen how both sides of the emerging development partnership could transcend their immediate interests of various types such as commercial benefits, local and international politics, etc. in order to make 1996, the UN designated International Year for the Eradication of Poverty, as the beginning of a new era when poverty will be only a matter of past history.

Bibliography

Asian Development Outlook 1995 & 1996, Asian Development Bank.

Australia's International Aid Program: 1990-92, AIDAB, 1992.

Australian Overseas Development Corporation: Statistical Summary 1993/94, AIDAB.

Australia's Overseas Aid Program 1995-96, Budget Related Paper No. 2, Canberra.

Daily Commercial News, Croll's Press Clips, 1 February, 1996.

Development Co-operation: 1994 Report & 1995 Report, OECD.

Global Economic Prospects and the Developing Countries 1995, World Bank.

Gounder, R., "Empirical Results of Aid Motivations: Australia's Bilateral Aid Program," World Development, 22(1), 1994.

Human Development Report 1994 & 1995, UNDP.

Official Financing for Developing Countries, IMF, April, 1994.

Statistical Yearbook for Asia and Pacific, UN.

Sustainable Development, Environment and Poverty Nexus, Asian Development Bank, December, 1993.

Sydney Morning Herald, 31 May, 27 June, 4 July 1995; 24 February 1996,

World Development Report 1994, 1995 & 1996, World Bank.

World Resources: 1994-95, Oxford University Press, 1994.

---

1 *Development Co-operation: 1995*, OECD, p. 8.

APPENDIX

Table 1

	New Zealand	Australia	United Kingdom	Canada	France	Germany	United States	Japan
1987	0.26	0.34	0.28	0.47	0.50	0.39	0.20	0.31
1988	0.27	0.46	0.32	0.50	0.72	0.39	0.21	0.32
1989	0.22	0.38	0.31	0.44	0.78	0.41	0.15	0.31
1990	0.23	0.34	0.27	0.44	0.79	0.42	0.21	0.31
1991	0.25	0.38	0.32	0.45	0.62	0.41	0.20	0.32
1992	0.26	0.37	0.31	0.46	0.63	0.39	0.20	0.30
1993	0.25	0.35	0.31	0.45	0.63	0.37	0.16	0.26
1994	0.24	0.35	0.31	0.43	0 64	0.34	0.15	0.29
2005	0.23	0.29	0.34	0.38	0 54	0.30	0.11	0.22

* Data until 1993 refer to the Federal Republic of Germany before unification.

The figure in 1994 refers to the unified Germany.

Sources:

World Bank, World Development Report 1994, Table 18 pp. 196-197.

OECD Development Cooperation Report 1994, Table IV-1 p. 74; Table VI-1 p. 111; & Table 46 p. I1-I2.

OECD Development Cooperation Report 1995, Table IV-1 p. 90; Table VI-1 p. 118.

Figure I-1: Trend in ODA program of selected OECD countries until 2005

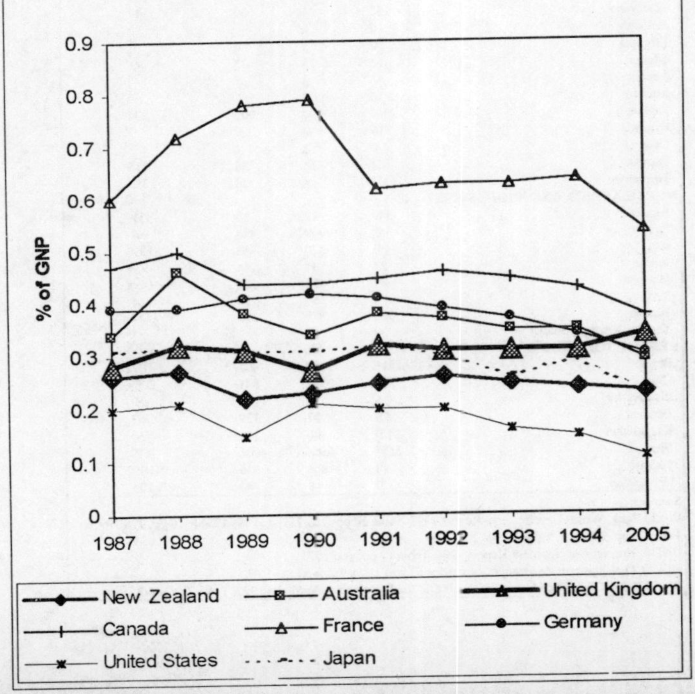

TABLE 2: **Official Development Assistance, Its Uses, and Other Capital Flows To Selected Developing Countries**

Country/Region	Net FDI in the Reporting economy (million $)			Forecast for net FDI (million $)
	1980	1992	1993	2005
(1)	(2)	(3)	(4)	(5)
PAPUA NEW GUINEA	76	400	763	5119
SOUTH PACIFIC				
Indonesia	180	1774	2004	4764
Malaysia	934	4118	4351	7147
Philippines	-106	228	763	7183
Singapore				
Thailand	190	2116	2400	5808
Burma (Myanmar)	0	3	4	4
Indo-China Region				
Laos	0	9		
Vietnam			25	
NORTH ASIA				
China	0	11156	25800	201528
Mongolia	0	6		
SOUTH ASIA				
Bangladesh	0	4	14	134
Bhutan	0	0		
India	79	151	273	1737
Nepal	0	4	6	30
Pakistan	63	275	347	1211
Sri Lanka	43	123	195	1059
INDIAN OCEAN ISLAND STATES				
Mauritius	1	15		
SUB-SAHARAN AFRICA (SSA)				
Indian Ocean SSA Countries				
Kenya	79	6	2	-46
Madagascar	-1	21	30	138
Mozambique	0	25		
Somalia	0	3		
Tanzania	0	0		
Other SSA Countries				
Angola			300	
Botswana	112	61	55	-17
Burundi	0	0		
Ethiopia	0	6	6	6
Ghana	16	23	25	49
Lesotho	5	3		
Malawi	10	0		
Nigeria	-740	897	900	936
Rwanda	16	2		
Uganda	0	3		
Zambia	62	50	55	115
Zimbabwe	2	4	28	316
NORTH AFRICA AND MIDDLE EAST				
Algeria	349	12	15	51
Egypt	548	459	493	901
Iran	0	-170	-50	1390
Jordan	34	41	-34	-934
Morocco	89	424	522	1698
Syria	0	67	70	106
Tunisia	235	379	239	-1441
Yemen (North & South)	34	0		
REST OF THE WORLD				
Brazil	1911	1454	802	-7022
Chile	213	737	841	2089
El Salvador	6	12	16	64
Jamaica	28	87	139	763
Kazakhstan	0	100	150	750
Mexico	2156	5366	4901	-679
Turkey	18	844	636	-1860
Uzbekistan	0	40	45	105

Sources:
World Bank, World Development Report 1992, Table 20 pp. 256-257; and 1994 Table 19 pp. 198-199; Table 21 pp. 202-203; Table 22 pp. 204-205.
UNDP, Human Development Report 1994, Table 19 pp. 166-167.
OECD, Development AssistanceCommittee Report 1994, Table 37 pp. h2-h5.
World Bank, Global Economic Prospects and the Developing Countries 1995, Table 7 pp. 84-85.

Table 3: **Australian ODA by Country at 1993/94 Constant Prices ($'000)**

	TOTAL				
Region/Country	1989/90	1990/91	1991/92	1992/93	1993/94
Papua New Guinea	366,139	346,178	341,951	337,423	338,957
South Pacific	115,606	112,082	119,082	120,345	125,568
ASEAN	234,854	238,554	238,384	268,209	248,964
South-East Asia	282,550	280,107	284,757	342,860	359,460
North Asia	46,263	41,864	60,648	77,436	87,578
South Asia	95,661	85,672	72,932	63,022	69,859
Indian Ocean Island States	10,865	8,385	8,883	8,381	6,586
Indian Ocean SSA Countries	27,855	20,174	21,819	38,965	28,523
SSA Countries	104,539	75,092	97,782	106,219	85,854
North Africa & Middle East	24,802	23,548	21,189	11,582	18,349
Rest of the World	6,821	6,886	3,301	4,545	3,958
Unallocable by country or region (a)	225,871	329,712	353,329	331,872	313,208
Total Official Development Assistance	1,272,401	1,310,611	1,357,822	1,401,643	1,410,815
	Percentage of Total Australian ODA				
Papua New Guinea	28.78	26.41	25.18	24.07	24.03
South Pacific	9.09	8.55	8.77	8.59	8.90
ASEAN	18.46	18.20	17.56	19.14	17.65
South-East Asia	22.21	21.37	20.97	24.46	25.48
North Asia	3.64	3.19	4.47	5.52	6.21
South Asia	7.52	6.54	5.37	4.50	4.95
Indian Ocean Island States	0.85	0.64	0.65	0.60	0.47
Indian Ocean SSA Countries	2.19	1.54	1.61	2.78	2.02
SSA Countries	8.22	5.73	7.20	7.58	6.09
North Africa & Middle East	1.95	1.80	1.56	0.83	1.30
Rest of the World	0.54	0.53	0.24	0.32	0.28
Unallocable by country or region (a)	17.75	25.16	26.02	23.68	22.20

	Forecast (% of Aust. ODA) 2004/5	**Forecast (% of Aust. ODA) 2009/10**
Papua New Guinea	10.30	4.38
South Pacific	8.34	8.17
ASEAN	17.31	16.96
South-East Asia	35.42	40.24
North Asia	14.32	18.06
South Asia	-3.55	-7.14
Indian Ocean Island States	-0.42	-0.83
Indian Ocean SSA Countries	3.20	3.66
SSA Countries	3.83	2.62
North Africa & Middle East	-1.46	-1.63
Rest of the World	-0.54	-0.90
Unallocable by country or region (a)	32.61	36.31

Source: AIDAB, Australian Overseas Development Co-operation: Statistical Summary 1993/94, Table 13 pp. 35-38.

Note:

(a) Includes contributions to multinational organisations, administrative costs and revenue.

15 INTEREST RATES AND INFLATION IN SOUTH AFRICA, 1970-1996

D J J BOTHA

Monetary theory, said Sir John Hicks, is less abstract than most economic theory. Monetary theory "cannot avoid a relation to reality, which in other economic theory is sometimes missing." These were his words when he delivered the Edward Shann Lecture here in Perth in 1967. It has been reprinted as Chapter 9 of his *Critical Essays in Monetary Theory*. The best work on money, he continued, had been done in relation to problems of the day. Monetary theory arose out of monetary disturbances, and he quoted as examples the many new ideas in the two great works of the century, Keynes's *Treatise* of 1930 and his masterpiece, the *General Theory*, six years later. What Hicks was in effect saying was that monetary theory ought always to be seen against the background of reality. It cannot hang in the air. David Hume argued in 1752 that in the long run it did not matter how small or large the money supply was; prices would adapt to it over time, when the situation would return to normal, with prices proportionately higher or lower depending on the nature of the change in the money supply. In 1848 J.S. Mill dismissed money as an "insignificant thing" except when it went wrong. Mill no doubt had in mind events such as the Bank Restriction of 1797 and the series of bank crises after the restoration of the gold standard in 1821 as examples of "money gone wrong" - all minor disturbances compared to what was to follow in the present century.

One is reminded of these classic views on money when one ventures to write about recent monetary policy in South Africa over the past quarter of a century. It was the most difficult period in the monetary history of the country. The monetary system was subjected to so many stresses that many of the policies adopted could be seen as crisis measures. This was especially true during the 1980s and beyond. The Nationalist government was on its last legs, sanctions were applied in earnest by a growing number of countries in the world, with dire consequences for real investment, international trade and the value of the currency, the Rand. We shall not describe the intricate details of these harrowing times[1], and after a brief background sketch, we shall focus rather narrowly on the policies which the central bank adopted over the years to combat the persistent inflation from which the country had been suffering for a long time. It could be said that inflation had become endemic in the country. Since 1974 the increases in the general price level exceeded 10 per cent, reaching an average of around 15 per cent for many years until the past two years, when it fell to below 10 per cent. When it approached that level - which was still unacceptably high by current international standards - satisfaction was expressed by many, including the central bank who regarded this as proof that its interest rate policy of some 16 years' standing was at last showing some signs that it was working! The past three decades conveniently coincided with the tenures of three successive Governors of the Bank - the South African Reserve Bank - and therefore also of their respective policies.[2] Briefly stated, the decade of the 1970s, the years of Governor de Jongh, was one of credit ceilings and other controls; the 1980s, of Governor de Kock, was the opposite, viz. the adoption of the philosophy of free markets under the lowering skies of world-wide sanctions and years of an impossibly complex political situation; the 1990s, under Governor Stals, saw the end of the apartheid era and the end to sanctions[3], but also the persistence of legacies of the past in the

---

I wish to thank Reneé Koekemoer, Department of Economics, University of Pretoria, for kindly collecting the statistics and drawing the graphs attached to the paper.

1 The Reserve Bank recently published a two-volume chronicle of events - in a limited edition - by Dr R.M. Gidlow, the first covering the era of the seventies, the second that of the eighties (see below). The best short reference is a highly informative and well-written paper by D.W. Goedhuys, "South African monetary policy in the 1980s: Years of reform and foreign financial aggression," in *The South African Economy in the 1980s*, Stuart Jones and Jon Inggs (eds.), special issue of *The South African Journal of Economic History*, September, 1994. Dr Goedhuys acted as adviser to the Governor of the Bank through most of the 1980s.

2 As in many other countries, monetary policy in South Africa revolves around the central bank, the Treasury and the money and capital markets. The central bank - the South African Reserve Bank - was established in 1921 as a public company with its shares quoted on the Johannesburg Stock Exchange. The government by law is the major shareholder. It also appoints the Governor. Money market institutions - discount houses and merchant banks - were first established in the mid-fifties on a modest scale. Monetary policy was limited to discount policies and minimum cash reserve requirements. Open market operations were first used as a viable instrument of monetary control in September,1973.

3 When Stals assumed office in 1989, however, he had to contend with the full blast of the world-wide antangonism against the apartheid system which by then had reached its peak. After the general election of 1994 he experienced the

form especially of inflation and problems around the balance of payments. The eras of de Kock and Stals provide remarkable examples of how politically conditioned - very closely politically conditioned - monetary policy can become. Monetary policy cannot escape the framework provided by those who wield political power. They, in turn, can - for good or bad - introduce policies that leave their mark on processes in the real sphere which inevitably and in a variety of ways affect the demand for or the supply of money in the system. This is how monetary policy, as Sir John Hicks has said, is inevitably rooted in reality.

As a brief background within the context of the limited objective of the present paper we shall say something about (1) controls over bank credit in the 1970s, and (2) the role of Bank Rate since the establishment of the South African Reserve Bank in 1921. This is followed by a critical discussion of the use of interest rates as an instrument of monetary policy by the Reserve Bank in recent times.

CREDIT CONTROL

In the period before 1980 monetary policy was characterised by an array of measures of direct control such as variable (often too high) liquid assets and cash reserve requirements, ceilings on bank credit, deposit rate control, exchange control and direct consumer credit controls.[1] The period of the mid-1960s to the early 1980s was one in which monetary policy was essentially based on a control over liquid assets. The various control measures meant that the market could not function properly. The Bank shied away from the use of interest rates as being too sensitive politically, interest being an important item of cost in the mortgage payments of home-owners and farmers, and interest charges on hire-purchase finance. A manipulation of interest rates as part of monetary policy was seen as being in the final analysis a burden on the common man, and the voter. This remains an important consideration, to which we shall return below.

Direct controls, as we know, can often be circumvented. This is what happened during the seventies. When borrowing from the banks was made difficult by the authorities, firms developed the practice of borrowing from one another, which meant that a sizeable volume of transactions could not be recorded in the monetary statistics. During

---

overall change in the political climate. But this had little noticeable effect on the economic situation in the country.

[1] This period is discussed in full by R.M. Gidlow, *South African Reserve Bank Monetary Policies under Dr T.W. de Jongh, 1967-1980*. Pretoria, South African Reserve Bank, 1995. Hereafter referred to as Gidlow, Vol. I.

the 1980s the controls were relaxed in favour of a cash reserve system that operated through open market operations and discounting at the central bank at Bank rate.

Until 1983 the issue of government bonds was done in unco-ordinated fashion by the Treasury, without reference to the current objectives and requirements of the monetary policy of the Reserve Bank. After 1983 the issue of government bonds was administered by the Reserve Bank, compatible with the aims of the open market policies of the Bank.

Another harassing regulation that became increasingly unacceptable during the 1980s concerned the so-called "captive capital market." Under the Bank Act of 1972 the government, in order to widen the market in government stock, decreed that institutional investors - mainly banks, insurance companies, pension funds - invest 10 per cent of their long term liabilities in prescribed investments, at least one-half of which was to be government stock of unexpired maturity of longer than three years. This took a substantial slice out of the market. But the funds invested in this way were not unaffected by current market trends. When bond yields were rising, the price of captive bonds fell below par, weakening the market valuation of investment portfolios; and when yields were falling, bond values rose, which did little to encourage institutions to invest in government paper. These regulations were abolished as late as the beginning of 1989.[1]

THE CHANGING ROLE OF BANK RATE

Since the establishment of the Reserve Bank in 1921 the role of Bank rate went through a number of phases. The Currency and Banking Act of 1920 limited the use of Bank rate to the discount of highly liquid short term trade bills, which did not allow the Bank much room to manoeuvre in an undeveloped money market. Very early on the Bank strove to encourage the use of trade and other bills and managed to persuade the banks to accept Bank rate as the general discount rate and also to "levy their overdraft and deposit rates in approximate accordance with Bank rate."[2]

The next development came in 1944 when the powers of the Bank as lender of last resort and its functions in regard to discount and open market policies were more clearly defined in the Reserve Bank Act of that year. A great stimulus was given to the development of an

---

1 This is described in more detail in Gidlow, Vol.I, pp.70-1, and also by Goedhuys, *op. cit.*, p.153-4.

2 Gidlow, Vol. I, p.48.

active money market through the establishment five years later of the National Finance Corporation. It happened to be the first money market institution in the country. Its function was to accept short term idle funds on deposit for investment in government and first class commercial paper.[1] This was followed in the mid-fifties by the formation of a number of merchant banks and discount houses, so that at the beginning of the sixties a fully fledged money market was in operation. During the decade of the 1960s the discount houses played an important role as an intermediary between the Reserve Bank and the commercial banks when the banks adopted the practice of holding call funds with the discount houses, which obviated the need for them to go the Reserve Bank for accommodation in times of a liquidity shortage. During this period the Bank rate showed very few changes, ranging between 5 and 6.5 per cent, done in steps of half a per cent at a time.

This system came to an end in September, 1973. Bank rate lost its pivotal role in the money market when it was ruled that in future discount houses could rediscount Treasury bills without limit at a rate of 0.5 per cent above the latest Treasury bill tender rate. Gidlow gives three reasons for this decision. First, it was felt that the asset portfolios of discount houses should reflect more closely the changes in the liquidity position in respect of call funds in the market. Under the previous arrangement they could maintain their portfolios through rediscounting at the discount window of the Reserve Bank. Second, by relating discount rates to the tender rate, the cost of central bank assistance would be more closely related to market rates. Third, it was hoped that under the new system the Treasury bill would be reinstated as the pivotal money market instrument.[2]

This was a rather novel decision in an era of controls, for under the new arrangement the "penal rate" system was done away with, and the Bank lost control over the cost of rediscounting paper at the discount window. The history of the ensuing period was one of an upward pressure on market rates, described as resulting from a "ratchet effect" in the market. When market rates were lower than the Reserve Bank rediscount rate, houses that had rediscounted paper with the Bank tended to sell paper in the market in order to buy back their paper from the Bank. The overall effect was an upward pressure on market rates. Conversely, when market rates were higher than the rediscount rate of the Bank, discount houses tended to buy paper at lower rates in the

---

1 The NFC was established under Act of Parliament, with 10 per cent of its capital held by the Reserve Bank and the rest by the private sector.

2 Gidlow, Vol.I, p.51.

market for sale at higher prices at the Bank. The overall effect again was an upward pressure on market rates.

This arrangement was abandoned in December, 1983. The Bank hoped to regain its influence over interest rates as part of overall monetary policy by quoting "a fixed, adjustable and differentiated set of rediscount rates for Treasury bills, Land Bank bills and bankers' acceptances" [1] that was higher for banks than for discount houses. It reintroduced Bank rate only in August, 1985, however, as the basic rediscount rate in the market, and in February, 1989, the privileged position of discount houses was brought to an end when uniform rediscount rates were quoted for all parties in the market.

The decade of the 1980s, as mentioned above, was characterised by the adoption of more or less completely opposite policy approaches to those of the 1970s. The quantitative-control approach of Governor de Jong made way for the free market approach of Governor de Kock. This was in line with international thinking, and it was hoped that by allowing markets to reflect true values, an indirect policy through qualitative credit control via interest rates would steady the increases in prices and the money supply. The result was that the rate of interest was subjected to a manipulation by the Bank as never before. Between 9th March, 1988, and 11th October, 1989, bank rate was raised seven times by 8.5 per cent to 18 per cent, with prime rate increasing to 21 per cent. The most common and persistent argument advanced by the Reserve Bank for this state of affairs has been that this was necessary in the fight against inflation. We now turn to this aspect in some more detail.

INTEREST RATES AND INFLATION

The rate of interest is one of the most complex of monetary instruments. The effects of, say, a rise in rates is not the same at all times, under all circumstances and in all countries. This has been well shown by empirical investigations over many years, e.g. the Oxford Study Group before the War, the investigations of the Radcliffe Committee in 1959 and later similar but more extensive research by the Porter Commission in Canada in 1964. This has shown the danger of generalising when assessing the effect of a change in the rate of interest on the economic process. It would appear that these findings have had no influence on economic theorising and model building, in so far as the rate of interest is almost always regarded as an important factor of

---

1 R.M. Gidlow, *South African Reserve Bank Monetary Policies under Dr Gerhard de Kock, 1981-1989*. Pretoria, South African Reserve Bank, 1995, p.73.

cost, leading to a high interest elasticity of the demand for credit. That need not, of course, be true.

Another aspect that has been lost sight of is the fact that the role of the rate of interest in the G7 countries is different in some important respects from what it is in the less-developed world. If the Bundesbank should increase German rates by one-half per cent, it could be expected that money would flow to Germany almost immediately. The same is true if this should happen in London, Paris, New York, Montreal or Tokyo. One-half of a per cent would attract funds from elsewhere. If a less-developed country should increase its rates by 1 or even 2 per cent, nothing may happen. Or there may be a slight inflow of speculative funds, depending on the country in which this happens.

In South Africa very much is expected of the rate of interest. It is supposed to attract funds from abroad after a rise, with beneficial effects on the state of the reserves and the balance of payments. It is also supposed to counteract the huge outflow of funds, a fact that has had nothing to do with the level of the rate of interest. But most of all, it has been used over the past sixteen years as the major instrument in the fight against inflation. The argument has been the same consistently over the years, viz. a rise in the rate of interest is firmly believed to dampen the demand for credit, reduce the increase in the money supply and bring down the increase in prices. Over the sixteen years nothing of the kind, however, has happened. Prices and the money supply have kept on increasing regardless of the level of interest rates.

Statistics over the years have regularly shown two disastrous trends in the economy, viz.

(a) Credit creation in the banking system traces out a monotonically, an almost exponentially increasing curve, one that is very obviously quite unrelated to what happens to the rate of interest. This is clear from *Graph I*. There was no stopping the increases in the credit extended by the private sector since the beginning of the 1980s.

(b) The productivity figures for South Africa, as shown in *Table I* are so ominously low as to jeopardise the chances of the country ever becoming competitive in international markets. The authorities have attempted to overcome this by resorting to a devaluation of the currency, with disastrous effects on the general price level in a country with a high propensity to import. Here lies the greatest single cause of the inflation. It has nothing to do with the level of the rate of interest.

Table 1: **Unit Labour Costs in Manufacturing (National Currencies, Base 1970)**

	USA	Japan	Germany	UK	Taiwain	South Africa
1980	194	202	176	425	271	272
1990	238	199	229	632	423	568
1993	246	219	263	700	461	1701
Output/Employee*	184	249	158	201	288	120
CPI*	372	308	238	759	405	1546

* = 1993 only

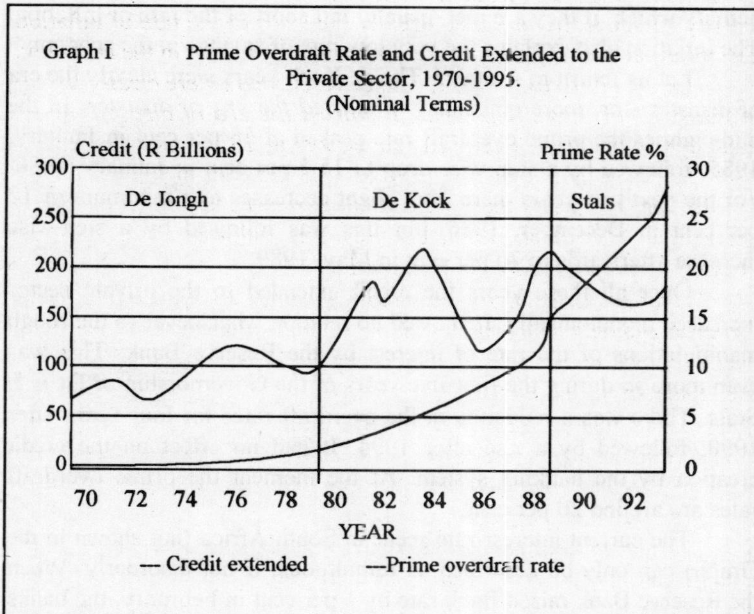

The monetary authorities over the years have consistently refrained from drawing the logical conclusion from these two trends. Had they done so, they would have realised that under South African conditions the rate of interest can in no way do what is expected of it. There is no known case in monetary history where such heavy reliance was placed on the rate of interest as the major weapon in the fight against a prolonged and persistent inflation. In South Africa it was done in the belief that the demand for credit was highly interest-elastic, a situation which the statistics show as clearly non-existent. Over the years it has had dire consequences for the economy.

The figures for inflation reveal the extent of the monetary problem. Taking 1970 as base year, the consumer price index for 1996 so far stands at 1913.98. With 1990 as base year, it is now 178.00. Put differently, in less than six years the price level has increased by 78 per cent on the base year 1990. A sum of R100 in 1970 was worth R5.24 in 1996; and a sum of R100 in 1990 only R56.18 in 1996. The inflation is continuing on its course despite a reduction in its rate of increase. This explains the continual requests and demands for increases in wages and salaries from virtually every sector of economic activity which, if they are met, usually fall short of the rate of inflation. The inflation also explains the very low rate of savings in the economy.

Let us return to *Graph I*. The de Kock years were clearly the era of disaster - or, more ominously, *it started the era of disaster*. In the mid-eighties the prime overdraft rate peaked at 25 per cent in January, 1985, followed by a step-wise drop to 15.5 per cent in January, 1986. For the next two years there were slight decreases to a minimum of 12 per cent in December, 1986, but this was followed by a step-wise increase afterwards to 20 per cent in May, 1989.

Over all these years the credit extended to the private sector increased monotonically. It showed no relation whatsoever to the rough manipulations of the rate of interest by the Reserve Bank. This was even more so during the first five years of the Governorship of Dr C.J. Stals. There was a reduction in the overdraft rates for four years after 1990, followed by a rise after 1994. It had no effect on the credit creation by the banking system. At the moment the prime overdraft rates are around 20 per cent.

The current interest-rate scene in South Africa (not shown in the Graph) can only be described as tumultuous, if not disorderly. When the Reserve Bank raised Bank rate by 1 per cent in February, the banks raised prime rates to 20 per cent, followed some days later by a sudden announcement from all the banks that they were raising prime rate by another 1 per cent. It was done without the knowledge of the Reserve Bank. This suspicious move caused questions to be raised by the Competition Board and in letters to the press. The banks quickly assured the public that this unilateral decision was reached quite independently, and denied any allegations of collusion. The matter is now regarded as closed. Since then one bank broke ranks and lowered its prime rate by 1 per cent. It is not clear at the time of writing whether others would follow suit.

Graph II Prime Overdraft Rate and Credit Extended to the Private Sector, 1970-1995. (Real Terms, Base Year 1970)

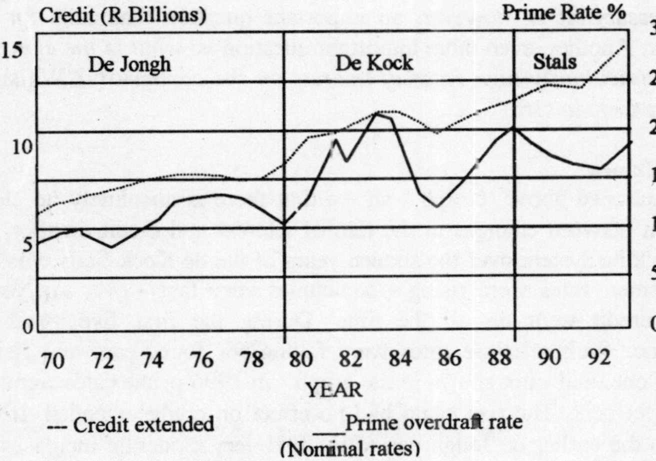

Graph III Prime Overdraft Rate and Credit Extended to the Private Sector, 1970-1995. (Real Terms, Base Year 1970)

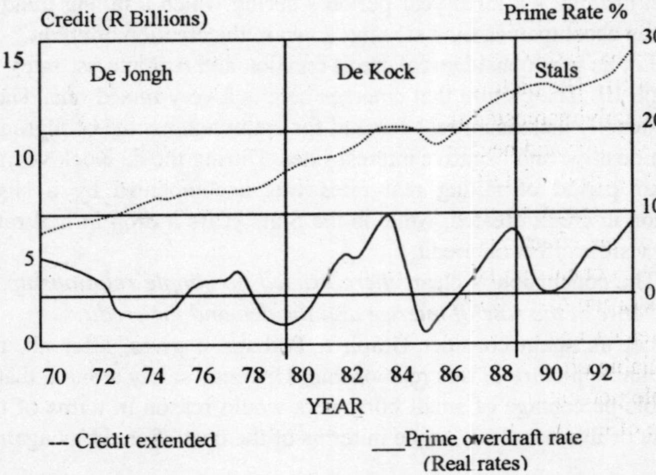

TWO IMPORTANT QUESTIONS

The figures discussed so far are all in nominal terms. Advocates of the present interest rate policy point out that this is misleading, that a different picture would emerge if real values were calculated. No one has apparently done it so far. To those who put their faith totally in the policy of high interest rates such a calculation would perhaps appear unnecessary. It is, however, an important question that calls for an answer. Another, even more important question is: *what is the effect of these ridiculously high rates of interest on the community?* We shall discuss them in turn.

Real Values

As mentioned above, Graph I shows that there is absolutely no close relation between changes in the rate of interest and credit creation by the banking system over the sixteen years of the de Kock-Stals eras. In the former, rates were rising - sometimes very fast - over six years while credit went up all the time. During the first five years of Governor Stals's tenure rates were falling for four years and rising during one, and - not shown in the graph - in 1996 prime rates went up to 20 per cent. The rise again had no effect on credit extended. If we turn to the earlier de Jongh period we find very moderate increases in the prime rate and equally moderate increases in the creation of credit.

Again, critics argue that the demand for credit in real terms would show a different picture. Graph II plots the real values of credit against the nominal rate of interest. In this graph the basic trends of the previous one reappear. We again find that periods of rising interest rates are accompanied by rising credit creation. In Graph II there was even an instance - a three-year period - during which a falling trend in rates was accompanied by a slowing down in the creation of credit.

Let us next consider real credit creation and real interest rates, as in Graph III. The picture that emerges here is a very mixed one. There was a steadily increasing real demand for credit against the background of both positive and negative interest rates. During the de Kock years a two-year period of falling real rates was accompanied by a slight reduction in credit created, while in the Stals years a drop in real rates had no visible effect on credit.

The conclusion is clear: *there existed no simple relationship, if at all, between the rate of interest and the demand for credit.*

Let us again consider Graph I. Perhaps it gives, after all, the most reliable picture of this relationship. One may safely assume that a negligible percentage of small borrowers would reason in terms of the real rate of interest. They argue in terms of the cost of credit as against the prospect of investing it profitably. Given favourable expectations the cost of credit assumes lesser importance. Further, the higher prices rise, the lower becomes the real rate. But this should not affect the investor unduly, for the price of his output would rise in concert with the general rise in prices. It could affect savings if, that is to say, savers happen to reason in terms of real values. The banks at the time, however, could provide in the increased demand.

Effect on the Community

A policy of high interest rates such as that which the Reserve Bank has been pursuing over some sixteen years has had the effect of shifting the burden on to the common man. The old argument that higher rates would curb investment demand has proved over and over again to have been a myth. Higher rates have not reduced investment demand, they have not attracted real investment under the conditions of uncertainty over this extended period, and they have not had the slightest effect on the pressure of inflation. The only sure effect of higher rates is on the common man. Higher rates bring him hardship in the form of a sudden increase in his mortgage payments - for housing and agriculture - and in the rates paid on hire-purchase contracts. Higher rates also increase the cost of servicing the national debt, a charge which is largely also paid by the individual. Large firms holding a dominating position in the market are not really affected by higher rates since these can often be passed on to the consumer in the form of higher prices. In this respect an anti-inflationary policy of high interest rates is fully counter-productive in so far as it constitutes an important force for further aggravating the situation.

There is only one party that stands to gain from this kind of policy. It is all those institutions that are in the business of advancing credit to the community. They suddenly earn more on funds advanced to borrowers. In South Africa at the present time the community owes the institutions R35 billions in mortgages on houses and apartments. An increase of 1 per cent in the rate of interest means that a sum of R350 millions in purchasing power per year is transferred to the institutions. Put differently, it represents a transfer of wealth from the poorer to the richer sections of the community.

The Reserve Bank has never shown a sensitivity for the socio-economic effects of its policies. The many hardships regularly reported in the public press after every increase in the rates have always left it unmoved. Criticism was always welcome, but invariably ignored. A unique exception to the rule occurred recently when the trade union Cosatu raised its voice against rumours of an impending further increase in rates after a similar increase some weeks before. It was the first time that organised labour has taken such a direct interest in monetary policy. An implicit threat of mass action managed to do what the logic of argument failed to do.

16 Governance of Marine Fisheries in the Development of Indian Ocean Countries

Nokome Bentley and Christine Halais

The Governance of Marine Fisheries: A Collective Concern

The countries bordering the Indian Ocean are varied, with different cultures, levels of economic development and forms of government. The one aspect they have in common is their connection with the same sea. For these nations the Indian Ocean is a vital source of food, income and cultural identity; the conduit for the transfer of these resources from the sea to the people is fishing. Not only do fisheries provide a source of food and income, they also generate a focus upon which cultural identity is often based.

The sea is a dynamic system within which biological material is constantly flowing; events in a discrete area of the ocean may have an effect on distant fisheries. The Indian Ocean differs from other seas with respect to marine productivity and requires specific solutions for fisheries management. It is therefore pertinent for countries of the Indian Ocean rim to arrive at an integrated policy as to the optimum management of their fisheries.

The current paper examines the patterns in marine fisheries in the Indian Ocean and the role of good governance in ensuring that they remain sustainable. Trends in marine fisheries production are analysed and their importance in development are discussed. Several examples of Indian Ocean marine fisheries are used to illustrate some of the potential threats to the sustainable management of these resources. The role of government in mitigating these threats is discussed and predictions are made for the future role of fisheries in the development of Indian Ocean countries.

A Desert Sea: The Indian Ocean in a Global Context

On the global scale, Indian Ocean fisheries are small, representing less than 9% of the world's total marine catch (*Table 1*), although more than 30% of the world's population lives in the countries which surround it. Furthermore, the Indian Ocean's catch is low in relation to its area, based upon which we might expect it to produce up to 17% of the world catch. Only the Atlantic produces a proportion of the world's catch equal to its relative size. The Indian and Southern ocean have lower catches and the Pacific greater catches than would be expected given a homogeneous distribution of fish and fishing effort over the world's oceans (*Table 1*).

Table 1: **Contribution of the major ocean basins to total marine fisheries catch in 1993, compared to their relative size**

Ocean	% Total Catch	% Ocean Area
Pacific	63.6	46.6
Atlantic	27.7	27.0
Indian	8.6	16.6
Southern	0.1	9.8

Source: FAO, 1994

The discrepancies between ocean area and size of catch may be explained in terms of the distribution of phytoplankton. These microscopic plants are the basis of oceanic food chains and are an important determinant of overall oceanic productivity. They are the primary source of production, which moves up through the food chain to fish and eventually humans. Areas of greater phytoplankton densities may be expected to support a greater fish population and therefore a greater fisheries catch.

Extensive areas of high phytoplankton concentrations occur in the northern parts of the Atlantic and Pacific oceans where there is strong tidal mixing, which upwells deeper nutrient rich waters and encourages phytoplankton growth. A similar situation exists off Argentina and the Faulkland Islands. Coastlines on the eastern edge of the northern and southern Atlantic and Pacific oceans experience upwelling events which also produce localised areas of intense oceanic production (*Figure 1*). The Indian Ocean is the exception in not having an upwelling on its eastern edge. This is due to the vagaries of ocean currents off Australia. The only major upwelling that occurs in the Indian Ocean is off Oman; this event is highly seasonal, only lasting for a couple of months in summer.

Another source of nutrient input into oceans is from terrestrial runoff which can produce localised areas of high production adjacent to river mouths. The Indian Ocean has such areas, adjacent to the humid areas of South-East Asia and the Indian subcontinent, at the mouths of the Indus, Irrawady and Ganges rivers (*Figure 1*). For the remainder of the Indian Ocean the surrounding land has low rainfall and river run off is minimal. Adjacent to much of Africa and Australia there is little river runoff and the seas mirror the lands in their relatively low biological productivity.

There is a strong positive correlation between phytoplankton densities and both current catches and FAO estimates of potential sustainable yields (FAO, 1982). The areas of greatest fisheries production are in the northern Atlantic and northern and south east Pacific, all areas of high phytoplankton densities. Although the western and eastern Indian ocean are large compared to other FAO statistical areas, current catches are small and close to or above estimated maxima, suggesting little potential for further expansion. As a consequence of its depauperate nature, the Indian Ocean is only able to sustain a lower fisheries production than other regions; this emphasises the need for good governance in exploitation of its limited resources.

LOCALISATION OF MARINE PRODUCTIVITY WITHIN THE INDIAN OCEAN

A correlation between phytoplankton density and fisheries production is also observed within the Indian Ocean. Most of the catch is taken in the north off Pakistan, India, Bangladesh, Myanmar, Thailand, Malaysia and Indonesia. (*Table 2*).

Table 2: **Marine fisheries catch (metric tonnes) by Indian Ocean Countries* in 1993**

LIFDC		**Developing**	
India	2486807	Thailand	712308
Indonesia	509280	Myanmar	625250
Pakistan	499159	Malaysia	394310
Bangladesh	312715	Iran	247000
Sri Lanka	202900	Oman	116472
Maldives	90012	Mauritius	21082
Yemen	85911	Seychelles	7000
Madagascar	85029	Reunion	2730
Tanzania	45000	French Sth. Tr.	500
Mozambique	25506		
Somalia	14600		
Kenya	4808	**Foreign**	
Comoros	7000	Spain	111353
		France	89974
Industrialised		Japan	60289
Australia	110672	Korea Rep	29879
South Africa	555	Former USSR	12384

Source: FAOSTAT data base, September 1996

*Note: Catch data are for the FAO definition of the Indian Ocean which includes only part of the South African coast (east of 30 degrees longitude). Country grouping according to FAO categories; LIFDC=low-income, food-deficit countries.

In contrast, fisheries production in the southwestern Indian Ocean is extremely low. The combined catch of Mozambique, Kenya, Tanzania, Somalia, Madagascar, the Comoros, Reunion, Mauritius and the Seychelles is less than any single of the aforementioned countries in the north.

Although this pattern has been consistent, the relative catches by each country have changed since the early 1970s. In particular, Indonesia and Thailand have increased their proportion of total production (*Figure 2*). The rapid expansion of the catch of these two countries, possibly due to increased technological sophistication of fishing methods utilised by them, is largely responsible for the decline in dominance by India.

About sixty percent of the catch has been taken by low-income, food-deficit countries, as defined by the FAO (*Table 2*). Countries from outside the Indian Ocean rim are taking an increasing proportion of the catch and nearly twice as much as that of the local industrialised nations.

Marine Fisheries as a Source of Food

Traditionally, fish and other seafood have been used almost exclusively for human consumption in the areas in which they were caught. These foods make important dietary contributions in terms of sulphur-containing amino acids, calcium, iron and zinc, nutrients which are often limiting growth.

Within the Indian Ocean, many people are dependent on fish as their main source of animal protein. The Maldives and the Seychelles have the first and third highest rates of fish consumption in the world. In numerous other countries, including the Comoros, Indonesia, Malaysia, Mauritius, Sri Lanka and Thailand, fish and seafood represent 10% of the animal protein consumed (*Table 3*). In large countries such as India, the coastal population also depends upon fish as its primary source of animal protein, although this is not evident from country-wide data which include a proportionally greater inland population.

Table 3 **Total animal protein consumption and the percentage provided by fish and other seafood in Indian Ocean countries in 1994**

Country	Animal protein consumption (g/person/day)	Fish and other Seafood (as % animal protein in diet)
Australia	102.4	4.3
Reunion	99.8	7.9
Maldives	83.8	51.7
Mauritius	81.5	10.3
Iran	77.2	1.5
Seychelles	76.9	26.2
World Average	72.5	6.5
South Africa	69.9	1.9
Myanmar	67.1	5.8
Malaysia	64.1	11.1
Indonesia	60.1	9.6
Pakistan	59.9	1.1
India	57.7	2.0
Yemen	56.8	3.6
Kenya	54.5	3.0
Thailand	53.0	14.6
Somalia	51.0	0.8
Madagascar	48.6	4.6
Tanzania	48.1	7.1
Sri Lanka	46.4	11.1
Bangladesh	41.7	6.1
Comoros	38.3	11.2
Mozambique	31.3	2.2

Source: FAOSTAT data base, September 1996

Trends in the consumption of fish in four Indian Ocean countries, Thailand, Malaysia, India and Pakistan are illustrated in *Figure 5*. These countries have been chosen because they have amongst the highest catches in the region and exhibit different patterns in growth of the fisheries sector and use of its catch. In general there has been no increase in the volume of fisheries export from these four countries. This has meant that as fisheries production has increased, domestic supply has also increased. An exception is Malaysia which has experienced a levelling of domestic supply due to a decrease in catches, and despite a net import of fisheries product (Figure 4). Malaysia is one of the few nations in the region in which catches have decreased.

Although there has been an increase in domestic supply, this has not always resulted in an increased supply of fish as food. In Thailand

and Pakistan, a large percentage of fisheries products was used as animal feed in the 1980s. (*Figure 6*). The increase in use of fish as animal feed may have contributed to the levelling off of fish consumption, as observed in these countries (*Figure 6*). In the early 1990s, the percentage of domestic supply used as feed decreased in both Thailand and Pakistan and there was a concomittent increase in consumption by humans. In contrast, since the late 1970s, Malaysia has seen a decrease in fish consumption which may reflect changes in consumer preferences.

Governance Options for Indian Ocean Fisheries

Fish stocks are a renewable resource which require effective management to ensure that they are exploited sustainably. This management, whether implemented by local communities or a central body, can be considered as a form of governance over exploitation. As with other types of governance, a range of factors will determine the most appropriate structure and scale for the management regime. The recent history of three Indian Ocean fisheries illustrate some of these factors.

Southern Bluefin Tuna: The Importance of Spatial Scale

The southern bluefin tuna is a large and valuable species which is highly sought after for its high grade sashimi flesh. Adults spawn off the south coast of Indonesia and the young move progressively southwards into the southern Indian Ocean and from there into the Atlantic and Pacific. In the 1970s and 80s, young tuna were caught off southern Australia for canning and large catches of a low value product were made. This combined with catches by Japanese vessels of the larger, more valuable individuals in the southern Pacific, Indian and Atlantic oceans lead to a decline in the global population.

The case of the southern bluefin tuna highlights the importance of considering the spatial scale of the population in determining the most appropriate form of governance. Highly migratory species require regional cooperation in research and management. In some cases it may be appropriate to extend this approach to integrated management. However, not all fish stocks are widely distributed. Those which have limited dispersal may be best managed at the local level. In these cases, local knowledge of the population dynamics of the exploited species may be valuable in management (Tisdell and Roy, 1998).

Persian Gulf Oil Spill: The Impact of Pollution on Food Production
Marine fisheries can be severely effected by development occurring in the adjacent terrestrial environment. The Persian Gulf oil spill of January 1991, was one of the largest oil spills in history (Goldberg 1991) . In the following year, landings of shrimp (Penaeus spp) in Saudi Arabia fell markedly, from about 4000 t in 1989 to about 25 t in 1992. There was an equally dramatic decline in an index of abundance used by fisheries scientists to monitor the population, from 205 in 1990 to about 1.5 in 1992. The biomass of spawning adults is estimated to have dropped to about 1.8% of the pre-Gulf War level (Shotton 1995). While the reason for these marked reductions in the shrimp population is not certain it appears that the oil spill smothered the important inshore nursery areas of the shrimp.

The spectre of marine pollution has been emphasised by conservationists groups for some time; so much so that we may have become complacent. However, as illustrated by the Persian Gulf oil spill, pollution can have serious effects on marine ecosystems to the extent of impacting on food production. With increases in population in many Indian Ocean countries, particularly in coastal cities, we can expect that the effects of pollution will become of greater importance to marine fisheries. In many places industrial development and the absence of human waste treatment are resulting in increased pollution. For example the Hoogly Estuary in West Bengal, India, is being adversely effected by untreated industrial discharge and this is likely to increase (Shotton 1995). Similar scenarios are likely to occur off coastal megacities such as Bombay, Calcutta and Jakarta, which are progressively expanding. The effects of chronic pollution are unpredictable but could have negative impacts on food production by marine fisheries. Such considerations highlight the need for integration of marine and coastal environmental management (Caddy and Griffiths, 1995).

West Australian Rock Lobster: The Beneficial Effects of Good governance
The fishery for West Australian rock lobster (Panulirus cygnus) is Australia's most valuable single species fishery, worth between A$120 - $200 million per year. Since 1907, catches have remained stable at above 10 000 tonnes. In 1963, it was the first fisheries in the world to implement a limited entry policy. However, a greater effort has had to be used in order to maintain catch levels, indicating a decline in abundance of the population. Although the management history has not

been perfect, the extinguishing of open access has probably saved the fishery from extinction. There has also been an investment in research which has aided significantly in management. In many respects the West Australian rock lobster fishery can be used as a model for others within the Indian Ocean. It is based on low quantities of a high value species and recognises the importance of fishers having property rights over the resource (Berkes, 1994) and the need for regulation to prevent the rapid expansion of fishing effort by people wanting to make quick money without regard to the future.

PROSPECTS FOR THE MARINE FISHERIES OF THE INDIAN OCEAN

The management of marine fisheries in the Indian Ocean must recognise the inherently low productivity of the area and focus on maintaining fisheries as a source of food whilst exploiting low volumes of high value species as a source of income. However, high value export products, such as shark fins, may lead to wastage and over-exploitation and should be closely monitored.

The importance of coral reefs and of mangroves, as nursery areas and habitats for exploitable fish populations, should be fully recognised. Coral reefs and mangroves have been degraded in all countries bordering the Bay of Bengal (Shotton 1995). Destructive fishing practices including blast and cyanide fishing, the use of coral for lime and in-fill of mangroves must be halted. Establishment of property rights over critical areas may arrest the degradation of coral reefs and mangroves by providing effective stewardship.

The scale of management should be matched to that of the fisheries stock. Negotiations currently underway to establish an Indian Ocean Tuna Commission are a step in the right direction. At the other end of the spatial scale, small localised stocks are probably best managed by promoting the public awareness, involvement and empowerment of local communities (Obura *et al*, 1996). Regardless of their form, all governments face the trade off between providing the maximum available resources to ensure the right to nutrition of the current population while at the same time ensuring the same right for future generations.

REFERENCES

Berkes, F. (1994) Property rights and coastal fishers. In: Pomeroy, R. S. (ed) Community management and common property of coastal fisheries in Asia and the Pacific: concepts, methods and experiences. International Center for Living Aquatic Resource Management, Manila. 1994. p 52 - 62.

Caddy, J. F. and Griffiths, R. C. (1995) Living marine resources and their sustainable development: some environmental and institutional perspectives. FAO Fisheries Technical Paper. No. 353. FAO, Rome. 1995. 167 p.

FAO (1982) Atlas of the living resources of the sea. FAO, Rome. 1982

FAO (1994) Yearbook of Fisheries Statistics: Catches and Landings. FAO, Rome. 1994

Goldberg, R. (1991) Marine oil spills. Academy of Natural Sciences. http://www.acnatsci.org/erd/ea/marine_oil.html.

Obura, D., Ilangakoon, A., Jayewardene, H. and Stone, G. (1996). Integrating marine conservation in the Indian Ocean: 1996 and beyond. New England Aquarium, Boston. 1996. 45 p.

Shotton, R. (1995) Western Indian Ocean. Review of the state of world fishery resources: marine fisheries. FAO Fisheries Circular No. 884. FAO, Rome. 1995. 105 p.

Tisdell, C and Roy, K. (1998) Governance, property rights and sustainable resource use: analysis with Indian Ocean Rim examples. Current publication.

Figure 1: Phytoplankton pigment concentrations (PPC, mg/m^3, image courtesy of NASA), 1993 fisheries production (dark circles; FAOSTAT database) and estimated potential yield (light circles; FAO 1982) for FAO statistical areas.

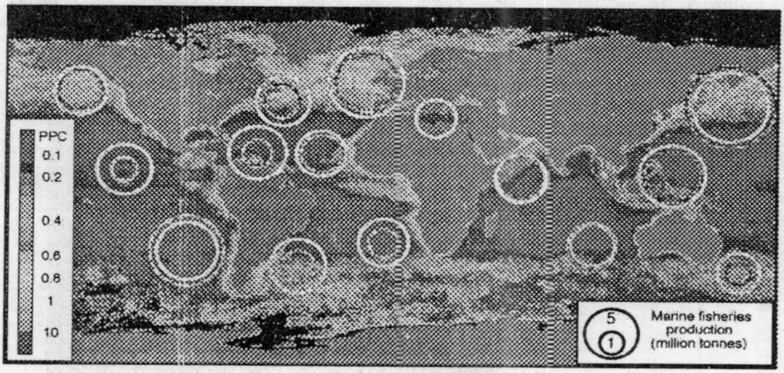

Figure 2: Changes in the proportion of Indian Ocean fisheries catch taken by various countries.

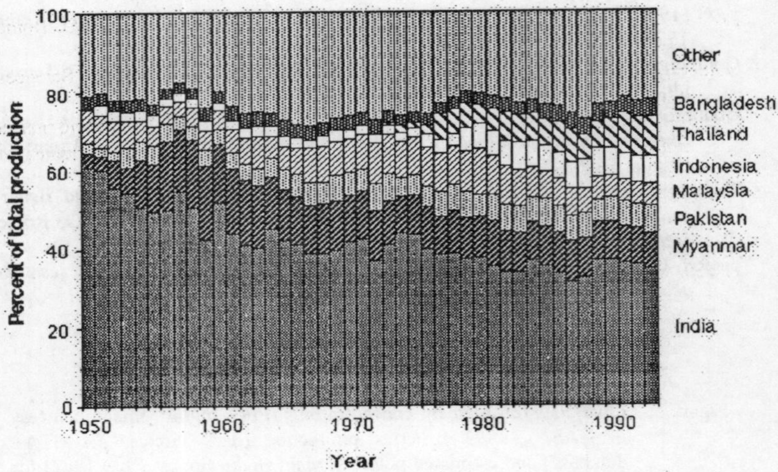

Figure 3: Proportion of fisheries catch taken by low-income food-deficit (LIFDCs), developing foreign and industrialised countries.

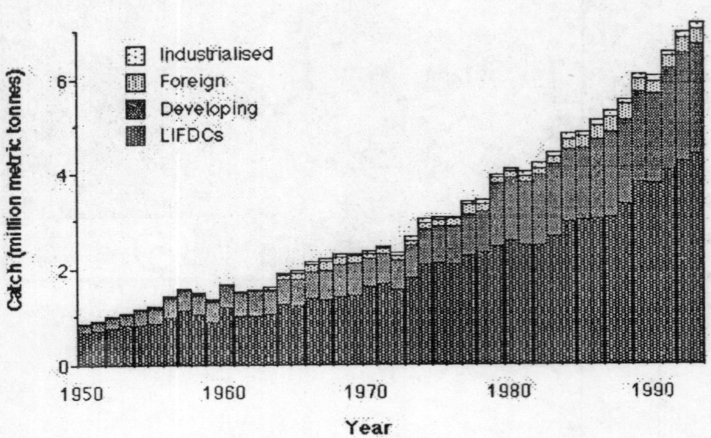

Figure 4: Changes in fisheries production and net international trade for India, Malaysia, Pakistan and Thailand.

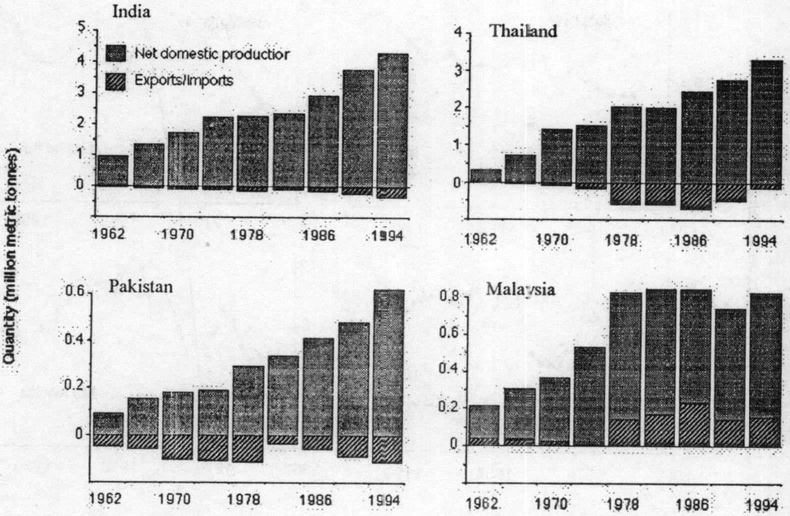

Figure 5: Changes in the use of domestic supply of fisheries products in India, Malaysia, Pakistan and Thailand.

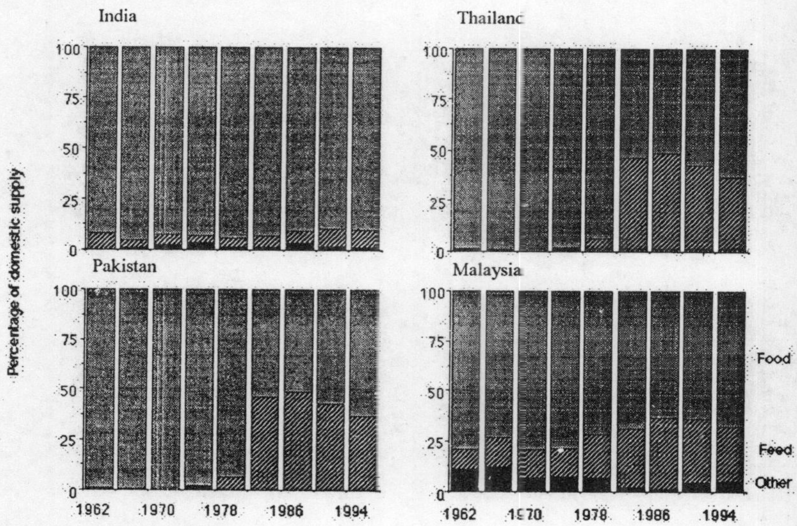

Figure 6: Changes in fish protein consumption in India, Malaysia, Pakistan and Thailand.

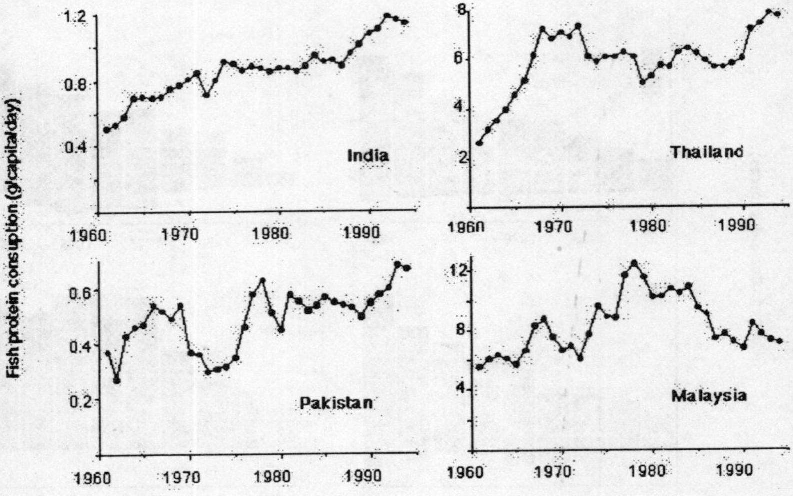

17 A Review of State Intervention, Welfare and Multinational Enterprises in India

Pradeep Ray

Introduction

The debate between market economists and interventionists on normative economics for developing economies is well known. The assertion of the former that the 'invisible hand' is an *efficient* way to clear prices and exchange is refuted by interventionists who maintain that contextual dimensions of a country may not warrant the fate of a country to be left to the realm of the invisible hand. In other words, efficiencies have no relevance, if in the aggregate the economy fails to respond to the *needs* of the poor and caters to the acquisitiveness of capital and *wants* of a few.

In the context of major shifts in global competition in recent times, the question of national development based on foreign direct investment (FDI) vs. local industry has become increasingly relevant. A change from a command type of economy to the more liberal type ushers in major shifts for local industry. The context in this paper is the nation state and the multinational corporation. The object is to synthesise knowledge about effects of multinational companies (MNCs) on local industry reported in extant literature and then associate the same with policy responses of the Indian state. A review of the policy responses of the Indian state and the behaviours of its national enterprises poses a sharp contrast to the pattern of indicative planning and innovation strategies of enterprises in Japan and Korea.

The arguments provided in this review were the views of the scholars cited and are intended to provide a linkage between theories of industrial development and efficiencies of MNCs *vis-à-vis* local enterprises as envisioned in the development and international business literature.

The Theory of Foreign Direct Investment

Since the time Hymer submitted his doctoral dissertation at the MIT in 1960, welfare effects of MNCs has been a topic of fierce debate. According to Lall and Streeten (1980) "it is not uncommon to find different writers accusing each other of 'bias', 'prejudice', 'subjectivity' or even 'extremism' when discussing the welfare effects of TNCs" (1980, p 47). But then, the question that arises here is: do these differences arise out of the fundamental antitheses between the doctrines espoused in classical and alternative theories of economics and society or are they not as contradictory in reality as enumerated in the theoretical abstractions?

The essence of the classical doctrine (in a line of direct descent from physiocrats) is the acceptance of the society in which they lived as a part of nature, and, the assumption of harmony of interest among the various sections of society. In other words there is no conflict, along Marxian lines between those who own means of production and those who do not. Whereas the classics had aimed at finding out how the system works in order to help it work better, Marx aimed at uncovering its contradictions in order to hasten its end through turmoil and revolution (Pasinetti, 1982).

Free trade theorists belonging to the neo-classical school such as Heckscher-Ohlin held that trade arises out of differences in factor endowments. However, the fact is, trade may arise not out of factor differences but on differences in product differentiation, economies of scale and production functions (Dunning, 1981). An area where much of welfare economics breaks down - especially the proposition that competition allocates resources efficiently and that there is a harmony between private profit maximisation and the general interest - is precisely the domain of the MNCs in imperfect markets. The efficacy of oligopolistic decision making of the MNCs refutes the basic presumption that foreign investments raise incomes and social welfare in recipient LDCs unless optimum conditions are distorted by protection, monopoly and externalities (Lall and Streeten, 1980).

The credit for pioneering a modern theory of foreign direct investment goes to Hymer (1960, 1976) who argued that if the world was characterised by the model of free trade the MNE would not exist. In a traditional Heckscher-Ohlin model of free trade, global welfare is maximised by nations producing according to their relative comparative advantage by different factor endowments. In idealised competitive situations no single firm can, by assumption, have access to any sort of special advantage which was not equally available to others. It is therefore a necessary condition of foreign direct investment (FDI) that the investing firm has some monopolistic advantage, not possessed by local companies. Hymer (1976, p 48) mentions both aspects of structural market failure as in Bain, and, cognitive failure as in Coasian economies of information and knowledge advantages that occur under vertical integration, the latter aspect dealt in extenso in Caves (1971) and the Internalisation Theory (Buckley and Casson 1976, Rugman 1975, 1981). On holistic lines, the eclectic paradigm of international production as a combination of ownership, locational and internalisation (OLI) advantages of FDI was provided by Dunning (1974, 1988, 1998).

The theory of foreign direct investment is thus a converse of the pure theory of international trade (Rugman,1981). The country specific advantage of a nation which leads to trade is replaced by a *firm specific* advantage internal to the MNE which leads to FDI. Its effect on market structure may be to induce a very high degree of oligopolistic concentration so as to impose the cost of diminished price competition, excessive product differentiation and so on (Lall and Streeten, 1980).

MNCs were seen, by Marxists among others, as entities which siphoned off wealth from poorer nations in favour of the rich. Hymer demonstrated that the multinational corporation's desire to *control* foreign operations was the central motive for direct investment and "is desired in order to remove competition between that foreign enterprise and enterprises in other countries."(Hymer, 1960, p25).

Historical underpinnings of international trade is suggestive of a pattern of exploitation by rich nations in the Marxist perspective. With its origins in the late fifteenth and early sixteenth centuries capitalism evolved under the Europeans, who upon mastering the art of long distance navigation roamed the seven seas, conquering, plundering and trading (Sweezy, 1972). Under the impact of the industrial revolution, the small capitalist proprietorship gave way to the corporation, permitting unlimited concentration and centralisation of capital and fostered by an elaborate financial superstructure of banks, securities markets, holding companies etc.[1] But maintenance of monopoly profits dictated a policy of carefully regulating the expansion of productive capacity with the result of an irresistible drive to move outside of and beyond its historical field of operation to penetrate new industries and new markets. According to Sweezy (1972), the British in India, the most famous case of all, had robbed and turned India into one of the poorest and most backward countries what had been one of the most advanced civilisations in the world.

Four hundred years after the advent of European supremacy, of the world's paramount 200 corporations, merely five countries (US,

---

[1] This argument has been elaborated well in Chandler (1962) who has traced the development of the modern M-form competitors at the turn of the century.

Japan, France, Germany and the UK) include 172 corporations. From a combined revenue of $3 trillion in 1982 to nearly double at $5.9 trillion in 1992 these mega-corporations enhanced their share of global GDP from 24.2 per cent to 26.8 per cent (Clairmont and Cavanagh, 1994).

THE GENESIS OF INTERVENTION

The mainsprings of inspiration towards control of multinational companies manifest in host governments' responses is a fascinating area of study. The zeal for self-sufficiency after years of colonial domination and a general suspicion of large multinational companies led India and many others like Mexico to opt for a command type economy. Such policy intervention, it must however be remembered, is a double edged sword, with the potential to tilt competition not only against the intended section of the economy but also the section it means to protect.

When increasing returns exist, the few firms that get a head start in an industry or the country that establishes an industry first may acquire a greater advantage in that industry than its resources could have earned in other sectors (Krugman 1988). Some industries may therefore, turn out to be strategic, offering the possibility of special advantage to those countries that get to specialise in them. The government can then indeed tilt competition in favour of a domestic industry, in a way that raises national income at foreigners' expense. In turn, this indicates that sophisticated government policies can do better than free trade, with a clever subsidy policy.[1]

The fundamental doctrines concerning the relatively young revisionist approach is found in the literature emanating from such scholars as Johnson (1982), Granovetter (1985), Pfeffer (1987), Thurow (1992), Scott (1994). The revisionist approach underscores the effects of state intervention in planning and control of industrial policy based on guided free-market enterprise. As a fitting prelude to this branch of thought Coase (1991), better known through his contribution to institutional economics argued "there is no such thing as a 'free market' or a 'level playing field' - these are concepts which live in the minds of economists but not on earth".[2] Elsewhere, Thurow (1992) reports "...international competition has become not just a contest between firms but a clash between national institutional systems as

---

1 Krugman cites example of national industries such as Airbus, Boeing etc.

2 Cited in M Rajan, 1994, Review Article: *Australian Business in the Asia Pacific Region: The Case for Strategic Industry Policy, Australian Journal of Management, 19(2), December* pp 231-237.

well".[1] In the criteria for developing industry, Scott (1994) captures the essence of distinction between the neo-classical systems and the revisionist approach as of a difference based on relative costs and market opportunities respectively. Whereas the neo-classical system underscores the importance of comparative advantage based on *factor endowments,* short term and consumer welfare (*a la* Heckscher-Ohlin), the revisionist approach bases appropriate choice of industries on *market opportunity* (size and growth prospects), long term implications and producers (Scott, 1994, p 11). The Japanese chose particular sectors on the basis of their long term opportunities, even if suffering comparative disadvantages and focused on market share, not short term earnings - all this while at the same time trying to shift resources from low to high growth sectors (pp 10-15).

'EFFICIENCY' OF THE MNE

But what is the fundamental point of dispute between nation states and the corporation *per se*? According to Rugman(1981) the major theme in the analysis of the multinational enterprise is its existence, as an economic creature, to *efficiently* produce goods and services from which it earns profits. Rugman argues that such roles as a transferor of technology, development agency or redistributor of income do not warrant a place in the multinational scheme of things. These goals come more appropriately, into the purview of national governments instead (1981, p 32). In other words, efficiency is both a means and an end in itself. In the parlance of organisational theory, it then implies 'efficiency' is equivalent to 'effectiveness'.

But then, the question of organisational domain consisting of the claims it makes with respect to products and services provided and populations served (Thomson 1961, Scott 1992) is left unanswered in economics. These claims immediately relate it to other organisations such as suppliers, competitors, customers, government etc that affect its behaviour and outcomes (1992, p 126). As opposed to the determination of behaviour by the preferences of a single individual or group, the behavioural-organisational model suggests that the firm is more about a mosaic of several groups - shareholders, directors, managers, secretaries, clerks, salespersons, foremen, workers etc. (Horst, 1974). The rational model of the neo-classical economists were thus challenged by the dominant coalition model which underscore the reification of the organisation as a single purposeful actor and

---

1 Cited in M Rajan, 1994, Unpublished Doctoral Dissertation, University of California, Irvine.

substitute the same by the negotiation process to set goals among dominant coalitions (Cyert and March 1963), (Pfeffer and Salancik 1974), (Scott 1992).

The open-systems view defines 'effectiveness' as the ability to detect and respond to subtle changes in its task environment (Scott , 1992, p 344). If we accept 'efficiency' as a pre-requisite for effectiveness (goal attainment), with built in conditions as minimising expenditure or maximising returns, it becomes evident that economists have been treating only the rational dimensions of the problem to the exclusion of contextual dimensions and bounded-rationality (Simon, 1956). Hence it becomes increasingly evident that mere consideration of the efficiency criteria is a rather narrow view of the enterprise, a kind of short-sightedness which has the potential to threaten the very existence of the enterprise no worse than it could affect adversely, the environment it operates in. But what is the ultimate effect of this efficiency in so far as it relates to the host economy and the indigenous entities it collides with?

Within the many theories of the multinational enterprise (MNE), the question of efficiency of MNE is interpreted as efficiency in oligopolistic decision making to secure their own expansion and survival by Hymer (1970). MNEs thus have the effect of enlarging the domain of centrally planned world production and diminishing that of decentralised market directed specialisation and exchange.[1] It follows therefore that a restriction on foreign direct investment or a policy to break up a multinational corporation may be the only way of establishing a higher degree of competition in that industry. This being an important rationale for the argument supporting protection of the infant entrepreneur, the developing countries need to devote an important share of their scarce national resources to build up national enterprises which may be used in bargaining with foreign oligopolists.

It is instructive to note that multinational enterprises may, if given a free hand, take over the leadership of the most dynamic technical and marketing based industries while promoting the expansion of domestic ancillary industries (Lall and Streeten, 1980). The final effect is likely to be that the local enterprises in the relevant sectors is reduced to secondary role though a few exceptional firms

---

1 Hymer argues "...(if) we had a regime of national firms (private or socialised) rather than multinational firms, the pattern of output would almost certainly be quite different than the one that is now observed. There would be more centers of innovation and probably more variety of choices offered to the customers as each country developed products suited to its particular characteristics" (Hymer, 1979, p 47).

who are well established in the market (especially state owned ones) may survive and remain competitive because of government protection.

However, alternatives of controlling behaviour of foreign affiliates and encouraging more competition from domestic firms, have been successful up to a point, but each has its own costs (Behrman, 1970). Extant literature reports predicted effects of MNEs on technical efficiency as both positive and negative in that, a positive effect might occur if the MNE as an entrant into a tranquil domestic oligopoly presses local enterprises to a higher level of technical efficiency (Caves, 1974). Among beneficial effects of foreign direct investment, the possibilities of injection of new technology, access to technological innovations, new managerial and marketing skills, competitive effect of domestic competition and improvement of quality and competitiveness (Lall 1993, Borner 1993).[1] Negative effects include increased industry concentration, a branch-plant outlook in the headquarter-subsidiary relationship (Hymer,1970,1976) and political implications for national governments. In political implications it has been suggested that MNCs undermine authority or sovereignty of national governments and weaken effectiveness of national policies (Borner, 1993). The imperialist world view of the Neo-Marxists and the Dependicia school argue that the MNC is the post World War II vehicle for imperialism and colonialism, the LDCs pitted hopelessly against the might of MNCs backed by the developed world (Borner, 1993, p 180).

DIVISION OF LABOUR IN THE MNE

Structural dimensions of major MNEs suggests that the MNE tends to create a division of labour between countries that corresponds to the division of labour between various corporate levels of hierarchy (Hymer 1970). Centralisation of high level decision making to certain key cities in advanced countries while the rest of the world is confined to lower levels of activity, may lead to the country dominated by foreign investment to develop a branch-plant outlook. Such a pattern contrasts quite sharply with the free trade system embodying both income equality and national independence.[2] The inequality and lack of

---

1 However from the theory of MNCs, we know at once, that while these are certainly possibilities under ideal conditions, in reality the nature and degree of these beneficial effects depend not only on certain contextual dimensions but also on the stage of industry in the home and host countries, the orientation of the MNC and indeed a whole host of issues too complicated to consider here.

2 To Dunning one of the most important distinctions is the behaviour of the individual units of the MNEs and the behaviour of MNEs in toto. But to explain the behaviour of the individual operating units of MNEs, compared with that of

autonomy denounced by Hymer is an inherent contradiction in the structure of international economic relationships between developed and less developed areas (Lall and Streeten, 1980). Additionally, this draws on the concept of 'home base' which is where strategy is set, core product and process development takes place and the essential and proprietary skills reside being the platform for global strategy (Porter, 1993). Frequently, affiliates of MNEs are geared not to meet their own objectives but to the enterprise of which they are a part and "decisions taken by MNEs on the use of resources by their foreign affiliates may be...neither in the latter's interests nor of those of the countries in which they operate" (Dunning 1974, p 269).

AREAS OF CONFLICT

Increasingly, the dilemma of FDI centers around uncertainties and misconceptions of the same by the two entities. While for governments it is the question of ensuring national competitiveness through MNCs vs. control over resources and interests, for MNCs it is balancing of global vision with local responsiveness. Governments can accept the presence or integrated MNCs, usually to bargain access to a large domestic market for an export-oriented investment with large positive balance-of-payments and employment effects (Prahalad and Doz, 1987). Whereas MNCs hope to achieve the much coveted competitiveness within the global systems, host governments strive to capture it within its national boundaries (Bartlett and Ghoshal, 1987).[1] Clashes with host governments over some aspects of their behaviour become inescapable which "..are likely to be greater, *inter alia*, the more a country pursues a policy of economic isolationism, the more the activities of multinational enterprises are in response to market imperfections and the greater the differences in incentives or/and penalties exerted by governments" (Dunning 1974, p 16).

The fear that national markets may become a battleground where MNCs depress prices to block one of its global competitors, with smaller national competitors becoming the first casualties is another

---

independent indigenous companies, the state of received theory seems less satisfactory. To do so one needs to turn to an explanation of the branch plant activities of firms, extended to include the specific characteristics of multinationalisation.

1 According to the authors, new industrial policies and trade barriers made restrictions more effective by preventing superficial MNC responses such as the establishment of local plants to assemble knock-down kits exported from the MNCs home operations. New foreign investment regulations defined specific levels of local content, technology transfer and a variety of other conditions from re-export commitments to plant location requirements.

concern of host economies (Prahalad and Doz, 1987). In maturing industries where MNCs become uncompetitive against local competitors, the most obvious response is to integrate across borders and have as few plants as possible to serve the entire world demand (1987, p 85). Thus integrated, these subsidiaries become difficult to regulate, their behaviour less predictable than subsidiaries of non-integrated (locally responsive) MNCs. National governments therefore regard them much more suspiciously, compounding an anxiety to intervene in their affairs more readily than the locally responsive types.

Effects of state intervention is most salient in the breaking up of the MNC into a dichotomous structure. That is, the clear separation of the MNC (subsidiary) from the MNE (parent) by forcing it to respond locally, conform to policies of import substitution and in a variety of ways behave perforce like local enterprises. In effect, the policy inducements making it compulsory for MNCs to behave more like multidomestic firms (Porter, 1986) are basically cutting off substantive firm specific advantages, or efficiency factors, by de-linking the rest of the enterprise from the subsidiary. Locally responsive MNCs are sometimes forced to 'reinvent the wheel' in the new atypical ESP (environment, structure and policy) conditions. The atypical ESP conditions also reinforces such phenomena. Lall (1981) notes that the ultimate effect of such policies might be that the MNCs are altogether discouraged to introduce the state of the art technology in host economies and reduce the roles of their subsidiaries to insignificant players in the international markets.

CHOICE OF TECHNOLOGY

One might ask, if it is better or worse for developing countries to rely less on FDI and more on arms length technology transfers to compete with MNCs? Available evidence suggests participation of multinational enterprises at arms length is not entirely immune from hidden infirmities.

The neo-classical economists assume that MNCs raise welfare by satisfying individual preferences in the market, income distribution being a non-economic matter. However, even as real incomes have risen in the advanced countries, the generation of demand for sophisticated products has thus become increasingly inappropriate to the needs of developing countries. Adoption of capital intensive technologies without modification to produce such products then lock developing countries into a technological trajectory determined by the developed engendering a dualistic pattern of development. A small high income sector absorbs almost all the country's investible resources, its infrastructure and skills, and generates demand among a small elite for the modern products produced in the sector. The remainder of the economy, encompassing the vast majority of the population, remains deprived of investment resources, modern technology or appropriate products, in conditions of extreme poverty (Stewart, 1993). This situation is reinforced by the presence of the so called 'entrepreneurs' who are merely penny pinching risk averters forever on the lookout for easy profits and importing blueprints of technology from foreign firms with blind inattention to the contextual dimensions or the presence of skills and infrastructure available in the country (Lindberg 1995, Bagchi 1995).

THE MODEL OF JAPAN

A prioritised pattern, delineating areas to invest, what technology to develop, what to import and which supportive policies to put in place characterised Japan's industrial policies. The Japanese experience shows that industrial policy can be an instrument for developing competitive advantage of national firms through the identification, development and control of certain industries to guarantee the economic health and effectiveness. A close relationship between industry, bureaucracy and the political parties ensured that they worked together to enhance the national and international competitiveness of Japanese firms (Sarathy and Samuels, 1987, p 34).

The initiative for competitive success, however, came from individual firms. The willingness to start an unfamiliar business and ability to assimilate new technology were the moving forces behind Japan's development (Odagiri and Goto, 1996). This was reinforced by the presence of engineers and entrepreneurs as Toyoda and Ayukawa who were willing to take risks and sustain efforts under adversity and the general ability of the engineers to absorb foreign technology. As in any late developing countries, reverse engineering was the first source of foreign technology. Visiting advanced factories of foreign producers, hiring foreign engineers and purchasing foreign technology were other important means. Technology transfer was made initially through foreign engineers and specialists, and later through reverse engineering, using licensing arrangements as stepping stones to self-sufficient technological capabilities (Baranson, 1990, p 164).

The distinctive characteristic in Japanese technology transfers have been the transfer through on-the-job-training with face to face contact instead of through manuals (Komoda, 1991). Indigenous technology was important not only on its own particularly in traditional industries but also in providing the ability to select among the technologies available in developed countries and in adapting and assimilating them to fit domestic conditions. MITI's role in collection and infusion of information regarding choice of technology thus appears to have been significant. Protection of domestic markets also played a significant role in Japan's post war industrial development at least until the early 1970s. Also as Hayashi (1984) pointed out the "linkage between new and old technologies made it possible for both to develop in mutually complementary fashion" (p 99).

The concept of Japan's industrial development based on being in the 1.5th place rather than the first or second, is explained well by Makino (1987) who suggests that 1.5 is precisely the position occupied by a company who develops a practical product from an abandoned invention - likened somewhat to the role of a foster parent. According to Makino, 'to foster a product that is still in the simple idea stage and put that into practical use is the basis of innovation, as well as the basic strategy that determines the outcome of a company' (1987, p 171). Makino cites example of Sony, Honda, Mazda who had taken up projects for industrialisation, from amongst many of the innovations that failed to bear fruit in the Western world.

THE KOREAN MODEL

The model of Korea reveals intervention had occurred in almost every aspect of industrial activity from protection of infant industries to promotion of large private groups, credit subsidies for selected activities, exports targets, growth of R&D and investment in the educational and institutional support (Lall, 1993). It also confined foreign entry to activities where local enterprises were unable to gain access or were deficient in advanced technologies, basically limiting FDI to areas where entry of foreign firms were compatible with development objectives of the country (Koo, 1985). This context, is suggestive of imperatives for indigenous technological effort for technological dynamism.

For infant industries, policy mechanisms to mitigate risks, secure stability and market protection from foreign competition were used extensively. Creation of large firms, known as *chaebols*, acted as an instrument to bring about scale economies and in turn to develop these strategic industries to lead exports (Kim, Lee and Lee, 1987). The important point of distinction with other developing countries was to be found firstly in Korea's well trained human resources and entrepreneurship which enabled the country to learn quickly from foreign capital goods and ensured independence from MNCs. Secondly, Korea differed from other developing countries in promoting big business in the discipline its state exercised over these *chaebols* by penalising poor performers and rewarding the good ones (Kim, Lee and Lee, 1987). And finally export promotion was the major policy imperative during the whole period in the rise of industrialisation in Korea.

The pattern of innovation fostered by the Korean republic informs the most important lesson as the layer by layer strategic plan executed by the mastery of a carefully deliberated policy. Korea seized opportunities as these appeared and promoted competitiveness of selective industries, not by restricting their scope as was done in the case of India, but by the very opposite means, i.e., by promoting the growth of big business to attain export competitiveness. State intervention, not market determined exchange, determined the challenge of Korea to the developed world in the vanguard of modern technology.

The unprecedented success of business enterprises in Japan and Korea illustrate the benefits of export orientation combined with strategic levels of government intervention (Lall, 1993). Classified thus as an 'outward looking strategy' Scott (1995) argues it permits high growth opportunities for those countries that opt for the same. On the other hand, the lessons of industrial strategy in the NICs suggest that the process of exposing industries to international competition has different implications for different categories of industries (Lall, 1993, p117). In one category are the competitive mature industries where the relatively simple technologies have been mastered and hence need to be exposed to world markets as soon as possible. In the other, there are enterprises that have complex technologies and are not currently competitive but potentially so if given time and support to relearn new skills and technologies. This category could be exposed to direct import competition gradually with selective assistance to upgrade their capabilities. Each of these temporarily protected industries however has to be persuaded or induced to enter export markets quickly in order to offset the disincentive effects of protection. This is perhaps the most important lesson of the industrialisation of Korea.[1]

Both Japan and Korea depended less on FDI than licensing and other arms length arrangements. A close scrutiny of their unprecedented growth in the world economy reveals that the NICs, rather than proceeding from innovation to investment to production, have taken a short-cut and focused on such mechanisms as reverse

---

1 The average rate of protection was very high for strategic industries. In others where technology was more complex and marketing was more elaborate protection had been relatively long lasting in order to provide a longer period of incubation (Kim, 1987)

engineering and the ability to operate production facilities according to competitive cost and quality standards. Thus, according to Singer, Hatti and Tandon (1991) "...the latecomer industrialisation model, based on borrowed technology, has been widely promoted as a possible model for the LDCs to follow in their efforts to upgrade their technology levels" (p 12). Active government involvement in indicative planning, dissemination of information and above all, development of favourable contextual dimensions as in roads, infrastructure, interest rates, without the stranglehold of industrial control, could be the argument for a recipe for success of Indian industries in the new global competition.

Let us now investigate patterns found in the real world to examine the theoretical concerns raised in extant literature and the policy responses that followed in India.

THE RATIONALE OF ECONOMIC PLANNING IN INDIA

The genesis of an overtly command type economy which India adopted after independence can be linked to the existence of somewhat singular contextual dimensions in India. The objective of development in developing countries is to increase *productive capacity* as non-employment in these economies is of a different nature from the unemployment in developed economies (Kalecki, 1976). The problem facing *mixed economies* is thus somewhat distinct from both developed and socialist economies, and is one of directing investment in the private sector. This is because to initiate large schemes of investment without a coherent plan will mean a great deal of wasted effort, where it will be necessary to plan not only the volume but also the structure of investment. Since the proper allocation between the production of necessities, non-essentials and investment goods is central, it will require much deeper government intervention. On the one hand, the state will have to invest in those branches of the economy in which private investment is not forthcoming and on the other, private investment will have to be licensed in order to prevent the upward deviation of the actual investment in some sectors of the economy from a planned level (Kalecki, 1976, p.29).

One of the reasons countries such as Korea or India that have taken a defensive approach by systematically limiting the role of foreign investment in economies is that they both suffered colonial domination and at independence wanted to rid themselves of foreign economic and political control (Wiegel, 1988). The objective of channelling the country's limited resources into desired directions which would lead to self sufficiency led India to choose a regulated economy beginning from the 2nd Five Year Plan. Three major objectives - those of self-sustained economic growth, reduction in inequality and a socialist pattern of society found importance in plans (Chaudhuri, 1978).[1] The low level of capital stock of the economy made the chief imperative to be an effort to increase the capital stock through a high rate of investment.[2] Self reliance even where this meant slower growth, domestic under-supply and higher prices became the basic philosophy of development (Stoever, 1989).

India encouraged import of technologies in specific sectors via arm's-length arrangements rather than FDI in the '60s and '70s[3] and deemed that once one Indian company has acquired a particular technology, it should be available to all companies (Lall 1981,1985, Stoever 1989). Under the Foreign Exchange Regulation Act (FERA), foreign ownership was limited to 40% of a company's equity as were limitations on dividends remitted, imports of equipment components and raw materials and the employment of foreign nationals in the country. This then succeeded in restricting the MNEs as well as the development of the external sector.[4]

The private corporate sector became subject to a battery of controls. The Monopolies and Restrictive Trade Practices Act (MRTP) labelled any firm over a specified size or with a dominant share of any market a 'monopoly house'. Additional restrictions of growth with complete absence of considerations of minimum efficient economic size and the presumption that public interest was always threatened by large size dominated the ethos of plans (Lall, 1985). The mechanism of licensed capacity creation in tune with plan targets with the object of prevention of concentration of monopoly power and balanced regional development meant in operational terms, the government actually planned target outputs for each industry (Mani, 1992). However in actual fact, the growth of output were far short of targets through the plans.

The policy induced barriers to entry actually increased, rather than prevented economic concentration in a host of industries. India's

---

1 India, *Planning Commission* 1956 chII, 1961 chI.

2 ibid. ch 5

3 In case of technical collaborations it prefers that payments be in the form of lumpsum rather than royalties or fees continuing over time. Where royalties or fees are allowed the government tries to limit them to 5% of the net ex-factory selling price and to a period of 5 years. Stoever, op. cit.

4 In 1950, India's share in world exports was 2%. By 1980, the figure had fallen to 0.4%. In the mid 50s India was the tenth biggest industrial power in the world. By the late 70s it had declined to the twentieth., R. Thakur, *Third World Quarterly*, Vol. 14, No 1, 1993

disappointing growth failed to make an impact on poverty, for, economic growth is not merely to be interpreted as a 'trickle-down' strategy, but rather as a 'pull-up' strategy, a process that can be biased by policy to benefit the poor' (Bhagwati, 1993). Weak growth was a reflection, in turn, of a feeble productivity performance stifled by extensive bureaucratic controls over production, investment and trade, inward looking trade and foreign investment policies, and a substantial public sector going well beyond the confines of public utilities and infrastructure. Finally, the combination of industrial licensing with import and exchange controls effectively cut off the rigours of competition and made possible the creation of a rentier, as against an entrepreneurial economy (Bhagwati, 1993). Elsewhere Datta (1992) reiterates that vested interests and rent-seeking elites dictated policies related to industrial and trade policies to the Indian politicians which resulted in the distortion of import substitution plan.

To suit restrictive industrial policies Indian industries developed management practices that reinforced their inward orientation. Rather than using production skills, industrialists managed their competitors through greasing the palms of the government officials (Minhas, 1991).[1] Abuse of the licensing system through pre-emption was an industry-wide malpractice even as it prevented new entrants from coming in and introducing competition. Clever accounting practices were seen as the main source of generating profits. Thus inward looking policies contrasted with outward looking ones initiated and concluded successfully in Japan and Korea marks the distinction of the Indian system with its East Asian counterparts.

Historically, the bias against integrated MNCs was obvious in the policies. A host of regulations such as phased indigenisation programs, local content and employment, import bans on raw, semi-finished and finished goods forced MNCs to conform to patterns of local responsiveness. Dilution of equity well below a critical minimum level, leading to sharing of interest by indigenous entities in some cases led to the waning of interest of the MNEs in their erstwhile subsidiaries. Typical cases in the 80s include Philips, Remington Rand, Gramophone Company of India and so on. However, the majority of MNCs in India that are well established and in general show a higher level of profitability, are better protected by mobility barriers than their local counterparts and show less vertical-local linkages (Kumar, 1990).

[1] B. Minhas, 'Public versus Private: Lessons of Economics, Economic Times, 6 June, 1991.

Economic Liberalisation and New Directions

Economic liberalisation in India was initiated in earnest in the early '80s and gained greater momentum in the mid '80s. Internal liberalisation, through partial reforms in industrial policy to the neglect of trade policy combined with the fiscal profligacy of the '80s led India to face an unsustainable balance of payments and fiscal deficit situation in the early '90s. As the Indian economy went into an unprecedented financial crisis in 1991, the threat of defaulting on international commitments, the denial of access to foreign exchange markets and the plummeting of foreign exchange reserves to only fourteen days' import became the circumstances in which India was obliged to undertake deregulation and restructuring under IMF auspices. The rationale of such policies rested on tight monetary policy with high rate of interest and devaluation of the currency with an object to reduce investment demand at home, make exports more competitive and attract foreign capital seeking higher rates of interest. These mechanisms were supposedly intended to ease the balance of payments situation and stabilise the overheated economy. Following the reasoning of Kalecki (1976) the question is, whether these recommendations would be suited to a developing economy facing under-utilisation of resources (Ghosh, 1994).

The triad principles of liberalisation, privatisation and globalisation made reforms in micro-economic areas such as industrial and trade licensing, privatisation of the public sector, and the acceptance in principle of the Dunkel Plan. The objectives of the Structural Adjustment Policy were modernisation of the industrial sector to achieve international competitiveness, faster growth with fall out effects on employment and a greater reliance on market forces instead of intervention to promote faster development (Ghosh 1994).

The question is, did the opening up of 'competition' in India amount to channelling of the nation's resources, infrastructure and technology to service India's elitist consumers to the neglect of essentials of the poorer sections of society? The new industrial policy of the Government of India scrapped artificial barriers to entry such as capacity restriction through licensing in all but 18 major industry groups (Mani, 1992). The large scale entry of MNCs into India facilitated by the new triad of economic reforms namely privatisation, liberalisation and globalisation ushered varied uses of entry strategies. Earlier, the US Tariff Commission's (1973) study of US MNCs reported by Lall noted the preference of MNCs for entering new markets by take-overs for reasons of immediate access to markets and brand names, control over proprietary technology, access to operating plants and personnel etc. In India, an ever increasing number of MNCs wresting control after economic liberalisation prompted top entrepreneurs to raise, albeit ironically, the question of bias against local enterprises in the new industrial policy. After the initial round of liberalisation a situation transpired such that whereas the Indian entrepreneurs were not allowed to raise their equity beyond 40 per cent, MNCs could hold 51 per cent under the new laws. The problem which arose out of this anomaly was the threat of take-over of Indian companies by MNCs. Even after policy corrections, the endemic problem of finding cash to raise equity in their words, was put as 'if we put all the money to buy our own equity, we will not have anything left to modernise and expand our companies".[1]

Casual observation suggests foreign corporations exploited their enormous financial resources to plough substantial capital into building brand advantages immediately following the lowering of policy induced barriers to entry. Companies like Pepsi Foods sunk Rs. 750 million in terms of losses - unthinkable to any Indian company. In 1993, Proctor and Gamble announced that it had totted up accumulated losses of Rs 280 million. In 1992 P&G had injected Rs 840 million into the Indian venture by increasing its stake to 65%. Raising of stakes in investment had the effect of raising entry barriers of the 'capital requirements' type (Bain, 1956) for new competitors while at the same time heightening mobility barriers (Caves and Porter, 1977) in the strategic group of MNCs and local competitors.

With liberalisation, it became possible for MNCs to become more integrated with other member companies within the multinational enterprise and draw on their mutual strengths. This, in turn, raised the possibility of MNCs to have lower local-vertical linkages and develop a more branch-plant outlook as previously suggested by Hymer (1976).

EFFICIENCY REVISITED

The entry of MNCs into increasing areas of the world economy was, in part, facilitated by the opening of the world economy under the Fund-Bank aegis (Purkayastha, 1994). In the latter 80's, the global economy witnessed FDI growing at round 25% per annum while world trade under 10% and GDP and output at around 2-3% (Lall, 1993). The rapid increase in the share of international production under control of MNCs reflects the 'efficiency' dimension - the growing economic strength of MNCs in innovation, services and finance apart from trade. Empirical evidence illustrates that global production is dominated by

---

1 Reported in the *Hindu*, New Delhi, 4.10.93

the strategic consideration of transnational corporations, some 24,000 in number owning one-third of the world's private sector assets with annual sales of 5.5 trillion US dollars (Ghosh, 1993). This phenomenon was postulated long ago by Hymer (1976) who remarked that economic forces in today's world are not the self regulating market responses of millions of atomistic producers and consumers, but the conscious outcomes of strategies of a few hundred global enterprises .

As the threat of take-over of the more dynamic sectors of the economy by MNCs looms, small players in India align with big MNCs in marketing intensive industries like soft-drinks. The case of Parle with Coca Cola and Duke with Pepsi are cases in point. In 1993, Hindustan Lever swallowed up the giant local Tata Oil Mills Company worth Rs. 4 billion to ".. provide quicker access to manufacturing capacities and be less expensive than organic growth."[1] Also evident is the fact that unless Indian companies are prepared to forgo controlling interest in their companies, MNEs tend to become increasingly reluctant to impart know-how. MNCs recognise that imparting know-how carries the risk of selling its ownership advantages to a competitor in a market they may enter through Internalisation.[2] Elsewhere, others local enterprises are suddenly confronted with the new belligerence of joint venture partners many of whom seek a controlling interest in Indian projects before parting with technology or brand names.[3]

Division of Labour within the MNE

If we assume that R&D is a corporate weapon to support product differentiation with the object of maintaining oligopolistic control, these higher level strategic (institutional) functions[4] are a key indicator of the relative importance of organisational hierarchies. The locational rigidity of R&D as a function illuminates this assumption (Howells and Wood 1993). Patel and Pavitt's (1991) work illuminates the observations in the foregoing. Using patent data from 686 large companies they conclude production of technology remains far from globalised, with majority of large firms keeping most of their technological activities at home. In 1968, only 6.1% of the US based

---

1 Narayan S, 1993, 'From Coup to Coup', *BusinessWorld*, August, Bombay, pp 18-25.

2 For a comprehensive explanation of the concept of internalisation see Buckley and Casson, 1976, *The Future of Multinational Enterprise, London*, Macmillan, pp 73-78.

3 Mathai, P and Narayan S, 1993, 'Fear of the Foreigner', *Business World*, November, Bombay, pp 18-29.

4 See Parson (1960) for a definition of the three levels of an organisation.

MNCs' R&D expenditure was split abroad. In 1977, the figure increased only marginally up to 7% (NSF, 1979:1)[1]. Again in 1985-89, only 9.3% of the R&D in US MNCs was split abroad (National Science Board 1991:10)[2]. A host of studies since the 1960s (Creamer 1976, Behrman & Fischer 1980, Hood & Young 1979; Pearce & Singh 1992) have indicated that growth in corporate R&D activity remains highly concentrated in the main advanced industrial economies of the world. A recent survey of 58 firms in India (50 per cent of which were MNC subsidiaries and the remainder were domestic firms and joint ventures) found that only 15 per cent had introduced new products based on distinct product or process innovation (Basu 1993). Most, simply introduced products of the firm's home nation product mix with least possible change.

Choice of Technology and the Dependency Problem

The record of the Indian private sector firms in the introduction of new products and processes, out of indigenous research is poor, albeit the existence of scientific and technological talent and competence in the nation (Chandra and Shukla, 1994). On a sectoral basis, out of a total R&D expenditure of Rs 48 billion in 1992, 80 per cent was spent by the central government, 7 per cent by state governments and only 13 per cent by the private sector. In 1991 the New Technology Policy of the Government of India under the item resources for R&D notes that the total R&D expenditure is only 0.9% of the GNP and the aim of the policy should be to increase it to 2 % of the GNP by 2000AD.

The long tradition of trade in India regard manufacturing as merely an add-on, with large business houses' roots in the same (Vyasulu, 1994). In trade, money is recycled quickly whereas in manufacture, the gestation period is long, margins are low and profits depend on turnover. Therefore the obvious question that arises is 'why get into this complex business when one can trade in MNC goods'? The government restrictions on FDI is a factor behind these coalitions, or tie-ups. The other side of the coin is the tendency of technology importers to usually maximise short run profits to the neglect of long term growth through self-reliance. This is compounded by the apparent oversight of the effects of technological dependence (Narayanan and Joseph, 1993).

Despite the elaborate system of approving technology co-operation agreement applications, most projects implemented in the

---

1 Cited in Howells and Wood (1993)

2 ibid.

private corporate sector have had little follow up action as to the actual compliance of the conditions, resulting in large scale distortion and fudging of actual facts with respect indigenisation. Very often, local indigenisation claims by some manufacturers have been deceptive, as they often arranged to procure the components through an independent third-party, showing on paper that components have been procured indigenously.

While liberalisation of the economy has provided MNCs a low cost opportunity to establish their brands in the Indian market, it has simultaneously provided Indian companies the opportunity to encash their *competitor's* brand names at the expense of their own R&D. With the simultaneous opportunity for internalisation and establishment of their brands, waning of interest in sharing brand names or advertising their association with Indian companies is discernible. Frequent attempts, in the early '90s, of wresting control over their brands as in the cases of Pepsi (formerly Lehar-Pepsi), Suzuki among others is manifest.

An example of dependence is captured well by Mani (1993) in the technology transfer and development pattern of the Indian telecommunications industry prior to the introduction of C-DoT in 1984. The Indian Post and Telegraph's Department in the '40s purchased the Strowger Exchange (telecommunications switch) at a high price of Rs. 11.2 million when the technology was already in the downward phase of the product life cycle. Even after two decades of manufacturing, the Indian recipient ITI did not learn the defect free manufacturing technique the rate of rejection being as high as 20% in the early '80s (Mani, 1995). The second major phase of technological change occurred when ITI decided to manufacture the Penta Conta Cross Bar exchange in the '60s - not only unsuited to the needs of the economy but also much of the R&D that followed got bogged down to adapting this inappropriate technology. Repeated import of technology even before the absorption of the previous one did not result in development of any significant skills that were necessary to induce technical changes.

In terms of nuances, the ability to master a technology depends on efforts spent on taking it apart, an appreciation of the *know-why* aspects, that is, the principles behind how a technology works. A mere 'operational level' of technological transfer does not engender self-sufficiency (Baranson 1990, Stewart 1991). The ability to expand and reproduce plant and its discrete components without foreign help is the next level of technology transfer, known as 'duplicative level'. To reach capabilities attained in the developed world, two more levels have to be crossed, namely the 'adaptive level' signifying the ability to adapt, reengineer products and processes, and, the 'innovative level' engendering the ability to develop next generation systems. Casual observation suggests that a substantial part of the Indian manufacturing sector is still at the operational level, locked into the technological trajectory determined by enterprises of the developed world (Stewart, 1991).

DEVELOPING INDIGENOUS CAPABILITIES

In the arena of strategic coalitions forged between large organisations of the developed world, over four thousand technology partnerships have been reported between 1980 and 1989 (Ghosh, 1993). The coming together of telecommunications and computers forged strategic alliances with chip-making companies even as high R&D costs double with each successive generation of chips. The cost of a new chip-making venture in the early '70s was about $2 million (Commonwealth Working Group, 1986). By the mid-80s, it had risen to $100 million and today stands at about $300-$400 million. The exorbitant R&D costs for new chips precludes any but the really large companies (and/or large state-supported ones) from entering this area (Purkayastha, 1994). It is therefore evident that unless there is substantial involvement on the part of government, the prospect of moving into strategic industries such as chip making for developing countries such as India appears pretty dim. This would call for an active leadership role of the Indian government, not unlike those of Japan and Korea, in contrast to the pseudo *laissez-faire* style of governance being pursued at the moment.

Development of indigenous semi-conductor/micro-processor industry with an adequate network of supporting local industries give the Hirschman type linkage effects to industries at the centre. In India the total absence of VLSI chip makers has put local industry at a disadvantage vis-à-vis the growing power of the NICs. But wherever Indian firms have innovated, the outcome has been beneficial. The Indian supercomputer cost only about $.05 million against several times that amount for the CRAY supercomputer from the US (Purkayastha, 1994). Parallel processing machines such as PARAM are efficient indigenous economic alternatives which need only conventional air-cooling compared to the elaborate climate conditioning required to run the Cray. The Centre for Development of Telematics (C-DoT) developed a digital switch comparable to the very best in the world, an area dominated by only 8-10 long established manufacturers from the developed world. C-DoT spent only Rs. 720 million ($28 million) up to March 1990 compared to the estimated cost of US $0.5 billion to $1 Billion spent by MNEs on developing similar technologies. Since C-DoT exchanges are modular they optimise the use of electronic components. Through its vendor development policy it has been able to build up an indigenous component industry and has reduced the foreign exchange component.

The rural population in India accounts for over 75% and yet has access to only 10% of the telecom lines, the tele-density being a low 0.08 per 100 inhabitants. Most consumer goods in India aim at small number of high income households, partly because the Indian firms and their MNC counterparts are within the technological trajectory determined by the MNE in the developed world.

AREAS OF CONFLICT: STATE INTERVENTION IN TELECOMMUNICATIONS

The case of C-DoT versus the telecom giants of six developed countries provides a fascinating study of half hearted interventionist policy with abandonment midstream and the move toward more market directed pattern of industrial development. Since the explosion of development costs of switches from a mere $50 million to about $0.5-$1 billion (Roobeek, 1988) there has been an increasing pressure for telecommunications giants to move out of their historic or geographic area of operations to recover the costs of development. These circumstances point to the importance of developing countries as an important market for their products (Mani, 1995). These oligopolies exert pressure on nationalistic regimes to open up their economies and are often aided by their home governments in convincing the P&T departments of host countries concerned to buy their products.

It has been shown that whereas the world market prices of digital switches prior to Indian market entry was much higher, the MNCs dumped their switches into India as a part of their entry strategy. This reduced C-DoT's output from 2 million lines a year to just about 1 million, with the rest of the orders being grabbed by the former. Prices (1994) charged by the MNCs for digital switches in their home markets and in India are shown in Table 1.

Table 1: **Prices of Digital Switches**

	Home*	India**
Alcatel	$335	$109
Ericsson	$325	$135
Fujitsu	$290	$241
Siemens	$450	$137

Source :**Telematics India*, 1994 (Local Switching),
** *Communications Today*, 1994 (Trunk exchange).

The anti-competitive effect, namely, the elimination of competition as a motive of the MNE (Hymer, 1960) is implicit in the data. On the other hand, the net consolation benefit to the Indian economy is the bargaining power leveraged from the presence of local competitors with comparable technology which, under a policy of blanket liberalisation, would have resulted in a weak bargaining strength and higher outflow of resources (Narayanan and Joseph, 1993) had C-DoT not developed switches of comparable range. The debate as to which is more desirable - the *consumer* based market argument or its anti-thesis, the *producer* based argument advanced by Scott (1994) is the moot point here.

Earlier, following the infant entrepreneur argument, the market for switching was reserved for C-DoT technology almost exclusively. The demand pattern for local switches of the department of telecommunications for the period 1992-97 is summarised in Table 2.

Table 2: **Purchase Requirements 1992-97** (in million lines for Local Switching).

	92-93	93-94	94-95	95-96	96-97	Total
Large Size (10,000+)	.88	1 03	1.21	1.36	1.52	6.00
Medium Size(2k-10k)*	.50	0 60	0.69	0.78	0.85	3.42
Small Size(<=2k)*	.35	0 42	0.49	0.55	0.62	2.43
	1.73	2 05	2.39	2.69	2.99	11.85

Source: *Communications Today*, Sep-Oct 1994.
*= Reserved for C-DoT

With economic liberalisation, orders for large switches have gone almost exclusively to the MNCs. The Department of Telecommunications argued that the massive investments needed for the expansion in such critical areas as telecommunications and infrastructure could not be mobilised unless FDI was allowed. With over 3 million line a year capacity, C-DoT licensees were faced with a large slump in the market. With orders from DOT being hardly one million, many of the licensees perforce shut down, effected layoffs and dumped the whole local indigenous industry.

The protection and subsequent withdrawal *before* allowing sufficient time for local indigenous industry to develop competitiveness illustrates yet another area of inept and half hearted government policy.

On the other hand, one can argue that contextual dimensions of India's economy in the early '90s was a circumstance which perforce led to this situation. Expediency of rational decision making in a crisis took precedence over arguments of the infant entrepreneur, the 'efficiency' of MNCs overrode the 'stakeholder' argument. Efficiency and not the effectiveness criteria scrutinised the MNCs.

CONCLUSION AND FUTURE DIRECTIONS

While FDI is on the rise in South Asia and indeed globally, the pattern of innovation strategy instituted in Japan and Korea reveals that these countries relied less on foreign direct investment, more on arms-length transactions, aided by an active involvement of their national governments to achieve global competitiveness. Second, their innovative strategies made a difference in their industrial performance and such nations came to be identifiable by the economic strategies they pursued (Scott, 1994). Third, an explicitly outward orientation (as opposed to inward looking ones such as in India) hitherto forced their entrepreneurial businesses to compete internationally relatively early. This in turn induced a competitiveness which would not have been forthcoming by competing merely on the home turf. Fourth, and above all, their insistence on learning from foreign experience and technology, reverse engineering and constant tuning to market opportunities rather than comparative advantage contributed to their success.

The absence of such policies in India reflects the government's failure to establish priorities in the use of scarce investible resources. The important question is whether the case for India is so simple, in that, a mere mirroring of either the industrial strategy of the NICs, or, the market directed exchange as argued by the IMF-Bank combine will suffice? Or, are there vast social and political dimensions that have to be considered before embarkment of a clear industrial strategy? The thrust for the new pattern of industrial development initiated by three angles such as supply side economists, aid donors and manufacturers of elitist consumption goods have all made India veer away from planning to market directed exchange (Datta, 1992). The task of rapid reform and globalising becomes daunting, if not completely untouchable, when one is confronted by the demographic characteristics such as 43%of the population living below poverty line (NSS consumer expenditure data for 1987-88), 48 per cent of the population above the age of 7 totally illiterate (Census, 1991) and a backlog of 28 million unemployed to which an additional force of 37 million to be added in 1995 (Planning Commission, 1990).

Admittedly, channelling India's vast array of 'slack resources' to build up infrastructure, education and health services would have beneficial effects. According to the noted economist Amartya Sen (1991)[1]

> *"I think that the question on public policy in India has sometimes been wrongly posed - are you in favour of government intervention or are you against it? The question in fact should be about the form that public policy should take. You can have positive intervention to remove illiteracy or the social inequalities between men and women. You can also have negative intervention where you can prevent people for doing something by licensing regulation or other restrictions. In India the emphasis has been on the latter to the neglect of positive intervention through public policy. To that extent I welcome market forces as I don't cry for the great negative restrictions and licensing."*

In curbing the MNCs, India over-extended itself failing to develop the crucial sectors of the economy and destroying the dynamism of not only the MNCs it intended to curb but also the local entities it meant to promote. On the other hand, complete removal of government controls could also have led to the problem of opportunistic behaviour on the part of the MNCs. Hence the government is squeezed between two extremes.

For MNCs, mere management of the efficiency dimension to the exclusion of claims of its stakeholders and inattention in its exchange as an 'open system' poses problems. In particular, inattention to the peculiarities of the context such as technical attainment, education and income distribution are ways to greater conflict with nation-states. Temporary exigencies apart, the MNC needs to place far greater emphasis on developing competitiveness as a locally responsive and yet globally active basis.

While Indian enterprises in general have had a poor track record in terms of innovation, it is remarkable that local enterprises such as C-DAC or C-DoT who developed the advanced generation computing and telecommunications systems, were promoted as a part of the technology mission of the Government of India and had the benefit of working as 'autonomous institutions' without the usual bureaucratic stranglehold so common in public sector organisations. The Indian government (or for that matter any other with similar concerns or objectives) could perhaps formulate their policies that would foster indigenous

[1] Reported in Indian Express, New Delhi, 21 December, 1991.

intellectual talent to serve national interests. For the MNCs on the other hand such resources represent a huge opportunity to enhance their profitability which is their major *raison d'être*.

BIBLIOGRAPHY

Bain J. S., 1956, *Barriers to New Competition*, Cambridge, Mass., Harvard University Press.

Baranson J., 1990, "Technology Transfers to India: Lessons for Chinese Industrial Development", *Research in International Business and International Relations*, Volume 4, Jai Press.

Bartlett C. and S. Ghoshal, 1992, *Transnational Management: Text, Cases and Readings in Cross-Border Management*, Richard D. Irwin Inc, Homewood, Illinois.

Bartlett C. and S Ghoshal, 1987, "Managing Across Borders: New Strategic Requirements", *Sloan Management Review*, Summer: 7-17.

Behrman J., 1970, *National Interests and the Multinational Enterprise*, Prentice Hall.

Behrman J.N. and Fischer W.A., 1980, *Overseas R&D Activities of Transnational Companies*, Cambridge, Mass., Oelgeschlager, Gunn and Hain.

Bagchi A.K., 1995, *New Technology and the Workers Response: Microelectronics, Labour and Society*, New Delhi, Sage aPublications.

Bhagwati J., 1993, *India in Transition -Freeing the Economy*, Oxford, OUP.

Borner, S, 1993, "The Multinational Corporation Competition", *Joint Ventures and Collaborations*, H. Singer, N Hatti and R Tandon (eds.), New World Order Series:10, Indus Publishing, New Delhi.

Buckley P.J and Casson M, 1976, *The Future of Multinational Enterprise*, London, Macmillan.

Caves R.E., 1971, International Corporations: "The Industrial Economics of Foreign Investment", *Economica*, 38, February, 1-27.

Caves R.E., 1974, *Economic Analysis and the Multinational Enterprise*, J.H. Dunning (Ed.), London, George Allen and Unwin.

Caves R.E and M.E. Porter, 1977, "From Entry Barriers to Mobility Barriers: Conjectural Decisions and Contrived Deterrence to New Competition", *Quarterly Journal of Economics*, Vol. 91, 241-61.

Clairmont F.F and J.H. Cavanagh, 1994, "World's Top 200 Mega Corporations: Foundations of the Economic Gulag", *Economic and Political Weekly*, Feb 5, 283-285.

Chandler A.D. Jr., 1962, *Strategy and Structure: Chapters in the History of the American Industrial enterprise*, Cambridge, Mass., MIT Press.

Chandra P and Shukla P.R., 1994, "Manufacturing Excellence and Global Competitiveness: challenges and opportunities for Indian industries", *Economic and Political Weekly*, Bombay, February: M2-M11.

Chaudhuri P., 1978, *The Indian Economy: Poverty and Development*, London, Crosby, Lockwood, Staples.

Creamer D., 1976, *Overseas Research and Development by United States Multinationals, 1966-1995: Estimates of Expenditures and A Statistical Profile*, New York, The Conference Board.

Cyert R.M., and J.G. March, 1963, *A Behavioural Theory of the Firm*, Englewood Cliffs, N.J., Prentice Hall.

Datta B, 1992, *Indian Planning At The Crossroads*, New Delhi, Oxford University Press.

Dunning J.H., 1974, *Economic Analysis and the Multinational Enterprise*, London, George Allen and Unwin.

Dunning J.H., 1981, *International Production and Multinational Enterprise*, London, Allen and Unwin.

Dunning J.H., 1998, Location and the Multinational Enterprise, *Journal of International Business Studies*, 19(1), First Quarter, pp 45-66.

Dunning, John H., 1988, "The Eclectic Paradigm of International Production: A Restatement and Some Possible Extensions", *Journal of International Business Studies*, 19(1), Spring :1-31.

Ghosh A., 1994, "Structural Adjustments and Industrial Environmental Concerns", *Economic and Political Weekly*, February 19: 421-426.

Ghosh A., 1992, "Planning Versus Market-Oriented Investment and Production: Indian Dilemma", *Economic and Political Weekly*, October, 17: 2280-2283.

Ghosh D.N., 1993, "Level Playing Field: A Mirage", *Economic and Political Weekly*, Bombay, December 4: 2633-2634.

Granovetter M., 1985, "Economic Action and Social Structure: the Problem of Embeddedness", *American Journal of Sociology*, 91: 481-510.

Hayashi, T., 1984, *Project on Technology Transfer, Tranformation and Development: The Japanese Experience*, The United Nations University, Tokyo.

Hood N. and Young S., 1979, *The Economics of Multinational Enterprise*, London, Longman.

Horst T.O., 1974, The Theory of The Firm, *Economic Analysis and the Multinational Enterprise*, J.H Dunning (ed.), London, George Allen and Unwin: 31-46.

Howell J. and M. Wood, 1993, *The Globalisation of Production and Technology*, Belhaven Press, London.

Hymer S., 1960, *The International Operations of National Firms*, (doctoral dissertation, Cambridge, Mass. M.I.T., published 1976).

Hymer S, 1970, "The Efficiency (Contradictions) of Multinational Corporations", *American Economic Review*, May, 1970, Vol. LX(2): 441-8.

Hymer S., 1979, *The Multinational Corporation: A Radical Approach*, Cambridge, Cambridge University Press.

Johnson C., 1982, *MITI and the Japanese Miracle*, Stanford, CA, Stanford University Press.

Kalecki M.,1976, *Essays on Developing Economies*, Sussex, Harvester Press.

Kim, L., J. Lee, J. Lee, 1987, "Korea's Entry into the Computer Industry and Its Acquisition of Technological Capability", *Technovation* September, 6(4): 277-293.

Koo B.Y., 1985, Korea in Multinational Enterprises, *Economic Structure and International Competitiveness*, J.H. Dunning (ed.), Chichester, John Wiley.

Krugman P., 1988, "Rethinking International Trade", *Business Economics*, April, 23(2)

Kumar N., 1990, "Mobility Barriers and Profitability of Multinational and Local Enterprises in Indian Manufacturing", *Journal of Industrial Economics*, 38(4), June: 449-463.

Lall S. and Streeten P., 1980 *Foreign Investment, Transnational Corporations and Developing Countries*, London, Macmillan.

Lall, 1981, *The Multinational Corporation*, London, Allen and Unwin.

Lall S., India, 1985, *Multinational Enterprises, Economic Structure and International competitiveness*, J.H. Dunning (ed.), Chichester, John Wiley.

Lall S., 1993, "Foreign Direct Investment in South Asia", *Asian Development Review*, 11(1): 103-119.

Lindberg P, 1995, "Managing and Organising for Advanced Manufacturing Technology", *New Technology and the Workers Response: Microelectronics, Labour and Society*, A.K. Bagchi (Ed), New Delhi, Sage Publications.

Makino N., 1987, *Decline and Prosperity: Corporate Innovation in Japan*, Tokyo, Kodansha International.

Mani S., 1992, "New Industrial Policy: Barriers to Entry, Foreign Investment and Privatisation", *Economic and Political Weekly*, August 29.

Mani S., 19952 "Output Growth, Technology Behaviour and Employment: Indian Electronics Industry under Liberalisation" in *New Technology and the Workers Response: Microelectronics, Labour and Society*, A.K. Bagchi (ed), New Delhi, Sage Publications.

Mathai, P and Narayan S, 1993, 'Fear of the Foreigner', *Business World*, November, Bombay, pp 18-29.

Minhas B, 1991, 'Public vs. Private - Lessons of economics', *Economic Times*, June 11.

Narayanan D and K.J Joseph, "Industry and Trade Liberalisation: Performance of Motor Vehicles and Electronics Industries", 1981-91, *Economic and Political Weekly*, February 20-27.

Narayan S, 1993, 'From Coup to Coup', *BusinessWorld*, August, Bombay, pp 18-25.

Nelson R and S Winter, 1977, "In Search of a Useful Theory of Innovation", *Research Policy*, 6: 36-37.

National Science Board, 1991, *Science and Engineering Indicators*, US Government Printing Office, Washington, DC.

National Science Foundation, 1979, "US Industrial R&D Spending Abroad", *Review of Data On Science Sources*, 33 (April), NSF 79-304, US Government Printing Office, Washington DC.

Odagiri H and Goto A, 1996 *Technology and Industrial Development in Japan : Building Capabilities by Learning, Innovation, and Public Policy*, Oxford, Clarendon.

Pasinetti, L.L., 1981, *Structural Change and Economic Growth – A Theoretical Essay on the Dynamics of Wealth of Nations*, Cambridge University Press, Cambridge.

Patel P. and Pavitt K., 1991, "Large Firms in the Production of the World's Technology: an important case of non-globalisation", *Journal of International Business Studies*, 22: 1-21

Patnaik P, "International Capital and National Economic Policy: A Critique of India's Economic Reforms", *Economic and Political Weekly*, March 19, 1994: 683-689.

Pavitt K and P Patel, 1988, "The International Distribution and Determinants of Technological Activities", *Oxford Review of Economic Policy*, 4(4): 35-55

Pearce R.D. and Singh S. 1992, *Globalising Research and Development*, Basingstoke, Macmillan.

Pfeffer J, and Salancick G., 1974, "Organisational Decision Making as a Political Process: The case of a University Budget, *Administrative Science Quarterly*, 19, pp 135-51.

Pfeffer, J., 1987, "Bringing the Environment Back In: The Social Contest of Business Strategy" in D.J. Teece (ed.), *The Competitive Challenge: Strategies for Industrial Innovation and Renewal*, Cambridge, M.A, Ballinger Publishing Company.

Porter, M.E., 1993, *The Competitive Advantage of nations*, London, Macmillan.

Porter M.E,1986 *Competition in Global Industries*, (ed),Harvard Business School Press, Boston.

Prahalad C.K., Doz, Yves L., 1987, *The Multinational Mission : Balancing Local Demands and Global Vision,* New York, Free Press.

Purkayastha, P., 1994, "New Technologies and Emerging Structures of Global Dominance", *Economic and Political Weekly*, Bombay, August.

Rajan M., 1994, "Review Article: Australian Business in the Asia Pacific Region: The Case for Strategic Industry Policy", *Australian Journal of Management,* 19(2), December.

Rajan M., 1994, *The Institutional Embeddedness of Corporate Strategies in Declining Industries: Capacity Adjustment Strategies in Structurally Depressed Industries in Japan*, Unpublished Doctoral Dissertation, University of California, Irvine.

Rao S.L., 1992, *Economic Reforms and Indian Markets*, New Delhi, 1992, Wheeler Publishing: 19-20.

Robinson J, 1969, *The Accumulation of Capital*, Macmillan Press, London.

Roobeek, A.J, 1988, "Telecommunications: An Industry in Transition", *The structure of European Industry*, H.W. de Jong (ed.), Dordrecht, Kluwer Academic Publishers.

Rugman A.M., 1975, Motives for Foreign Investment: The Market Imperfections and Risk Diversification Hypotheses, *Journal of World Trade Law*, 9 (Sep-Oct), pp 567-73.

Rugman A., 1981, *Inside the Multinationals*, London, Croom Helm.

Sarathy R., and Samuel R., 1987, "Corporate Responses to Industrial Planning", *International Marketing Review*, 4(2), Summer: 33-45.

Scott W.R., 1992, *Organisations: Rational, Natural and Open Systems,* New Jersey, Prentice Hall.

Scott B.R., "Economic Strategy and Economic Performance" in *Australian Business in the Asia Pacific Region - the Case for Strategic Industry Policy*, I. Marsh (ed.), Melbourne, Longman.

Simon H.A., 1956, *Administrative Behaviour*, New York, Macmillan.

Singer H., Hatti N., and Tandon, R., 1991, *Joint Ventures and Collaborations*, New World Order Series:10, New Delhi, Indus Publishing.

Stewart F, 1991, "Technology Transfer for Development", *Joint Ventures and Collaborations*, H. Singer, N Hatti and R Tandon (Eds.), *New World Order Series:10*, New Delhi, Indus Publishing.

Stoever W., 1989, "Foreign Collaboration Policy in India: A Review", *Journal of Developing Areas*, No. 23c, July: 485-504.

Sweezy, P., 1972, *Modern Capitalism and Other Essays,* Monthly Review Press, New York.

Thakur R., 1993, "Restoring India's Economic Health", *Third World Quarterly*, 14(1).

Thomson V.A., 1961, *Modern Organisation*, New York, Knopf.

Thurow L.C., 1992, *Head to Head, The coming Economic Battle Among Japan, Europe and America*, New York, William Morrow and Company.

Vernon R., 1974, "The Location of Economic Activity", in *Economic Analysis and the Multinational Enterprise*, J.H. Dunning (ed.), Surrey, George Allen and Unwin.

Vernon R., 1966, "International Investment and International Trade in the Product Cycle", *Quarterly Journal of Economics*, May: 190-207.

Vyasulu V., 1993, "New Economic Policy and Technological Change: Towards New Initiatives", *Economic and Political Weekly*, July 17-24: 1515-1520.

Weigel D. E., 1988, "Investment in LDCs: The debate Continues", *Columbia Journal of World Business*, Spring: 5-9.

18 PROBLEM OF CHILD LABOUR IN INDIA: NORMATIVE ISSUES

S GUPTA

POSITION OF CHILD LABOUR IN INDIA

Despite the Constitutional directives against abuse of children, the magnitude of the problem of child labour has been of serious proportion from time to time. The Census of India Report 1981 revealed that 5.55 percent of total work force was in the age group of 0-14 in 1981. Among males 4.47 percent were in the age-group of 0-14 while among females 8.65 percent of workers were in the age group of 0-14. Child labour in livestock, forestry and fishing accounted for 15.36 percent of female workers and 13.90 percent of male workers, the total percentage of child labour in this category being 14.21 percent.[1] The Census Report (1981) further revealed that 12.55 million child labourers were in the rural areas and 1.05 million child labourers were in the urban areas. The number of child labourers was the highest in Andhra Pradesh (1.80 million); next came Madhya Pradesh (1.63 million) followed by Maharashtra (1.45 million). The percentage of child labour to child population was also the highest in Andhra Pradesh followed by Karnataka. Cultivators, agricultural labourers and household industry accounted for a large number of child workers in this age group. It is interesting to note that the percentage of female child workers was higher than that of male child workers in these categories. Even in construction, trade and commerce, transport, storage and communication and other services the percentage of female child labour was higher than that of male child labour. It is also interesting to note that number of child workers was higher than that of non- workers.[2] The 1991 census figures for child labourers are not yet available. But the UNICEF estimates indicate that the official estimate

1 These figures have been taken from the Census of India Report, 1981. The figures exclude Assam. Also see the *Table I* in the Appendix, *Table I* also shows the percentage of child labour to child population

2 *Table I* in the Appendix shows the distribution (percent) of child workers by Industrial Categories and by Broad Age Group. *Table II* shows the child workers and non-workers classified by age and sex.

of child labourers in 1993 was 17.5 million and the unofficial estimate is 50-100 millions.[1] By including child labourers who work but are not paid, the Operations Research Group of Baroda arrived at an estimate of 44 million child workers (Weiner 1991, ch.1). In 1996, it was estimated that the total number of child workers in India was about 20 million. Child labour is to be found in both rural and urban areas. About 86% of the child labour in the country is engaged in family labour alongside parents in the agricultural sector (Eswaran 1996). In urban areas female child labourers are very often engaged in the household sector for cleaning utensils, washing garments, and cleaning the floors of the building, etc. They are also sometimes engaged in other activities like their male counterparts. Male child labourers are sometimes engaged in tea stalls or shops in the market apart from being put to work in construction, trade and commerce and transport sectors. In the rural sector, child workers, both male and female, are engaged in the agricultural farm, livestock, forestry, plantation, fishing, household sector and even in mining and quarrying.[2] Legislation related to regulation of child labour in India concentrates on the following issues : (1) minimum age for employment of child worker, (2) a minimum period of work per day and forbidding work of child labour at night, (3) prohibiting certain types of job for children and (4) medical examination of all working children. During the British regime, the Employment of Children Act 1938 prohibited the employment of children below the age of fifteen in any occupation connected with railway transport or with any port authority. It further laid down that child workers below the age of fourteen should not be engaged in (i) *bidi* making, (ii) carpet weaving, (iii) cement manufacture, (iv) cloth printing and dyeing and waving, (v) manufacture of matches, explosives and fire works, (vi) mica cutting and splitting, (vii) shellac manufacture and soap manufacture, (viii) tanning and (ix) wood cutting.

The Factories Act, 1948 prohibits employment of children below 14 years of age in a factory. The Act also prohibits employing children in the age group of 14 to 17 years at night and the children between 14 and 15 years for not more than four and half hours a day and that also

---

1 Sources of these figures are : UNICEF, *The State of the World's Children 1995* (New York : OUP 1995) pp 66-85. It has been guessed that very often the official data regarding child labour do not reveal the truth. Also see the Report on `Child Labour in Asia' prepared by a Committee in Australia to recommend where Aus AID may contribute to alleviate the situation.

2 Report on Child Labour in Indian Industries, Labour Bureau, Ministry of Labour, Government of India, Simla, 1981, P.7.

in one shift. The child workers shall not be allowed, according to this Act, to work on machines which are considered dangerous and shall not be asked to clean, lubricate or adjust any part of prime mover or of any transmission machinery while the same is in motion.

The Mines Act, 1952 prohibits the employment of children in mines and also prohibits the presence of a child worker in any part of the mine which is below ground or above ground where any mining operation is going on.

The last piece of legislation to protect the interests of the child workers in India is the Child Labour (Prohibition and Regulation) Act, 1986, which prohibits the engagement of child workers in certain employments and regulates the conditions of work of children in certain other employments which are hazardous in the organised sector.[1] But this Act which replaces the old Act of 1938 adding one more process into the existing list, viz. 'building and construction', does not say anything about the eradication of child labour.

ECONOMICS OF CHILD LABOUR

The problem of child labour should not be viewed simply in the context of labour law which calls for immediate dismissal or withdrawal from work of children below the age of 14 or 15 since such action may in fact be to the contrary of the children's immediate welfare. Apart from the immediate measures required for the protection of child workers, the plan should include measures against the underlying causes of child labour.

The employment of child labour is basically an economic problem. Abject poverty of the parents forces the children to do some work for earning their livelihood.

The contribution of child labour income to the family income is significant in some cases. In a micro-level study of child labour in four districts of the state of Tamil Nadu in 1986-87, Sumangala and Nagarajan (1993; 121) found the following distribution of the contribution of child labour income to the family income in a sample survey of 400 child labourers and their families: In 15.25% of the families, the contribution was up to 10% of family income, in 41.5% of the families between 11-20%, in 22.73% of the families between 21.30%, in 12.5% of the families between 31.40%, in 4.75% of the families between 41.-50%, in 1.25% of the families between 51-60%,

---

1 For details of the legislation regarding prohibition and regulation of Child Labour in India, see *Young Hand at Work : Child Labour in India*, edited by Manju Gupta and Klaus Voll (Atma Ram and Sons, New Delhi, 1987).

in 0.25% of the families the contribution was above 71%. The role of the child labourers in holding the family above the poverty line in large number of cases is also significant (Sharma and Mittar, 1990 : 109). There is little dispute in the literature about the causes of child labour. Poverty is cited first as the cause of child labour. Statistics indicate that the incidence of child labour is larger in the economically backward and drought-prone areas than in the urban areas. While it is argued that the degree of poverty is the indicator of the incidence of child labour, it is also argued that child labour not only perpetrates poverty it now also constitutes its fundamental cause (Burra, 1995 : 143). If poverty is the principal cause of child labour, it is not the only or the sufficient cause. Illiteracy and the lack of education, commercialisation of agriculture generating surplus labour in the farm sector, and the promotion of export industries requiring cheap labour are also the contributory factors to the growth of child labour.

The majority of child labourers all over the world hand over their earnings to their parents or guardians. Their work is essential to meet the minimum requirements of the household in most of the cases.

The notion of children of the poor working with their parents is centuries old. But there have been changes in the nature of the work with time. Changes in the economic system or mode of production are associated with changes in the structure of labour. The economic justification for child labour may be examined from the standpoint of a demand-supply framework (Bhatty 1996). The demand for child labour comes largely in the form of wage employment in the sectors like industry, domestic establishment, households, commercial enterprises and in the agricultural sector where the child workers assist their parents or family members. This does not cover bonded labour and self- employed street children. Regulatory provisions of the Factory Act which forbid employing child labourers in hazardous jobs compel the most of child labourers to seek employment in the small scale sector. Wages paid to children are always lower than those paid to the adults in the same job. Employing child workers at much lower wages than adults and compelling them to work for long hours is profitable for employers in the small scale sector. The child workers are normally paid remuneration at piece-rate system. Not only that, the children do not form unions and they are less likely to leave the job if they are remunerated regularly, although at low rates. The employers can maintain their full control over the child workers who "can be coaxed, admonished, pulled up and punished without jeopardising relations". [Singh et al 1980 : 152-155]. The benefits derived by the employers from employing child labour are many and it has been found that the producers would rather stop their production than hire adult workers because of the substantial reduction in profits (Kanbargi 1988, Burra 1995).

Another factor influencing the demand for child labour is that child labourers are supposed to be better and more sincere in work than adults at tedious, mechanical jobs which require dexterity rather than training and skills. They are, as such, demanded for labour-intensive jobs in the primary sector and also in the non-primary small scale sector. Therefore, not only does employing child workers keep the wage bill low, it also acts as a disincentive to modernise the industrial unit since raising its capital intensity would be a costly proposition (Bhatty, 1996). It has also been noticed that child labour is considered as an asset to the employers also in export-oriented industries since they can be easily laid off in case of slackening demand without compensation, and can again be employed at cheaper rate in case of increasing foreign demand for these goods. In India, in the handloom and the handicrafts sectors, exporters take advantage of this flexibility in employing child labour. Fluctuations in demand in the export sector also lead to fluctuations in the demand for child labour.

The supply of child labour is contingent upon the economic condition of the family to which the child labourers belong. As long as poverty continues to exist, it would be difficult to totally eradicate child labour. It is commonly believed that the families of the working children are so poor that their survival would be threatened if they are removed from the labour force. They not only earn their livelihood through work, they also contribute to the family fund for the very existence of the family.

The ILO Report on *World of Work* (1996) states that child labour is not only found in domestic and industrial use, but also in prostitution in which children, especially girls are increasingly found. The ILO Report has given a strongly worded statement that "The AIDS epidemic is a contributing factor to this trend, as adults see the use of children for sexual purposes as the best means of preventing infection. The laissez faire attitude of the authorities in charge of national and international tourism is also largely responsible for the current situation". This is a moral issue which can be checked if the Government of a country sincerely and seriously enforces restrictions on immoral trafficking.

As regards the supply of child labour in the agricultural and the industrial sectors, the apologists hold a different view. They believe that their work is some sort of apprenticeship which would help them to acquire the required skill as good artisans in future life, and that if they are sent to schools instead of going to work, they would be detached from the village economy or from the small scale sector. This detachment from the village economy or the small scale sector, according to them, may not guarantee white collar jobs when they become educated adults. The proposition here is very weak in substance. Some questions may be raised in this context. How much are the children contributing to their respective families? Can there not be any alternative way to supplement this income for the affected families if the children are withdrawn from the work? How is the productivity of the children and their capacity to earn higher wages affected during their life time as a whole because of their being added to the labour force at an early age? How would the modernization of the industry with improved technology affect child labour? Finally, what would be the total cost of the economy as a whole if it is to depend on ever-increasing illiterate and unskilled labour force?

We may here refer to some findings of some researchers which may provide answers to these questions. Wiener (1991:33) has observed that ".... it remains unclear how much worse off the family will be if the children were in school. Financial contributions by children to household income are small". Wiener has also referred to the finding of Nasir Tyabji that "the amount added by the child to household income seems to be small" (1991:55). It has also been revealed that even the families above the poverty line send their children to work for maximising family earnings or for preventing their children from remaining idle without sending them to schools. Allowing the children to work is not always a matter of survival of the family. A researcher in this field has found that in many cases earnings of the children have been used by their parents for conspicuous consumption (sometimes for consumption of alcohol).[1]

Even on the demand side, the argument for employing child labour at lower wage rate is very weak since it may adversely affect the efficiency and quality of the labourers in the long run when they become adults. Bhatty (1996) has cited the example of WIMCO factory which makes matches more profitably without child labour and with better technology than other match manufacturers. Burra (1987) has compared a brass factory in Thailand with one in Moradabad and found that the former did not employ child labour and used a better technology than what was used in Moradabad, and had output of better

---

1 This is the finding of Vidyaben Shah. He made this observation at a seminar on "Combating Child Labour in New Delhi" in April, 1995. Reference to this matter is to be found in the paper of Bhatty (1996).

quality. The basic issue here is, depending on child labour even in the small scale sector does not permit introduction of sophisticated technology and as a result both quality and quantity of output suffer. Burra (1987) has also found that child labourers who are pushed to work at the primary stage of their life may even face the risk of unemployment in later life. Very often children have been employed in hazardous activities violating the norms and very often they encounter accidents. The economics of child labour in the demand-supply framework very often ignores the normative aspects of the problem.

It appears that while poverty of the bulk of the population is the most important cause of child labour, the prevalence of child labour is also responsible for poverty since the children do not get the opportunity of being educated and acquiring sufficient earning capacity when they become adults. Health, nutrition and education which are the basic ingredients of human development are denied to the child labourers who are compelled to work for their respective families. The fact of being a low income country is not sufficient for defending the cause of child labour.

Historical comparisons with Sri Lanka, Vietnam, Tanzania, Uganda, Zaire, Burma, Kenya and China show that compulsory education for the children has ensured decreases in child labour.[1] This has not yet been found in India. The ILO Report (1996) observes that in the majority of the countries where child labour is of critical importance, the action taken so far to combat it has in no way been proportional to the extent and the gravity of the problem. Many governments have left it to economic growth and legislation alone to provide the solution. But experience suggests that unless specific measures like human development and social development are taken, growth in itself rarely benefits the very poor and legislation means little when it is not vigorously enforced.

NORMATIVE ISSUES OF THE PROBLEM

It is acknowledged that child labour should be eradicated. It is also admitted that child labour cannot be eradicated within a short period and that only legislation alone cannot solve the problem. The denial of opportunity to children for their proper physical development and education is an issue of serious nature. It is true that the problem of child labour is basically an economic one; but it has far-reaching social

[1] Weiner (1991) has shown that of the 14 countries in the world with population more than 15 million and per capita income less than $ 500 in 1989, India ranks ninth in literacy behind all the countries mentioned here. India is ahead of Ethiopia, Nepal, Sudan and Bangladesh in this respect. Also see Bhatty (1996).

implications. Keeping in view the problem of poverty which prepares the ground for employing child labour, a way has to be found to give the child the necessary education in his receptive years. The National Commission on Labour in India feels that "this can be ensured by fixing the employment hours of children so as to enable them to attend to schooling. When the number of children is adequate, the employers, with the assistance of State Governments should make arrangements to combine work with education".[1]

Apart from enforcing compulsory primary education for the child labourers, another measure for dissuading the entrepreneurs and factory owners from rushing for cheap child labour is the introduction of minimum wage for child workers. This measure is not an alternative to education. It is possible that just as making school mandatory would reduce the supply of child labourers, so raising their wage rate and thus the cost of their labour would lower the demand for them. With children no longer available at cheap rates, child labour may lose much of its attraction to the employers. The market would automatically readjust to this situation with a shift from the demand for better-paid child labour to better-paid adult labour.

The Supreme Court of India has ordered that the employers who have recruited child workers in the hazardous jobs will have to give compensation to each of the child workers to the tune of Rs. 25,000/-. But loopholes in the legislation have been taken advantage of by the employers to avoid the compliance with this directive of the court. Statutory protection to child labour does not guarantee the abolition of the system.

The Government of India has not officially abandoned its objective of ending child labour and enforcing compulsory primary education for the children. Accepting that child labour is the consequence of chronic poverty - not its cause - the Government appears not to be very strict in enforcing the remedial measures, particularly the implementation of compulsory primary education for the children. The Government made 'amelioration' and not `abolition', the primary thrust of its National Policy on Child Labour in 1987. This policy embodied a mixed prescription. Child work was allowed in less hazardous jobs through greater regulation, and on the other hand declared to set up 500,000 new non-formal educational centres to enable children both to work and study. Under the National Child labour Policy the lot of child labourers may improve. But the fear is

---

1 See the Report of the National Commission of Labour, India, 1969, Para 27-39.

that ameliorating the problem would not help much to eradicate the problem.

But our view is different. We feel that compulsory education for the children would be a better proposition than combining work with education. There are some norms arising from the inherent dignity of human beings and these are recognised in international covenants accepted by different countries irrespective of their levels of development. It is imperative for these countries to adhere to these norms. India was a signatory to the first ILO convention on prohibition of child labour in 1919. To invoke the pretext of poverty and economic compulsions in a less developed economy for the transgression of universally accepted values regarding the inherent dignity of human beings is to accept the perpetuation of universally condemned abuses [ILO 1983 : 20]. In India, there is no doubt that there have been some improvements in poverty levels but there has been no corresponding improvements in the prevalence of child labour (Bhatty, 1996). There has also not been much improvement in literacy rates.

It must be recognised that even with the strongest of legislation and the most efficient implementation machinery, child labour cannot be eradicated overnight. It should be done in phases. But first of all, it must be recognised that giving indulgence to child labour on the pretext of poverty and underdevelopment without giving the children the opportunity to be educated and to get the benefits of health and nutrition is unethical. The first step should be to remove children from working in hazardous occupations and to create conditions to gradually eliminate child labour.

Any programme for eradication of child labour should begin with creating an atmosphere where people will realise that it is unethical to deny a child of the opportunity of going to school and also creating a consciousness about the evils of this practice in the society, in the minds of parents, labour contractors, entrepreneurs, politicians and labour leaders. Article 45 of the Directive Principles of State Policy (Part IV of the Indian Constitution) directs the state to provide free and compulsory education for children up to the age of 14 years and this was to be achieved within 10 years from the commencement of the Constitution. We have a long way to go. In West Bengal, school education up to the higher secondary level has been made free for many years. But it has not been possible to ensure that all parents send their children to schools. If every school-going poor child were to be given a stipend along with one free nutritional meal, it would pursuade the parents to send their children to schools since the money from the stipend would somewhat offset loss in income and the free meal would ensure a better, healthy growth of a child (Gupta, 1987 : 162).

Compulsory primary education must be introduced and this should be accompanied by improvements in the education system. The rigid school curriculum should be changed so that it incorporates training in crafts along with reading, writing and basic mathematics. Even a cultivator or a landless agriculturist should have the minimum education and that should be imparted to him in his childhood - this should be the norm in introducing compulsory primary education. Compulsory primary education is undoubtedly the most effective tool in keeping children away from the labour force. Parental apathy is definitely a constraint in sending the child to school. Along with compulsory primary education, arrangement may be made for adult education programmes imparting knowledge of sanitation, health care and nutrition as well as creating an awareness that pushing children to work is detrimental to the mental and physical growth of their children. This may be helpful to remove the parental apathy (Gupta, 1987 : 162). The 1981 Census of India revealed that only 9.17 percent of the main male child workers in the rural areas had attained the primary education level while only 4.95 percent of the main girl child workers in rural areas had studied up to the primary level. The situation improved over a decade up to 1991 but not significantly. In India, bonded labour where children have been pledged to landlords and factory owners, creates a hurdle to the child workers going to schools. In India there are about 10 million children who are in some form of bondage despite debt bondage had been formally outlawed in 1976. In India, the female children who, because they are destined to leave the family after marriage, are considered less worthy of an education than boys, are more suited to contribute to family income. Parental apathy to send the children to school is particularly much evident in case of female workers. Apart from parental apathy, another constraint in eradicating child labour is the hidden strength of the vested interests who intend to perpetuate this evil only for their own private interests. It has been revealed in a study made by Juyal (1986) that mafia gangs on the pay roll of big factory owners forcibly bring children to work and no form of protest is allowed. There have been many cases in Mirzapur - Bhadohi and Firozabad where social activists against child labour have been eliminated. Child labour has been the unfortunate creation of a class of labour which can be forced into work and discarded at will (Gupta 1987 : 165). Had there been strong political will to eradicate child labour, an atmosphere could have been created where parents, employers and politicians would feel guilty and made to realise that sending children to work is unethical and that it is their duty to give back to children their basic right of a carefree childhood. The children can also be motivated to demand education and a good life. Apart from enforcing compulsory primary education steps should be taken to implement the existing Acts and also to undertake rehabilitation programmes for children. A suitable population policy based on family planning programmes should also be pursued since all welfare programmes for children in the forms of giving food, medical care and education may come to nought if the birth rate is not brought under control. The non-Government organisations and the village *panchayets* could also play an important part in making the people understand the urgency of family planning.

Compulsory education is definitely the remedy for child labour that the Union Government and State Governments should employ. In Kerala, the literacy rate is the highest in India (which was 89.8 percent in the 1991 Census and which is estimated to be 93 percent in 1996) and the percentage of child labour to child population is the lowest in that state. The Kerala experiment is a concrete proof that neither widespread poverty nor low per capita income could be posited as barriers to the adoption of compulsory education. Kerala has consistently spent about 36-38 percent of its budget on providing a universally accessible education system which is far above the state average for India. One significant aspect of the Kerala experiment is that schooling of children has been carefully organised around work, rather than functioning as an alternative to work. Most of the schools remain closed for 160 days a year, this enables seasonal work and the educational calendar to be conveniently reconciled.

Besides the measures required to protect the children, the underlying causes of child labour should be considered keeping in mind the economic issues, and the social attitudes and sensibilities. According to the statistical survey conducted by the ILO as many as 25 to 40 percent of children under 15 years of age are economically active in various developing countries.[1] While the children should be compulsorily sent to schools to ensure a decline in the number of child workers, employment strategies should be so designed that viable income opportunities may be created for the poor through poverty alleviation programmes. The system of education should also be made attractive to the children and there should be a system of mandatory attendance enforced by local pressure groups. This might help to check the influx of children into the labour force. The social and religious

---

1 ILO Report, *World of Work*, 1996.

organisations can play an important role as pressure groups in not only providing literacy and non-formal education but also in removing the parental apathy in sending the children to schools.

Non-government organisations can act as identifying and monitoring units to tackle this problem, and public opinion against the abuses of child labour can thus be mobilised.

CONCLUSION

Problem of child labour is basically due to abject poverty of the people. Total eradication of child labour is not possible in a developing economy like India. But child labour should not be encouraged on ethical and social considerations. To check the growth of child labour, poverty alleviation programmes along with measures for compulsory education of the children should be vigorously implemented. Legislation to check the abuses of child labour should, no doubt, be enforced. But this is not sufficient for the eradication of the problem. The numerous holes in the legislations should be plugged, and the hazardous work should be clearly identified so that child labourers, so long as the problem has not been solved, may not be employed in hazardous work. On balance, the provision for an adequate education system for the child workers is the most practical way to combat child labour. What is most important is to awaken a feeling in the minds of the parents of the children that their sons or daughters should not be denied of the opportunity of a decent life which is primarily contingent upon education. Actually, the political will is lacking in most of the states of the country to eradicate the problem. The normative issues of the problem should be highlighted and the non-government social organisations as well as religious or missionary institutions may be asked to mobilise public opinion in favour of compulsory school attendance of the children. To overcome the parental apathy in sending the children to schools, some sort of financial relief for the child's family should be provided for. Children of the poor going to school may also be awarded stipends. This may enable the family to send its children to schools. The problem has far-reaching social implications and to tackle the problem, changes in social attitudes to child labour must be changed. So long as child labour cannot be eradicated, steps should be taken to ban child labour in hazardous areas and to regulate the conditions of works in other areas. Along with this, provision should be made for proper nutrition, health and compulsory education of the children.

REFERENCES

Bequele, A. (1986) - *Child Labour : A Briefing Manual* (Geneva, ILO).

Bequele, A. and Boyden J. (1988) *Combating Child Labour* (Geneva, ILO).

Bhatty, Kiran (1996) - "Child Labour : Breaking the Vicious Circle", *Economic and Political Weekly*, Bombay, February 17.

Boyden, J. and Myers, W. (1995) : "Exploring Alternative Approaches to Combating Child Labour : Case Studies From Developing Countries" (Occasional Paper, Child Rights Series, No. 8, Geneva, ILO).

Burra, Neera (1987) : Report on Child Labour in the Pottery Industry of Khurjua, Uttar Pradesh (Mimeo), DANIDA, New Delhi.

____(1995) : *Born to Work : Child Labour in India*, Oxford University Press, New Delhi.

Dinesh, B.M. (1988) *: Economic Activities of Children : Dimensions, Causes and Consequences* (Delhi, Daya Publishing House).

Eswaran, M. (1996) : "Fertility, Literacy and the Institution of Child Labour" (IRIS - India Working Paper No. 26, Maryland).

Ghosh, Arun (1992) : "Child Exploitation and Abuse : A Global Phenomenon". *The Report of the First Asian Conference on Child Exploitation and Abuse*, Calcutta, India, December 17,19, 1990 (New Delhi, B. Mallik).

Gupta, Manju (1987) : "Proposals on How Child Labour can be Eradicated" *in Young Hands at Work : Child Labour in India* - Edited by Manju Gupta and Klaus Voll (Atma Ram and Sons, New Delhi).

ILO (1983) : *Report of the Director General, International Labour Conference*, 69th Session, Geneva.

_____(1996) : *World of Work*, Geneva.

Juyal, B.N. (1986) : "Child Exploitation in Carpet Industry - A Mirzapur - Bhadohi Case Study", ISI Seminar.

Kanbargi, R. (1988) : "Child Labour in India : The Carpet Industry of Varanasi" in Assefe Begnele and Jo Boyden (eds), *Combating Child Labour*, ILO, Geneva.

Kumar, S. (1993) : "Child Labour and Education" in *Children at Work* (eds) B.P. Singh and S. Mohanty (B.R. Publishing Corporation, Delhi).

Mahtre, S.L. (1995) *: Child Labour Legislation in South Asia : A Documentation and Analysis* (UNICEF, Regional Office).

National Commission of Labour (1969) : India, New Delhi.

Sharma B.K. and Mittar V. (1990) : *Child Labour and Urban Informal Sector* (Deep & Deep Publications, New Delhi).

Singh, Musafir et al (1980) : *Working Children in Bombay : A Study*, NIPCCD, New Delhi.

Sumangala, M. and Nagarajan B.S. (1993) : *Economics of Child Labour and Fertility* (B.R. Publishing Corporation, Delhi).

Wiener, Myron (1991) : *The Child and the State in India*, Oxford University Press, New Delhi.

Report on Child Labour in Indian Industries (1981) : Labour Bureau, Ministry of Labour, Government of India (Simla).

Report on Child Labour in Asia (1996) : Committee for AusAID Contribution to alleviate the Problem of Child Labour.

Report of the National Commission of Labour, India (1969).

APPENDIX

Table 1: **Distribution (per cent) of Child Workers (main plus marginal) by Industrial Categories and by Broad Age Groups, 1981.**

	Industrial Category	Persons 0-14	Males 0-14	Females 0-14
I-IX	Total Workers	5.55	4.47	8.65
I	Cultivators	5.05	4.13	8.11
II	Agricultural Labourers	8.98	8.42	9.69
III	Livestock, forestry, fishing etc.	14.21	13.90	15.36
IV	Mining and quarrying	2.30	1.49	7.47
V	Manufacturing, processing, servicing and repairs:			
	(a) Household Industry	5.76	4.29	8.77
	(b) Other than Household Industry	3.22	2.58	8.35
VI	Construction	2.42	1.68	8.06
VII	Trade and Commerce	1.86	1.80	2.58
VIII	Transport, storage and communications	0.58	0.54	1.68
IX	Other Services	1.76	1.28	4.05

Source: Census of India Report, 1981.
Figures exclude Assam.

Table 2: **Main Child Workers, Marginal Child Workers and non-Workers Classified by Age and Sex.** (Figures in Millions)
(Percentages are in Brackets)

Total Rural Urban	Age Group	Population			Main Workers			Marginal Workers			Non-Workers		
		Total	Male	Female	Total	Male	Female	Total	Male	Female	Total	Male	Female
Total	0-14	263	135.8	127.2	11.2 (4.3)	7.4 (5.4)	3.8 (3.0)	2.4 (0.9)	0.7 (0.5)	1.7 (1.3)	249.4 (94.8)	127.7 (94.0)	121.7 (95.7)
Rural	0-14	205.4	106.1	99.3	10.2 (5.0)	6.7 (6.3)	3.5 (3.5)	2.4 (1.2)	0.7 (0.7)	1.7 (1.7)	192.9 (93.9)	98.8 (93.1)	94.1 (94.8)
Urban	0-14	57.6	29.7	27.9	1.0 (1.7)	0.7 (2.3)	0.3 (1.1)	0.06 (0.1)	0.02 (0.0)	0.04 (0.1)	56.5 (98.1)	28.9 (97.3)	27.6 (98.9)

Source: Census of India 1981 Report.

Part III

Closing Address

19 INTERNATIONAL CONFERENCE ON GOVERNANCE ISSUES AND SUSTAINABLE DEVELOPMENT IN THE INDIAN OCEAN RIM COUNTRIES

MICHAEL BEHAN

CLOSING ADDRESS

Could I say, at the outset, how nice it is to be back at my alma mater. The University of Western Australia has one of the better campuses in Australia, if not the world. If universities are about quiet contemplation, then this is the place to be. I would also like to make a couple of opening comments: the first a disclaimer that I am not a theorist. I have spent the last twenty years in politics, nine of these as a Senator, nearly three as President of the Senate, and before that as a party official. So I have spent a good deal of time trying to put other people's theories into practice.

Secondly, while I have always been interested in international affairs, and in particular in development aid, my role as President of the Senate has drawn me further into this area. It has, for example, involved a lot of travel. It has also involved hosting overseas delegations, receiving ambassadors and being very well briefed on international affairs. It is an interesting coincidence that the last ambassador to present his credentials to me as President of the Senate before I relinquished the position was His Excellency Ambassador Chialo of Tanzania, who has been with us throughout the Conference. All of this has involved me much more deeply in international affairs and explains, in part, why I am now attached to the Centre for Development Studies at Edith Cowan University.

I came to this Conference to learn, and I must say that I have learned a lot, and have enjoyed the interchanges and meeting with some very pleasant people with very fine minds. I hope, then, that you will forgive me for 'shooting from the hip' in exercising the privilege of making these concluding remarks.

As I have been thinking about the Conference four issues have exercised my mind above others. The first was stimulated by Professor Paige Porter who, in her opening remarks referred to the fact that the term 'globalisation', so glibly used by all of us these days, refers solely to economics and trade; that it says nothing about political or social concerns; that there is no effective globalisation, for example, of government or (and here I may be expanding on Professor Porter's views) of politics or labour. This was taken up later by Professor Robert Schrire when he made the point that good governance in a domestic context (he was referring to South Africa) is made much more difficult by globalisation.

It struck me that the question of globalisation provides a backdrop for everything that we have been discussing. There is no doubt that nation states, whether developed or developing are less significant - less powerful, less able to influence events - than they were. Large transnational and multinational companies (and I use these terms descriptively not pejoratively) have turnovers bigger than the GDP's of many of the countries with whom they deal. They, together with the major developed nations where they are based, influence the direction of events, leaving most national governments to respond reactively.

So, globalisation, with all its difficulties and challenges, particularly for developing countries, must always be prominent in our consideration of questions of governance.

The second issue which has exercised my mind, and the minds of most of us I suspect, is that equally over-used term 'sustainable development'. If we take the most frequently quoted definition of Gro Harlem Brundtland: *'Development that meets the needs of the present without compromising the ability of future generations to meet their own needs'* can we any longer regard this as possible? Some, like Professor Kar have expressed doubts, and I know that others do too. Does any of us seriously believe that we can offer a billion Chinese, as just one example, the profligate lifestyle in Western developed countries, without massive and catastrophic environmental degradation?

Binayak Ray[1], in his paper, quoting from a collaborative study with Robin Ghosh re-defines sustainable development as: *'A rate of economic growth that is required to ensure a steady and long-term improvement in the standard of living of a population at large'*. All of this has implications for Western developed nations which I will come back to.

The third issue which has troubled me is what is meant by governance. A variety of approaches has been taken - from the World

---

1 This paper is not included in this volume.

Bank definition referred to by a number of speakers to more specific and focused examples. Professor Kelegama's excellent case study[1] of Sri Lanka places considerable emphasis on the strong and focused leadership of President Premadasa in achieving strong growth together with substantial economic and social reform, even if this was at the expense of human rights considerations in dealing with the insurgency. Interestingly, and all too rarely, Professor Kelegama referred to the interplay between political and social considerations and economic considerations in shaping policy. It is frequently forgotten or misunderstood that a climate of acceptability must be won if lasting economic reform or 'structural adjustment', as we call it when applied to developing countries, is to be achieved. In any democratic system governments do not act in a vacuum. They are constantly and understandably conscious of public reactions to their policy proposals and actions.

Professor Hamid took an equally useful but different slant on governance, listing a range of rules and regulations through which the Government of Bangladesh could have improved on an already impressive economic record, while Dr Sam Makinda, in his interesting description of the clan structure of Somalia, demonstrated that even this tortured, damaged and apparently chaotic country is not without governance, even if this is poorly understood by the United Nations and its agencies. There were other, quite different approaches such as that by Professor Botha, who defined governance in relation to monetary policy.

It struck me that the question of governance might well be applied in reverse to developed nations. In our comfortable democracies we have reached the point where poll-driven governments are being forced by populist demands into mean-spirited and inward-looking policies which include cuts to development aid programs. Governments, even if they know better, find it difficult to bring about a real re-distribution of global wealth. This has happened over recent years with the Republican resurgence in the United States, and it is happening here in Australia now.

I see very little hope, when we are driven by ignorant opinion, that our forms of government will ever permit the sort of reduction in living standards which is essential if the world's limited resources are to be shared more fairly and without environmental damage. I must say that I like the idea, proposed by Professor Tisdell that those countries

---

1 This paper is not included in this volume.

which have an accumulated stock of, say, greenhouse emissions or forest usage should pay for the privilege.

I am embarrassed by the fact that Australia's contribution to overseas aid is now down to 0.28% of GDP and falling, against a UN target of 0.7%. I thank Binayak Ray and Dr Dutta for their useful contribution to an understanding of aid statistics. And I do not blame the current government exclusively, the rot was started by the Labor Government of which I was part, and is being driven by liberal economists in Treasury and Finance.

Fourthly, we have talked a lot about corruption, again without agreeing on what we mean by it. Although again there have been some very useful contributions. I was delighted to hear about Transparency International, which I had not heard of before. I notice that Isabel Blackett of Transparency International focused our attention on 'grand corruption', while Binayak Ray and others pointed out that identified corruption is not, in some countries an impediment to development, whilst in others it is. In this regard the paper by Robin Ghosh and Abu Siddique on types of corruption is a useful starter. And the series of questions put 'off the cuff' but very cogently by Abdul Hamid provide useful further pointers for research.

Corruption is such a variable thing. I am reminded of two personal experiences. The first was at a conference in Japan. I had presented my business card to a Thai member of parliament and former Admiral. He commented on the fact that I was Chairman of our Parliament's Corporations and Securities Committee and, rubbing his fingers together, indicated that there must be plenty of money in such a position. He seemed surprised when I told him that it involved only a small allowance. The second, at a more petty level, was on a recent visit to Sydney when the taxi driver asked me what amount I would like written on the receipt. Again he seemed surprised when I suggested that the receipt should be made out for the amount on the meter.

Finally, since I could not take the matter further at the time and I now have the opportunity, I challenged Professor Robert Bruce on the question of the training in Australia of Indonesian military personnel. I wanted to take the matter further - to put the case for constructive engagement rather than isolationism. We may well come under criticism for engaging Indonesia in the way that we do, but if we do it well and without compromising our principles, and use every opportunity at our disposal to express our concerns on human rights issues, then this is infinitely better than isolating them.

It is very easy for the United States and Europe to be critical of our relations with Indonesia. They do not live here. And I have the feeling that the strength of feeling about issues is in inverse relationship with one's distance from them.

I would have liked to have had time to comment on some of the other papers and to recount some personal experiences with the question of governance in Africa, but applying the maxim that good things when short are twice as good, I will stop now and simply thank the organisers and you, the participants for allowing me the privilege of this final say.

INDEX

The Centre for Migration and Development Studies (CMDS)

CMDS is an advanced research centre located within the Department of Economics at The University of Western Australia. The Centre's research interest revolves around theoretical aspects of the migration-development process, the impact of permanent migration on Australia's socio-economic development, and the impact of migration in general on processes of socio-economic changes in developing countries. It also conducts applied research on various developing regions. Its current focus is on South Africa, Indian Ocean island states, South Asia and the Middle East with special reference to intra-regional migration; economic development and change; role and effectiveness of economic aid; sustainable development and environment; economic liberalisation and trade reforms; and tourism in relation to economic and social change. The Centre has already achieved national recognition in both government and academic circles in Australia.

Academic and research staff associated with CMDS have extensively published in refereed journals and authored numerous books dealing with developmental issues. The Centre is very active in organising international seminars and conferences on contemporary topical problems. In the past it has been successful in attracting research grants from both national and international organisations such as UNESCO, AusAID, the National Centre for Development Studies (NCDS) and the West Australian Government.

The Centre's principal researchers are: Dr M A B Siddique, Emeritus Professor R T Appleyard, Associate Professor R Gabbay and Associate Professor R N Ghosh. The researchers of the Centre are often invited to present papers at national and international conferences.

The Centre is always ready to consider quality research papers relating to migration and development for publication.

For further information please contact:

Dr M A B Siddique
Director
The Center for Migration and Development Studies
Department of Economics
The University of Western Australia
Nedlands WA 6907, Perth, Australia
Telephone: +61-8-9380-2941 Facsimile: +61-8-9380-1016
Email: asiddiqu@ecel.uwa.edu.au

ASPECTS OF INDIAN SOCIETY AND ECONOMY

Aspects of Indian Society and Economy

[IN THE NINETEENTH CENTURY]

[*A study based on an evaluation of the American Consular Records*]

VINAYSHIL GAUTAM, M.A., PH.D., F.R.A.S.,

School of African & Asian Studies,

University of Sussex, England

and

St. Stephen's College,

University of Delhi, India.

MOTILAL BANARSIDASS

Delhi Varanasi Patna Madras

Head Office: Bungalow Road, Delhi 110 007
Branches: Chowk, Varanasi 221 001
Ashok Rajpath, Patna 800 004
6 Appar Swamy Koil Street, Mylapore,
Madras 600 004

Edition: 1986

ISBN: 81–208–0057–5

Printed in India by Narendra Prakash Jain at Shri Jainendra Press, A-45 Naraina, Phase I, New Delhi 110 028 and published by Shantilal Jain for Motilal Banarsidass, Delhi 110 007.

For,

Prof. D. A. Low

FOREWORD

Few will deny that the nineteenth century was a creative age in Indian History and witnessed the decline of the old order and the foundation of the new. This was particularly so in the socio-economic field. Several scholars have worked on this aspect of the development, yet it will not be wrong to say that our knowledge of this subject is still rather limited.

It is a matter of great satisfaction, therefore, that Dr. Vinayshil Gautam, one of the most promising Indian scholars of the younger generation, has prepared this painstaking account of social and economic conditions in India in the nineteenth century on the basis of the reports of the American Consuls stationed in Calcutta and Bombay. By doing so he has not only opened up a new source for the history of India in the nineteenth century, which had not been tapped uptill now by anyone, but also presented before us a balanced picture of Indian society and economy in the nineteenth century. He has not accepted anything uncritically, but checked whatever information he has gathered from the American Consular reports by referring to other relevant sources. At the same time he has carefully delineated the conditions under which and the purpose for which the American Consuls wrote their reports. He has also added a chapter on Indo-American trade in the nineteenth century. All in all, the present study represents a valuable addition to the existing literature on India in the nineteenth century and should be found useful by all serious students of the subject.

Jawaharlal Nehru University,
New Delhi, India.

Bimal Prasad
Professor of South Asian Studies

CONTENTS

PREFACE

The task of a student of social history of modern India is at once absorbing and challenging but on occasions it can also be exasperating. Lack of adequate data which plagues so many branches of history handicaps the writing of a convincing social history too. Hence there is a perennial quest for new sources and improvement of methodological tools which could take the available data the greatest distance possible. This essay is a small effort in both these directions.

One's interest in social history took one far afield and after having drawn a blank with some sources it was quite a thrill to hit upon the American Consular Records. Most unexpectedly one did strike oil after several drillings. But, as so often happens with a new source, it was realised that these Records were useful not only for the reconstruction of social history but for the redoing of some other branches of history too. It was a difficult task to resist the temptation of exploring all the possibilities in this one effort but 'discretion being the better part of valour' it was considered advisable to restrict the study to the socio-economic evolution alone. It was some satisfaction to realise that having chartered the area of social and economic history for the work the problem was one of dealing with two branches of history intimately correlated with one another and which also lent an insight into each other's evolution.

However for such a study of these Records it is not as if the plunge could be taken straightaway. This is so partially because the nineteenth century in India was a strange century in more ways than one. What with a colonial situation here and the need of accomplishing the double revolution of liberalism and nationalism it was complicating the understanding of the subject still further to realise that the attitude or the policy of the United States (the writings of whose representatives are sought to be evaluated here) towards India was not an autonomous variable in this century but was dependent to a very large extent on the relations of the United States with the United Kingdom. A relevant analysis of the American Consular Service was therefore essential. It was not unoften that in the course of the research I was reminded of a comment made by Prof. D. A. Low as early as January 1969 on this project : 'Perhaps you have an over-ambitious scheme'.

Not being an angel perhaps I did rush where wiser men might have feared to tread. The result of the effort is now before you to see and assess. I was, indeed, charmed by these sources perhaps because amongst other reasons it is one of the few non-governmental sources with an all India or as nearly all India perspective as one might conceivably get. Being an 'overtly' third person empirical account of persons not really 'involved' in the scene was an added attraction. Exploring it was both fun and education.

Greater was the satisfaction because it helped me in formulating certain models which had appeared to emerge from my dablings in missionary papers, folk literature, folk art and a limited amount of field work.[1] To go into those details would really be outside the scope of this essay and a passing reference has been made to such aspects here only because the Consular Records helped confirm an impression which had grown on me by my association with these different types of source material. The work therefore provided an occasion to me to hazard the duality model of 'traditional unit' and 'colonial unit' for the evolution of the Indian society. It is needless to add that for one's purposes it would mean an almost equal emphasis on the economic factors as on the non-economic. It was natural therefore to drift into the field of economic history proper where too one has proposed certain methodological innovations. The researchers in the field might like to consider it.

Another interesting dimension which emerged spontaneously from the survey of the economic scene was the narrative of the Indo-American trade relations. A brief survey of this facet of Indian economy for the whole of the nineteenth century is also given in the book.

Left to myself I would have probably liked to spend considerable more time in processing, myself, some of the data

1. after all in a proverbially stable society like pre-industrial India, with a comparative absence of written records, it is possible to project one's vision by about a century or so backwards after a careful field survey.

presented here. To do so would have been most fruitful but realising that research is a continuous process I thought the better of it. It was perhaps as important to place these Records on the map of Indian historical research as it was to analyse them. The first job had to be performed with a sense of urgency for the sequel to it would be a challenge to be met by more than one researcher in the field with specialisation in their respective areas of interest. I decided to perform the first duty, and confined myself merely to introductory comments on some of the areas which these Records covered even at the risk of being told that I should have spent still more time in analysing them. I was, indeed, reminded of what William Penn said somewhere. The exact quotation is : 'I have undertaken a subject that I am very sensible requires one of more sufficiency than I am master of to treat it, as in truth, it deserves..... but since bunglers stumble upon the game as well as masters though it belongs to the skilful to hunt and catch it, I hope this essay will not be charged upon me for a fault if it appear to be neither chemerical or injurious and may provoke abler pens to improve and perform the design with better judgment and success'.

My other reason for getting this essay in print, when I did, is a slightly personal one. Frankly nearly four years of research on this aspect of modern Indian history had left me tired and stale. Besides the major portion of the printing was done on the eve of my departure to the School of African and Asian Studies, University of Sussex, England. To leave it unpublished would have meant a delay of another couple of years, perhaps. It was not worth the price.

The obligations, inspiration and sustenance in any work of this type are many. I will not even claim to be exhaustive, nevertheless I would like to record my appreciation and gratefulness to the following persons for what they did for me in the course of this study : Profs. B. B. Misra, D. N. Sharma, R. Kumar, A. Prasad, M. N. Das, Sarup Singh, Mrs. K. Sharma, Miss D. Sharma, Messrs S. N. Aggarwal, M. L. Mehra, Vijayshil Gautam, Kumaresh Misra, Zubair Ahmad and the authorities and the staff of the National Archives of India, Maharashtra State Archives, Tamil Nadu State Archives, Sapru House Library, Rattan Tata Library etc. I would also like to record my thankfulness to

Dr. P. Misra for having generously lent to me some of the micro-film reels in his possession and helped me in more ways than one.

To Prof. D. A. Low I am grateful for having ever been encouraging and always keeping in close touch, in sincere acknowledgement of which it was thought fit and proper to dedicate this work to him. Prof. Bimal Prasad, my teacher in my university days as a student, has been very gracious in having kindly agreed to write the foreword to this book.

Messrs Motilal Banarsidass have been very obliging in the course of the publication and I feel particularly happy to thank Shri N. P. Jain and Shri J. P. Jain for many kindnesses personal and professional.

And finally to the unnamed one too my no less sincere and grateful appreciation for being around in a solicitous way.

Vinayshil Gautam

ABBREVIATIONS

S. Doc.	*State Document* (Department of State, U.S.)
H. Jol.	*House Journal* (Ref. American Senate & American House of Representatives)
H. Doc.	*House Document* (Ref. American Senate & American House of Representatives)
Cong. Globe	*Congressional Globe* (Ref. American House of Representatives)
H. Rpt.	*House Report* (Ref. American Senate & American House of Representatives)
Op. Attys. Gen.	*Opinions of Attorney Generals, Collection of* (American)
C.D.	Calcutta Despatches
B.D.	Bombay Despatches
Ames mss.	Ames Library Manuscripts
N.A.I.	National Archives of India, New Delhi
M.f.	In Microfilms

CHAPTER I

Introduction

Formulation of the Problem

To this day there is no essay available which seeks to trace the Indian social and economic scene in its entirety throughout the nineteenth century. Perhaps no such satisfying attempt can be made for a long time to come, because the regional histories on which such a study would necessarily be based are only beginning to be written. The need however remains to tap such sources also which had an all-India or as near all-India perspective as was possible for that period. Among such sources the American Consular reports in India undoubtedly rank very high.

This essay is a humble effort then to use such a source to trace the social and economic condition of India in the nineteenth century. Yet it is not exclusively based on Consular reports because to do so would have been to expose oneself to the charge of credulity. Throughout it has been one's effort to keep testing the Consular and other descriptions on the framework of such evidence as available : both Governmental and non-governmental.

There was one other obvious advantage in making such a study viz. the American Consular reports would overtly have been a 'third-person-account' of the Indian situation. 'Third-person' because Americans were not active political participants in the colonial situation of India, where Indians and Britons were concerned. 'Overtly' because on the face of it Americans being a different nationality could possibly be free from bias towards either of the two parties concerned. Yet this was a postulate which needed to be analysed scientifically before it could be accepted, and the attempt in itself was worth making.

This, then, was the major concern in such an analysis as is attempted here. But the story could unfold itself only in a particular context. And to make a scientific survey it was essential to get this context right.

This context was of a study in a colonial situation. When

the U.S. Consuls were accredited to Calcutta and later elsewhere they could not be accredited to a geographical entity, but had to address themselves to a government. The 'government' in this case was that of the East India Company—a joint stock organisation holding territory ! Could such a 'government' receive diplomatic representatives ?[1]

That was a separate matter and shall be studied in a subsequent chapter. But what is significant is that the area of operation of the American Consul was essentially that of British India. As the British territories expanded so did the sphere of activity of the Consul. Again British behaviour in India was not an autonomous variable but was dependent on many factors included among which would be British thinking at home and the world situation affecting their Empire. Hence to have a proper appreciation of the colonial situation in India one has to keep in mind such factors also. And a proper understanding of the colonial situation at that, is important because America through its Consuls was not touching a free India directly, but a dependent India through England. Hence American attitude towards India was to a very large extent guided, if not wholly determined, by its relations with England.

Then again the colonial situation in itself was not a static one in India through the nineteenth century but was constantly developing and changing. Gradually the power of the East India Company had to be contained and slowly taken over by the Crown. The process begun in 1793 saw its culmination in 1858 aided by the catalyst of 1857. But this consummation was only to mark the beginning of another process which reached its climax in the administration of Curzon.

Hence it was a dynamic situation in which the Consuls had to operate. What contact they had with princely and non-British India was also through English administration in the country.

If the Indian situation was a dynamic one no less fluid was the American situation the writing of whose representatives one seeks to use here. The Consuls would have been more than human if they did not bring with themselves a carry-over of the conditions at home as also their prejudices. Hence to make a scienti-

1. Benjamin Joy in a letter to the Secretary of State, U. S. A., Calcutta, dated Nov. 24, 1794, Calcutta Despatches, hereafter written as C.D.

fic study of their statements it was important to know their background. It would not merely suffice to present an abridged history of the United States but the need would be to present an authentic and relevant account of America of the period of our study, based again on original sources.

One need hardly point out that America of 1905 was not the America of 1865 or of 1790 in any sense of the term : be it politics, territory, military, people or even culture. In 1790 America's population was less than four million. The whole settled area was less than the area of the present State of Texas. The people were poor and backward in industrial development. The amount of internal trade was small, even in proportion to the scanty population. Militarily and economically they were very weak.[1] The power-packed, prosperous image of America is definitely of a later date.

Hence for a proper scientific understanding of the reports of the Consuls it was necessary to have a rough idea of the changing patterns of American history and foreign policy itself, which had its projections in the Consuls.

The upshot of this all was that the essay, like some of Shakespearean plays, developed a very essential sub-plot or thesis which though a little less important than the main thesis nevertheless became an integral part of the larger picture.

In fact it was interesting to note that both the United States and India had been together a part of the British Empire in the eighteenth century and the happenings in one area had tangibly influenced the developments in another—one such specific instance was the American War of Independence.[2] Hence this was a special type of relationship where one was an ex-colony of England and the other was contemporaneously one.

Such a study was bound to raise some interesting side issues like the varied facets of imperialism in the nineteenth century. How did the British in India treat a country which had been their colony ? Could any new world patterns be detected for the

1. Day, Clive : *A History of Commerce*, p. 469.

2. Gautam, Vinayshil : "Some aspects of the effects of American War of Independence on India", *Journal of Historical Research*, Vol. XIV, No. 2. The paper brings out how the American War of Independence tangibly altered and affected the political situation in India.

nineteenth century ? What if any were the nature or direct contacts between India and America during this period ? What was the volume and graph of trade between them ? What was the system of operation of U.S. Consular service in general and in India in particular ? etc. etc.

Hence it was an absorbing if challenging task one set out to do.

This was made particularly so because of the uniqueness in our history of nineteenth century and the special relevance it has for us today.

Through the nineteenth century, then, which was a century of the growth of commerce and stagnation of agriculture; of growing prosperity of the commercial classes and increasing poverty of the rural masses; of rising prices and stationary wages; of increasing export of food grains and the existence of an endemic state of hunger among a substantial section of country's rural poulation; of the inadequate measures of relief and ineffective agrarian legislation; of attempts at modernisation of India's medieval economy and increasingly sharp rises and falls in the economic prosperity graph of India, it was one's attempt to use the U.S. Consular reports for an objective picture.

As has been pointed out in the Chapter giving the conclusions there were some disappointments in not finding all the answers one was looking for and from the fact that the sources themselves at times proved inadequate. Nevertheless to have been able to say all that one has said from the standpoint elaborated above was itself a matter of some satisfaction. At least a beginning had been made.

The Nature of Basic Sources

An introduction to the nature of basic sources used for this work is desirable as they have never been, to the best of one's knowledge, the subject of serious study either in India or any where else. Moreover they are an unusual set of collection providing invaluable information on the various problems outlined above.

It would not be too much to suggest that fifteen years ago such a study would not have been at all possible in India. A protracted visit to the United States would have been imperative to have a look at the basic documents. But the process of micro-filming documents helped to solve problems. Acquisitions going into about fortyfive reels from some half dozen libraries and repositories in the United States had to be looked into and examined.[1] These were to the exclusion of the primary source material which were the Consular despatches from Calcutta and Bombay spread over some thirty micro-film reels. They covered the period of 1792 to 1906 in the first instance and 1838 to 1906 in the second. The Calcutta despatches are spread over 17 reels or volumes. In addition to this there are certain supplementing reels which one shall refer to later. While being unreservedly grateful to the National Archives, Washington, for having undertaken such a publication one only wished there was more system in the micro-filming of the documents. There are numerous instances of two or three documents being interspersed among each other.[2] Thus leaving the researcher the problem of not only analysing the documents but quite literally trying to piece them together like a jigsaw puzzle.

Again many documents are duplicated[3] i.e. are printed twice in the same reel which from the point of view of research is at times really quite confusing. The difficulty becomes all the more time-consuming when there are two reproductions of the two different documents almost identical[4] in nature with a few verbal differences. Almost a word for word study involving comparison had to be undertaken only to end in the conclusion that semantical differences did not really involve a difference in the substance of the document.

These various reels containing the documents from Calcutta Consulate General of United States of America contain not only the despatches of the Consul but a host of other evidence or reports e.g. newspaper clippings, Gazettes, Legislative Council

1. See Bibliography.

2. The classic example being provided in Vol 3, Calcutta Despatches, where notification no. 3020 of Government of India has interspersed among it proceedings of the Legislative Council, notifications of appointment, military reports, promotions report etc. etc. (C. D.)

3. Benjamin Joy in a letter to Edmund Randolph, Secretary of State, U. S. A., dated Nov. 24, 1794, Calcutta, Vol. 1, Calcutta despatches. (C.D.).

4. James Higginson in a letter to Secretary of State, U. S. A., dated July 12, 1868, Calcutta, Vol. 1 (C. D.) and the letter immediately next to it.

proceedings, American Congressional Records, Court reports, various contemporary pamphlets which might be of interest to the Consulate, resolutions of Chambers of Commerce, notifications of the Government of India, private papers of the various people etc. etc. The problem however being that not infrequently they suffer from bad documentation. It would be obvious from a reflection for example that the exposure is of a newspaper clipping. But it would almost begin with the text making no meaning whatsoever and end as abruptly, leaving the researcher very much on his own to make what sense he can out of the whole thing.[1] The clippings, had they been neatly cut and/or properly filmed they could have been far more useful. What is far worse from the accuracy point of view is that at times not even the name of the newspaper, or the date of the particular issue is available.[2]

It is further to be kept in mind that the American Consulate General in Calcutta was *not* meant for the Indian subcontinent exclusively but was for a larger area which covered a section of South East Asia also. Included among this would be Ceylon[3], Burma[4] and also the complex around Singapur.[5] It might be helpful to point out here, (as has been substantiated in a subsequent chapter[6]) that it was the American policy to cover the world of its interests with a network of Consulates. These were intended to safeguard the interest of American citizens, shipping and nation in that area. Hence it would be unnecessary even to seek to try to establish a congruity of areas of our (i.e. Indian) interest and American interest then. As a result of this not every thing in these reports is of relevance for one's study. The areas of Burma have merited, however a little more attention than other areas because they fitted in with the Indian economy. The British annexed Burma for trade reasons and kept it firmly together with British India. Incidentally one noted that during the

1. e. g. Vol. 8, 10 (C. D.)
2. e. g. Vol. 14, 15 (C. D.)
3. Vol. 1 Bombay Despatches, hereafter referred to as B. D.
4. e. g. see Charles Huffnagle's letter to Daniel Webster, Calcutta, dated Jan. 1, 1851 (C. D.)
5. U. S. Vice Consul in a despatch to the Secretary of State, U. S. A., Calcutta, dated April 28, 1858 (C. D.)
6. See Chapter III

time of famines the rice surplus of Burma helped British India to tide over problems. Hence with independence when the rice of Burma was no longer available to India on same terms as earlier, in times of famines, they (famines) assumed a disturbingly different shape. This is a factor which has not been too often kept in mind even in otherwise good works of research.[1] Because of all this the Calcutta Despatches assume a very large significance.[2]

The Bombay Despatches are also significant. In a collection of eight the micro-copies consist, for the most part, of despatches addressed to the department of State by United States Consular officials at Bombay between October 12,1838 and August 11, 1906. These despatches with very few exceptions are arranged in chronological order; their contents being registered on Roll 1 of the micro-copy.[3]

Interspersed throughout the series are some documents other than despatches from United States Consular representatives at Bombay. Occasionally there are some memoranda prepared by State Department officials, letters from the Treasury Department, and communications from private citizens of the United States.

Both these sets of despatches cover a wide range of economic, political and social subjects. Some are covering letters from enclosures of a routine nature forwarded by Consular officials to the Department of State, such as tables of Consular fees received, of arrivals and departures of American vessels, of trade statistics and of other data collected in ordinary course of Consular duty. After 1870 upon receipt by the Department of State, most statistical enclosures were removed from their covering letters and distributed among various other records of the Department of State, or in case of enclosures relating to fiscal affairs of the Consulate, of the department of Treasury.

The entire series was discontinued on August 14, 1906, when the Department adopted the practice of filing incoming and outgoing correspondence by subject.

1. e. g. See Bhatia, B. M. : *Famines in India* 1860-1905, it is surprising how Dr. Bhatia has overlooked the point completely.

2. The dates of Calcutta despatches which have been micro-copied on separate rolls is given in the appendix No. II.

3. The dates of Bombay despatches which have been micro-copied on separate rolls is given in the appendix No. I.

Further there are two micro-film reels available in India at the National Archives, New Delhi, relevant for our period which contain instructions (except circulars) from the department of State to the Bombay Consulate. Unfortunately they cover only the period between 1894 to 1906. Termed as "records of the United States Consulate in Bombay" they have their own use.

The other sources used are such as are being regularly used hence there is no need to introduce them as such.

The Scheme

The periodisation of this work is from 1792-1906. This is to include in totality all the Consulate records of Calcutta and Bombay. The first available Consular letter is in 1792.[1] And this process of filing records is disbanded on August 14, 1906.[2]

In these records whatever is relevant to the Socio-economic history of the sub-continent of India has been used. There is no specific territorial delimination either save what is self-imposed in records. As has been mentioned earlier on the attempt is to tap a non-regional source and a 'third-person' account to attempt the socio-economic scene of India in the nineteenth century.

The chapter-wise[3] division is as follows :

Chapter II : *Aspects of U.S. History and the American Consuls in India* : the approach ; a survey 1792-1906—from the birth of the nation to 1792,1792-1796 : Benjamin Joy, 1796-1843 : a period of no consular representation, 1843-1847 : James B.Higginson, 1847-1861 : Charles Huffnagle, 1861-1862 : James Lilly, 1862-1871 : N.P. Jacobs, 1871-1881 : A.C. Litchfield, 1881-1884 : H. Mattson, 1884-1886 : J.A. Leonard, 1886-1890 : B.J. Benham, 1890-1893 : Samuel Merrill, 1893-1897 : Van Leer Polk, 1897-1906 : R.F. Patterson, 1906-H. Michael.[4]

Chapter III : *Aspects of principles and practice of U.S. foreign policy and India* : Some fundamental facets of American

1. Benjamin Joy in a letter to the President of United States, dated Dec. 9, 1792, Newbury Port (C. D.)

2. Vol. 1 (B. D.)

3. It was thought advisable to give the detailed subdivision of the various chapters here rather than with the contents, where one sought to present the fundamental structure of the study.

4. These are the names of the various American Consuls at Calcutta.

foreign policy with special reference to the 19th century; England, America, and India ; U.S. Consular Service and India ; the office of the U.S. Consul in India.

Chapter IV : *Facets of Indian Society in the nineteenth century*: The framework; some strands of the social history of India : Glimpses of social life in western India; Glimpses of social life in Eastern India ; British rule in India and social change.

Chapter V : *Facets of Indian economy in the nineteenth century*: The nature of Indian economy in the nineteenth century; 1792-1857 : the years that set the pace ; 1858-1880 : the years of healing and growth ; 1880-1906 : the years of drift.

Chapter VI : *Facets of Indo-American trade relations in the nineteenth century* : 1792-1833 ; 1834-1865 ; 1866-1880 ; 1881-1906.

Chapter VII : Epilogue.

Two points before one concludes.

There were no American Consular representatives in India between 1796-1838 hence no Consular despatches are available. However, an attempt has been made to fill the gap in the narration by other sources for the sake of continuity and better composite understanding of the later developments of the nineteenth century. It is significant that Indo-American trade relations continued to exist during this period, in spite of the absence of Consular representation.

Wherever a point has been substantiated with an e.g., either in the text or the footnote, care has always been taken to select a representative example.

1. It was thought desirable to deal with the Indo-American trade relations separately from the previous chapter because of two reasons : first to dispel the popular notion that no such relations existed it was essential not only to substantiate one's thesis but also be exhaustive and to include it under Chapter V then would have made the already big chapter on Indian economy still bigger, second, the topic itself is significant enough to merit separate treatment.

Chapter II

Aspects of U.S. History and the American Consuls in India (1792-1906)

"..... the area of operation of the American Consul was essentially that of British India... the colonial situation was in itself not a static one in India through the nineteenth century... the process begun in 1793 saw its culmination in 1858 aided by the catalyst of 1857... this consummation was only to mark the beginning of another process which reached its climax in the administration of Curzon...... (on the other hand) The consuls would have been more than human if they did not bring with themselves a carryover of the conditions at home as also their prejudices. Hence to make a scientific study of their statements it was important to know their background....."

Introduction p. 10-11.

The approach

As observed in the Introduction this study is basically an exercise in having an overtly 'third-person-account' of the Indian social and economic condition in the nineteenth century. But the fact that it is a 'third-point-of view' account does not necessarily make it either impartial or correct. Prejudices of one order or another are as likely to weigh in even the understanding of the situation as in the presentation by the observer in this case as in any other.

As such during the course of one's study certain methodological safeguards have to be taken. It is equally essential to know the background from which these observers emerged, for that would explain much of that they say and much that they do not say. This is especially significant when the observers are not operating as individuals in their personal capacity but rather as representatives of a country in their official capacity. The condition back home is bound to weigh with them heavily. And the whole problem becomes much more intense and complicated when it is spread over as large a period as the present work is.

Emerging and consolidating first as a nation, then facing the problem of Slavery and Reconstruction to pass on to fresh industrial strength which enabled it to make its weight felt in international affairs, America which came out of the nineteenth century was in many significant ways different from the America that entered it. It is further to be kept in mind that all the while the country was acquiring more and more territory thus increasing the number of constituent States—though American history stands testimony to the fact that this was not an unmixed blessing. All this lends to American history a peculiar character all by itself because United States is the only country in the world to enlarge itself so systematically. The behaviour and reports of the representatives of such a nation then, have to be assessed very carefully.[1]

1. The task is facilitated by the fact that these consular reports, despatches etc. are not of public character but are of a confidential nature which were sent to the department of State of United States to keep the home Government *correctly* informed about the Americans interest in India as well as the situation here. Hence the likelihood of errors of commission are reduced.

Further more it is essential to keep in mind the context in which the U.S. Consuls in India operated. Their sphere of activity, as has been pointed out, was British India, which itself was neither a fixed territorial or legal concept through the whole of the nineteenth century. Hence the context itself was a fluid one.

In the following pages the period of 1792 to 1906 has been chronologically sub-divided as amongst the period of tenure of the U.S. Consul Generals in Calcutta[1] and a brief outline of American history[2] for that period is also provided. Along with these are noted, as per the same division, the important landmarks of the fluid Indian context in which the U. S. Consuls had to operate. This, it is hoped, will lend clarity to the understanding of their work as assessed in this essay.

A Survey : 1792-1906

From the birth of the nation to 1792 : After initial failures and experiments in independence a new national constitution was drawn up in 1787 and it went into operation in 1789. The year 1788 was spent in trying to secure the approval of the people of United States to the new instrument. The strongest and most eloquent appeal for ratification by the States was made in a series of articles known to history as "The Federalist", written by Hamilton, Jay and Madison in their effort to win the people of New York to adopt the new frame of government. "No nation" argued the Federalist, "No nation acquainted with the nature of our political associations under the Articles of Confederation would be unwise enough to enter into any international arrangements with the United States." "We are a discredited nation," said the authors, and not the least eloquent of their papers were devoted to a consideration of the

1. The reason why the tenure of the incumbents of the Calcutta office was accepted over the other alternative of following the tenure of the incumbents of the Bombay is that Calcutta office enjoyed definite superiority over Bombay Office, see Chapter III.

2. References have also been made to the European Scene as and when such references were deemed absolutely indispensable for the understanding of the theme.

proper method of conducting international relations in contrast with the pitiful weakness in that respect, of the Confederation.[1]

Their efforts were crowned with success and in the next year a full-fledged national government with a real executive, a real legislative and real judicial department came into being.

But before one launches into a more specific discussion of the developments in America it would be meaningful to take cognizance of some major developments in Europe in particular which would ultimately effect both India and America.

From about the middle of the eighteenth century changes and developments were taking place which would play a vital part in a realignment of the balance of power among the nations of the world. The Industrial Revolution caught on in right earnest. The Seven Years War further changed the balance of power among nations and with the signing of the Treaty of Paris on Feb. 10,1763, England was left the leading colonial power of the period.

In America itself 1789 was a busy year with Congress creating the departments of State, of the Treasury, and of War. The Supreme Court was formed with John Jay as Chief Justice. Within two years ten amendments to the Constitution (known as the Bill of Rights) were ratified by the States and became a part of the Constitution.

About the election year of 1796 the undercover struggle for control of the government was growing in intensity between the Federalists and the anti-Federalists or Democratic-Republicans.[2] But John Adams' three vote victory was an indication of the rising tide of Anti-Federalists Republicans, who would eventually engulf bickering Federalists.

On the Continent itself the French Revolution was a genuine menace to the established order of things there but had by then perhaps attempted more than it could take.

1792-1796—*Benjamin Joy*

As has been suggested in the Introduction American attitude towards India was to a very large extent guided by

1. *The Federalist*, Nos. xxii and esp. LXIII ; see also XI, LXIV and LXX.

2. See *Inaugural address of John Adams*, March 4, 1797, Senate Chamber, Philadelphia.

the American relations with England even at this early date. As a matter of fact, at around this time the differences between America and England were becoming particularly acute. To settle all of the outstanding disagreements without war was a difficult thing, for they had been piling up since 1783 and included debts, western posts, loyalists as yet uncompensated, as well as neutral rights, the rule of 1756, and the desire to trade with the British West Indies. Any apparent yielding to Great Britain outraged the Jeffersonian party, the Democratic-Republicans, for they were all for France and for helping France, even at the cost of a war with England. But a small group of Federalist Senators, representing the New England shipping interests, were equally determined that there should be no war. They suggested to the President that he send a special envoy to England, they told him whom they wanted sent and how he should be instructed.[1] So in 1794 John Jay was dispatched to get whatever concessions from England, he could and as much as was possible.[2] In return for all the demands he made on England Jay had very little to offer.[3] However, this Treaty is a significant landmark so far as relations of America with India are concerned and the operation of U.S. Consuls in India goes. In the uncertain condition that Bengal politics and commerce was then it was vital to English interests that America not align with other European powers against her here. Such an alliance would have tilted the balance of power

1. Hayden R., *The Senate and Treaties*, 1789-1817, p. 92 ; Bemis, S.F. *The Jay Treaty, a study in Commerce and Diplomacy*, p. 210-12.

2. *American State Papers, Foreign Relations*, I, 470-3.

3. "Jay's task was an almost impossible one because England was definitely the more powerful nation, but he certainly made the best of a very bad job. Britain agreed to evacuate the western posts and to stop patronising the Red Indians and Canadian fur traders. She agreed to a scientific finding of the disputed boundaries in the northeast and the northwest. The United States promised to pay England the much discussed debts, and England promised to compensate the United States' merchants for the illegal seizures. England even went so far as to let the United States share in her precious West Indian trade. But she absolutely refused to give up her rights to seize, block or otherwise obstruct natural commerce, she would not give up the Rule of 1756. Moreover Jay brought back an enlarged rather than a diminished contraband list.—Malloy, W, : *Treaties and Conventions*, I. 590, 601. Bemis, S.F. *The Jay Treaty*, p. 261.

against the English interests. Hence, after this treaty America gets at the hands of the English the 'most-favoured nation' treatment in India. This was of course an attempt to prevent the Americans from becoming disgruntled. However that may be, it certainly helped the American relations and commerce with India to grow.[1]

However, as Benjamin Joy had noted he could not receive recognition as the Consul General of America in Calcutta but had to rest satisfied with the rank of a Commercial Agent.[2] This was natural because there was an obvious anomaly in a Joint Stock Company organised for trading purposes receiving Consuls or Ambassadors like a sovereign power. That the ineffectual Moghul Emperor would not have been able to prevent such a recognition had he even opted for it, is another matter. *De jure* sovereignty still lay vested in him and only he could receive diplomatic representations.

The fact that American Consul chose to petition the English Governor General[3] rather than the Moghul Sovereign does not necessarily bespeak his ignorances of affairs Indian. Being interested only in trade and port matters[4] it might have appeared the most obvious and meaningful thing to do.

Further more it need hardly be pointed out that the English parliament in the 'post-Regulating-Act-mood' as it was, would never have approved such recognition at the hands of East India Company, any way.

However, Benjamin Joy went back to America in 1796.

1796-1843[5] : *A period of no consular representation*

When Benjamin Joy returned to America he had hoped to come back to India. But the climate here was uncongenial for

1. See Chapter VI.

2. J.H. Harrington, Sub. Secretary, Council Chamber, in a communication to Benjamin Joy, U.S. Consul in Calcutta ; Calcutta dated April 21,1794.

3. Benjamin Joy in a letter to the Secretary of State, U.S., Calcutta, dated Nov. 24, 1794.

4. See Chapter III.

5. The U.S. Consulate at Bombay had started operating, however, from 1838.

him and his doctors advised him against it.[1] From then on to 1843 there was no consular representative of U. S. at Calcutta. Perhaps this itself was a reflection of the straits that the home (American) government was in during the period.

Nevertheless a survey of the period would be fruitful because despite the absence of Consular representative, Indo-American trade relations continued.[2] A survey would further help in, not only lending a meaning to the subsequent developments of American History but also by implication, explaining why American interests went unrepresented in India for nearly four decades.

Thomas Jefferson was at the helm of affairs from 1801 to 1809 and during his period the U.S.A. not only gained a fair deal of stability but developed a certain degree of confidence also where foreign relations were concerned. In his second inaugural address he was to declare with a gratifying sense of achievement to the American people that "In the transaction of your foreign affairs we have endeavoured to cultivate the friendship of all nations, and especially those with which we have the most important relations. We have done them justice on all occasions, favoured where favour was lawful and cherished mutual interests and intercourse on fair and equal terms..."[3] The fear of Napoleon failed to intimidate the growing Union. Ohio was admitted as the 17th State and approximately 900,000 square miles of land were added to the nation in Louisiana Purchase made during the following year. American citizens went out far and wide especially in the Asian-African region.[4] In 1803 Jefferson sent Captain Edward Prible against Tripoli. The nation dropped the cloak of neutrality with which Washington had enveloped its foreign policy and under Jefferson began a policy which can be termed aggressive nationalism.

Contemporaneously in Europe Napoleon's defeat of the

1. Benjamin Joy in a letter to the Secretary of State, U.S.A., Boston dated, Jan. 24, 1796.

2. See Chapter VI.

3. *Inaugural Address of Thomas Jefferson*, March 4, 1805, Capital building Washington D.C.

4. Gautam, Vinayshil : 'Some aspects of the trade relations between United States of America and Mauritius :' *Proceedings Volume* thirty first session of the Indian History Congress, Dec. 1969, Varanasi.

Austrian forces in Italy marked the emergence of France as a major world power. Napoleon himself was crowned Emperor of France on Dec. 2, 1804 at Notre Dame.

However, America's prosperity bubble burst when British orders in council and decrees by Napoleon impaired American commerce. By 1807 Jefferson was forced to retaliate with an embargo prohibiting American ships from carrying goods to foreign ports. Although this act was widely criticized, in the election of 1808 Jefferson's candidate was still able to poll 122 electoral votes for president to Federalist C.C. Pinckney's 47. It is to be noted that Jefferson's decision was a set back to America's rule as prime neutrals in a warring European order and in turn affected America's trade relations with India.

By this time in the United States of America there was already developing a pattern, a strong leader elected to two terms of office would refuse a third term and would pick a Successor whose thinking most closely paralleled his own. Washington chose Adams, Jefferson chose Madison.[1]

In 1810, Napoleon married Maria Luisa, Spanish colonies revolted in Venezuela, Uruguay, Paraguay, Chile, Argentina and Mexico with Peru following suit in 1811. King George III of England was declared insane in 1811 and the Prince of Wales became regent. In 1812 Napoleon invaded Russia and in the same year America declared war on England.

The peculiar thing about this war was that any sea man who had emigrated to America from England was considered to be a deserter from the British Navy and was treated as such, rather than as a naturalized American citizen. No wonder in the second inaugural address Madison commented, "... and now we find them, in further contempt of the modes of honourable warfare, supplying the place of a conquering force by attempts to disorganize our political society, to dismember our confederated Republic...."[2]

1. Compare Jefferson's first inaugural address to James Madison's first inaugural address to see a striking identity in the political philosophy of the two leaders. In a way this helps to explain why Jefferson selected Madison over Monroe as his immediate successor.

2. *Inaugural address* (2nd) *of James Madison,* March 4, 1813, Capitol building, Washington D.C.

The British blockade of American ports and harbours brought on a general price inflation due to scarcity of goods. On June 1,1813, the British 38 gun frigate Shannon captured the U.S. 38 gun frigate Chesapeake, a boat which incidentally had visited India earlier.[1] During this war Washington city was captured and burnt on Aug. 24 and 25, 1814 due to poor leadership of American troops, and American prestige had sunk very low indeed.

It is no wonder then that the Consular Services of the United States suffered a severe set back in and around this period and were in many places discontinued. In India itself not uptill the late '30s or early '40s of the nineteenth century were the services resumed. But this is a subject which shall at great length be dwelt upon in some of the other chapters.

It might be pointed out heıe that the fall of Isle de France a little earlier into English hands had further closed another avenue of contact between the United States of America and India.[2]

The next two decades in American History were of steady building up, Monroe concentrated on building up a steady strong force, of a strong standing army and an adequate Navy, backed by a militia trained and ready for quick action. His ideas for the armed forces are remarkably similar to our present day system of a regular Army, Navy and Air Force, backed by trained reservists. Monroe also had the idea of the creation of coastal fortifications.[3]

An attempt was made in this period, also to pay attention to the consolidation of internal state of production. "Our manufactures", said Monroe, "will likewise require the systematic and fostering care of the Government possessing as we do all the raw materials, the fruit of our own soil and industry, we ought not to depend in the degree we have done on supplies from other

1. O.C. 3 Oct. Proceedings Volume (1787) Foreign Department, N.A.I.

2. Gautam, Vinayshil : 'Aspects of the role of Isle de France in contacts between India and the U.S.A. (1773-1810). *Summary of papers* : thirtieth annual session of the Indian History Congress, Bhagalpur, 1968.

3. *Inaugural address* (1st) *of James Monroe*, March 4, 1817, Capital Building, Washington D.C.

countries.........It is important too that the capital which nourishes our manufacture should be domestic, as its influence in that case instead of exhausting, as it may do in foreign hands, would be felt advantageously on agriculture and every other branch of industry. Equally important is it to provide at home a market for our raw materials as by extending the competition it will enhance the price and protect the cultivator against the casualties incident to foreign markets....'[1]

Times changed and within a matter of few years America was enjoying a period of prosperity and rapid expansion under the able statesmanship of Monroe and Adams. An example is the origin of the Monroe doctrine. It was set forth in the following declaration "......The American continents, by the free and independent condition which they have assumed and maintained are henceforth not to be considered as subjects for future colonization by any European powers. But with the governments who have declared their independence and maintain it .. we could not view any interposition for the purpose of oppressing them or controlling in any other manner, their destiny by any European power in any other light, than as the manifestation of an unfriendly disposition towards the United States."[2] This meant, if the independent nations of the Western Hemisphere were molested, war with the United States could result. It is understandable that during this period there would be a lul in America's relations with the Eastern Hemisphere.

The visit of the aging Lafayette and his son in the fall of 1824 climaxed Monroe's second term.

Now it was Russia's turn to step into the world spotlight. Early in 1825 Russia and Britain signed a treaty to determine the boundary between Russian and British America. Nicholas I was soon to declare war on Persia and in 1828 on Turkey. The Russian menace grew also on the North Western Frontier of India.

United States of America under Jackson was left pretty much alone to expand. The Mississippi, formerly considered the nations perimeter, now became the jumping off place for new

1. *Inaugural address* (1st) *of James Monroe,* March 4, 1817, Capitol building, Washington D.C.

2. *Monroe Papers*, message to the eighteenth Congress on Dec. 2, 1823.

explorations into the western vastness. Jackson made a bid to purchase Texas from Mexico but was rebuffed. Beginning in 1830 with the first covered wagon train blazing a trail to the Rockies under the guidance of Jedediah Smith and William Subbtle, the trickle of settlers westward became a flood. Unrest in Europe had also caused a large increase in immigrants.

By 1833 Britain's Reform Bill of 1832 was making itself felt in Parliament, where the nations growing manufacturing interests began to be represented. The death of William IV on June 20, 1837, and the accession of Queen Victoria ushered in a new era for Great Britain. The following year England sent her first large group of settlers to New Zealand. Still unaffected by foreign unrest America's amazing expansion westward continued. Arkansas became the 25th State, June 15,1836 and Michigan followed January 26, 1837.

On May 24, 1844 Samuel F. B. Morse used his new telegraph to send a message from Washington D.C. to Baltimore, Maryland. Thus a new dimension was added to the means of communication. On August 29, 1842 the treaty of Nanking ended the Opium War between Britain and China with Hong Kong being ceded to England. 1843 saw the British Conquer Sind and proclaim Natal a British colony. In the first instance adequate care was taken to see that American involvement was in all cases safeguarded.[1]

However, from the above going narration it is easy to see why United States of America did not find it feasible to send any consular representative to British India, as a replacement in the situation left vacant by Benjamin Joy, for such a long period.

The strained relations between England and America, weak condition of United States, administrative and economic involvement with domestic problems and almost a continual condition of growth and expansion, were definitely some of the most significant contributing causes for the absence of U.S. Consuls in this period in India.

1843-1847 : *James B. Higginson* : The British India that James B. Higginson came to in 1843 was in very many ways different to the British India that Benjamin Joy had left. The

1. P.C. 21-22 proceedings vol. (1839) foreign department, N.A.I.

British power was now firmly established in India though the stewardship of East India Company had not been formally abolished. The 'French menace' was no more, Marathas were vanquished and out of the race for supremacy over India, Sind was annexed, Sikhs were friendly, Gurkhas subdued, Burmese driven out of Assam, Afghanistan under a friendly ruler and Russian menace finally at an end.

No wonder Higginson found it feasible to go about his job as a Consul in a smooth business-like way without much really to bother about.

1847-1861 : *Charles Huffnagle* : The Congress of Paris in 1856 had ended the Crimean war. Here, the British were finally induced to admit some of the rights of neutrals for which the United States and the nations of continental Europe had been contending since the days of the armed neutrality of 1780. The declaration of Paris said (1) that privateering was abolished (2) that a neutral flag would protect the enemy's goods, except contraband (3) that neutral goods, except contraband, should not be liable to capture under the enemy's flag and (4) that a blockade was not a blockade unless it was made effective. These principles had been insisted upon by the United States many times in its relations with England. Instead of taking advantage of this great step forward in International law, the United States refused to adhere to the Declaration of Paris, because it did not go far enough and protect private property at sea.[1] But Europe, and particularly England, could not move that fast. However, since the United States had long contended for these propositions, the Declaration of Paris could not help but remove some more long standing causes of irritation between the United States and Great Britain and render naval warfare more humane in accordance with the wishes of the United States. The whole episode is curiously illustrative of a tendency sometimes seen in American foreign policy to cry for something and then refuse what it asked for because of the form.[2] Nevertheless in the given circumstances Indo-American relations were bound to be more cordial.

1. Moore, J.B., *Digest of International Law*, VII, 561; J.D. Richardson's *Messages*, V, 412.

2. Hyde, C.C., *International Law, Chiefly as interpreted and applied by the United States*. II, 392.

At the turn of the half century the perimeter of the civilized world had begun to shrink with an ever-increasing rapidity. The spread of telegraph, the laying of the first trans-Atlantic cable between the United States and England, the increased replacement of sail by steam—all these innovations brought the peoples of the world—and thereby of India and America also closer together with each passing year. England under Victoria exploited these factors to great advantage, increasing her colonial empire in all parts of the globe.

James Buchanan the fifteenth President of the United States was elected at a time when a strong personality was needed to lead the nation (1857). But instead of taking a firm stand on the question of slavery, he tried to please both sides, apparently motivated by the desire which he termed 'to live in grateful memory'[1] of his countrymen. Even in his December 4, 1860, address to Congress Buchanan would be non-committal. His failure to take any stand would be unsatisfactory both to Southerners and Northerners. Lincoln's inauguration would see seven States already seceded from the Union, with the first shots on Fort Sumter only five weeks away.

This period is also very significant in the history of India if only because of the happenings of 1857 which not only marked the passage of power from the East India Company's hands to the Crown of England but also the last major struggle on part of the traditional Indian aristocracy to maintain its position. If one were attempting a political history of India the Consular reports for this period would, again, be an invaluable source of information.[2] The different petty states and quasi sovereignties were being gradually annexed and absorbed, and their inhabitants brought more directly under the influence and protection of British Laws.[3]

1861-1871 : *James Lilly* (1861-1862) ; *N. P. Jacobs* (1862-1871) :

Abraham Lincoln who succeeded Buchanan to begin with used four references : the Constitution, Clay's speech of 1850,

1. *Inaugural address of James Buchanan*, March 4, 1857, Capitol Steps, Washington D.C.

2. See Gautam, Vinayshil : Nana Saheb Peshwa : an assessment, a review article in *Samiksha*. Vol. 3, No. 1

3. Annual Consular report for 1862-63, Calcutta dated Sep. 30, 1863.

Jacksons' nullification proclamation and Webster's reply to Hayre.[1]

The thirteenth amendment introduced in Congress on Feb. 27, 1861, was finally passed on February 1, 1865 and notified on Dec. 18, 1865 only a month before Lincoln's second inauguration. The progress of war had about that time been far more than what Abraham Lincoln termed "reasonably satisfactory."[2] The South was beaten and General Lee had sent out peace feelers only two days before the inauguration.

Lincoln's policy of reconstruction in the South had met with rising opposition in Congress where power-hungry radicals clamoured for revenge. After the death of Lincoln these men felt Andrew Johnson—a poor white whose home had been taken over by South—would listen to their furious demands for vengeance. Johnson's rejection of these vengeful policies touched off a concerted campaign to undermine the President. Faced with a two-thirds majority in both Houses and a Senate, Johnson saw his vetoes over-ridden again and again—with disastrous results in a South pillaged by carpet-baggers. These men moved in and took control of the defeated states under an authority granted them by the first three Reconstruction Acts, all passed over Johnson's vetoes in 1867.[3] It is to be noted that Congress also passed the Tenure of Office Act, which in essence provided that the President could not remove those officials appointed or approved by Senate without the consent of that body.

While the South was struggling with reconstruction great progress was being made in the North in industry, commerce and education.[4]

During the first term of Ulysses S. Grant America had grown in territory and population even further and was beginning to feel the first feeble stirrings of new ideas and ideologies that would

1. *Inaugural address* (1st) of Abraham Lincoln, March 4, 1861, Capitol Steps, Washington D.C.

2. *Inaugural address* (2nd) of Abraham Lincoln, March 4, 1865, Capitol building, Washington D.C.

3. Gautam, Vinayshil : "Reconstruction period in United States' history—some observations," read at an Inter-disciplinary Seminar, Hyderabad, May 1969.

4. Many new universities had been chartered e.g. University of Minnesota (1851) ; University of Illinois (1867) ; West Virginia University (1867) ; the University of California (1860) ; etc.

eventually exert profound influences on the American way of life. In December 1869 Wyoming Territory granted the first woman suffrage in the United States. Labour Unions began to spread throughout growing American industries. In May 1869 a golden spike was driven at Promontory Point, Utah, commemorating the completion of the first transcontinental railroad. About the return of seceded states southern States Grant had claimed, "When my first term of the office of Chief Executive began, the country had not recovered from the effects of a great internal revolution, and three of the former States of the Union had not been restored to their Federal relations."[1] Grant was apparently in error as there were four southern states readmitted to the Union after he took office : Virginia, January 26,1870 ; Mississippi, February 23, 1870 ; Texas, March 30, 1870 ; Georgia, July 15, 1870.

This period did not witness any event of fundamental importance in India so far as the American Consuls were concerned. However, the Civil War of America had its echoes in India both in matters of economy generally[2] and trade particularly[3]. In the former case Indian cotton industries received a boost which in turn influenced the social scene, at least, of Western India;[4] in the latter case for the period of the Civil War the number of American ships visiting India was reduced nearly to zero.

1871 *to* 1881 : *A.C. Litchfield* : The post civil war growth of the American nation continued. There was a tremendous influx of men, women, and children, from many parts of the globe. The country's businessmen were perfecting principles of mass production. Each year saw new improvements on basic inventions—the telephone, the electric light, the steamboat, the steam engine, the telegraph—that were to become the backbone of American industry. The steel mills were running full blast, and the young oil industry, led by a financial wizard named John D. Rockefeller was growing rapidly. In fact around 1877, it is commonly assumed, America crossed the threshold into an era of industrial expansion. This in its turn was to show in a grow-

1. *Inaugural address* (2nd) of Ulysses S. Grant, March 4, 1873, Capitol Steps, Washington D.C.
2. See Chapter V.
3. See Chapter VI.
4. See Chapter IV.

ing influence in world affairs of the United States. However not until after 1898 was this influence felt in South Asia. So any relevance of this increasing economic strength, so far as the American Consuls were concerned was only to be looked for in the boosted America's commercial contacts.

Naturally now the stature of American Consul in India was far superior to what it was even two decades back. The office was being extended all the diplomatic recognition and respect that was due to the representative of a significant nation. The officiating head of the Calcutta Consulate was invited[1], by the Viceroy to be present on the occasion of the assumption by Queen Victoria of the title of "Empress of India"[2], in the absence of the regular Consul General.[3]

1881-1886 : *H. Mattson* (1881-1884), *J.A. Leonard* (1884-1886) : The 80s of the nineteenth century were to mark the beginnings of a new prosperity in United States, with the entertainment industry coming up,[4] sports becoming more popular, ten storey buildings coming up in such places as Chicago for organisations like Home Insurance Company. In the east the opening of the Brooklyn Bridge May 24, 1883 after 13 years of construction was cause for a great celebration.

In India for a part of this period Ripon was the Governor General. He was a true representative of Gladstonian Liberalism. He not only concluded a mild treaty with Afghanistan, restored the Ruler of Mysore to his territory, repealed the Vernacular Press Act but also among other things introduced the western version of Local Self Government.[5] The American Consul noted these changes in his observations of the Indian scene, and a new dimension was added to his duties.

1. Vice Consul General in a letter to the Secretary, department of State, U.S.A., Calcutta, Oct. 13, 1876 (C.D.)

2. *Gazette of India* (Extraordinary) Simla, Friday August, 18, 1876.

3. R. Macallister in a letter to the department of State, U.S.A., Calcutta, Oct. 13, 1876 (C.D.)

4. P.T. Barnum, made news in 1881 by combining his 'greatest show on earth' with Bailey's rival circus and "Barnum and Bailey" became a familiar name to generations of Americans young and old.

5. The need for such an institution can hardly be doubted after the following description of the Calcutta port, "...there is neither a warf or a quay...at low waters the passengers and his baggage are still borne on an hand barrow by coolies, through the mud to the shore and the cargoes must even then be discharged into boats, thence on coolies heads through the same mud and up the steep bank..." The needs of urbanisation had to be met.

Incidentally, as a Viceroy and Governor General, Ripon had a soft corner for America and this naturally helped the United States and India to draw closer.[1]

1886-1897: *B.J. Benham* (1886-1890), *Samuel Merrill* (1890-1893), *Van Leer Polk* (1893-1897): By 1889 a new name began to loom large on the political horizon of America, that of Theodore Roosevelt. As an aggressive champion of civil service reform both before and after Harrison's election Roosevelt earned the public's confidence and trust, but developed powerful enemies. Benjamin Harrison who was inaugurated on March 4, 1889, could only express noble sentiments,[2] but being basically meek and pliable Harrison never had the courage to break with his wealthy backers and place the country's welfare above the private interests to whom he owed his victory.

Britain's influence dominated milllions of the world's population. Throughout the continent the Industrial Revolution was itself to undergo a revolution, as electricity began to come into use, although coal and steam were at the time still the chief sources of power. As the world approached the last decade of the nineteenth century preparations were being made for a world fair to be held in Paris, a fair in which British India also participated.[3]

The Columbian Exposition and the Chicago World Fair also attracted world-wide attention in the early 90s with nearly

1. The following extract from an interview that the Consul General had with the Viceroy would illustrate the point :

"Yesterday I had the honour to be formally presented to His Excellency the Viceroy of India, the Marquis of Ripon, at the Government House, and as he expressed such warm feeling of friendship and admiration for the Government and people of the United States, I have thought it worthy of reporting the interview to the Department. Among other things His Excellency the Viceroy said in substance that his visit to the United States and his connection there with a movement to settle differences and promote friendshipbetween the United States and England he regarded as the most pleasant incident of his life. He was happy to believe that among the people of both countries there now existed such a feeling of genuine respect and friendship that nothing could estrange them from each other..."

—Despatch no. 8 dated Dec. 14,1881, Volume 12.

2. See *Inaugural address* of Benjamin Harrison, March 4, 1889, Capitol Steps, Washington D.C.

3. See Vol. 14 (G.D.) for a comprehensive list of articles sent to the fair.

every country including British India being represented. In 1893 strikes were still tying up British industry.

America too was in no comfortable position financially at this time. When Cleveland was called upon to run for the Presidency again he made tariff reform the chief issue of the campaign and won. Nevertheless the inexorable world-wide freezing of economic activity was not to spare United States of America.

In India itself the period saw the beginnings of the nationalist movement. But this is neither reported by or commented on by the American Consuls. This seems strange, situated as they were in Calcutta—Eastern India, the centre of such activities.

On the contrary there is positive evidence to the effect that Americans as a nationality were the favoured ones of the English.[1] In fact the American Marathi Mission in Western India used to hold its meetings at times even at the residence of the Collector.[2]

Perhaps the explanation for this lies in the commercial relations of the United State sand British India. In the post 1877 developments of American economy it was very helpful to have intense trade contacts with India; in fact the figures of export and imports to the United States register a positive rise around 1880.[3] This sort of relationship not being uncongenial to the English it was natural for them to have a kindly eye towards the Americans.

1897-1906: *R. F. Patterson* (*July* 1897 *to March* 1906), *William H. Michael* (*March* 1906—) : William McKinley was the last veteran of the Civil War to be elected President. He won his first term of Presidentship because of his advocacy of a high protective tariff and a sound currency based on the gold standard. He had however to lead the country against Spain in War. Once committed he threw the full force of the army and navy into the scenes of action—Cuba, Guam and Philippines—with the result that victory was achieved in less than a year—the shortest war in American History. The Filipinoes, however,

1. See the proceedings Board of Trade for Calcutta and Bombay ports for the years 1793-96. N.A.I.
2. Annual Report of the Marathi Mission for 1889.
3. See chapter VI.

resented American rule as much as they had Spain's. Under their leader, Aguinaldo, a long guerrilla warfare began that dragged on for another two-and-a-half years. Despite this unpopular suppression of the Filipino insurgents McKinley was at the peak of his career in 1900. With the colourful, well liked Theodore Roosevelt as Vice-presidential candidate McKinley easily won the Presidency for the second term. When he was assassinated a few months after his inauguration in 1901 and Vice President Theodore Roosevelt became President the imperialist camp had reason to expect that expansionism would be further encouraged.

In India Lord Curzon had become the Governor General since 1899. And the period of his administration marks the apogee[1] of the imperial system which had been built by Dalhousie and his post-Revolt successors. The year 1906 was to see the emergence of leaders like Tilak on one hand and institutions like Muslim League on the other. There can be no doubt that India was on the threshold of another distinct phase of its modern history.

Now for the first time, because of its involvement in Philippines, United States had to keep an eye on its South Asian Consulates also from a political point of view. U.S. Consulates in India could and did furnish some very material support to the American interests in Philippines,[2] indeed for a while the American Consulates in India also represented the Cuban interests.[3]

There was at the same time perfect cordiality between the representatives of the U.S. and British Government on the diplomatic level and the attitudes during the Delhi Durbar of 1902, confirm it. Wrote the Consul General of U.S. to the Assistant Secretary of State about the Durbar itself "It will be the most magnificent oriental display.... Mrs. Patterson and I are among the Viceroy's invited guests..."[4]

1. Spear, P. : *The Oxford History* of India, Part III, p. 304.

2. e.g. Despatch no. 24. Vol. 6 (B.D.)

3. Letter of Consul General of U.S. to department of State, U.S., Bombay, dated August 19, 1902 (B.D.)

4. American Consul General at Calcutta, to the department of State, despatch no. 194, Oct. 29, 1902 (C.D.)

There were often political situations also related to India which required policy decisions on the part of U.S. government during this period. The Boer War was one such instance. On January 11, 1902, Consul W. T. Fee was writing from Bombay to David J. Hill, Assistant Secretary of State, Washington that a number of Boer prisoners confined in the old fort at Ahmednagar, Bombay Presidency, had applied to him for information with regards to grants of land in the United States which might be open to Boer settlement at the close of the War in South Africa.[1]

And this was only natural because they had obtained information from newspapers and other sources that some of American railroad corporations or possibly some of American Western States or territories had made special offers and inducements for Boer settlements.[2] That the results of the Boer War took such dimensions also needs to be noted.

Having thus briefly noted some aspects of American History which are relevant to one's study, as also the relation of American Consuls in India vis-a-vis these, in a dynamic Indian context, one has the needed canvas for drawing out the Consular activities as also assessing their reports in a particular way.

1. American Consul at Bombay, to the department of State, despatch number 137, Jan. 11, 1902 (B.D.)

2. Ibid.

CHAPTER III

Aspects of Principles and Practice of U.S. Foreign Policy and India (1792-1906)

"Hence for a proper scientific understanding of the reports of the Consuls it was necessary to have a rough idea of the changing patterns of American foreign policy itself which had its projections in the Consuls.........America through its Consuls was not touching a free India directly but a dependent India through England. Hence American attitude towards India was to a very large extent guided, if not wholly determined by its relations with England.......What was the system of operation of U.S. Consular Service in general and in India in particular?"

Introduction. p. 10-11

Some fundamental facets of American foreign policy with special reference to the 19th century

American foreign policy is an expression of American history. American history, in turn is an integral part of the history of mankind. The context is the historical record of all nations, that long and tragic record which Gibbon described as "little more than the register of the crimes, follies and misfortunes of mankind."

Before the United States acquired roughly its present dimensions it was considered doubtful that democracy was at all possible on a scale larger than that of the Greek city State.[1] Alexis de Tocquevelli, visiting the United States in 1830's believed that the country was doomed because of the incompatibility, as he saw it, of democratic process with the effective conduct of foreign relations. "Foreign policies" he wrote "demand scarcely any of those qualities which are peculiar to a democracy, they require, on the contrary, the perfect use of almost all those in which it is deficient..........A democracy can only with great difficulty regulate the details of an important undertaking, preserve in a fixed design, and work out its execution in spite of serious obstacles. It cannot continue its measures with secrecy or wait their consequences with patience."[2]

Today many cite the statesmanship of the founding fathers in America as the supreme example of political wisdom in action. But it did not look that way at the time, and the men themselves seemed less than monumental. The Secretary of the Treasury, in 1791 maintained confidential relations with the British representative in Philadelphia and in effect conspired with him against the official policy of his own country, which the Secretary of the State was trying to carry out.[3]

The degree to which the members of the Commission to negotiate a peace with Britain at the end of the Revolutionary War—Franklin, Jay and Adams—allowed themselves to act independently and in conflict with one another would be almost

1. Halle, Louis J. : *American Foreign Policy* (theory and reality) p. 16.
2. Tocquevelli, Alexis de : *Democracy in America*, I, p. 243.
3. Bemis, B.F. : *The American Secretaries of State and their diplomacy*, II. p. 29, 34.

unthinkable today. Bad faith towards one's colleagues as well as one's allies, was common place.[1]

As the constitution has been since 1789 the instrument through which the United States has been governed, it is well to look a moment at the provisions it made for the conduct and control of foreign relations. Coincidentally with International Law the Constitutional Law of the United States is the supreme law with other nations.[2] Treaties which are made with foreign nations are part of the supreme law of the land, and they override prior laws made by Congress or by any State Legislature, although of course subsequent laws made by Congress may override treaties.[3]

The control and conduct of foreign relations is not under the constitution given to any one of the three departments of government. To the President is given the right to send and to receive ambassadors. To the President and the Senate is given the power to make treaties and other international obligations and bargains. The carrying out of such treaties and other international obligations is partly the work of Congress and partly the work of the executive. The enforcement of treaties as law and the interpretation of treaties within the United States is given to the Supreme Court of the United States which has subsequently taken over the admiralty jurisdiction. Congress by its power to regulate trade may, however, seriously interfere with policies which the President has initiated. The Judicial Department has expressly disclaimed any share in the framing of policies.[4] Having broadly clarified the fundamentals it will be helpful to cite a concrete case.

The fur trade on the north-west coast of North America was a significant point of interest for many countries. In fact, individuals from such distant places as India were interested in it.[5] A small inlet on the western shore of Vancouver Island known as Nootka sound, was the centre of the British, Spanish and Russian fur trade, and the three were anxious to secure it. Thus there was prospect of war in Europe and such a war was

1. Halle, Louis J. : *American Foreign Policy* (theory and reality) p. 32.
2. Wright, Q : *The Control of American Foreign Relations*, p. 145.
3. Mathews, J.M. : *The Conduct of American Foreign Relations*, p. 190-2.
4. Jones vs U.S., 137 U.S. 202 (1890).
5. Public Department, O.C. 24 Jan., 1786, No. 40, N.A.I.

going to be a war between two neighbours of the new Republic. As the British and Spanish territories adjoined American on three sides there was every likelihood of American territory being used as a highway of attack. Pitt sounded out his allies in Europe and then decided that the best way to get at Spain would be to send troops from Canada across the United States and capture Spanish Louisiana.[1]

The British Minister accordingly sounded out the Washington administration in the matter. This put up squarely to the Government the question of whether the United States was to continue to be just a convenient factor in the European political situation. Washington's cabinet was divided. Jefferson, always distrustful of England, advised against letting the British through as a matter of policy. He argued that England would inevitably win such a war and if England got the Spanish territory in North America, it would be surrounded on three sides by British territory and would never get the much needed right to navigate the Mississippi.[2]

Hamilton took the exactly opposite view and insisted that since England would certainly win such a war, America would be at England's mercy anyway and it would be better to have England under obligation to America, so that they might share in the fruits of victory and possibly obtain New Orleans.[3]

John Adams presented the sanest view of the matter, for he pointed out that by following the law on the subject America would find the best way out of the difficulty. Any act by which the United States permitted her soil to be used as an avenue of attack by one belligerent on another would be a violation of neutrality. It was clearly to America's best interest to remain neutral in a fight in which America had no concern.[4]

From this mass of conflicting advice Washington formulated a policy of neutrality which was to be the American ideal for the century.

It is to be noticed while studying the history of American

1. Manning, W.R. : "The Nootka Sound Controversy", "*Am. Hist. Assoc. Repts.*, p. 412-19.
2. Jefferson's *Writings*, II, 100, VII 568.
3. Hamilton's *Works* IV, 48.
4. John Adams *Works* VIII, 497.

foreign policy or the career of the American diplomatic corps that although the Constitution permitted United States to send out "ambassadors" none were sent out in the nineteenth century. Instead America deliberately chose to send out only those of the second rank, in the diplomatic classes, namely "ministers". This was done in the theory that an ambassador represented the sovereign of a country and that Americans had done away with sovereigns, and thereby it would be more dignified and appropriate to have all American envoys ranked as 'ministers'. The result was quite the opposite as the American minister had often to wait patiently in an outroom while the Ambassador of Turkey took precedence over him merely because he was an ambassador and the American was but a minister.[1]

England, America and India

It has been maintained earlier that the American official relationship with India was to a very large extent guided, if not determined, by America's relationship with England. As such a passing reference to this facet of one's study will only help one in obtaining a more objective picture. At the risk of painting with bold strokes, it is one's impression that between the period 1792-1906 ignorance, provincialism crudeness and self-righteousness on the part of democratic America was constantly irritating to the arrogance, haughtiness and insolent contempt for the ex-colonials which characterized aristocratic England of that day. The legacy of misunderstanding which the American Revolution had left in its wake had been accentuated and magnified by the 'offences' of British sea power which led up to the War of 1812.

Moreover, it is to be pointed out that the American Revolution was not a 'neat' one and was in this sense anatypical. That it is one of the few instances of the kind where a community whose majority consists of the emigrants from a particular country rise in rebellion against the mother country is a commonly appreciated fact. But what is not equally well recognized is that not all inhabitants then of what is now United States of America were anti-British or pro-Republican. There was a strong section

1. Schuyler, E.: *American Diplomacy* (N.Y. 1886) 109-13, Foster, J. W. *The Practice of Diplomacy* (Boston 1906) p. 21-23.

among them of the 'loyalists', many of whom in the ultimate analysis took refuge in Canada. Hence in the few immediate decades of post-Independence in American History, United States' relations with England were positively of a most sensitive type. Add to this the fact that the boundary question had yet to be settled in all its details one sees the relationship in the proper perspective.

Is it any wonder then that the first Consul of United States to India went unrecognised ?[1] The issue then, was not merely if a joint stock company could receive a duly accredited envoy of a sovereign power or no. In fact, it was not really till the late thirties of the nineteenth century that one sees the Consulate of America taking some root in India and that also albeit reluctantly.[2] Hence as has been said earlier the real use of the study of such papers as are available in American sources about India is not so much in what they have to say about American 'policy' or 'attitude' towards India but rather in a scientific study of what they say about India itself.

The difficulties of such a scientific analysis are obvious and hence the need of establishing the proper canvas for a fruitful study. The Treaty of Ghent in 1815 left the most important disputes between the two nations unsettled and the end of the war discovered both sides feverishly at work building naval armaments for the next war of the Great Lakes. But if the people of two countries had to spend the next century learning to understand one another, the two governments soon realized that they could not afford to spend too much time glorifying their own questionable military records and trying to belittle the other side.

In 1817 President Madison decided that the competition of naval armaments on the Great Lakes would impoverish both nations and inevitably lead to war. The obvious alternative of an agreement on both sides not to maintain a navy on the Lakes, was too apparent to escape notice and the American Minister at London, John Quincy Adams, suggested to Lord Castlereagh:

"It is evident, if each party augments its forces there with a view to obtaining the ascendancy over the other, vast expenses

1. James B. Higginson in a letter to the Secretary of State ; Calcutta, July 12, 1848. (C.D.)

2. See Vol. I, (B.D.)

will be incurred and the danger of collision augmented to a like degree."[1] So in spite of Parliamentary opposition Castlereagh finally accepted the American proposition.[2]

Even without the formality of a treaty, Secretary of State Richard Rush arranged with the British Minister Charles Bagot an agreement by which both nations agreed to maintain in the Lakes only such vessels as were necessary to police the waterways. President Monroe was careful to submit this agreement to the Senate for its consent[3] and thereby wrote into American foreign policy the principle of disarmament as a means of preventing war. The peace on the Canadian border is to a very large extent due to this.

But in the years following 1818 Anglo-American relations were seriously affected by not a few psychological and mental troubles which still frequently disturb relations between two countries. A new generation was growing up in America which was being fed on the legend of the victories of their country in the wars of Revolution and of 1812. On the other hand in the first part of the nineteenth century, however, English travellers in America and other English literary people were writing somewhat patronizing memoirs of their residence in the young Republic or books about it, which expressed contempt for the queer experiment in democracy being tried out in the New World. Sidney Smith insolently inquired what of intellectual or artistic merit an American had produced. Mrs. Trollope wrote her *Domestic Manners of the Americans* in a general vein of captious criticism which was hardly improved by Dickens' *American Notes.*

In view of this general attitude on both sides of the water, it is a great tribute to the diplomats that they managed to keep the peoples of the respective countries out of constant warfare. Another influence was steadily growing stronger to keep the peace.

With the gradual surrender of the old Mercantilist Navigation System, England admitted the right of the United States to trade with her colonies, because among other things, it was evident that the colonial monopoly idea was more disastrous to the British Sugar colonies than it was to foreigners. British

1. *House Document*, No. 471, 56th Congress, Ist Seas. p. 5.
2. Hansard's *Debates* xxxiii, 376-8; 567-91; Adams', J. Q., *Memoirs.* III, 287, 329.
3. *Edinburgh Review*, xxxiii, 78.

cotton interests were also involved and this is one of the facets where India looms large as a factor which Americans had to take due cognizance of. But the advent of free trade in England (1846) and the final surrender of the Navigation System (1849) was an admission of the fact that England could no longer produce enough food to supply the wants of her growing population, and that she could not, within herself or her colonies produce all the raw material required to keep her mills and factories going. England simply could not afford to go to war with the United States, because she derived the bulk of her cotton supply from the southern states, and because her population would starve without the regular shipment of grain, beef and pork from overseas. A war would mean the serious interruption of that food supply.[1]

In addition to this the old landed aristocracy of England was giving way to a new type of commercial and industrial aristocracy, who had made money from the numerous wars, or 'entrepreneurs' who had made the most of the factory system before the advent of protective legislation, or colonial magnates. These people had often, big investments overseas which would have been seriously jeopardized by a war with the United States. There was that rising class of industrial capitalists whose money was not tied up in big estates in the south of England, or plantations overseas. This new ruling class had made itself felt in the Great Reform Bill of 1832. The party alignments had changed. The Tories who went out with Wellington in 1830 were by no means the same Tories who came back with cotton mill magnate Peel in 1841. The old Whigs who identified themselves with Charles James Fox were not of the same type of mind as Bright and Cobden in the new era.[2]

It is no wonder then that diplomatic difficulty after diplomatic difficulty was irritated into life only to be smoothed out when sober second thought made it clear that these two nations simply could not afford to make war on one another. Naturally the American Consuls in India were left undisturbed or were per-

1. Cunningham, W. : *Grow of English Industry and Commerce, Laissez Faire*, p. 624.

Newton A.P., *Cambridge History of British Foreign Policy*. II, 233.

2. Dorman, M.R.P.: *History of the British Empire in the* 19th Century-II, 355.

haps even slightly patronised.

If this is the story of how Anglo-American relationships affected the behaviour of Americans in India in the first half of the nineteenth century, there is no great variation to this in the second half of the nineteenth century. In fact as shall be seen in the following chapters the second half of the nineteenth century witnessed a further strengthening of these tendencies whose faint beginnings one notices earlier. It is in this perspective that the pattern of behaviour of the American Consuls can actually be understood.

The only exception to the above going generalisation was the period of the American Civil War when the relations between the Federal Government and Her Majesty's Government became somewhat strained because of the help that the latter gave to the Confederate States. Though this may be a departure from the general concept of amity between America and Britain it does not disturb the larger thesis that the only way to discern a meaning to the behaviour and have a key to the proper understanding of the statements of the U.S. Consuls in India is on the larger canvas of Anglo-U.S. relationship. In fact the U.S. Civil War and the consequent strain between England and America had great impact on India especially in the Bombay Presidency.[1]

The disputes between England and United States themselves arising out of the controversies of the Civil War in America were settled by the arbitration treaty signed in Washington in 1871.

At about the same time the vexed questions of impressment and expatriation were settled by a treaty in which Great Britain gave way completely to the American point of view, and acknowledged that each nation must fully and faithfully recognize naturalization acquired under the laws of the other nation. No longer would the British take American citizens from the decks of American vessels under the pretense that they were English by birth. The Americans had not finally taken the position that naturalization ends a former allegiance until 1845, and not until 1868 had this been embodied in the Statutes of the United States.

1. Gautam, Vinayshil : "Some aspects of Social life and customs in the Poona districts : 1870-1880" *Maratha History Seminar Papers*, Shivaji University Publications, Kolahpur. (1971)

In the treaty of 1870 England consented to cease questioning the right of a person to so change his allegiance, and another source of irritation was laid at rest.[1]

A number of other problems crept up between England and the United States like the Venezuelan and Alaskan arbitration which included among other things problem of territorial adjustment and boundary settlement. This was quite a natural problem for a growing and expanding nation like the United States.

In fact it was not until 1906 that a treaty was made for the settlement of America's last boundary disputes with England, and that provided for commissioners to discover and fix the line of the 141st. degree west longitude which marked the division between Canada and Alaska upto the Arctic Ocean.

The synchronisation of the latter date of our study and the end of the boundary disputes between England and the United States is significant. It only helps to underscore the peculiarity and uniqueness of this period in Anglo-American relations. That so much tension and clash of interest would be resolved so amicably is a matter of no small credit to the personalities concerned. Naturally all this affected Indo-American contacts also. And it is not surprising that but for a brief patch, during the period of the American Civil War, Indo-American contacts remain steady for the whole of one's period of study.

Theodore Roosevelt a few years before his death remarked:

"Moreover I am prepared to say what five years ago, I would not have said, I think the time has come when the United States and the British Empire can agree to a universal arbitration treaty. In other words, I believe the time has come when we should say that under no circumstance shall there ever be a resort to war between the United States and the British Empire and that no question can arise between them that cannot be settled in judicial fashion."[2]

This was the changed voice of United States speaking be-

1. Hyde, C.C.: *International Law Chiefly as Interpreted and Applied by the U.S.*, I, 662-5;

Malloy, C. : *Treaties and Conventions*, I, 691.

2. Quoted in, Rhodes, J. F.: '*McKinley and Roosevelt Administrations*', p. 260.

cause the war of 1898 had marked as it were the beginnings of a new era.[1] America itself had acquired a considerable Empire and could now hope to share the experiences of the "mother country" in this new sphere of its activity. The sentiments attributed to Walter Page[2] would be shared by many in America.

Many of the subsequent American attitudes to India's problems as a part of the British Empire could possibly be traced to this.

U.S. Consular Service and India

Though the United States of America had sent its consuls in places of its interest in as early a period as 1792 it was not uptill some thirty years or so, later that the system was regularised. The code of behaviour for American Consuls in places such as Mauritius (Isle de France) was very undefined and they could have great latitude for independent decision. Their independence was, of course, increased by the great geographical distance which existed between them and America as, of course, the great time it took for messages to pass to and fro.

From 1831 however the whole system began to be more closely drawn together but the organisation was only comparative and as shall be seen in the following description not uptill 1906 even, the Consular Service of America had any semblance of the compact set up which the present day diplomatic services have.

It is moreover to be realised that there was no exclusive Consular Service for India on the part of U.S.A. but that the Consulate System in India was an integral part of the worldwide set up which the Americans had. As a result thereof, very often the peculiar needs of India were not taken care

1. Gautam, Vinayshil : 'Some aspects of the attitude of United States of America in India' : 1901-1905; *American Government and Politics*; S. Chand & Co., Delhi ('72)

2. "Blood carries with it that particular trick of thought which makes us all English in the last resort. Thus despite the fusion of races and all the great contributions of other nations to her hundred millions of people and her incalculable wealth, the United States is yet English led and English ruled." in Hindricks, *Life and Letters of Walter H. Page*, I, 258; many would of course, be also inclined to doubt this, broad statement of Mr Page, and one could read, for it, Rossiter, W. S., "What are Americans," *Atlantic Monthly*, LXXVI, 270.

of and that changes in the system were introduced only when a larger need for such a change in the service was realised.

Yet before one goes into a study of the actual pattern of the Consular service two observations have to be made. First, of course, as has been substantiated earlier is that during the period under study U.S.A. approached the Indian situation very largely through Britain. And this was natural also, for India was part of the worldwide British Empire. What then, is of one's interest, is the fact that the few Consulates that U.S. had in India did not form an independent unit but that in the U.S. Consulate Service, it is the Consulates in the British Empire that had a separate identity for themselves. This is of course notwithstanding the fact that the Americans had after 1840 a separate Consul General for British India posted at Calcutta.

A natural corollary therefore from the above-mentioned facts, is that U.S. did not have any specific policy towards India as such during the period under study. Matters related to India hardly ever reached the policy making level and what decisions were to be taken with respect to India were dealt with more during the routine course of things. Hence, it also seems natural to conclude that what can really be discovered during the period is a set of 'attitudes', towards India and not really a 'policy'.

A word in clarification might help. If there is any thing outstanding about the American nation it is the great scope for individual initiative. Every thing need not be channelised through nor does it wait for the help of, the fairy god-mother of welfare state. If the individual wishes to do anything, it has all the scope and opportunity to do so. America's relationship with other parts of the world also amply bear out this pattern. And this is also true of America's relationship with India. Hence the Consular Service in India becomes as much a source of documentation of the American's activities in India as it is a storehouse of information of what actually happened in India itself.

With this brief reference to the nature of the Consulates in India it might be worthwhile to take a glance at what exactly these Consulates were doing and how they were expected to operate from 1830 onwards.

Piecing together the various documents in a chronological

order, a picture as the following emerges.

In January 1831, U.S. Consul Strobel wrote to the Secretary of State reporting on the regulation of American Consular system made upon an examination of returns received. This was done (i.e. the reporting) in pursuance of the State Department circular of 10 June, 1830. Nor was this a cursory or incomplete report but was exhaustively undertaken in which relevant comparisons were made to the prevailing Consular system of other European countries.[1] This report was not universally welcomed but met with certain amount of opposition by the Woodbury Commission on U.S. Commerce. Happily President Jackson was in favour of revising the laws regulating the Consular system and this he made known in the annual message. And finally the whole thing was referred to the Commission of Foreign Affairs.[2] In the long drawn out procedure of representative legislation the process of change is necessarily slow. On March 16, 1838, American Consul at St. John, Montgomery presented a memorandum to the House of Representatives proposing revision of U.S. Consular system.[3] This was followed on March 23, 1840, by one known as Reed, Representative from Massachusetts who brought a motion forward to entrust the Commission on Commerce to enquire into expediency of changing the Consular system, so as to pay the Consuls by salaries. This would obviate the necessity of their serving as merchants in order to make a living. This was, of course, agreed to by the house.[4] But in actual terms it did not achieve much as the subsequent events were to prove. On January 7, 1842, again a motion was brought before the house by Wood of New York, this time directing the Commission on Commerce to consider the propriety of introducing a bill requiring all consular and commercial agents of U.S. to be U.S. citizens, abolishing fee system, and classifying Consular service.[5] This was, of course, duly agreed to, also by the house. Not only was there a mounting pressure on the part of various members of the house but several lobbies of the house were

1. 21.2. S. doc. 57, 4.
2. 22.1. H. Jol , 17, 39.
3. 25.2. H. doc. 467, 2; H. Jol. 631.
4. 26.1. H. Jol. 651.
5. 27.2. H. Jol. 127.

also busy exerting pressure for a change as their commercial interests were being hampered in the prevalent state of affairs. May 4, 1842, saw the presentation of a memorandum on behalf of Baltimore shipmasters to U.S. House against the appointment of foreigners to consulships and praying reorganization of Consular system—which was, of course, in a hangover of the Anglo-Saxon tradition referred to Commission on Commerce.[1]

Yet it would be a mistake to presume that during this period there was only a plea and a case for what we might like to term today as a 'rationalization of the system'. The opposite current was also there and E.H. Foster, Senator from Tennessee remarked against such a move and moved an amendment to the resolution regarding operations of Consular officers.[2] However, on June 17, 1846, U.S. Select Committee led by Campbell on alterations in Consular system did recommend the substitution of salaries for fees and was adverse to subjects of foreign powers fillings posts of American Consuls.[3] And thus a great change was brought about in the system itself which saw its reflection in the Indian context also. U.S. Consuls in India after all, were only a part of the larger net work. From this period onwards there is an increasing awareness in the American circles of the importance of Oriental trade. And on Nov. 28, 1846, A.H. Palmer submitted to the Secretary of State, Buchanan a report on oriental nations with which U.S. had not made treaties; it not only recommended special mission to open commercial relations; but also proposed a Consular plan.[4]

Yet as has been pointed out earlier it would be misleading to suggest that these memoranda, reports or bills of change were accepted and acclaimed universally. The bill which was introduced in March 1855 met with heavy weather and on June 2, 1855 U.S. Attorney General Cushing was giving his opinion on so much of act of March 1,1855, in connection with Sec.3,

1. 27.2. H. Jol. 783.
2. xiii Cong. Globe, 188.
3. 29.1. H. rpt. 714.
4. 29.2. H. exdoc. 96.

act of March 3, 1855, amendatory thereof as related to appointment, salary and duties of consuls of U.S.[1] This was not enough either, on July 14, Attorney General Cushing gave, as he was asked, his opinion in the matter of functions of Consuls.[2] Perhaps this is a solitary case of the law stepping in to define diplomatic responsibilities in the nineteenth century. And when all arguments of the conservatives failed, the last infallible one—economic—was used by them. To stall change from the traditional system R.M.T. Hunter, Senator from Virginia commented on Feb. 19, 1859, urging economy in expenditures for diplomatic and Consular services[3] which conceptualised and perpetuated a bane against which Theodore Roosevelt was to murmur against some 45 years later.[4]

The U.S. Consular Service continued to be fundamentally unaltered during the remaining period though minor events like opening of new Consular agencies or closure of some old ones did take place as per needs of the situation.

In 1906 the system of filing Consular despatches was radically altered.

The office of the U.S. Consul in India

The American Consuls were usually appointed from among the leading businessmen of a place. As the post was not salaried[5] this was always the more convenient process for getting people to fill the situation. On his appointment the person concerned had to obtain two sureties from the United States[6], usually of men of social standing and resident there. He had also to take an oath of allegiance to the Constitution.[7] After such and other formalities were over he had to apply for recognition[8]

1. vii. Op. attys. gen. 242.
2. ibid. 342.
3. Cong. Globe, 35.2., 1145.
4. ed. Lewis, Alfred Henry : *A Compilation of the messages and speeches of Theodore Roosevelt* (1901-1905), p. 847.
5. See Vol. I, (C.D.) ; Vol. I, (B.D.)
6. Charles Huffnagle in a letter to James Buchanan, Secretary of State, U.S.A., Calcutta, dated Dec. 20, 1847 (C.D.)
7. ibid.
8. Charles Huffnagle in a letter to the United States Minister at London, Calcutta, dated July 20, 1848.

to the British, authorities in India, which once the diplomatic relations between England and America had been established on a firm footing, was never delayed in coming.

The American Consul in turn recommended, on application, some persons for the post of Vice Consul or Consular agents for the various ports within his jurisdiction which had American Consular agencies.[1] Usually preference was to be shown to persons of American citizenship[2] and there was reluctance to have an incumbent with British citizenship. The latter could have easily created complications.[3] Such persons could also be businessmen who were residing for a while, anyway, in that particular part of the country, as per needs of their main vocation.[4] Because of the great distance from the home government very often the Consuls did not even wait for the formal sanction on their recommendation but took it for granted.[5] The home authorities also obliged.

There was a Consul General in Calcutta[6] and a Consul

1. e.g. Despatch no. 312, Calcutta, dated August 4, 1880, (C.D.). The American commercial agents placed in the various ports used to take care of American interests there as well as serve as feeders of all type of relevant information to the main Consular offices at Calcutta or Bombay as the case might be.

2. Benjamin Joy in a letter to the Secretary of State, U.S.A., Boston, dated Jan. 24, 1796 (C.D.)

3. "...for should a subject of the kind of Great Britain be appointed it be quite in the power of the Government there to send him to Europe a prisoner whenever they saw fit, unless some convention with that country is made to prevent it ; their India Act gives full power to the Governor of any of their settlements to deport any British subject from the other side of the Cape of Good Hope that is not actually in the service of the British King......if there should be a necessity for appointing a British subject to that office and one who has not the Company's permission to reside there, that they should feel themselves in rather an awkward situation respecting the mode of treating him, as they are enjoined by their orders from home not to allow any person to remain there without the Company's permission."

—Benjamin Joy in a letter to the Secretary of State, U.S A., Boston, dated Jan. 24, 1796 (C.D.)

4. e.g. James Lilly, Consul General of United States at Calcutta, from April 15, 1861 to Nov. 25, 1862. (C.D.)

5. James B. Higginson in a letter to the Secretary of State, U.S.A., Mirzapur, Dec. 4, 1843. (C.D.)

6. See Vol. III (C.D.)

in Bombay.[1] And though their relationship was never expressly defined, it was commonly assumed that Calcutta was the superior office. Not only by virtue of its designation but also by the fact that it was in the same city which had the seat of government for British India, Calcutta was ranked higher and this showed itself in the precedence which Calcutta got in the diplomatic protocol.[2] There was also an instance where an officer of the Bombay office was severely pulled up for permissive negligence in having himself designated Consul General in one of the newspapers.[3] Nevertheless the Consular offices were free and independent in many matters. It (Bombay office) neither routed its despatches to the State department in America through Calcutta nor did the Calcntla officials have any say in the appointments of Bombay Consulate. There was some friction also over the respective spheres of jurisdiction of two offices.[4]

However neither could be deemed as headquarters in their own right for they were both subsurvient to the London office of the American diplomatic corps. The American minister in London was the last word in many matters. This further lends weight to the thesis that America's diplomatic relations with India were routed through London and hence were to a very large extent dictated if not wholly determined by America's relationship with England.

Because of the inbuilt vagueness of the whole system and lack of good communication very often removal of Consuls was

1. See Vol. II (B.D.)

2. At the time of the Delhi Durbar of 1902 the head of the American Consulate General at Calcutta was invited to it by the Government of India. The American Consul at Bombay did not figure in the picture at all. See despatch no. 194 of Oct. 29, 1902 (C.D.)

3. See Vol. 16, (C.D.); Vol. 6, (B.D.)

4. Towards the beginning of the twentieth century there was a mild controversy about the respective territorial jurisdictions of the Calcutta and Bombay Consulates. This was primarily because of the proverbial vagueness about most of the things of the U.S. Consular service in nineteenth century. See despatch no. 225, of June 13, 1903 (B.D.) However nothing much came out of this controversy because no great change in territorial jurisdictions were brought about because of it; only the conventions received formal sanction now e.g. Calcutta office got confirmed its jurisdiction over Madras. See the answer of the Calcutta office to despatch no. 320, dated July 26, 1906 of the Bombay office (B.D.)

not formerly intimated but was conveyed to them only by the arrival of the new incumbent. Naturally enough this was a cause of annoyance with the out-going official.[1] As a matter of routine in the absence of the Consuls the Vice Consuls officiated.[2]

Even small matters like the appointment of a clerk or messenger had to be reported home and approval sought.[3]

It is no mere coincidence that all the American Consulates or Agencies were situated at ports. They were not basically meant to be a diplomatic link with the area in which they were situated, as indeed they would be expected to be now. Rather they were there primarily for commercial reasons, to take care of such details of trade and transaction as would be in the interest of their mother country. This would involve various duties of which high level politics or diplomatic exchange would form an incidental part. Being at a port would naturally facilitate their work.

These Consulates or Agencies were expected to take care of the interest of the American ships which would arrive there, as also of any grievance that may have arisen among the seamen during the voyage.[4] At times differences on the ocean and/or land would take violent form involving American citizens, and result in a court case. In such an eventuality the Consulate would helpfully arrange for an advocate for any of the needy (American) parties.[5] However, such and such like gestures were not always supported by the home authorities from the financial

1. Despatch no. 3, Calcutta, Dec. 14, 1843 (C.D.)

2. See the bitterness of J.B. Higginson in the letter to the Secretary of State, U.S.A., Mirzapur, dated Feb. 24, 1848 (C.D.)

3. e.g. despatch no. 180, Calcutta, dated June 24, 1902 (C.D.)

4. e.g. there was some criticism of the way the American skippers were using the Sandwitch Island crews and a private American citizen wrote of this to the Secretary of State, U.S.A., see letter of A.B. Ely to the Sectary of State, U.S.A., Boston, April 9, 1851 (C.D.) and subsequent documents show that follow up action was taken, and the American Consul investigated he whole question.

5. e.g. the murder case involving American citizens Francis S. Very, Theodore Sidgway, William Stiltz and Edward Ree where the U.S. Consulate General in Calcutta had to provide advocates for them. See letters no. 1 to 5, between dates Jan. 9, 1851 to Jan. 10, 1851, as also U.S. Consuls General's letter to Francis Very (Sr.), Calcutta, dated Feb. 3, 1851, (C.D.)

point of view.[1]

The Consulate was also expected to maintain a register of the arrival and departure of American ships, their tonnage and the goods they carried.[2] Periodically the Consulates were expected to transmit to the department of State various forms which included digest of the invoice book, register of official letters sent, arrivals and departures of American vessels, return of deceased American citizens, names of all persons employed at the Consulate concerned and rent and miscellaneous expenses with vouchers in quadriplate.[3] The number of vouchers required to be sent varied and at times it could be as many as six.[4] Similarly Consular fees had also to be accounted for and transmitted to the department of State.[5]

These consular offices would naturally be well supplied with laws and regulations.[6] And it was a part of their job to pass bona fide information about India to United States and *vice versa* as the need might be. The regularity with which survey of India reports were sent to United States is amazing.

In course of time as the work of Consulates grew it became necessary for them to maintain an archives. Ready references had to be available as well as a proper cataloguing had to be there. Papers which had passed between the Consulate and the State department, or the Consulate and the Government of India, or any princely state would be required in a growing situation of complicated diplomatic relations. But the archives took time to evolve and in 1880 the Calcutta Consulate archives was inadequate in many ways. The various circulars and instructions received from the State department, though neatly bound were not indexed till as late a period as 1871.[7] Soon after the

1. See the pitiful letter of Charles Huffnagle, American Consul General at Calcutta, to the fifth auditor's office, Treasury Department, U.S.A., Calcutta, dated Jan. 10, 1851, (C.D.)

2. Vice Consul U.S. in a despatch to the Secretary of State, Calcutta, dated March 1, 1844. (C.D.)

3. e.g. despatch no. 279, Calcutta, dated January 16, 1880 (C.D.)

4. despatch no. 301, Calcutta, dated, July 2, 1880. (C.D.)

5. Vice Consul U.S.A. in a letter to the Secretary of the State, Calcutta dated August 7, 1846. (C.D.)

6. e.g. despatch no. 155, Vol. 17 (C.D.)

7. despatch no. 303, Volume 12 (C.D.)

need for keeping an office copy was realised for all out-going despatches. As a rule press copies were not used for any part of the correspondence of the Calcutta Consulate.[1] There was also some fund with the Consulates for the distressed seamen of the United States which was given to the needy seamen as per their needs.[2]

This brings one to the role which these Consulates were expected to play towards the private citizens of the United States in India. The reports are impressive in the way they keep account of individual Americans, their problems and property.[3]

These reports begin with recording that 'no passport is needed[4] to visit British India' and end by mentioning the absolute necessity for one.[5] Hence, the reports themselves mark a graph of the attitude of the British in India in some matters.

In a way these reports also show how the Consular service in India evolved from its rudimentary beginnings to a fairly well established organisation with all the trappings of a diplomatic office. In the beginning even small items like the U.S. flag or the Consular seal were a luxury[6] being available only through repeated requests and almost unending patience. Financial stringency at times verged on the ridiculous[7] and many provisions of the Consular regulations the Consuls refused to implement as being utterly derogatory to their position to enforce. But slowly things changed for the better till more method was introduced in the system. Clerks were appointed and

1. despatch no. 303, Volume 12 (C.D.)

2. U.S. Vice Consul in a letter to the Secretary of State, Calcutta, Feb. 4, 1846 (C.D.)

3. e.g. despatch no. 173, Bombay, August 7, 1902. (B.D.). This is a unique case where the American missionaries settled in India are also given the same protection by the Consulate as would be available to an ordinary American citizen.

4. See Vol. 1, (B.D.)

5. despatch no. 193, Vol. 17 (C.D.)

6. e.g. U.S. Consul General in a letter to the Secretary of State, U.S.A., Calcutta, July 15, 1851 (C.D.)

7. ibid.

messengers hired. The office of the Consul became salaried from feed.[1] And round the turn of the century talk was on for putting up electric fans in the Consulate offices.[2] Like other human organisations the Consulate service also had its human jealousies and pettinesses. Signature campaigns were at times conducted[3] and allegations and counter allegations were made while the accuser and the accused vied with each other in calling one another false. Washington headquarters were very often dragged in the picture.[4] But it is unnecessary to over play this aspect of the Consular service.

What was perhaps one of the most useful and positive services rendered by the U.S. Consulates to the American nation was the incentive that they gave to the American industries by informing the men behind them about where exactly lay an opening for them, marketwise.[5] It is not surprising therefore to hear at times even the British Parliament bewailing the gains

1. despatch no. 20, Bombay dated May 26, 1898 (B.D.)

2. despatch no. 166, Vol 17, (C.D.)

3. The following extract from the letter of N.P. Jacobs, Consul General of U.S. at Calcutta to the department of State, dated March 23, 1861 will speak for itself.

"...Having been informed that by this mail will go forward to Boston for additional signatures and thence to the department of State, a paper containing false, malicious and libellious charges against my official and personal character intended to effect my official stand and my personal reputation, both at home in the U.S. and in this city, I most respectfully and yet most urgently request that the paper itself on the receipt of the department at once be forwarded to me... (so that I may) be enabled to institute in the High Courts of India, suits for libel and defamation against the parties originating and circulating and who by false representation have obtained the signature of various other persons and firms to the paper aforesaid and also against the parties last mentioned for signing and other by endorsing the slanderous matter which I am given to understand the said paper contains, unless these parties fully and publicly apologize to me, therefore—I respectfully ask for the original paper, since owing to the rules of court here prevailing not even a certified copy will suffice as a basis of suit while the original is in existence."

4. N.P. Jacobs in a letter to the department of State, U.S.A., Calcutta, dated March 23, 1867 (C.D.)

5. This is a point which has been discussed in Chapter VI.

of Americans in Indian markets.[1] But this would be so only towards the closing years of our study when the American Consular Service in India had nearly perfected[2] its tools both of gathering information and transmitting it.

1. despatch no. 153, dated June 12, 1901 (C.D.)
2. The opening note to Vol. I (B.D.)

CHAPTER IV

Facets of Indian Society in the Nineteenth Century

"... (an)...effort...to use such a source (American Consular Papers) to trace the social...condition of India in the nineteenth century..it has been one's effort to keep testing the consular and other descriptions on the framework of such evidence as available..."

Introduction p. 9

The Framework

As is commonly realised exactitude in periodisation so far as social history or development is concerned is a very elusive task. As such the period 1792 to 1906 can conveniently be taken to mean approximately the nineteenth century. Social history and nineteenth century in India bring to the mind of a, student of history certain concepts, notions and figures, the more 'eye catching' among which would be movements like abolishment of Sutee, female infanticide; widow remarriage; notions of religious reform, religious revivalism; individuals like Raja Ram Mohan Roy, Ishwar Chandra Vidyasagar, Syed Ahmad, Vivekanand etc. etc. A very neat and composite picture. A process which has been viewed by a renowned scholar in the following words: "Modern Indian renaissance is essentially a change of spirit and a reorientation of outlook of the vast multitude of this continent through various forces in the new world of the nineteenth century."[1] While this can be considered a good definition of renaissance, which section of the society was affected by this remains an open question. One wonders if this 'renaissance' ever touched the *masses*. The doubts are further confirmed by the realisation of the fact that in terms of social evolution Indians are on many points exactly where they were hundred years back. The learned scholar has, in the above referred book, made some over-simplified generalisations for the whole of the sub-continent on the basis of his few tentative conclusions about Bengal. This has been an error with some of the other historians also; and this sort of analysis confuses a proper understanding of the Indian social scene.

India, while undoubtedly being one cultural unit, is composed of several cultural sub-units many of which are at varying levels of social evolution.[2] The result being that the whole nation is not on one wave length as it were. This is partially so because geographically the whole sub-continent was never under the direct control of the Colonialists and as such

1. Datta, K.K. : *Dawn of Renascent India*, p. VI.

2. Gautam, V. : 'Some aspects of social change in the Bhojpuri speaking area, 1858-1920 : a case study of a traditional unit in a colonial setting" *abstract of papers*, 28 *International Congress of Orientalists*, Canberra.

was not equally exposed the catalytic influences of the Industrial-technological culture. This variation in response is very well brought out by the comparison of reports of the American Consulates emanating from Bombay and Calcutta. And this hypothesis goes a distance in explaining the different patterns of evolution in Western and Eastern India—one being so organised and methodical and the other so disorganised and confused. The particular source study with which this book is concerned, thus gives an added and vital dimension to the study of social processes in India. For as is well accepted, for the study of a pre-industrial, non-literate (*not non-educated*) society such as nineteenth century India sources are very few and at times discouragingly inadequate. The American Consular records go a distance in fulfilling this need, for most of their accounts are based on empirical observations of their agents who travelled deep into the country for trade purposes and observed accurately and incisively. The bulk of the evidence is so great as to permit the writing of the separate evolutions of Eastern and Western India merely on the basis of the Consular reports and other American reportings. This could indeed be a worthwhile exercise if only to give one more dimension to the study of the social history of the country. The comparative value of the same source of reporting from widely differing areas of the country has already been noted.

In another way these reports were found useful viz. the evolution of a theoretical framework of reference for the understanding of the Indian social scene. While the quest is still on for a viable framework, some scholars have tended to accept the conceptual frame of 'Western Impact and Indian response'.[1] Elsewhere it has been suggested that this will be an inadequate[2] framework of reference for it is neither possible to understand the western impact nor quantify the Indian response without first having understood what the Indian situation was. Hence a three phase approach to the problem was considered advisable : viz. (1) a study of what was the Indian situation, (2) a study of

1. This is evident in such an analysis as undertaken in P. Knaplund's '*Britain, Commonwealth and Empire*' (1901-1955) etc. etc.

2. Gautam, V.: "'Social life in the 'Poona districts' " 1870-1880, *Maratha History Seminar Papers* ('71), Shivaji University Publications, Kolahpur.

what were the instruments of social change and then only (3) what was the resultant. It would be inadvisable to skip the first two phases to reach third.

The U.S. Consular reports give an excellent account of the first phase namely what some aspects of the Indian situation were. This is also an account which stands the tests of corroborative evidence. Besides they give a very graphic account too of some of the instruments of social change e.g. law, communication, education etc. They have some light to shed both on the urban and the rural sectors. As such they are an useful set of evidence.

The remaining part of this chapter is divided into three sections viz. some strands of the social history of India, glimpses of social life in Western India and glimpses of social life in Eastern India and finally one tries to see if any meaning can be read into them.

Some strands of the social history of India

Heirs to the tradition of Renaissance, Reformation, Industrial Revolution and French Revolution by the nineteenth century Europe had attained not only something qualitatively different from the rest of the world but also found itself superior to the rest of the world in armoral strength by virtue of its technological superiority. Naturally the overflow of these dynamic peoples from Europe, around the world was further intensified during this century. England being the first of the industrialised nation was understandably in the forefront. This historical process had far-reaching significance for the more traditional, meditative and non-technological cultures of areas such as India, China, Japan etc. They had to either adjust to the new value scale or face the alternative of extinction. That the Indian culture has survived so far in spite of its domination by one of the most pursuasive of occidental cultures—English—is by itself something amazing.

To understand this process of interaction merely an 'impact—response' analysis will not do. As has been said earlier the Indian situation, which, to borrow a term from sociology, would be called 'T_1' (i.e. Time 1), must be understood. The American Consular reports processed from this point of view would be a mere abstraction unless preceded by a brief analysis of what appear to be the fundamentals of the situation.

The areas which the American Consular reports deal with—viz. the Eastern and Western India—bore the brunt of the English impact. And it has been noted earlier that there were contrasting patterns of response from the two areas.

In the earlier phase of the colonial situation the Gujarat bourgeoisie fared better than any other regional bourgeoisie and certainly more so than the Bengal bourgeoisie. This was partially so because they had been traditional leaders in terms of trade and had a special type of crop specialisation. They also had the advantage of not facing the brunt of English competition in the earlier phases of English domination and it is perhaps more than a coincidence, an index of their social sophistication, that in the course of American help to Indian experiments in cotton cultivation in the nineteenth century the American citizens found this area very responsive and socially receptive to experimentation techniques.

It is to be noted that the Bengal Presidency and its adjoining regions (referred to in this book as Eastern India) coming under British rule earlier had to deal with greater number of English officers and free traders. Besides Western India in facing the Middle East was face to face with a more meaningful region, commercially, than was Eastern India in facing the South East Asia. Socially Gujaratis had no inhibitions to sea-travel while the East Indian was always in danger of losing caste. Moreover the so-called 'drain' was almost entirely from the Bengal region. And when one keeps in mind the fact that throughout greater part of this century the English military machine in the Western and also at times Southern India was being financed from the surplus extracted from Eastern India it is easy to understand, partially, their subsequent ematiated state. It is therefore a viable hypothesis that under the Ryotwari settlement of Western India there was generated a well-to-do middle stratum of peasants which serving the purpose of the 'meso-structure' could absorb the industrial-technological values of the west and pass them into the main stream of that section of the Indian society. This could not be so in Eastern India for the 'meso-structure' was not present to absorb any values. The monopolistic system of the English was far more total there and prevented any such development.

Hence if the social history of the country in the modern period till 1947 be considered as partially, the history of the attempt of the society to accomplish a double revolution then the contrasting patterns of the two areas of American reporting become very clear. This double revolution would mean the one against British colonial domination and the other against her own unchanging, unyielding segment of tradition. In Europe for example the upsurge against the *ancien regime* was a simple affair, for as it has been noticed by some, it was one and the same thing e.g. Bourbon monarchy was two enemies in one—both an obstacle to nationalism and liberalism. In India in so far as the past appeared as the traditional system of caste and family life that was the stumbling block for liberalism. The British Raj itself took the place of European legitimacy and stood in the way of the emergence of nineteenth century national self-determination. Some feel that had the British identified themselves squarely with the Indian tradition the problem of the Indian social reformers would have been solved by attacking both the enemies in one. For it is felt that they (reformers) were constantly getting, "their wires crossed. They had to attack the British but defend the Indian past which the British attacked, or at least endangered. Or else logic compelled them to defend the British rule and attack the Indian past, and get the British rule to help them in this attack."[1]

The fact of the situation is different, however, for, for the most part of this century the British did *not* have a consistent policy towards the Indian social tradition ranging as it (the policy) did from Orientalism to Utilitarianism, to Paternalism interspersed with various patches of indifference. Hence it is that the problems of social evolution which was faced by Orientalists was different to that faced by Ram Mohan to that faced by Sayed Ahmad to that faced by Tilak. Besides, the Indian tradition did not consist only of the obsolete and irrelevant and so the Indian social reformer had not always to choose between the so-called grey and the white alternatives of the Indian and the Occidental tradition.

As the American reports help in identifying, there were grave sociological, economic and geo-political factors involved

1. Mazumdar, R.C. : 'Rammohun Roy and Bal Gangadhar Tilak on Social Legislation', *Journal of Indian History*, Vol. XLV, No. 133.

in a particular type of social movement. In many of the traditional units[1] of Eastern India, because of the stunted economic growth during this period, the heavy indebtedness, the progressive fragmentation of land holding, the chronic state of industrial backwardness, the phenomenon of migrant labour as well as the introduction of the rule of law in a later period as also the introduction of modern means of education and communication, there is a peculiar type of social growth. Furthermore the widely prevalent view that the social reform movements of the first half of the nineteenth century evolved into the nationalist agitations of the second half of the nineteenth century is an over-simplification of the whole problem. It is true only in as much as some of the reformists movements were really revivalist in content.

During the nineteenth century these issues did not always come into the open very sharply. If one looks at the case of Ram Mohan Roy, for example, one will find that he opposed tradition. He criticised castes and the institution of child marriage, and was greatly influenced by the European liberal spirit. He wanted to start a new rationalist religious movement and envisaged the possibility of cutting loose from the moorings of ancient India. The Society which he founded became a great humanitarian influence in Bengal, but his real objectives, which were totally anti-traditional, were soon lost sight of.

On the other side one has Tilak (who emerges towards the end of one's period of study) and who proceeded in every respect in the opposite sense. He set up cow-protection leagues; opposed the English, and had nothing against violence. He based himself squarely upon traditionalism and objected to any kind of social reform through the English aegis, especially to the raising of the age of child marriage. He raised a storm of opposition to the Age of Consent Bill—(it violated religious duties, he said) and he denounced every Hindu supporter of it as a traitor to the faith. He always added that his opposition was grounded on the belief that no reform must come from the English, and that once the English were out and India free, he

1. Gautam, V.: 'Introduction to the Social history of the Bhojpuri speaking area in India as reconstructed from folk-literature.' *'Society and Culture'* Vol. III, No. 2.

would then look into the matter of reform himself. This was merely a rationalisation. Tilak was a traditionalist and summoned up tradition to defeat the English.[1]

It is significant to note that the way Ram Mohan Roy and Tilak wanted to tackle the issue of child marriage varied greatly. It was bound to be so because child marriage is a very ancient institution of India and served a far-reaching purpose. In a sense it is one of the cornerstones of the rigidity of the joint family and caste systems.

By introducing the future wife into the family of her husband at an early stage, she became part of that family. And the husband in turn was prevented from looking for a sexual partner and a wife for himself. The early sex impulse, therefore, did not drive him beyond the family circle. And what adult sex initiation the wife could not provide, being all too young, was at times provided by the wife of the elder brother—who quite ambivalently besides being the next thing to the mother could be a person with whom an individual as brother to the husband could flirt with. Thus all the adolescent urges were internalised and the joint family served as an excellent bulwark of the traditional agrarian society. With the coming of the industrial age and the universalisation of the monetisation process all this had to go. The nuclear families tended to emerge and the traditional fabric of Indian society destroyed or at least questioned. This confrontation with the traditional and modern elements was aided by economic evolution including agricultural and land tenancy condition. As is understandable in Eastern and Western India—areas of the sub-continent under influence of direct if varying nature of colonial domination the process was intense. The American reporting, though helpful largely for understanding T_1, is a significant piece of evidence (also because it is a third person account) in this direction.

Glimpses of Social Life in Western India

The greater part of Western India throughout the nineteenth century was not a well-knit unit so far as communication

1. See Mazumdar, R.C. : 'Rammohun Roy and Bal Gangadhar Tilak on Social Legislation,' *Journal of Indian History*, Vol. XLV, No. 133, for a very interesting discussion on the subject.

was concerned. This was primarily because of the nature of the tarrain of the area. The town of Ahmadnagar then was one hundred and twenty miles east of Bombay and the town of Sholapur was in its turn some one hundred and thirty miles south-east of Ahmadnagar, but by rail Sholapur fell some two hundred and eighty two miles distant from Bombay. Ahmadnagar and Satara were not on the line of the railroad.[1] The roads were not too good either and a look at the geography of the area is enough to show the inadequacies of the waterway.

If the major towns of the region then were connected in this cursory manner one can well imagine the plight of somewhat out of the way areas. Koina valley would be typical of many pockets which would be cut off from all contacts with the outside world for spells ranging at times to four months.[2] Rains would very often be responsible for these. Naturally the development in such pockets would be very much in isolation—explaining in a number of ways the "peculiarities" which they at times seem to have evolved. What influence the policies of the administration might have had in regions such as this remains anyone's guess.

At the hub of the rural world, as Ravinder Kumar points out, lay the village "community". And at the head of this community stood the village headman or *patel*, the leading member of the caste of cultivators or *kunbis* who dominated the village. The dominance of *kunbis* determined the conditions for a harmonious relationship between the cultivators and other social groups like the *vanis* or the *bullotidars*, who played such an important role in making the village self-sufficient.[3] Yet the dominance of the *kunbis* found expression primarily in social styles. The village community managed the internal affairs of the village and shaped its relations with the political authorities at Poona, the capital of Maharashtra, through the intermediate and counterpoised institutions of an hereditary landowning aristocracy, and a bureaucracy created for the collection of land revenue.[4]

1. L. Bessell and C.W. Park in a letter to N.G. Clark, Ahmadnagar dated Aug. 21, 1874. N.A.I.

2. Henry J. Bruce, in a letter to Clark, Mahabaleshwar, dated May 20, 1878. (B.D.)

3. Kumar, Ravinder: The Deccan Riots of 1875, *Journal of Asian Studies* XXIV, Aug. 4, 1965 p. 613.

4. Ibid.

Through the larger part of the nineteenth century[1] a typical village in this region continued to be a miniature world, self-sufficient in itself and geared to a style of life which required a minimum contact with the outside world.

Nevertheless towards the end of the second quarter of the nineteenth century there is a perceptible rise in the stature of the *vanis* in the rural sector of Maharashtra.[2]

It is however interesting to notice that both the "upward" movement of some classes in the "social hierarchy" and the "downward" movement of others left the form of social sanction against an individual or group very much unaltered, that is of course, when and where the sanctions had to be applied. An example will serve to clarify the point. When the unrest of 1875 was just about gathering force the ryots of Kallas in Indapur agreed on what was referred to as *sama patra* and this pointed out that any member of their caste i.e. the *kunbi* cultivating the land of a *vani* will neither be allowed to come to caste dinners nor intermarry amongst his own society. Such person will be considered an outcaste.[3] This not only illustrates the nature of social sanctions but also shows how the village was fragmented along caste and functional lines.

Furthermore the dislocation caused by the Civil War in United States and by a series of bad harvests had together helped to create an unusual amount of unrest in the rural areas during this time. The unstatesmanly revision of the land tax by Francis then only aided the unrest.

It is unfortunate however that this 'rural upheaval' (i.e. of change in position of *kunbis* and *vanis*) was not matched by simultaneous industrial growth. That would have at least given an outlet to some dispossessed peasants to find alternative employments in cities. Nineteenth century in Maharashtra, as Ravinder Kumar rightly points out, is not even noted for the rise of cities.

1. Coats, T. : Account of the Present State of the Township of Lony, *Transactions of the Literary Society of Bombay* III, London 1823, pp. 183-250.

2. e.g. See the *Report of the Deccan Riots Commission*, (Bombay 1876) II, Appendix C, 66-69; for a more detailed description of the process on a much wider territorial and time canvas see Ravinder Kumar's "*Western India in the Nineteenth Century.*"

3. *Report of the Deccan Riots Commission*, Vol. II, *Sama patra* by the villagers of Kallas, dated May 7, 1875.

Through greater part of the century there is conspicuous lack of planning on the part of contemporary administration, and for good or for evil the individual had to fend for himself. The last factor has been taken by some as freedom of individual initiative.

Perhaps the administration was incapable of taking on many things that one expects it to take on today. And this is especially obvious when once the power had passed from the hands of the decadent Maratha administration to the English. Of the inept no one expects anything but it is different when once persons who boast their efficiency in matters of administration come to power. An example would establish the point. There was a case of a pretty large establishment in the Ahmadnagar city (in 1874) requiring a water connection for its premises. All that the municipality could do in a case like this was to *give permission* to the establishment to take the connection. To lay the pipe from the city aqueduct to the premises, to build a reservoir there (which in this case would cost Rs. 250)[1] etc. would all be the concern of the individuals interested. Yet there was an inordinate delay in the sanction. It would appear that the administration was content to leave things alone, even let situations develop the way they would, so long as people did not question the basis of the existence of the administration which in this case was colonial.

However, one thing which was common to both towns and villages was the reaction to Christianity. Hindus and Muslims had not yet learnt to accept Christianity.

Christians in general and missionaries in particular were equally eager, now, to root their religion in the soil. Naturally enough they had taken up to indigenous techniques of *Kirttan*[2] etc. for popularising their belief. At a particular instance when one Pastor Kasambhar with his singers was giving *Kirttan* in one of the villages near Parner something unhappy took place. The Christians had taken water from the public well of the area and a few of the villagers were angry on this account. Just at the close of the *Kirttan* a volley of stones was thrown at the company. One or two of them were hit but not seriously. The pastor and

1. Minutes of the meeting of the Marathi Mission of the A.B.C.F.M. held at Ahmadnagar, Oct. 20—Nov. 2, 1875.

2. Annual report of the Mission of the American Board among the Marathi people for 1874, Ahmadnagar.

his company withdrew to their tent and several stones were thrown at them from a distance under cover of the darkness of the night. Complaint was then made to magistrate who promised to punish the guilty men if they could be identified.[1] Not only does this case illustrate the prevalent law and order situation but also shows that the concept that all classes have equal right of air and water just did not exist.

Even so it would be wrong to believe that among the Hindus and Muslims rank itself there was any cleavage in feeling when it came to attack on Christians. The high and the low caste would join hands in denouncing the Christians. One comes across numerous instances especially in Satara district where the high castes and the Mahars were together in their antagonism to them (i.e. the Christians)[2].

The missionaries and the newly converted Christians also richly paid back the compliment by showing an utter distaste for the religious beliefs and practices of indigenous religions. An extract from one of the letters will illustrate the point, "We rejoice that Moharram is past. The last especially has been a week of noise and hub bub. At all hours, day and night, parties of excited Mussalmans were passing our house, and shouting 'Haidos Dhula' or 'Hussan Husin' as they belonged to one or another sect. The procession must needs pass through the streets that bound our yard on the North, East and South—flounting their banners, swinging their torches and exhibiting themselves and their enthusiasm. Some were dressed in their finest in brilliant red, yellow and green or in purest white. Some dressed and painted themselves to personate tigers, bears, ascetics English soldiers etc. etc. Each one tried to make as much of himself as possible and attract attention.

Yesterday afternoon the tabuts were carried through all the principal streets of the city and were then 'cooled' by being thrown into well. The tabuts, called tazias sometimes are imitations of Mussalman tombs in the frame of Bamboo and covered with tinsel and bright coloured enamelled paper."[3] One can even

1. Annual report of the Mission of the American Board among the Marathi people for 1874, Ahmadnagar.

2. Items from Satara contributed for the Marathi Mission report for 1880. N.A.I.

3. Henry J. Bruce, in a letter to N.G. Clark, Ahmadnagar, dated March 21, 1872. (B.D.)

be grateful for the distaste that the missionaries developed for Indian festivals and customs for at least it helped them to give a graphic account of the happenings nevertheless. About Holi as was then celebrated in this region they had equally strong views, "...Holi which lasts for five days is the noisiest and filthiest feast of the Hindus. This is no time for street preaching, the people are mad on their idols and their customs."[1] Though there was good Hindu-Muslim religious amity, these religious festivals, especially ones like Moharram could very often be occasions for fanatical outbursts against the government or individual Englishman.[2] Assassinations like that of Judge Norman in Calcutta or Lord Mayo at Andamans must have made the English very wary. It appears special police precaution was taken to prevent outbreaks of violence.[3]

The nature of Hindu-Muslim relationship has been referred to above but what is equally worthy of note is the position that Hindusthani or Hindi enjoyed especially in the second half of the nineteenth century. Evidently it was in good usage, with schools being at times provided with teachers exclusively for Hindi.[4] Even on the streets it appears to be commonly used and widely understood. Naturally enough it was used as a medium of public speech. What is more, Hindi/Hindusthani had not taken on any communal overtones. Muslims accepted it as much as their language as much as any one else. In fact there are cases where the public speaker or the missionary records that Hindusthani[5] addresses drew large number of Mohammedans—who normally did not attend.

If this be some facets of the social life and customs in the relatively more sophisticated and urban pockets of Western India, equally important were areas which were developing in comparative isolation. Koina valley is one such significant area which can be taken as a case-study.

1. Henry J. Bruce, in a letter to N.G. Clark, Ahmadnagar, dated March 21, 1872. (B.D.)

2. ibid.

3. ibid.

4. Minutes of the meeting of the Marathi Mission of the A.B.C.F.M. at Ahmadnagar, Oct. 23—Nov. 5, 1872.

5. Records of the meeting of the Marathi Mission of the A.B.C.F.M. at Ahmadnagar, Oct. 16 to Nov. 4, 1898.

The people there, apparently, had some customs which seem very singular. There was no soap for washing and no salt for food in the valley. There was no oil for burning and people had no lights except their fires. They had no locks or other proper fastening for their doors—when they fastened them with strings and left their houses the monkeys come, unfastened the string and stole whatever they could from the houses.[1]

These people observed one day in honour of their gods and declined to do any work on that day. This day could be celebrated either on a Friday, Monday or a Tuesday—depending on which particular God they wished to please. Once a month the Gods went out[2] on a hunting excursion and the people accompanying them bore torches before them. The people of this valley had full faith in an oracle. An example would show how it worked. When a man wished to go anywhere or do anything he sought the permission of his God. He would take two leaves from a certain tree and wetting them place one upon the right leg and the other upon the left leg of his idol-God. On becoming dry, of course, the leaves would fall off. If the one on the right leg fell off first God was supposed to be favourable and permission was granted. But if the one on the left leg fell off first it meant that permission was withheld and the man would on no account act contrary to it.[3]

Similarly the food habits were slightly unusual. The principal food in ordinary times was a kind of gram used only by mountaineers. Sickness was common in this area and modern medicine was unknown. During famine large number of the people would be reduced to the necessity of subsisting on roots and a certain kind of porous tree the body of which was dried and ground into flour and made into a tough kind of bread.[4]

Famines, of course, being times of difficulty and trial would reduce any community to its bare fundamentals where

1. Henry J. Bruce, in a letter to N. G. Clark, Mahabaleshwar, dated May 20, 1878. (B.D.)

2. For the description of another journey by a God of the Marathi region see, Karve, Irawati : On the Road (a Maharashtrian pilgrimage), *Journal of Asian Studies* XXII, Nov. 1, 1962, pp. 13-29.

3. Henry J. Bruce, in a letter to N. G. Clark, Mahabaleshwar, dated May 20, 1878. (B.D.)

4. ibid.

principles of behaviour are concerned. This is amply borne out by the findings of the investigation committee which went into the famine conditions of 1878-79 in some parts of this area. Involved in it were Dr. Ballantine, Dr. McDonald, Dr. McKiller and S. B. Fairbank. They inspected towns and villages in the Sholapur and Kaladgi collectorates as to food supply, health and means for preparing and sowing their fields.[1]

The devastations wrought by these famines would be terrible with the population in 1879 being less than half of what it was seven or eight years ago.[2] In the 1878-79 season there were prospects of a good harvest but the rats destroyed that.

It is relevant to one's study to note the people's reaction in such a situation. Of the various types of rats which abounded, causing havoc to thousand of square miles of cultivable land two types i.e. the *Kok* and the *Mittad* were susceptible to rain and many were destroyed. But the *Jerboa* rat did not succumb to rain. They had to be destroyed. But the people would not kill them because they thought that these rats were their relatives and friends of last birth, especially those who had died in famine conditions.[3]

This naturally brings to mind the nature and extent of education that was prevalent there in this region. Though strictly speaking one would treat it as an instrument of social change, it might help in giving a fuller picture just to narrate here a few major aspects of education as it then was. English education was only beginning to pick up. In most parts of Western India there was an unexpected absence of those classes in the colleges whom the English thought would have been first to opt for this system viz. the landed aristocracy and the well-to-do commercial middle classes.[4] So evidently it would be wrong to assume that the average man on the streets had an 'education' which would help him to tide over the superstitious beliefs which he had by

1. S.D. Fairbank in a letter to N. G. Clark, Ahmadnagar, dated June 27, 1879. (B.D.)

2. ibid.

3. ibid.

4. "Not only is any class like that of the sons of the zemindars entirely wanting in our colleges, but also the native merchants of Bombay themselves seem to have most narrow views as to the value of collegiate education". *Annual Report of the Director of Public Instruction in the Presidency for the year* 1866-67 (Bombay, 1867), pp. 31-32.

tradition inherited.

However, among the students in the English Colleges the dominance of a few groups was obvious. Of all college students before 1885 the Brahmins were on an average about 43%, Parsis about 23%, Gujarati trading castes around 7%, Goanese Christians about 6%, European and Eurasian Christians around 6%, Prathus (i.e. the traditional scribal caste here) about 4%. No other single community averaged as much as 3% of college students in this period.[1]

So far as the question of syllabi was concerned variety in the undergraduate course before 1880 was found only in texts selected annually for university examinations. All students were examined in five subjects: English literature; history, including political economy; moral philosophy and logic; mathematics and a classical language. Elphinstone College was able to offer a voluntary course in natural sciences with the appointment of a Chemist in 1868, but after lecturing for eight years without benefit of laboratory or demonstration apparatus he dismissed his efforts in 1875 as a "waste of time on the part both of the professor and of the students."[2] With Sir Richard Temple, a strong believer in technical education, becoming the Governor in 1878, it was time for a change.

It was time for change indeed, for even on the surface of a traditionally stable society faint rumblings of questioning and unrest could be heard. This was again the period in which organisations like *Poona Sarvajanik Sabha* were to begin agitations in this region. As Ranade pointed out the first prerequisite for progress was belief in progress itself—for progress to be achieved it has first to be desired.[3] The revolution of rising expectations and the growing commitment to social mobility and economic growth have to be there.

1. These figures are worked out from tables of caste and community of students in government and private high schools and colleges which appear in the annual reports of the Director of Public Instruction, Bombay for most years from 1870-1885.

2. *Annual Report of the Director of Public Instruction in the Bombay Presidency for the year* 1874-75, Appendix A, pp. 143-44.

3. Ranade, M.G. : "The exigencies of progress in India", *Quarterly Journal of the Poona Sarvajanik Sabha*, April 1893 (though Ranade did not sign this article it is commonly assumed that he wrote it).

Glimpses of Social Life in Eastern India

Eastern India in the nineteenth century, like the rest of the country, was predominantly agricultural. Hence it would be in order to begin any survey of social life there by taking a look at the conditions of agriculture. It is to be noted that the method of cultivating the soil and harvesting and threshing in general and wheat in particular continued to be predominantly the same as it was centuries earlier. Because of the conservative disposition and caste prejudices of the farmer there was great difficulty in inducing him to invest in modern agricultural implements or to do anything differently from the way his father and his father's father did before him. And in fact, there was not, owing to the extreme cheapness of agricultural labour, the necessity for improved and labour-saving agricultural implements and machinery in India, which existed in United States and many other countries.[1]

In Eastern India the tiller of the soil leased a little patch of ground consisting ordinarily of about 5 to 10 acres[2] and with his rude plough, often little better than a forked stick, with an iron point, he hitched on to his small pair of bullocks and scratched over his patch, which he then sowed by hand and covered with a bamboo harrow or drag constructed like a ladder and dragged crosswise.[3] He reaped his grain with an old fashioned sickle and tramped it out with cattle and winnowed it by pouring it through the air when there was sufficient breeze, or if not he would create the breeze with a rude kind of hand fan.

And yet with all his simple and primitive methods he could successfully compete with even those in U.S. so far as the production of wheat was concerned. This factor can be well understood if one takes into consideration, the facts that the Indian farmer's entire farming outfit represented a capital of not more than \$ 40.00 or \$ 50.00 and his hired help (if he should require any) could, and did work feed and clothe himself according to the Indian fashion, for an average, throughout the wheat growing provinces, of about \$ 2.50 per month.[4]

1. Despatch no. 36, Vol. 13. (C.D.)
2. See *Famine Commission* (1880) *Report*, Part II, pp. 115-6.
3. First Annual Report of B.F. Banham, Consul General of U.S. at Calcutta to the department of State, U.S.A.
4. Despatch no. 36, Vol. 13. (C.D.)

The indigenous day labourer in Eastern India either at farming or other unskilled employments did not seem ambitious to get rich or even financially independent. Of his wages he would spend about $ 2.40 for food consisting principally of rice and dal and occasionally some fish and the balance was invested in clothing and incidentals.[1] This condition of things, when there was a failure of crops as sometime occurred from extreme drought, resulted in the great famines of India. Because of lack of any saving, naturally deaths were many of such 'daily' workers.

But Eastern India has too long been equated only with famines, floods and the consequent misery of human life. There is another facet of Eastern India also, that of prosperity, happiness and gaiety. Towards the middle of the nineteenth century this part of India was particularly prosperous and opulent, in spite of the scars of 1857. One almost said because of them, because that had lead the Britons to put their administrative and financial house in order.

The prosperity and wealth of some of the people continued to be in advance of that of the Government, as a natural result every apparent avenue to wealth was crowded with an eager throng of such competitors.[2] Speculation was rampant, assuming in its extravagance the most ludicrous forms. Apothecary and shoe shops, tailors and jewellers, livery, stall and hotel keepers with a limitless number of other projectors had suddenly as "Joint Stock Companies Limited" thrown their prospectuses and shares for one or more lac of Rupees each, upon the market and had them quickly absorbed by the ordinary man.[3]

Naturally all types of manufactures sprang up ranging from Cotton to Hemp and received a tremendous boost.

However, manufacturing in India continued to be at this time in its infancy and had in no branches except the manufacture of cotton and jute attained anything of importance.

The impetus given to the culture of cotton by the high prices during the American Civil War coupled with the facts

1. Despatch no. 36, Vol. 13. (C.D.)

2. Consular Annual Report for the year 1862-63.

3. Consul General's letter to the department of State, U.S., Calcutta dated Sept. 30, 1863 (C.D.)

that cotton yarn and its twist were imported into India and that labour was much cheaper here than elsewhere seemed to have turned the attention of capitalists in that direction. Although the cotton mills had been in operation in India before that time, yet from want of proper management or some other cause they did not prove uniformly successful.

That industry could be said by fourth quarter of the 19th century to be fully established and likely to increase further.[1] There were then 15 mills in operation in Bombay with about 450000 spindles and 4833 looms, and in Calcutta 4 mills with 106000 spindles and 200 looms. With the raw cotton at hand, cheap labour rapidly becoming skilled and import duty on cotton yarn and twist, of 5%, and a home demand on cotton yarns and manufactures to the value of $ 84000000[2] annually, there seemed to be every encouragement for investments and no reason why every pound of goods of such quality as could be manufactured from Indian cotton and required in the country should not be manufactured here. The imposition of a duty of 5% on cotton manufactures was by no means intended as a protection to Indian manufacturers but was simply for custom revenue. On the other hand the imposition in 1875 of a duty of 5% on "raw cotton, not the production of continental Asia or Ceylon"[3] was generally regarded as legislation on behalf of Manchester and on this ground the mill-owners of Bombay addressed a 'memorial' to the Government of India praying that the duty might be remitted. Their social standards were being affected because of the economic strain.

However the parallel and perhaps a more important industry in the Eastern part of India was the manufacture of jute which had rapidly developed within the last few years of the third quarter of the 19th century. Although slightly depressed around

1. Mill put forward the view that best chance for the development of Indian industry was through growth of export trade in Cotton, Indigo, Sugar, Coffee, etc. to the markets of Europe. The same view was held by the Government of India during this period. An increase in foreign trade was interpreted by it as an index of development and prosperity of the country. See S. S. Raghavaiyagar's "*Memorandum on the progress of Madras Presidency during the last forty years of British Administration*" (1893), p. 307.

2. Despatch No. 151, Volume 10. (C.D.)

3. Annual Consular Report for the year 1875.

1876 owing to a large surplus of jute manufacture having been thrust upon the market, a year since, the fact had been established that the Calcutta manufactures could compete successfully the best managed concerns in any other part of the world.[1] This was clearly admitted by one of the largest manufacturer of jute at Greenock, Scotland, who was then stripping his machinery from his mills and sending it to Calcutta. The indications were clear that Calcutta would in due time to become the great jute manufacturing centre of the world.

Turning to flax and hemp it is commonly assumed that the new industry of the manufacture of flax and hemp twine and canvas was started by the founding of a mill with a full set of machinery for twine and 50 looms for canvas by an enterprising American by the name of Richard Macallister. He had already put in operation during the year 1872 and '76 a large cotton mill with 4400 spindles and 100 looms, 2 Jute mills with 600 looms.[2] Hence it can be affirmed without any doubt that there was a sustained condition of prosperity for a good section of the nineteenth century in Eastern India which opened up tremendous avenues of individual enterprise and initiative. Dispossesed landowners and landless labourers from Champaran, Arrah and Gorakhpur could find new avenues for raising their status in society and not just of making a living. Money economy became a convenient social lever. Because of growth of manufacture and industries the 'traditional unit"[3] of East India Society met the 'colonial unit'[4] among other things by the phenomena of migrant labour, thus facilitating cross pollination of ideas and life.

1. Annual Consular Report for the year 1875.

2. Despatch No. 151, Volume 10. (C.D.)

3. Gautam, V. : 'An introduction to the social history of the Bhojpuri speaking area in India—as reconstructed in folk-literature. "*Society and Culture*" Vol III No. 2 analyses this point adequately. It is pointed out there that a 'traditional unit' because of oneness of dialect, a fair homogenity of culture, common exclusive set of heroes and the custom of intermarriage among the inhabitants of the region subject to caste restrictions etc. is a unit of social action and therefore of study of social change. It survives by moral weight and not political authority. In Eastern India some such units would be the Bhojpuri unit, the Maithili unit etc.

4. By 'colonial unit' is meant a unit of territory which shares at the very minimum a common authority capable of maintaining itself and propagating its values and recognised as such by others. The unit needs no

However it would be wrong to presume that all who went out towards industrial or production centres came back millionaires. Many who went out poor came back poor, maybe a shade better, but by no means opulent. The newly emerging industrial commercial centres needed labour and the labour came from the rural areas, especially of Bihar and Eastern Uttar Pradesh. It floated to such places as Calcutta or the plantations of Assam. Such wide ranging opportunities and great physical mobility was bound to enfuse a lot of dynamism into the Eastern India Society. Transport and communication improved aiding this process. Later on in the chapter one will have occasion to talk of these instruments of social change. The Eastern India in the nineteenth century was, indeed, passing through a set of experiences it had never known before.

So much activity could not leave law and legal structure unaltered which in any case was most uneven at this time. Because of the conflicting character of Hindu, Muslim, English laws and other local custom and traditions the tenure of landed property was most vexatious and uncertain. The courts of course permitted each of them to act upon the laws of their several communities.[1] But in course of time this would have to be systematised.

New laws and regulations had to be passed too to regulate manufactures and inventions at an early date. In 1859 was passed an act for granting exclusive privileges to the inventors.[2] An invention not publicly used or known in U.K. or

particular sanction as such because it derives its sanction from the coercive power of the state and unlike the traditional unit has no moral weight. It was in India the creation of the colonial power for its own administrative ends, at times quite arbitrarily created, at times cutting across many traditional units at the same time. Nevertheless these arbitrarily created units such as 'districts' were very often advanced outposts of the 'modern' value scale. Often enough they would also have industrial centres, as around the urban centre of Calcutta which would mean that the contrast with traditional—agricultural India would be even more heightened.

1. Annual Report for 1862-63. (C.D.)

2. By this the inventor of any new manufacture could petition the Governor General in Council, for leave to file a specification thereof. Every such petition had to be in writing in a particular type of form. Upon such petition the Governor General of India in Council, could make an order

India before the application for leave to file this specification was to be deemed a new invention within this act.[1]

As has been noted all this industrial activity did affect the social norms. And even before the evils of the traditional society could be eradicated some evils of the modern society had been ushered in. All sorts of bluffs would be practised on the consumer, especially in a growing market economy. An example will illustrate the point. During this period there was a good market in India for American Kerosene Oil[2] and it enjoyed a large amount of goodwill, but was costlier than some of the other types of oil available. What the unscrupulous dealers would sometimes do was to transfer inferior type of oil into American Kerosene Oil tins and sell them off as such.[3] This example is only cited here as an illustration of a type of social value that was prevalent at that time. There is no evidence to presume that this matter engaged the attention of the Government with any seriousness, but perhaps it was in no mood or position to bother with such 'trifles'[4] either. In a far more obvious situation demanding its interference it had to act with almost inhibiting caution for fear of hurting popular feeling. One is referring to the reaction that was

authorising the petitioner to file a specification of the invention. Before making such an order the Governor General of India in Council could refer the petition to any person or persons for enquiry and report. After the completion of formalities the petitioner was entitled to exclusive privileges for 14 years from the time of filing specification, and subsequently it could be renewed for another term not exceeding 14 years. Of course the order to file the specification had also to describe the invention. False statement in declaration was punishable as perjury. Exclusive rights were also to cease if the government declared it mischivous etc. to public. The importer of an invention, if not the actual inventor, was not to be deemed as such.

—The Calcutta Gazette, No. 43, dated Saturday, May 28, 1859.

1. "The definition of an invention in this case was an invention not publicly used or known in U.K. or India before the application for leave to file this specification to be deemed a new invention within this act."

—The Calcutta Gazette, No. 43, dated Saturday, May 28, 1859.

2. Despatch no. 36, Vol. 13. (C.D.)

3. See Annual Consular Report for 1886-87.

4. Collection of district reports : Zillah Gorakhpur : Ames mss. N.A.I.

witnessed to the prompt action of the Government when plague was suspected in Calcutta. There was panic in the city, among the indigenous population, more from the fear that the *Zenana* (the women's apartments) would be violated in the house to house inspection, the enforcement of segregation and the separation of families as was done in Bombay[1], Poona[2], Karachi and other places and that quarantine would prevent their escape from the city, than the fear of the plague itself.[3]

However the publication, of the measures that were to be adopted, by the Legislative Council, and the assurances of the Lieutenant Governor helped to allay the excitement and many who had decided to leave the city decided to watch the development of the disease. This was no small tribute to the tact and success of governmental measures.

Fortunately the disease itself came at a time (April-May 1898) which was the least advantageous to its spread, and the measures adopted helped to prevent its adopting a virulent form ;[4] for had it done so the contemporary condition of the indigenous quarters being what they were, with their narrow crowded streets and insanitary conditions would have fallen easy prey to it and the epidemic would have succeeded not only in sweeping away a large proportion[5] of the population but also in destroying a

1. The following extract would demonstrate the difficulties that the government had to face in the enforcement of health measures because of the prejudices of the people and the inadequacies of its own resources in similar circumstances in Western India, "In order to eradicate the plague, which is sweeping off over 200 people every day, the Plague Committee appointed by Government has been using such strict measures as seemed to be necessary. The people conceal cases, hence there are search parties accompanied by soldiers, who enter houses and search for the sick and take to hospital those found suffering with plague. This is very bitterly resented... Care has not always been taken to have Mohammedan women examined by lady doctors and this has been resented as against their customs and religion...On Wednesday last...a crowd gathered and attacked the search party." —J.E. Abbot in a letter to J.L. Barton, Mazagaon, dated March 11, 1898.

2. See Gautam, Vinayshil : 'A note on the use of Maratha Mission papers as a source of social history of Western India for the last three decades of the nineteenth century', *Proceedings of fortieth Historical Records Commission Meeting*, Madras, pp. 89 to 97.

3. Consul General in a letter to the department of State, Calcutta, May, 4, 1898. (C.D.)

4. ibid.

5. Despatch no. 55, Vol. 16.

large section of the foreign commerce on which Calcutta so largely depended for its prosperity.

British rule in India and Social Change

From the above going description and one's knowledge of social history of India in the nineteenth century it should be possible for one to comprehend in a more relevant fashion the significance of 'the instruments of social change' which are described in the Consular papers.

Briefly then, it is well-known that until the end of eighteenth century India was a prize for European marauders and traders. However from the trial of Hastings onwards, in the wake of English moral revival, India became an object of interest as well, to the improving, reforming Englishmen. The whole process, involving Missionaries, administrator-reformers, Indian pioneers of change, Utilitarians and others, saw its culmination with Bentinck. In the years following the departure of Bentinck and Macaulay from the scene and the death of Ram Mohan Roy the reformist enthusiasm began to ebb. Even among the Indians there was no great leader to spearhead such a change. In fact, the 40s and the 50s lacked any ideological cast. Old impulses had waned and new ambitions and rationalizations had not been clearly formulated. 1857 did that. In the pre-Revolt period the English reformers had looked to India for the realization of radical hopes. Frustrated at home, in this post-Revolt period however it was the autocrat who sought in India a field to fulfil ambitions stymed in England.

However to go into the motivating forces of history is neither the intent or purpose of this study. In practical terms all that matters is what actually happened. Social history like any other branch of history can only be worked out in such terms.

What one is seeking to establish is that it is immaterial for one to try to understand why the British did what they did, so long as their actions had material effects. From this point of view the pre- and post-1857 distinction melts away and there is a certain uniformity in their activities in India, e.g. establishment of a certain concept of law, aiding education, furthering transport facilities etc. The whole of the nineteenth century and more becomes one unit from this point of view, all serving a very relevant purpose of social change.

Among such catalysts for change law emerges as one of the first. The concept that ultimately all Indian people should confirm to one set of uniform secular laws[1] came in with the English or the modern period, however one prefers to view it, and this was a change of a fundamental order. The traditional multiplicity of laws varying from community to community, and at times within the same community was quite confusing, to say the least, and it was attempted to do away with them. However, it is to be noted that in the beginning the English too were averse to questioning the accepted traditional modes of enforcements of laws in India.[2]

Furthermore the notion that even the executive was subject to certain laws and could not be arbitrary in the medieval sense of the word gradually took deeper root through the nineteenth century. Undoubtedly important as this concept of 'Rule of Law' might be it would be well to remember that there was no parity in the enforcement or enforcing authorities of law between the English and European white on one hand and the 'natives' on the other hand. Perhaps it is too much to expect that such utopian equality would be observed in a colonial context. The impeachment of Warren Hastings and some other such stray cases would be exceptions that prove the rule.

But beyond this controversy about the perfect or imperfect implementation of the 'rule of law' is another point which merits attention viz. that this view about the position of the executive is far removed from the ancient Indian concept of the ruler being 'annadata' i.e. 'one who feeds' or the medieval concept of 'mabadaulat' i.e. 'I by the kingly authority of being myself'. Now, abstractions of what the human society considered the ideal were to rule and that too in the shape of law. No individual could govern in his own right and if the executive did something for the ruled it was not a matter of grace or charity but it did so because it was there explicitly for that purpose. The concept of the state was changing.

Here it would be worth noticing that in India the cycle of divine right of kingship, the Social Contract, the Idealist, the

1. See Annual Consular report for 1862-63, Calcutta dated Sept. 30, 1863.

2. Consul General, Calcutta in a despatch to the department of State, U.S.A., Calcutta, dated Sept. 30, 1863. (C.D.)

Utilitarian, the Socialist theories did not occur in the same sequence or the periodicity as they did in the West. In fact there is no such systematised conceptualisation possible for India, because violations of one type or another can be detected. On one hand Social Contract was conceived of in India in as early a period as that of *Mahabharat* or Kautilya's *Arthashastra* and on the other even in late seventeenth and a good section of eighteenth century the kings here continued to rule as if they had the divine right to it. So what is important to note is that the principles of English rule gave a jolt to this framework of existing situations, and as it were, inducted a new stream of liberal thinking in matters of both administration and framing of society.[1] One is aware of their shortcomings from the ideal or desirable point of view but to deny them this credit would be less than fair.

The way education developed during this period has been referred to at some lengths in the section dealing with Western India, in this chapter. Unhappily the reports from Calcutta do not have much to say about this at all.

Through the nineteenth century changes were being brought about on the Indian scene in another very radical manner. Long lines of railways were being opened and trunk roads being established which opened the interior for many thousand miles to cities of the Board.[2]

At the end of 1880, 8611 miles were open for traffic of which 6693 miles were on the 6′6″ gauze, 1850 miles on the metre, 27 miles on the 4′, and 40 miles on a 2′6″ gauze.[3] Attention had chiefly been given to the lines which served political and military purposes on the North Western Frontier, in Rajputana to which point it was proposed to extend the line in the course of time. The construction was then going on interrupted from time to

1. Stokes, Eric : *The English Utilitarians and India*, pp. 249-50.

2. Consul General, Calcutta in a despatch to the department of State, U.S.A., Calcutta, dated Sept. 30, 1863. (C.D.)

3. Despatch no. 325 (Vol. 12) of the Calcutta Consulate to the department of State, U.S.A. This despatch is a very exhaustive one and has been very carefully compiled. Relevant information was sought from the various government departments and the appropriate publications used for it. In the normal pattern of the working of the Consulate this information was checked and verified. There can be no doubt about the authenticity of its information.

time by the state of affairs in the districts. In fact, the portion open from Sukkur to Sibi a distance of 133 miles was laid in 101 days, a rate of progress unparalleled in the annals of any railway network of the period; and this too with great shortage of material. It is another matter that the work had been sanctioned as a political measure. There are 'perhaps few if any instances in the world' says the American Consul General, 'where the railways have been pushed forward with such rapidity'.[1] They (i.e. the railways) were expected to stimulate trade, and agricultural industry, penetrating as they did a country where safe and regular communication was not a very common thing, contemporaneously. A nation was being woven together more closely and avenues were being opened for the individual to discover a personality.

The railway bridge which was then being constructed on the Ganges at Varanasi was the most formidable work of its kind ever undertaken in India. The river at that point then was about 3,000 feet wide and the bridge was to consist of seven spans of 416 feet each between centres of peers, which was to be constructed of brickwork, having for their foundation solid blocks 65 feet long by 20 feet broad encased in an iron shell. The wells had to be sunk to a minimum depth of 90 feet and possibly to 150 feet below the bed of the river.[2]

Considering that growing and better means of transport and communication are instruments of social change this period indeed is of seminal importance for the following years of modern Indian history. Not only in the North but in peninsular India too a great deal of work was on. Several extensive canals were in the course of construction through the country which would not warrant railways. On the long term basis it was hoped that by the means of these and like public works agricultural produce would be eventually moved so rapidly that famines could be chained if not conquered altogether.

Uptil the last quarter of the nineteenth century a total sum of £123,124,000 had been expended upon railways in India; the average expenditure from 1848 to 1878 was upwards of four million pounds per annum.[3]

1. Consul General of U.S. in a letter to the Secretary of State, U.S.A., Calcutta dated Jan. 19, 1881. (C.D.)
2. ibid.
3. ibid.

The total amount of freight carried during the year 1878 was 7876,000 Tons and the aggregate number of passengers exclusive of season ticket holders, 43,144,000. The total expense of working and maintenance for the year 1880 which can be considered an average year, was £5,774,000. The total number of locomotives employed 1946, and of vehicles 41740 of which 5760 were passenger cars.[1] The figures speak for themselves.

These details have been given at some length to establish clearly the rate and enormity of expansion and the incidence of usage of this means of transport and thereby underscore the tremendous social revolution which would be on beneath the surface. That it took a fair deal of time to show out in the open only emphasises the vastness of the Indian society and the implied difficulty of making instantaneous impact thereon.

The Indian society having agriculture at its base, has indeed evolved its own value system which is slow to react to any external pressure or change. It is not just a nomad-tribal group which could be overwhelmed by the industrial-technological value scale. In the Indian context therefore there is no vacuum to be filled up and as such there is always a struggle between the traditional and the modern—the traditional at times displaying great resilience and streaks of, what others would like to call 'modern'. At times even the decadent aspects of traditionalism triumphed over the happier features of modernity by virtue of there being lack of adequate infra-structure of social change. For example from around the third decade of the nineteenth century, in Bengal, the agrarian society there was to a great extent under the influence of external pressure due to the introduction of new legal concepts. Later on in the century it was to result in two significant historical events—the indigo revolt and the agrarian rising in the Pabna district. Yet the forces of tradition ultimately nullified the effect of these legal concepts and rendered them infructuous. Stable as the Indian social scene is, it was not unoften that industrial-technological value system instead of altering the decadent aspects of traditional value system, were themselves modified or rendered temporarily inoperative by the latter.

1. Despatch no. 325, Vol. 12. (C.D.)

However changes would result ultimately because of fundamental innovations touching the every-day lives of the people as in the building of railways. Even if they be laid essentially for military or political purposes the fact their being there is not altered. People would learn to use it and travel fast from one place to another irrespective of the intent and purposes for which they were constructed.[1] This would in turn create effective physical mobility and thereby enable an individual not only to choose the community to which he would like to belong but also break away from his original parent community if he so chose to. A man of Malda could take residence in Lucknow and settle there for good if he so chose and vice versa. An individual was no longer tied to his original surrounding with the same intensity as earlier.

As the Indian society moved towards modernisation, as can be imagined, there was talk of introduction of sophisticated scientific techniques of quicker communication like telephone.

One can view the condition as it existed in 1880 for example. 1880 has been selected by one as the representative year because for the first time, that year as never before there was considerable talk in Government and commercial circles on the question of introducing the telephone exchange system into the larger towns of India. There were also wild rumours to the effect that certain private concerns were thinking of setting up limited telephone exchanges with the help of American firms.[2] Later on two English firms arrived on the scene and there was infinite wrangling till the Home Department issued an order making the job of laying telephone exchanges, exclusively a Government concern. Naturally enough the American Consul was not too happy with this Government take over and it is best if his sentiments are reproduced in his own exact words. "In this as in many other things of a similar nature the Indian Government shows its unwillingness to surrender to private parties, anything which promises a remuneration if monopolised by themselves."[3] Such sentiments are understandable from the representative of a

1. Gautam, Vinayshil : "Some primary sources for Bihar Studies", a paper read at a Seminar on Bihar Studies, Patna, July, 1970.

2. Consul General of U.S. in a letter to the Secretary of State, U.S., Calcutta, dated Jan. 19, 1881.

3. Ibid.

nation where private enterprise receives so much of accent and emphasis.

It may help to underscore the spirit of the times if it is mentioned that it is around this period that the first electric railway was laid in India. This was put into successful operation by some enterprising Germans, in the Zoological Gardens at Calcutta. No doubt this venture was one only of novelty and amusement but it did give hopes of the days to come.[1]

It might also be mentioned that in 1879 tramways were put into successful operation in Calcutta and were greatly patronised by Indians. The rails were laid in the street in a way as not to cause inconvenience to the general public at all. And still the comfort of the car was left unimpaired. As the Consul noted it gave great credit to the private company laying these lines.[2] This process can be considered a definite mile-stone in the growth of urban communities in India.

This has led many people to look upon the British rule in India as a great benefactor of social change deliberately brought about. Others feel that there is hardly anything to be grateful for, for such changes as they did bring about were basically intended to serve their own political or other ends and whatever transformation they caused was only incidental. Neither of the two statements could be valid for the whole of the nineteenth century and depending on which period of the century one is dealing with both the statements could be true.[3] The fact of the matter, however, is that change was brought about which did help in altering the value system of the people. To what extent this change was brought about is another very interesting question to which various types of speculative answers have been hazarded. The Consular reports provide little clue to that—unless it be by process of comparison of reports of two different periods. As the century rolled on new factors such as the coming to maturity of the middle classes, growth of an occidental form of national consciousness, etc. impinged themselves onto the situation.

1. Despatch no. 325, Vol. 12. (C.D.)
2. ibid.
3. Compare Vols. 4 and 11 of, (C.D.)

Slowly the industrial-technological age was beginning to take birth in India. The process was so slow as to be almost imperceptible. In the given situation of growing modernisation, industrialisation, urbanisation etc. the traditional values were bound to be challenged. Expulsion from caste dinners or social excommunication would not be deterrent enough for the individuals who were non-conformists. One is too close to the nineteenth century to view it objectively but it was undoubtedly a great century. It was great if for no other reason because the average individual Indian began to discover a personality. The concept of a common man began to grow, crystallise. He—the average individual Indian—was no longer just a part of a social unit of a paternalistic order where all his behaviour would be dictated to him, as it were. He, as a person, could also exist.

This realisation was to take a long process. Even today for the greater part of the country this realisation has little or no social manifestation. The emergence of an individual in any conformist order is a long drawn out process and beset with many confrontations with the traditional value system. Many aspiring, but weak, individuals crumble and succumb. The brave who fight their way to freedom are few. But then these few brave have also the responsibility of defining a new social order which would replace the old. This is again no easy challenge. The nineteenth century opened all these questions and more. The Indian society still blunders on groping for an answer which the historical process alone can provide.

CHAPTER V

Facets of Indian Economy in the Nineteenth Century

"...(an)...effort...to use such a source (American Consular Papers) to trace...the economic condition of India in the nineteenth century...it has been one's effort to keep testing the Consular and other descriptions on the framework of such evidence as available..."

Introduction p. 9

The Nature of Indian Economy in the Nineteenth Century

The inter-relation between social developments and economic situations is too obvious a thing to need comment. It was not any different in the nineteenth century India. There too, no less than elsewhere, correct dimension of social forces cannot be assessed without a knowledge of the economic framework. Similarly social, cultural and religious factors too help in understanding the economic situation—in fact they also accelerate or retard economic change. Certain practices may be meaningless and uneconomic in the total context of human welfare yet they may help in maintaining the stability of the society. In that case its adjustment with economic processes becomes essential. As such, for a student of social history, it is not difficult to realise that economic evolution is not after all an autonomous variable.

It ought to be also recognised that some of the most pressing of the socio-economic problems relate to the operation of the society as a whole rather than to the utilities or disutilities which are supposed to motivate individuals! The status of women, the caste system, the joint family system, the attitude towards some of the animals, religious beliefs and practices are only a few of the non-economic factors relevant to the study of Indian economic evolution, as in any time, during the nineteenth century also.

If, indeed, one is interested in the functioning of the society as a unit of study as well as its properties as a functioning society then the behaviour of the whole cannot be explained just in terms of the behaviour of individual constituent units. Social scientists have to apply the logic of modern Physics according to which the aggregates of things acquire properties which they do not already possess as individuals. All this makes the understanding of the actual nature of the Indian economy in the nineteenth century quite a complicated one, the conspicuous lack of data calling really for methodological innovations rather than anything else. And it is here that social history is no more just a companion to economic history but becomes something more—perhaps even providing a clue to the understanding of the latter.

An illustration will clarify the point. In the thirties of this century when economic thinking had to face the challenges of the real world of stagnation and depression the economists were impressed by their methodological inadequacies. It is little wonder then that as early as the publication of the *Tract on Monetary Reform* Keynes was unable to limit himself to an argument on inflation purely in terms of the level of cash balances. He was constrained to consider the cash habits and policies of the public, of the business world, of banks and of central banking authorities. In fact while discussing the social effects of the changes in the value of money, Keynes introduced the threefold classification of society into the investing class, the business class and the earning class and took care to say that such a division corresponds to a social cleavage and are actual divergence of interest. (Keynes: *Tracts of Monetary Reform*) Later Keynes used the term *Rentiers*, *Entrepreneurs* and the *Salariat* to represent classes which may be either responsible for the inflationary process or may be victims of it. The bearing of these social groups on the economic process has now been distinctly recognised. Thus a broadly sociological approach is now considered relevant not only to the theory of the trade cycle but also to the theory of economic growth. Very recently attempts have been made by French economists to subordinate the stocks-and-flow concept to the concept of group behaviour. Indeed, Aujac, defines inflation as a situation where monetary relationships are disturbed by actions and reactions of *social groups*, whether for political, economic or other reasons."[1]

As suggested earlier, perhaps the key, then, to the understanding of the real nature of the nineteenth century economic situation lies in such a methodological analysis. Sociological factors like the rise of the various middle classes may hold the key to the problem. Evidently the percentage of re-investment of the production surplus in Western India was greater than in Eastern India. Even the American Consular records lend credence to this belief.[2] Perhaps such evidence as is available, coupled with the data harvested from such untapped sources as these Records would enable a pattern analysis of developments

1. Ganguli, B N. : 'Rethinking on Indian Economics' '*Presidential address*, at the 38th annual conference of Indian Economic Association, Poona, Dec. 26, 1955.

2. See Vol. 5 (B.D.) and Vol. 12. (C.D.)

such as those of the middle classes or various types of industries. The exact regions as well as types of the growth could then be identified which could in turn offer an insight into the nineteenth century Indian economy especially with reference to such debatable issues as the 'drain'.

Prof. T. Raychaudhuri has summarised the present thinking in the following words: "The debate as to whether the Indian economy under the British rule was characterised by growth or stagnation or progressive impoverishment has not yet come to an end. The major reason for the inconclusive character of the debate is the inadequacy of the relevant quantitative data......The thesis of India's progressive impoverishment as a result of colonial exploitation by Britain was strongly put forward by the nationalist writers on the Indian economy from the days of Dadabhai Naoroji onwards. The position taken by the 19th century nationalists was accepted by their 20th century counterparts....(also) sophisticated arguments are put forward to prove that there was considerable economic development in India during the 19th century and at least the early years of the 20th century, and that if this process of development was not quantitatively as impressive as one might expect, the blame cannot be laid at the door of colonial rule."[1] He goes on to suggest that there is one further possible line of analysis which has not been specifically applied to the Indian case, but can have obvious relevance to it: that the impact of the world market forces and the development of the social overheads stimulated a limited degree of growth in the economy, but the nature of this growth was such that it could not by itself lead to the stage of economic development described as that of sustained economic growth.[2]

This coupled with a sociologically biased analysis is perhaps the solution to the problem. For it must be stated that national income statistics of this period are based to a large extent on daring guesswork alone because of inadequate records both on agricultural and non-agricultural production.

Nevertheless to be conversant with the present state of thinking on the century the table given on the facing page will

1. Mazumdar, R.C. (ed) : *Struggle for Freedom*, p. 829.
2. ibid.

Estimates of per capita income in India : 1850 to 1900[1]

Year	Estimated by	Per Capita Income (Rs.)		Price of Paddy (Average of Madras and U.P. Prices) Rs. per Maund	Per Capita Income in terms of Paddy Maunds	Per Capita Income (at 1873 Prices)
1850	Digby	30.0		0-15-0	32.0	—
1867-68	Naoroji	20.0	25.0	1-10-0	15.4	24.35
1875	Atkinson	30.5				
1880	Digby	22.5	25.0	1-10-0	15.4	24.05
1882	Baring and Barbour	27.0				
1895	Atkinson	39.5				
1899	Digby	18.0	29	2-6-0	12.7	23.13
1901	Curzon	30.0				

1. From. V.V. Bhatt's : *Economic Change and Policy in India*, p. 19. Sources : (1) Dadabhai Naoroji, *Poverty and Un-British Rule in India*. (2) William Digby, "*Prosperous*" *British India*. (3) Fred J. Atkinson, "A Statistical Review of the Income and Wealth of British India" in *Journal of the Royal Statistical Society* LXV, 1902. (4) Daniel, Thorner, "Long-term Trends in Output in India" in *Economic Growth : Brazil, India, Japan* edited by Kuznets, Simon, Wilbert Moore, Joseph Spengler. (5) Government of Bengal, *Report of the Land Revenue Commission*, Vol. II. (6) Government of India, Department of Commercial Intelligence and Statistics, Index Number of Indian Prices, 1861-1931. All these estimates may broadly indicate the trend in *per capita* income during the latter half of the nineteenth century particularly as the personal bias of the estimaters have been removed by combining two or three estimates for years fairly close to each other and made by persons with dissimilar bias, and the estimates are made comparable by converting them in real terms.

The *per capita* income estimates, at current prices for this purpose, are converted into estimates in terms of maunds of paddy by multiplying each of them with the current average price of paddy in Bengal and the United Provinces. Then Dadabhai Naoroji's estimate for the year 1867-68 is combined with that of Atkinson for the year 1875, while Digby's estimate for the year 1880 is combined with that of Baring and Barbour for the year 1882. Similarly the estimates of Atkinson, Digby and Curzon for the years 1895, 1899 and 1901 respectively are combined. Digby's estimate for the year 1850 is left out as it could not be combined with any other estimate by a person with dissimilar bias.

be of help. It has been worked out from a cross section of the conflicting evidence available.

This declining trend in *per capita* income in the second half of the nineteenth century has to be viewed in the context of the already poor conditions in the first half of the century. The deterioration in the fortunes of the textile industry of the period is common knowledge. It was in such a situation that Bentinck said that, "the bones of the cotton weavers are bleaching the plains of India."[1]

Having, then, briefly seen the general nature of the economic condition of the country for the century one can turn to a more carefully detailed analysis of the period, dividing it into three sections of (1) 1792 to 1857, (2) 1858 to 1880 and (3) 1880-1906. All these dates have obvious significance in the context of this work or otherwise. As shall be seen during the course of the survey around both the dates viz. 1857 and 1880 close distinct eras in the economic history of the country.

However, before moving on to that, it is worth noting the peculiar character which the British rule lent to nineteenth century India. In fact economic planning on the grand scale is never likely to be successful over a tract of time, and the old English colonial system furnishes a good example of the friction which may be generated by a well meant endeavour to regulate the commercial and industrial life of scattered communities from a distant centre. London serving as the metropolitan centre was the nerve centre of the entire system. Of this there were a number of satellites throughout the British Empire, three fairly important ones being situated in the Indian sub-continent : Bombay, Madras, Calcutta. Yet a system of 'eternal dependency' was tried to be floated by pursuing such policies as refusal of permission to the colonies to build markets of their own—as it was feared that in the long run they may turn out to be competitors. Not only this but vessels were earmarked and cargoes were to be discharged in English ports alone. Such a system could do comparatively little good even to the permanent interests of the 'colonial power' and certainly no good to the colony.

1. Quoted in Strachey, John : *The End of Empire*, p. 52.

1792—1857[1]: *The years that set the pace*

The year 1792 is of little or no significance, in the economic history of India but since one's study begins from that year it has been duly noted here also. What it shall signify for one's purposes, however, is the last decade of the eighteenth century. 1857 is important because after the Revolt far-reaching changes were brought about in the economic structure of India.

Dr. Francis Buchanon, who was the first statistical inquirer employed by the British Government and who did much travelling around the beginning of the nineteenth century, has left valuable records for the state of Indian economy at the turn of the eighteenth century. It is quite obvious from his account that by the end of the eighteenth century India had attained a high degree of development in agriculture and variety in industries. This in turn showed itself in the general prosperity of the country,[2] which meant that trade was bound to rise.

Writing about the first quarter of the nineteenth century a contemporary author Horace Hayman Wilson remarked ,"That the trade (of Bengal) has augmented during the period under examination is undeniable; but it has not increased in the degree which is sometimes supposed and in many instances it has sustained serious injury from the extension of the Commerce of Great Britain in the East."[3] He was a very careful, cautious and well balanced person, and was further at pains to underline the fact that there ought to be a cautious reception of the confident theories which contemplated no bounds to the wealth and capabilities of Bengal.[4] Such an idea was clearly ridiculous and was at the root of much of the foreign excesses in Bengal and in turn originated from the stories of the fabled east.[5]

1. As has been noted earlier there are no Consular despatches available for the period 1796-1838. However, that phase has been sought to be filled up through various other sources in order to lend a completeness to the picture and coherence and meaning to the post-1838 developments.

2. See Martin Montgomery : *History of Eastern India*, Vol. II.

3. Wilson, Horace Hayman : '*A review of the external Commerce of Bengal* (1813-14 to 1827-28), p. iii. N.A.I.

4. ibid, p. iv

5. In fact as Horace Wilson commented further : "British India is a poor country and must remain so whilst its population has a perpetual tendency to exceed the means of subsistence." This also points clearly to the factor of over population in the area. ibid, p. iv.

Indeed a large portion of its scanty capital was annually abstracted to enrich and swell the resources of Britain.

If the trade of this area was receiving so much attention in that period it would be a fruitful thing to try to see what were the usual terms on which merchandise was brought and sold.

Sales of foreign imports were invariably effected on a credit of three to four months excepting spelter which was usually sold at a credit of 7 months. The discount thus allowed was not a bonus but the buyer was entitled to it by a long established usage and demanded it as his due. When purchases were effected by a third party, the amount of discount obtained was certainly passed to the credit of the individual on whose account the purchase was made, the negotiator of the bargain was only entitled to his brokerage or commission : either from his principal that is, he who employed him to make the purchase or the seller according to the settlement previously made.[1] The rate of discount allowed by the seller was always uniform in every article and did not vary in any class or kind of manufactured cottons. In some descriptions of metal the rate of discount and terms of credit varied as the accompanying list would show[2]—

British white and grey piece goods	3 months	8 p.c.
Yarns and grey piece goods	8 months	8 p.c.
Metals		
Bird shot	3 months	8 p.c.
Brass shot	4 months	10 p.c.
Brass toaf (China)	4 months	10 p.c.
China white copper ware	4 months	10 p.c.
Copper sheet	4 months	10 p.c.
Copper bolt	4 months	10 p.c.
Copper nails and composition nails	4 months	10 p.c.
Copper tiles-Ingots-Cakes and bricks	4 months	10 p.c.
Coffee pegs and slabs	4 months	10 p.c.

1. Despatch no. 18, Vol. 2. (C D.)
2. ibid.

From here onwards extensive data is quoted in the hope that others might like to use it . As these Consular records are still in microfilm reels and by and large Calcutta Despatches are not available to the average researcher in India, or for that matter, probably anywhere outside the United States, it was thought that extensive quotations will help.

Copper Ole	4 months	10 p.c.
China cash	4 months	10 p.c.
Iron flat square-bar bolt	3 months	8 p.c.
Iron-nails and rods	3 months	8 p.c.
Iron hoops plates and sheets	3 months	8 p.c.
Iron rice bowls	3 months	8 p.c.
Iron indeihs flat and square	3 months	8 p.c.
Iron pig	3 months	8 p.c.
Iron anchors	3 months	8 p.c.
Iron cables	3 months	8 p.c.
Lamitter single and double	3 months	8 p.c.
Lead peg and sheet	3 months	8 p.c.
Leaf gold	3 months	8 p.c.
Quick silver	3 months	8 p.c.
Iron bottles	3 months	8 p.c.
Spelter sheets (even)	7 months	10 p.c.
Spelter nails	7 months	10 p.c.
Spelter plate	4 months	10 p.c.
Steel British	3 months	8 p.c.
Steel blistered	3 months	8 p.c.
Steel cash	3 months	8 p.c.
Steel Iping	3 months	8 p.c.
Steel Indish	3 months	8 p.c.
Tin block	3 months	8 p.c.
Wire copper	3 months	8 p.c.
Wire brass	3 months	8 p.c.
Wire iron	3 months	8 p.c.
American Tar	3 months	8 p.c.
American Detel	3 months	8 p.c.
American Rosin	3 months	8 p.c.
Coal Tar	3 months	8 p.c.
Coal	3 months	8 p.c.

Purchases of East India produce are usually effected for *cash without any discount.*

No bounty was given by the Government on country produce exported whether to foreign countries, the United Kingdom or the colonies, nor was any difference made between British, American or other foreign flags. The only allowance made by way of encouragement to the producers was on the exportation of cotton when the transit duty levied in the North West provinces was paid back to the exporter in shape of drawback and this was equal in all vessels whether British or foreign and to all countries without discrimination.

The customary charge of commission for purchases and shipping goods/merchandise of a different descriptions was as follows :

The Commercial List Rates of Commission and Mercantile Agency[1]

	Per cent.
1. On the sale purchase or shipment or bullion gold dust coin, jewellery, pearls and precious stone	1
2. On the purchase when in funds on sale of indigo, silk, copper and opium	$2\frac{1}{2}$
3. On the purchase of ditto when funds are provided by the agent	3
4. On sale or purchase of other goods	5
5. On the sale or purchase of ships, factories, houses, lands and all property of allied description	$2\frac{1}{2}$
6. On returns for consignments if made in produce	$2\frac{1}{2}$
7. On ditto if in bills, bullion or treasure	1
8. On goods and treasure consigned and all other property of any description referred to agency for sale which shall be afterwards withdrawn; and on goods consigned for conditional delivery to others, and so delivered; (on invoice amount at the exchange of 2 s per rupee)	$\frac{1}{2}$ com.
9. On making advances or procuring loans of money for commercial purposes when the aggregate commission does not exceed 5 p.c.	$2\frac{1}{2}$
10. On ordering goods or superintending the fulfilment of contracts, or on the shipment of	

1. Proceedings of the meeting of Bengal Chamber of Commerce, Calcutta, dated December 3, 1849.

		Per cent.
	goods where no other commission except that of account is derived	$2\frac{1}{2}$
11.	On guaranteeing bills, bonds or other engagements and on becoming security for administration of estates for contracts, agreements, etc. and to government for the disbursement of public money when the funds of the individuals are insufficient to cover the risk	$2\frac{1}{2}$
12.	On del credere or guaranteeing the due realization of sales	$2\frac{1}{2}$
13.	On executorship or administration to estates of deceased persons	5
14.	On management of estates for executor of administrator	$2\frac{1}{2}$
15.	On chartering ships or engaging tonnage	$2\frac{1}{2}$
16.	On advertising as the agent of owners or commanders of ships for passengers on the amount of passage money, whether the same shall pass through the agent's hands or not	$2\frac{1}{2}$
17.	On procuring freight or advertising as the agent of the owners or commanders; the commission to be calculated on the gross amount of the entire freight	5
18.	On effecting insurances or writing orders for the same whether on lives or on property	$2\frac{1}{2}$
19.	On settling insurance losses and averages and on procuring returns of premium	2
20.	On purchasing/selling or negotiating bills of exchange	1
21.	On debts or other claims when a process at law or arbitration is incurred in claiming them	$2\frac{1}{2}$
	If recovered by such means	5
22.	On bills of exchange returned dishonoured	1
23.	On collecting house rent	$2\frac{1}{2}$
24.	On ship's disbursement	$2\frac{1}{2}$
25.	On negotiating loans on respondentia	2
26.	On granting letters of credit	1

	Per cent.
27. On sale or purchase of government securities and bank shares on every exchange or transfer, not by purchase from one class to another	½
28. On delivering up government securities and bank shares or depositing them in the treasury	½
29. On the amount debited or credited at the option of the agent, within the year, less the balance brought forward and all items on which a commission of 5 p.c. has been charged	1
30. On all advances not punctually liquidated, a second commission may be charged as on new advance, provided it do not occur within the same year	
Brokerage when actually paid is considered a separate charge.	

One could now turn to the customary brokerage on the sale or purchase of merchandise.

On the sale and purchase of piece goods and metals the purchaser paid the brokerage. On the former at about 6 as. to 8 as. per 100 Rupees, on the latter about 1 per cent. When the seller paid the brokerage the broker was not permitted to take a brokerage also from the purchaser—the general usage however was for the purchaser to pay the brokerage. On the sale or purchase of sugar and salt-petre the seller always paid the brokerage. If he happened to be an Indian merchant he was allowed the Anna per maund, if European the percent or the Anna per maund as might be agreed on at the time of the sale. On the sale or purchase of rice seeds and the like goods by indigenous merchants, the seller invariably paid the brokerage. On the sale of silk, silk corahs, choppehs etc. the seller paid the brokerage; where European houses sold these goods they allowed a brokerage of the percent. On indigo transactions both seller and purchaser frequently paid brokerage as might be agreed upon beforehand.[1]

1. Consul General of U.S. in a communication to the department of State, U.S., Calcutta, dated Jan. 2, 1852. (C.D.)

On purchasing a produce the price agreed upon included the usual *dastoori* and brokerage which was on sugar 5 as. per maund, on salt-petre 3 as. per maund, on rice and grain 1 as. per maund, on shellac 12 as. per maund, on lac dye 12 as. per maund, silk 2 as. per sect. On silk corahs, choppehs and bacedaunoes Rs. 3 in cargo of 20 pieces. Rum four pieces the gallon old measure, oil 2 as. per maund, jute 4 as. per bale. On sugar 4 as. per bag, on salt-petre 4 as. per bag.[1]

Rice and grain 4 as. per bag, shellac Re. 1 and 8 as. per charab, lac dye Re. 1—8 as. per cherab, silk Rs. 7 per square bale of 2 maunds, Rs. 4 per bound bale goods, silk corahs, silk choppehs, rum marking and exporting 8 as. per hhd, pressing and examining charges excepted, oil as. 9 per hhd, castor-oil from Rs. 4- as. 8 per chest, jute Rs. 3 per bale.[2]

All transit or frontier duties or imports except on the articles of Cotton (which was refunded to the shipper on exportation by sea 'as a drawback') had been abolished by then. The expenses of transportation from the place of growth and manufacture to the port depended very much on the distance and the nature of the country through which the goods had to pass. These terms were to remain so for the rest of the century, with minor variations.

In a way India was then placed in a most fortunate position because almost everything she produced was in constant and boundless demand in Europe and almost every article of importance required in Europe was found increasingly in India.

Exports[3]

Average of five years	*Merchandise* £	*Treasure* £
1834-39	11071529	251069
1839-44	13789769	462795
1844-49	15675044	1320503
1849-54	14899594	646469
1854-59	22187736	850605

1. *Supplement to the Calcutta Gazette,* Calcutta, Wednesday Feb. 6, 1850.
2. ibid.
3. From : Speech of James Wilson in the Legislative Council of India, Saturday, Feb. 18, 1860, printed in *Supplement to the Calcutta price current and market report.*

The import breakdown for the same period would be as follows:

Imports[1]

Average of five years	*Merchandise* £	*Treasure* £
1834 to 39 average	497000	2345000
1839 to 44 ,,	7691428	2762164
1844 to 49 ,,	9131612	3073249
1849 to 54 ,,	10756134	4474107
1854 to 59 ,,	15365934	11223107

Taking the exports and imports of merchandise and treasure—and there was really no distinction between the two—one notices that the trade of India had grown up during the period and increased in these tables from a total sum (exports and imports together) of £13847289 in 1833-34 to one of £60219660 in 1858-59.[2] This was a sure proof of the steady prosperity of the country. Because of this great demand for exportation in the later years the prices of country products had gone up a great deal. It is often possible to take an over simplified view of India's prosperity or otherwise during the colonial period and this need not always be the correct picture.

It is interesting to study the effects produced upon the interests of the cultivators of the soil by this enlarged trade. One could take a look at the return showing the number of estates in the permanent settled districts brought to sale in each year since 1834 to 1859, for default of rent. In the first year of the period, estates representing an annual rental of Rs. 4,81,403 were sold for rent; in the next year 1835-36 the sales represented an annual rent of Rs. 950,608. In the year 1858-59 the sales represented a rental of only Rs. 14,493 while the average of the last seven years showed a rental of only Rs. 65,326 being little more than $\frac{1}{9}$th of the former average. Again if one refers to the arrears of the land revenue at the end of each year one finds that from a sum of upwards of 4 crores

1. From: Speech of James Wilson in the Legislative Council of India, Saturday, Feb 18, 1860, printed in *Supplement to the Calcutta price current and market report.*

2 ibid.

(£ 4000000) in 1834, in 1859 they had dwindled down to a mere nominal sum.[1]

This prosperity was to be credited to the changed attitudes of the post-1857 period. However, that shall be dwelt upon in the next section.

1858—1880 : *the years of healing and growth*

The expenses of 1858 had been excessive, caused by the enormous military establishment rendered necessary by the Revolt and the Mutiny. Government had been forced to propose a series of new taxes, on opium and salt and incomes, which caused great dissatisfaction. However, the execution of the greater parts of these obnoxious measures were indefinitely postponed by the arrival of James Wilson one of the best political economists then. He was known to favour a push to public works such as Railways to the utmost extent, thus opening the country and enabling the products to come to the market more fully.[2]

Other measures were also taken to boost trade, for example it was decided to reduce the duty upon all the articles in the tariff, for every one of them, save tobacco, which then bore a duty of 20 per cent to 10 per cent, showed on the decline. Even as a matter of policy there were many considerations which in the views of the Government rendered this a desirable step. Looking then to other articles of trade that reduction from 20 to 10 per cent could raise the imports again to the rate they stood at before 1858. There was a consensus for giving every opportunity for the produce of the country to increase and for commercial intercourse to be enlarged.[3] It was obvious that as a general rule when the products of India had to find a foreign market and in cases in which they entered into competition with foreign countries the direction of export duties had to be such as to place Indian products in those countries at an advantage with their foreign competitors—in point of fact it could not be

1. Despatch no. 3, Vol. V. (C.D.)
2. *Supplement to the Calcutta price current and market report*, Feb. 1860.
3. The speech of James Wilson in the Legislative Council of India, Feb. 18, 1860, Vol. V. (C.D.)

deemed that in such cases an export duty fell chiefly upon the producer who cultivated it.

Again there were some articles of raw material which merely passed through British territory for shipment from its ports. The article of sheeps' wool was one such. A large quantity was imported into Bombay from Cutch and from 'countries beyond Indus'[1] and exported chiefly to England. In 1859 that wool was charged an import or a transit duty of no less than 10 per cent. Wool produced in India paid an export duty of 3 per cent. And it was being realised that for a large trade in wool to be developed from Indian frontier hills the transit down the Indus had to be improved and the Railway to Multan to be finished.

There were two other articles of considerable export which arose chiefly in consequence of the Russian War viz. hemp and hides—the competition which those had to bear in English markets with products of other countries made the export duty bear heavily upon them. It was proposed to place them also in the free list.[2] Then again the article of jute was in the same category. It was one of the great raw materials used in England which competed with coarse hemp of Russia and the production of which it was English interest to promote. The duty upon the export of tea was only £ 2500 and it was also placed in the free list. Books were already free and it was proposed that prints, maps and work of arts should be included.

It cannot be denied that the Revolt of 1857 had infused in the people instead of lethargy a state of intense activity. In a personal testimony James Wilson commented "when I had the good fortune as Secretary to the India Board in 1849 to pass the first two Bills through Parliament for railways in India I was told by those who had long experience in India that the natives could not use them. We have on this side of India two extensive pieces of line from here (Calcutta) to Raniguni and from Allahabad to Kanpur. Those who have seen the rush of third class passengers on holiday in Belgium can form the best idea of the use made of these lines by railways. What we

1. The speech of James Wilson in the Legislative Council of India, Feb. 18, 1860, Vol. V. (C.D.)

2. ibid.

require is the completion of those lines at any cost but quickly and we shall see a result for which the most sanguine is not prepared."[1]

Another result that flowed from these measures and much more important and more interesting than any, because it affected directly the great masses of people, individually so helpless, was the benefits of extended commerce upon the land. It did not also leave the labourer untouched. In fact it would be no exaggeration to say that such was the increased demand for improving labour that the rate of wages had risen in many districts,[2] two folds and in others three folds during the previous few years. And it is in this context that the earlier envisaged measures have to be understood.

As a follow up measure on March 3, 1860 was passed a bill for the establishment throughout India of a paper currency, the principal points of which would be as follows :

The notes could only be issued by the Government and by the Government alone payable to the bearer in sums of Rupees 5, 10, 20, 50, 100, 500 and 1000 and these notes would be a legal tender in payment of all debts, land revenues and other government dues included. The country was to be divided into three presidencies and a number of subordinate circles, each containing a central bank of issue. All notes were redeemable in cash either at their place of issue or at the principal treasury of their presidency.[3]

Wilson whose name is also associated with the introduction of this paper money intended to use this as a source of income on large scale. *An Oordoo or Hindostanee Exposition of the New Indian*

1. See *proceedings* of the Legislative Council of India debate on Feb. 18, 1860, Vol. V. (C.D.)

2. *Hindu Patriot*, March 10, 1860.

3. See Vol. V, (C.D.). It is to be noted that since the convertibility of the notes every treasury was bound at all times to keep in reserve $\frac{1}{3}$ of the cash paid in exchange for notes, the remaining $\frac{2}{3}$ being at once invested in government securities, the interest derivable from this would be public profit. The whole system was to be under the control of currency commission one for each presidency with an incharge for each circle, they were to be totally independent of the executive government. A public statement about the cash reserved in the treasury was to be made each month. Private banks were to be restricted from issuing notes as is the case at present.

Paper Currency for the information of the Natives of India published by the Government of India in 1860 said : 'The effect of such a currency will indeed be the same as if a silver mine or a gold mine had been discovered in the plains of Hindoostan, or in the valley of the Ganges.'[1] Wilson did not advise the creation of a Government currency issuing bank in India like the Bank of England, but adopted the banking principle in issuing paper money, whereby, following the then practice in the Bank of England, two-thirds of the notes in circulation were to be against Government securities.

What is to be observed here is that gradually these measures were bringing about the modernisation of Indian finances.

Samuel Laing, Wilson's successor as Financial member arrived from England in January 1861 but was not to stay here long. Before he finally left the country in 1862 because of ill health, Laing advised a future Financial Member of India, Richard Temple, to seek distinction in active administration, for as Laing told him, the heroics of Indian finance were over.[2] The Government's search for permanent increase in income by new taxation as announced in the Financial Notification of February 1859, in the event, practically reduced itself to increased salt duty, which Canning did not really like. The chief new tax in the period of post-Revolt financial reorganization a truly modern one, viz. income tax, which people in north India viewed as a Mutiny tax, was allowed to expire in 1865. It had produced less than £ 2 millions a year, and much criticism and bitterness.[3] But with returning peace and revival of trade, income from land revenue including forest and excise increased by a million pounds every year from 1858-59 to 1862-63 ; income from salt improved by about £ 2 millions, and income from customs duties by one million, during the same period, 1858-59 to 1862-63. Thus it may be said that the returning peace and prosperity, a timely small windfall in income from opium, and what was most important, bold reductions in military expenditure, more than any innovation in taxa-

1. See Home Department (Public) No. 8, April 20, 1860. N.A.I.

2. Sir Richard Temple, *The Story of My Life* (London, 1896), I, 135.

3. Bholanauth Chunder in his *The Travels of a Hindoo* (London, 1869), I, 437, tells us that in 1860 throughout Hindustan the income tax "is regarded as a national punishment for the Rebellion".

tion, finally restored equilibrium after the financial crisis created by the Mutiny of 1857.[1]

But it was not all smooth, non-controversial sailing throughout. Even as the dust settled while noticing that in all that related to management of Loans, Budget and Audit and general organization and management, British India had gained through Wilson's and Laing's labour some wondered,[2] at what cost ? Would the loss of Wilson and Ward, Laing's breakdown, the damage to Trevelyan's official repute and the interruption to his usefulness, the increased acerbity of local jealousies, the consequent delay and loss of time in effecting real reforms—would these be balanced by what was gained ? Indeed was British India's gain equal to what it might have had if what Canning had begun early in 1859 had gone on undisturbed by external interference ?

During the whole period of this recasting of Indian finance a very live controversy had raged over the wisdom and convenience of imposing direct taxes. A controversy which, as is well known, had involved a number of leading personalities of the time. This was not to end even with the stabilisation of other issues but continued roughly for a couple of decades more—till around 1880.

After one successful experiment in 1867-68, licence taxes were permanently introduced in the presidencies in 1878. The chief direct tax of modern finance, the income tax, failed because of the opposition of the Anglo-Indians and rich Indians, in a second experiment during 1869-72, but succeeded with the income tax of 1886, which became permanent, and thereby opened a new epoch in Indian fiscal history.[3]

1. Laing acknowledged the importance of reduction in military expenditure in ending the post-Mutiny financial crisis. In his budget speech of 1861 he paid a tribute to the Military Finance Commission : "If the future historian of India should have occasion to mention, that in the year 1861, India was saved from a great Financial danger, that history will be very imperfectly written if it omits the names of Colonel Balfour, and his colleagues, Mr. R. Temple, and Colonel Simpson." See Laing's Financial Statement, p. 5.

2. Letter to Canning, June 11, 1861, in Martineau, *Frere* I, 326.

3. The Government in urging the income tax from 1859 onwards had good reasons for doing so. Without an income tax, Europeans in India,

The relation between Indian economy and agriculture is obvious. Especially during this period the Indian agriculture was experiencing great developments, however unequally spread among the rural masses might be its benefits. Yet this state of prosperity not being scientifically created could not be taken as something achieved with effort and would well vanish from one year to another.

Furthermore the picture painted till now indicates the commercial revolution through which India was passing. But this, while bringing prosperity to those engaged in trade and commerce did not necessarily effect the average agriculturist favourably. Indeed the revolution was not a natural growth from within but was imposed from above by the compulsions of the country's colonial economy. The unfortunate part, especially about this period of one's study is that the great expansions of trade caused by the construction of the railways and opening of the Suez Canal was matched neither by the development of modern industries nor by a similar increase in agricultural production, whereas all the while population continued to grow and rural unemployment increased.

It would be fruitful then for the understanding of the country's economy to take a survey of the major crops—cash and cereal—grown at that time. It would not only indicate which way things were developing but also where exactly stood Indian economy.[1]

official and mercantile, paid no direct tax to the Government and bore little share of the burden of the state. As to taxing native zemindars and other high income groups, an income tax was not unfair, nor oppressive on incomes above fifty pounds or 500 rupees a year, the lowest income schedule carrying a rate of one per cent in the unsuccessful income tax of 1869-72 levied by Sir Richard Temple

1. For this the U.S. Consular reports—annual and periodical—are of invaluable use because they give a heap of information reliably compiled. And they also used more than one source for the conclusion. The difficulty however is that in working out the annual reports the Consuls found it impractical to compile correct tabular statements relative to the trade and navigation. The monthly reports of several custom houses and the annual report of the Government however, were very often used for statistical information. The British India Government on the other hand always took a very helpful attitude and even where reports were not available in print and were needed by the Consuls he was furnished by the department of Revenue, Agriculture, Commerce, etc. the required data or by the Collector of Customs etc. the various facts and figures needed.—Despatch no. 151, Vol. 10. (C.D.)

Cotton : With scarce an exception both as regards soil and climate, every portion of the vast Peninsula was favourably adapted to the growth of this article and had a capacity to equal any demand. This was also true of British Burma, from whose principal port, Rangoon, many cargoes were beginning to clear direct for England and the Continent. The high prices prevailing had drawn from India supplies of unanticipated magnitude. In return therefore came back immense sums of silver and gold disarranging and demoralizing financial operations and institutions not only in the Presidency cities but seriously affecting those also of the great commercial and monied centres of the Globe. The balance of trade abroad was in favour of India, in India against the cities.[1] Of the specie imported in this great mass passed into the interior and was there absorbed, but into no sterile or unfruitful soil. For if a portion be hoarded the remaining had paid off the indebtedness of the *ryots* (petty) land-holders, furnished him with improved agricultural implements, permitted him to clear the surrounding jungle and add to his small holding, land fitted for cultivation.[2]

And as the cotton gins in many instances at government expense had been distributed and presses erected throughout the country the crop was consequently coming forward, generally well cleaned, well pressed, and in good shipping order. In quality however, it did not compare with American cotton. The various experiments to introduce Orleans, Sea Island, with other foreign varieties were failures. And these experiments were still continuing some 40 odd years later.[3] The indigenous staple was said already to have improved under more thorough modes of cultivation. Three years of prosperity had placed the Indian cultivator of cotton in a favourable position to compete with his fellow labourer throughout the world on the production of that article.

It is difficult from the published statistics to form any estimate as to the quantity of cotton grown in India. Following

1. Despatch no. 75, Vol. 7. (C.D.)

2 Consul General of U.S. in a letter to the Assistant Secretary of State, Calcutta, dated Oct. 28, 1864. (C.D.)

3. See Volumes 6 and 7. (B.D.) ; Despatch no. 15[illegible], Vol. 10. (C.D.)

is the statement and valuation of shipment from the ports and for the year mentioned.

Raw Cotton

1862-63[1]

	Quantity (Cwt.)	*Value* (£)
Calcutta	363856	1399117
Madras	506785	2143400
Bombay	3010563	13256201
	3881202	16799317

1863-64[2]

	Quantity (Cwt.)	*Value* (£)
Calcutta	401663	2152128
Madras	597995	4103000
Bombay	3325463	25177690
	4325121	31432818

Although rice was king, cotton held the first place of importance for an article of export. The high prices which ruled during the Civil War in the United States had led to the investment of large amounts of capital in the cultivation of cotton in India and fortunes were made with great rapidity, most of which were however lost by an unwise calculation on the part of cotton growers and speculators that the war was to be prolonged indefinitely. Whereas when everything was invested and large calculations made for the future, the War ceased and the price of cotton went down.[3] Nevertheless the production continued to be much larger than formerly. The shipments in 1873 amounted to lbs. 627,209,725 valued at

1. Despatch no. 75, Vol. 7. (C.D.)
2. ibid.
3. Despatch no. 151, Vol. 10. (C.D.)

$ 665220095 and of cotton yarns and manufactures to the value of $ 2233951, add to this consumption of the mills of India of lbs. 83164836 worth about $ 9148137 and one has a valuation of $ 77904097 for the entire crop.[1]

Indigo : The cultivation of indigo was carried on all over Bengal proper and in the North Eastern Provinces along the course of the Ganges.

The average quantity produced annually was about 120,000 maunds, until 1858 when disturbances broke out in Bengal owing to the farmers' refusal to cultivate indigo whilst other crops for which their lands were equally suited promised better returns. These caused a material decrease in the cultivation and the higher rents and enhanced value of labour subsequent to it kept down the average product to 100,000 maunds.[2]

The average area required to produce one maund of indigo was about 18 *beeghas* or about 6 acres and the area under indigo cultivation was about 600,000 acres.[3]

The cost of production varied in the different provinces, on an average it was reckoned at Rs. 40 per maund, exclusive of interest on the block or cost of the indigo factories.

The sowings in Bengal and in the districts adjoining it to the West, took place in October and during the following Spring. The October plant was cut in June and the Spring cultivation was ripe by the commencement of July. The manufacture therefore commenced in June and continued uninterruptedly until the end of July and in some districts the middle of August. In Tirhoot and North Eastern Provinces the season was later and the manufacture continued until September. The plant in these provinces yielded a second cutting the following year.

The best quality of indigo was produced in Bengal proper, and in Tirhoot and the lowest qualities in the Doab. The quantity of indigo production in each province was on an average as follows.[4]

In Bengal including Purneah and Bhagalpur	35,000 maunds.

1. Consul General of U.S. in a despatch to the department of State, U.S.A., Calcutta dated Nov. 24, 1875. (C.D.)
2. Despatch no. 75, Vol. 7. (C.D.)
3. ibid.
4. Consul General of U.S. in a communication to the department of State, U.S., Calcutta dated Oct. 28, 1854. (C.D.)

In Tirhoot and Monghyr	35,000 maunds.
Benares and the adjacent Provinces	15,000 maunds.
Doab	15,000 maunds.

The crop for 1864 was estimated at 95,000 maunds. The industry was almost entirely under the management of Europeans and as a rule the money invested was European. In the few cases in which Indian capitalists had invested in the business, they had generally employed European managers.[1] The out-turn usually amounted to 80,00,000 lbs. The crop seems to have been on extremely uncertain one and though at times this industry had paid handsomely, investments in it were considered hazardous. Indeed the investors had to be abundantly able to stand a bad year or two to be at all certain of success.[2] Drought would in certain seasons almost ruin the crop, while extensive rains would wash the plants out, robbing them of much of their rich colouring matter. One of the best years for production of indigo was 1843-44 when the crop amounted to 12500000 lbs. The crop in the year 1873-74 roughly mounted to 9124000 lbs. in round numbers, valued at $ 11300000. Of this amount England took to the value of about $ 7600000, France $ 1500000, the Mediterranean port $ 1200000, America $ 350000, Russia $ 300000 and all other countries $ 350000.[3]

Opium: This was a government monopoly. The raw produce in many instances came from governmental estates and in some others was procured by advances to Zamindars and native princes. However the Government retained the handling and control until sold by its own auctioneers in Calcutta and Bombay. The actual receipts from this article for the year 1863 was the enormous sum of £ 8655476.[4] There is little reliable data available as to number of acres under cultivation, capital invested, or labour employed in the production of opium.

1. Annual Report for the year 1874-75, Vol. 10. (C.D.)
2. ibid.
3. Consul General of U.S. in a communication to the department of State, Calcutta, dated Nov 24, 1875. (C.D.)
4. Despatch no. 75, Vol. 7. (C.D.)

The following extract from the financial statement of Hon. Sir C. E. Trevelyan may be of interest so far as the financial importance of opium goes:[1]

"The increase in the revenue of India during the last 5 years, corrected according to the actual account is as follows:

1858-59	..	£ 16060788
1859-60	..	£ 39705822
1860-61	..	£ 42903234
1861-62	..	£ 43829472
1862-63	..	£ 45148752

The most important event of the current year 1863-64, in its bearing upon the finances has been the depressed state of the money market. The first symptoms of this appeared at Bombay in October and throughout the last six months of the year, revenue has suffered from its injurious influence. Upon the opium revenue the effect has been particularly marked. The average price of the Calcutta sales during 1862-63 was Rs. 1429 a chest. The average price during first 6 months of 1863-64 was Rs. 1371. The average price of the 5 sales which have since taken place is Rs. 1100. At Bombay owing to the scarcity and dearness of money which afterwards extended to China and caused a serious fall in the prices there, the taking out of the opium poppies at the fixed rate of Rs. 600 a chest was almost suspended."

Naturally enough all this led to caution among the governmental circles and it was soon declaring its intention not to increase the area of cultivation of opium.[2] Nevertheless every endeavour to enhance the productiveness of that already under cultivation continued to be made. For this purpose liberal advances were being made for the construction of wells for irrigation purposes and for measures to enrich the soil and every encouragement was held out to stimulate interest of the indigenous cultivators. A system of honorary distinctions was introduced or revived and several thousand rupees were expended annually in presentation of broad cloth, shawls, turbans and other articles which served as a mark of honour to each of the cultivator engaged in growing paddy as have distinguished themselves by

1. See Vol. 7. (C.D.)
2. Despatch no. 151, Vol. 10. (C.D.)

their exertions and success.[1] To prevent frauds by adulteration and false weights a complete system of checks was introduced.

Jute : The cultivation had a local interest from a very remote period but it was comparatively an unimportant production until about the sixties of the nineteenth century. (In point of fact, shipment of jute to England was mentioned even during the last decade of the eighteenth century[2].)

In the year 1828-29 a separate account of it as an article of export, was first kept at the Calcutta Custom House and the amount exported was 180 tonnes valued at £ 75. In 1835-36 the export was 621 tonnes. In 1850 its cultivation was largely extended and exports amounting to 21139 tonnes. From the year 1874-75, the cultivation continued to increase until the exports took the 4th place in the trade list of Calcutta, amounting during the year 1872-73 to the enormous total of 367784 tonnes. During the year 1873-74 and 1874-75 by reasons of drought and decline in the markets which were doubtless overstocked the amount produced declined so that the exports showed a falling off to 274539 tonnes. A large share of this apparent decrease was due also to the increased consumption of the fibre in the Indian manufactures set in operation during this period.[3]

Tea : The cultivation of tea which was beginning to take such a high place among the industries of India, was of comparatively recent introduction and development. About the year 1833 an indigenous tea plant was discovered in the jungles of Assam which unlike the ordinary or China plant, was really a tea-tree growing to an average height of about 20 ft.[4] Although it was sometime before this plant was fully admitted to be tea, the Assam indigenous gradually grew to be recognized as the most valuable in the English market.

About the time of this discovery, the Government of India was devoting a great deal of attention to the cultivation of China tea plant in India. These also proving successful the China plant was largely introduced to cross-graft so that in Assam by the

1. Annual Consular report 1862-63. (C.D.)
2. Despatch no. 151, Vol. 10. (C.D.)
3. See Consul General of U.S. in a despatch to the department of State, U.S.A., Calcutta, dated Nov. 24, 1875. (C.D.)
4. ibid.

third quarter of the nineteenth century the tea cultivated was mostly a hybrid variety. In fact, the more it partook the nature of Assam indigenous the more valuable it was supposed to be.

The production and export of tea nearly doubled, between 1865 and 1875[1] and there were over 66 companies, investing huge amount of money in this industry.[2] In fact there seemed to be no limit to the possibilities of this kind of industry. The American Consul General was led to suggest from all this to the State department that the Indian tea plant could flourish well in southern California where Chinese labour could be utilised for it.[3]

Wheat : Talking of wheat and its method of cultivation in India the U.S. Consul General commented:[4]

"The method of cultivating the soil, and harvesting and threshing wheat in this country is in the main, the same as it was centuries ago, and from the conservative disposition and caste prejudices of the native *ryot* (farmer) there seems to be great difficulty in inducing him to invest in modern agricultural implements, or to do anything differently from the way his father and his father's father did before him."

The quotation needs no comment and is symptomatic of the condition of Indian agriculture.

The following table[5] is for the total export of wheat from

1. 170000 acres of land had been taken up for tea cultivation in the year 1862-63. Of this area 27000 were cleared up and planted affording employment to nearly 28000 labourers and several hundred of other respectable folk as clerks. The value of tea produced and exported to England for the year 1862-63 was estimated at £250000.

—Annual Consular report for the year 1862-63. (C.D.)

2. There were at this time (around 1865) 45 Joint Stock tea companies in actual operation. Their shares were quoted in the Calcutta exchange but their field of operation was confined mostly to the provinces of Assam and Cachar. Plantations were however then being opened with success in the Chittagong area also. Enormous dividends had been declared by the older established companies and large and increasing ones by those of more recent date—announcing the assured success of that which was no longer an experiment.

—Annual Consular report for the year 1862-63. (C.D.)

3. Consul General of U.S. in a despatch to the department of State, U.S.A., Calcutta, dated Nov. 24, 1875. (C.D.)

4. Despatch no. 36, Vol. 14. (C.D.)

5. Despatch no. 36, Vol. 13. (C.D.)

India for thirteen years and in a way shows the entire history of wheat production in India, for the period, so far as it had become an article of export.

Year	Cwt.
1867-68	299385
1868-69	275481
1869-70	78208
1870-71	248522
1871-72	637099
1872-73	394010
1873-74	1755954
1874-75	1069076
1875-76	2498185
1876-77	5583336
1877-78	6340150
1878-79	1044709
1879-80	2195550

Rice : The amount of rice and paddy exported from the whole of British India[1] in 1874-75 has been 869647 tonnes against 1300000 tonnes for Burma, Bengal[2] and Madras.

The fact that American or Carolina rice commanded double the price of Indian rice, in the English market led the Government of Bengal to institute careful enquiries regarding its cultivation and to make an experiment on an extended scale, with seeds procured from America but the experiments were only partially successful and the conclusion[3] arrived at by the Government of Bengal seemed to be that the superiority of the

1. Consul General of U.S. in a despatch to the department of State, U.S.A., Calcutta, dated Nov. 24, 1875. (C.D.)

2. "The districts of whole of Bengal proper or the great alluvial and deltaic plain between the Himalayas and the Bay of Bengal and of Orrisa or the deluvial territory between the hills and the sea connecting the province with Madras, a level area of nearly 100000 square miles uninterrupted by a single hill, rich in black mould and of boundless reproductive fertility, subject to recurrent inundations and enjoying natural facilities such as no other country in the world possesses for internal commerce and irrigation constitute the great rice producing districts for Bengal" : '*Rice trade of the World*' a report, by Mr. Cotton, Secretary to the Government of Bengal, Vol. 10, (C.D.)

3. Despatch no. 151, Vol. 10. (C.D.)

Carolina rice was the result of careful cultivation only and that an artificial supply of water alone was required to make its cultivation a success. But perhaps in coming to this conclusion the Government was oversimplifying the problem and overlooking the climatic factor involved.

The scarcity of staple crop and famine : It would be recalled that during the year 1873 the want of rain in Bihar and the north part of Bengal, upon which this area depended for the maturing of the full crop of rice, the most important of all the crops, and for saving the seeds for crops which would be reaped the following Spring, had caused widespread want, and threatened those sections of India with all the horrors of terrible famine.[1] Because of lack of reliable reports from agricultural districts, many of them far from ordinary routes of travel, it was impossible to determine with any degree of accuracy the seriousness of the threatened calamity and so the relief measures which were undertaken by the Government had necessarily to be extravagant in nature.[2]

During the latter part of January 1874 Sir Richard Temple who had been financial member of the Governor General's Council was associated with Sir George Campbell the then Lt. Governor of Bengal and deputed to visit[3] the distressed districts and help organise effective measures of relief. On April 8, Sir Richard Temple had himself become Lieutenant Governor.

The measures of relief[4] finally fixed upon were the energetic prosecution of work upon roads, canals, tanks[5] and other internal improvements, with a view, in so far as possible, to provide work for the destitute as well as to secure some return for the lavish expenditures made on their behalf.

1. *Gazette of India* (Extraordinary) Calcutta, Friday, Nov. 7, 1873.
2. Consul General of U.S. in a communication to the department of State, U.S., Calcutta, dated Nov. 14, 1873. (C.D.)
3. '*Minutes*' by Richard Temple, Governor of Bengal.
4. Smith, Baird *Report*, Section I, paras 20-28.
5. It might be pointed out here that for agricultural improvements there was an act which provided for advances of money by the Government to any landlord or tenant desiring to make an improvement in any land of which he was in possession or occupation, i.e. *Land Improvement Act* (XXVI of 1871).

It was a comparatively easy thing to plan works of public improvement and to obtain the needful supply of rice for food, since British India possessed an excellent corps of engineer officers, and British Burma and Orissa had produced unusually abundant crops of rice, but to distribute this rice amounting to upwards of 400000 tonnes (about eight times as much as the largest crops ever realized in the United States)[1] throughout the distressed districts was indeed a difficult task. The magnitude of the undertaking can be realised by considering a few figures relating to the expenditures, the means used and the results obtained.

The districts threatened had an aggregate of 40,109 square miles with a population of nearly 18 millions of which number it was estimated nearly 4,000,000 would require relief, for which purpose the Government had allotted the enormous amount of 404,000 tonnes of rice. From Burma alone the amount of rice ordered (and delivered in about six months time) was 289,534 tonnes valued at $ 936457900 exclusive of freight.[2]

To transport this rice from railway stations and main water courses over rough road or where there were no roads, for distances ranging from 20 to 155 miles, 212800 drought bullocks, 1350 camels, 14000 pack animals (mostly mules and ponies), 2340 country boats and 23 steamers were employed. There were in all about 2300 relief circles or districts, large and small, 158 of these were regularly organised under Government officers, in most of which field hospitals were established, supervised by members of a Special Medical staff collected for the purpose.[3]

The staff of all grades employed in relief operations amounted to 6960. The public works undertaken were 6626 miles relief roads, 380 miles Sone Canal works, 90 miles Gunduck embankments and 198 Northern Bengal Railways.

The expenditures by Government after deducting amounts realized from sales of rice etc., amounted to about 6,000,000 pounds sterling or about $ 30000000. The total number of per-

1. Annual Consular report for the year 1874-75. (C.D.)
2. ibid.
3. ibid.

sons subsisting on Government rice was estimated at $4\frac{1}{4}$ millions. Of this number, 1770732 were employed on public works and paid in rice, between 6000,000 and 700,000 were on charitable relief and the balance bought Government food.[1]

Relief operations extended as far as October 1874 and the famine very materially affected the shipment of rice during the year 1873-74.[2]

1880-1906 : *the years of drift.*

1880 has been chosen as the year roughly around which new trends are discernible in Indian economy. For one thing after 1880 till about 1895 India was free from any major agricultural calamity or severe economic distress for the masses of the population. It is true after 1895 some disturbances did occur, but keeping in mind that there was nothing else which made 1895-1906 exclusive years it was thought best to keep them included under the larger head. Besides there were other trends which began around 1880 and continued through till beyond 1895 e.g. laws to regulate production and export.[3] It need hardly be stated that 1906 had to be accepted as the closing date because of obvious compulsions.[4] Furthermore from around 1880 it is possible to detect the beginning of a different phase in the production of some items also like tea. Among other things the years 1880 to the end seemed also to be characterised by a singular policy of drift on the part of the Government. After having once put back the economy on a fairly sure footing following the rebellion of 1857, the government seemed satisfied to move from day to day so long as its colonial requirements from this colony were being met satisfactorily. To look for any dash or enterprise in its policies during this period would be perhaps misplaced. Moreover by now the Indians were beginning to realise that basic rights as human beings were being denied to them under this alien rule. They were bound to protest and agitate initially for the removal of disabilities and ultimately for the total independence of the country. The economy of such a period would

1. Annual Consular Report for the year 1874-75. (C.D.)
2. *Orissa Famine Report* I p. 97.
3. See the case of 'Salt-petre', despatch no. 319, Vol. 12. (C.D.)
4. There are no Consular reports, as such, available for post-1906 period.

necessarily be different from the earlier phase. What was the economy then during this segment of the nineteenth century and a little beyond ?

The currency : This period was of great significance so far as currency problems and their ultimate solution was concerned. So it might be helpful to begin with to know the extent of fineness, weight etc. of the various coins in circulation. The table[1] given on the facing page may give the picture in a nutshell.

Next one takes up the Copper coins which were legal tender for fractions of a rupee only.

Copper Coins[2]	*grain*
A double piece or half anna	200
A piece or quarter anna	100
A half piece or one-eighth of an anna	50
A pie being one-third of a pice or one-twelfth of an anna	$33\frac{1}{3}$

Yet it would be a mistake to suppose that no variations from the standard weight and fineness was allowed. Indeed it would have been a most unnatural thing to attempt because such precision would not have been physically possible then. The following account might give some idea of what exactly was the extent of permissible variation.

'For *gold coins* an amount not exceeding two-thousandths in weight and two-thousandths in fineness.'[3]

'For *silver coins* of a rupee and half a rupee the allowance in weight was five-thousandths and the allowance in fineness was two-thousandths. For quarter of a rupee the allowance in weight was seven-thousandths and the allowance in fineness was three-thousandths. However for eighth of a rupee the allowance in weight was ten-thousandths and the allowance in fineness was again three-thousandths.'[4]

1. Despatch no. 292, Vol. 12. (C.D.)
2. Consul General of U.S. in a despatch to the department of State, Calcutta, dated April 28, 1880. (C.D.)
3. Letter of Finance Secretary to the Government of India addressed to Consul General of U.S. ref. despatch No. 292, Vol. 12. (C.D.)
4. ibid.

Gold Coins[1]

	Pure gold grains	Alloy grains	Total weight grains Troy
A double gold mohar or 30 Rs. piece	330	30	360
A mohar or 15 Rs. piece	165	15	180
Two-thirds of a mohar or 10 Rs. piece	110	10	120
One-third of a mohar or 5 Rs. piece	55	5	60

But no gold coin was legal tender in payment or account.

Silver Coins[2]

These were legal tender in payment of all engagements.

	Pure silver grains	Alloy grains	Total weight grains
A Government Rupee	165	15	180
A half rupee	82½	7½	90
Legal tender for fractions of a Rupee only			
A quarter or 4 annas piece	41¼	3¾	45
An eighth of a Rupee or 2 anna piece	20⅝	1⅜	22

1. Despatch no. 292, Vol. 12. (C.D.)
2. ibid.

It is, however, interesting to note that the coins of native states had the same status in British India as the coins of foreign countries. They were not allowed to circulate.

As authorized by the Indian Paper Currency Act (Act iii of 1871) paper currency did circulate in India but the metallic currency largely exceeded the paper issue. The Government also held a reserve of metal and of government bonds against its issue of paper, equal in amount to that of whole paper issue. It obviously speaks of the stage of the money economy that India was in at that period.

A statement of the paper in issue and the silver held in reserve against it was published monthly in the official Gazette of India.

As per laws of economics naturally enough the relative value of the various currencies in the world would vary. This would, of course, also effect the trade relations in a world of ever expanding commerce. The U.S. department of Treasury took due note of this and issued periodically what was known as a circular "estimating and proclaiming in United States money of account, the values of standard coins in circulation of the various nations of the world." In 1880 it appears there took place one such major fluctuation in the rate of Indian rupee as compared with the U.S. dollar, and this all those connected with Indo-U.S. trade were specially asked to note on the American side.[1] This did not happen all of a sudden but was rooted in historical causes. The standard coin in circulation then was the Rupee and the Half Rupee. The Rupee of course was the unit of the money of account. Silver was the legal standard measure of value. The standard weight of the Rupee was 180 grains Troy, and its fineness 11/12. The Rupee thus contained 165 grains of pure silver.[2] Hence the importance of silver in the economy was obvious.

But in Europe France's defeat at the hand of Germany had set in motion a circular process which in turn was draining France of all its silver. Alarmed by the situation, the govern-

1. State Department circular No. 18, dated March 20, 1880 to American Consulates.

2. Letter of Finance Secretary to the Government of India addressed to the Consul General, U.S., Simla, ref. No. 1603.

ment of that country virtually suspended the coinage of silver. Following this, the United States Congress passed in February, 1873, an Act "revising and amending the laws relative to the mints, assay offices, and coinage of the United States". The seventh section of this law deprived silver of its right of being coined into full legal tender money on either government or private accounts. This and other similar measures proved half-way remedies. By providing for the purchase of a considerable amount of silver, they did prevent a sudden contraction of the volume of money available. But by refusing to admit free coinage of silver they failed to increase the money supply so as to meet the demands of a rapidly increasing population. Besides, the adoption of gold standard by European countries threw much of the silver into disuse at a time when the world supply of the white metal was constantly increasing.[1] The cumulative effect of these factors was a steep decline in the value of silver in terms of gold, and with that a fall in silver currency.

The Indian rupee, being a silver coin, experienced this fate. In 1871 the rupee was worth $23\frac{1}{2}$ d. ; in 1878 it had fallen to $19\frac{3}{4}$ d., and by 1892 it was reduced to 14.9 d. But the depreciation in currency did not result in the rise of prices in India. As noted by the Royal Gold and Silver Commission of 1886, the prices in the silver currency countries till the close of that year had fallen 30 per cent at an average from the gold base and silver measured in gold had declined at a rate almost exactly equal.[2] Thus, the exchange value of silver had remained almost constant, for silver and commodities had not changed in their relations to each other. That is, an ounce of silver could be exchanged for the same quantity of goods as before. The purchasing power of silver in India was unaffected while gold was at a high premium.

This added to the advantages of India in its export trade. When silver dropped in the London market, it was to the advantage of the English importer to buy in India rather than the United States. With a certain number of pounds sterling he could buy more rupees than before and with each rupee, he

1. For figures see *The National Bimetallist* (Chicago, March 11, 1892), 333.

2. House of Commons, *Second Report of the Royal Commission appointed to enquire into the changes in the relative value of Precious Metals* (London, 1888), 72.

could get as much goods in India as he could before silver was demonetized. Thus, he could sell his goods more cheaply than the importer from the United States, who had to pay for his consignments in gold.

This was repeatedly pointed out by the American bi-metallists and agrarians as an argument against gold mono-metallism. "In exporting to gold standard countries", wrote Wharton Barker, the editor of the *American* in 1896 "the Indian wheat grower......has enjoyed and is enjoying a very considerable bounty—gold as measured by the rupee being at a premium of over sixty per cent."[1] Replying to the argument that the increased Indian export was due to improved transportation in that country and the opening of the Suez Canal, the *National Bimetallist* compared the figures of the Indian and the American exports to Europe, and pointed out that the demand for Indian wheat in Europe rose from 13 million bushels in 1881 to 50 million bushels in 1891 while that for the American produce fell from 150 million bushels to 55 million bushels. "It is perfectly obvious", the paper concluded, "that there must have been some other cause than railroad building and completion of the Suez Canal. The cause has been the difference between gold values and silver values, stimulating the exports, not only of India but of Argentine and other countries having currency cheaper than gold."[2] The *Bimetallist* also attributed the rising export of Indian cotton to the same fact.[3]

The currency situation gave a fillip to the Indian manufacturing. Since the purchase of goods involved a conversion of Indian silver into gold at a loss, the Indian began to manufacture for himself. The same considerations induced the investment of British capital in the Indian cotton mills, for a given number of sovereigns could buy a greater number of rupees, and each rupee did as much work as it ever did in India. As a result of this encouragement, the total number of spindles in Bombay rose from 450,000 in 1873 to 4,000,000 at the close of 1894.[4] This enabled India not only to meet a considerable

1. Wharton Barker, *Bimetallism* (Philadelphia, Barker Publishing Co., 1896), 146.
2. *The National Bimetallist*, March 11, 1892, 327.
3. ibid, 315.
4. ibid, 315.

portion of its own demand for cotton goods but also to capture markets in China and Japan. The consumption of British goods in these countries remained stationary.

From the American point of view, this development had two effects—both adverse. The American exports to these countries suffered a setback. It was also feared that the English and European manufacturers, frustrated in their efforts to expand markets in the silve rusing countries of Asia, might look to the United States for the consumption of their goods.[1] The currency situation, thus, lengthened the shadow of Indian danger to the farming and manufacturing interests of the United States.

From the Indian point of view, however, silver posed a different problem. The Government of India had to remit large sums of money annually to England for the home charges, and its remittance in gold meant an increasing amount in silver, as the latter fell in value. This the Government of India considered an additional tax on the people of that country. The remedy was a reduction of the home charges, but the Viceroy, Lord Lytton, in 1878 proposed to raise artificially the value of the rupee. Only half way steps were taken to achieve the objective. The fall in the rupee continued.

The Indian authorities attributed their failure to some of the circumstances prevailing in the United States. In 1886, the Viceroy thought that the uncertainty regarding the policy of the United States was an important cause of anxiety. Later, he explicitly stated that the fall in the price of the rupee was due to speculation in America regarding the repeal or modification of the Bland Act.[2] Therefore, the Government of India urged the British Government to enter into some arrangement with the United States before the International Monetary Conference at Brussels in 1892.[3] The British Government ignored the suggestion, and nothing came of the deliberations at Brussels. All attempts to arrest the fall in the Rupee ended in frustration.[4]

1. Wharton Barker, *Bimetallism*, 110.
2. Telegram of the Indian Viceroy dated January 12, 1886, and February 6, 1886, quoted in Romesh Dutt, *The Economic History of India in the Victorian Age* (London, 1956), 582.
3. A.S. Ghosh, "*India's Case for Silver*", 478.
4. Dr. D. Tripathi has discussed all this very well in some of his writings to which due acknowledgement is made.

It was imperative to reopen the whole question of silver. The British Parliament, therefore, referred the problem of Indian currency to a committee under the chairmanship of Lord Herschell, then the Lord Chancellor. On the recommendation of the Committee, the Indian mints were closed in June, 1893. It is interesting that Lord Herschell based his conclusion, among other things, on a fear that the repeal of the Sherman Act in the United States might throw an enormous amount of silver into the market and thus, lead to a further fall in the value of the rupee.[1]

The closing of the Indian mints had immediate effects on the United States. Within forty-eight hours of the announcement of the Indian authorities[2] silver fell in New York market from 82 cents to 60 cents per ounce, and all the silver mines in the United States were closed,[3] heralding the monetary panic of 1893.

There is no doubt that the demonetization of silver in India "led to, or hastened the repeal of the Sherman Act in America" in November, 1893. Thus within four months, two countries, one being the largest silver producing and the other the largest silver consuming one, prohibited the purchase and the coinage of that metal.

This caused great hardships in both the countries. In the United States, the prices fell and the mine-owners and the miners became almost destitute. In India, the bullion value of the rupee fell so much as to reduce considerably the difference which previously existed between its face value and bullion value. This hit the manufacturing classes as well as the common man. Since the banking system was undeveloped in India, the people were accustomed to hoarding their savings in the form of ornaments. As a consequence of the closing of the mints, these hoards could be sold at 3/5th of their face value or at a loss of

1. House of Commons, *Report of the Committee Appointed to Enquire into the Indian Currency* (London, 1893), 9.

2. The Indian authorities were only a puppet in the hands of the British Government, and they had to follow the dictates of the government at home. Since the former had no freedom of action, Indian authorities and British Government have been used interchangeably here.

3. Ritchie to Butterworth, March 2, 1896, U.S. Senate Doc. No. 235, 54th Congress, 1 Session (1896) 11.

forty per cent. But owing to the grave anxiety about the future of silver, the dealers in India were charging at least an additional ten per cent to cover all risks. Hence the total loss to the people of India was fifty per cent of their savings.[1]

Under these conditions, the interests of the United States and India warranted the reopening of Indian mints. This would open the door for greater consumption of the silver produced by the western states of America, and would also increase the value of the silver hoards in India. The Indian economic circles felt that a policy of bi-metallism in the United States might force the British Government to re-monetize silver in India in order to prevent a flow of silver from that country to the United States. A considerable section of population in both these countries looked with hope at the presidential election of 1896. William J. Bryan, who ran on a silver platform, had active support of the silver states and the moral support of the Indian economic circles.[2]

With the defeat of Bryan, the hopes of India vanished. A country the future of which depended on what served the interests of the British Government could hardly carry on any effective agitation. The silver interests in the United States, however, continued their efforts to get the Indian mints reopened. Their leader and chief spokesman in Congress was Senator Edward, the expert on currency problem of the world. William McKinley, who favoured an international agreement to solve such problems had been voted to the presidency in 1896 on a gold standard platform, and had little hope of any cooperation from England. In order to placate public opinion in the silver states, however, he despatched Wolcott to Europe in 1896 on an unofficial mission to explore the possibilities of a joint action.[3]

In the meantime, Congress appointed a Bimetallic Commission in 1897. Senator Wolcott was its chairman with Senator Adlai E. Stevenson of Illinois and General Charles J. Paine of Massachusetts as members. All of these were men of pronounced

1. *Congressional Record*, XXV, 479.
2. ibid, 486.
3. Thomas Fulton Dawson, *Life and Character of Edward Oliver Wolcott* (privately printed, no date), 654.

bimetallic views. Their mission evoked considerable hope in India, for their main proposal was to reopen the Indian mints.[1] France needed little persuasion, but Britain, being a creditor nation with a gold standard, had little interest in raising the value of silver. An appreciation of gold was to its advantage. To sidetrack the issue, therefore, the British Government referred the question to the Indian authorities for their advice. Senator Wolcott and his colleagues considered it a mere formality. To their great surprise, however, the Government of India rejected the proposal. The Commission's efforts proved abortive.[2]

This was not only the defeat for the protagonists of silver but underlined the singular callousness of the British towards the real good of the Indians. The imposition on them of a gold exchange standard could not be taken to mean anything else.

Agriculture : Agricultural interest was in a very poor condition and there had been little change in the mode of production over the course of centuries—a fact which one notices to be true, for many parts of the country, even today. Yet the richness of the soil made up for comparatively, primitive techniques.

Cotton : Though during this period Indian raw cotton was finding new market in China, Italy, France and Australia efforts to improve the quality by using American seed had been in vain. The Times of India[3] contained the following remark on the cultivation of cotton and the same facts applied largely to other products and explains the difficulty in obtaining reliable statistical information on Indian agriculture for the period, "According to the annual returns, the outturn for the year 1880/81 in the North Western Provinces and Oudh was 65·2 lbs. per acre, which was 2·2 per cent over the average of the preceding year. The average price the cultivators received was at the rate of Rs.15·8·2 per maund or Rs. 11·11·7 per acre. From this the *ryots* have to deduct the cost of cultivation rent and taxes, and it will not take long to ascertain how little they have left. The marvel, however, is that these same men continue the

1. Thomas Fulton Dawson, *Life and Character of Edward Oliver Wolcott* (privately printed, no date), 666.

2. ibid, 679.

3. *Times of India* dated December 7, 1881.

losing game year after year. The real truth is that the returns are utterly valueless. The *ryot* (cultivator) invariably understates the production from a desire to keep his neighbours, his *bunias* and the Government officials in ignorance of his real condition. He is afraid that if the *Sirkar* (Government) found that he was making any money he would have increased taxes imposed upon him."

It is significant to note that the American Consul General in his reportings notes how the opening of railroads into the interior had made transport cheaper and thus helped in the increased cultivation of cotton.

Tea : Tea came in by a separate category of itself because its interest was pushed with much energy by European planters and capital. A concerted action on their part had opened a large market in Australia[1] in around 1880's. The American markets continued receiving good attention also.

Manufacture : The proverbially cheap Indian labour was an asset any time so far as manufacture was concerned. In fact there it had no competitor then save perhaps the Chinese Empire.

The Indians were, as of tradition, naturally proficient at all sorts of handicraft, they were very patient, enduring and accurate "they live on simplest diet and are glad to work for 10 to 15 cents a day" noted the American Consul General at Calcutta.[2] Because of abundant raw material such as cotton, jute, tobacco, paper material, wood and pottery clay, the crafts were encouraged. The introduction of machinery in India for manufactures had of course been largely a post-Revolt phenomena. This had naturally given a great impetus to the industry and contributed to a certain degree to the well being of the people.

Around the beginning of the third quarter of the nineteenth century most of the mills were owned by foreign capitalists but the Indians were beginning to see the advantages of such set ups and a couple of decades later Tata were to try to establish their own mills in iron industry.[3]

1. Annual Consular report for the year 1880-81. (C.D.)
2. ibid.
3. Consul General of U.S. in a communication to the department of State, U.S., Calcutta, dated January 8, 1882.

There were other types of manufactures and industries however which were present even then, e.g. the cotton industry. However, such gestures like the abolition of import duties on cotton fabrics and yarns of coarse texture which were the only kinds produced in the Indian mills at the instigation of the Manchester merchants who have an influential party at home, had placed the Indian manufactures at a disadvantage, and the Indian mill-owners with the raw material at hand and with cheap labour still found it difficult to compete with the skilled labour of Manchester.[1] However, this was not enough to satisfy the Manchester merchants and at that time they were making strenuous efforts towards the total abolition of import duties with a view to check all progress of their Indian rivals, and to induce the Indian Government to make up the loss of revenue thereby occasioned by the imposition of direct taxation.

Trade—imports and exports: The imports of merchandise were increasing. As the American Consul pointed out in 1880-81 the total value was about $ 201,235,337 being $ 42,000,000 in excess of the imports for 1879-80. Out of the sum of $ 201, 235,337, 34.31 per cent were goods free of duty, 60.69 per cent were dutiable goods. Out of the free goods $ 60,033,210 in value were imported from the United Kingdom, $40,000,000 or two-thirds being the value of British Cotton twist and grey piece goods exempt from duty.[2]

Of the dutiable imports, those from the United Kingdom amounted to $105,137,326. Thus out of the whole imports of merchandise no less than $165,770,539 came from the United Kingdom being 82 per cent or more than four-fifths of the whole.

This clearly demonstrates the calculatedly unbalanced trade ratio that the English maintained in India in favour of themselves. Principal articles of merchandise imported according to their importance during the year ended March 31, 1886[3] were as follows : Cotton Goods (including twist and yarns);

1. Consul General of U.S. in a communication to the department of State U.S., Calcutta, dated Jan. 8, 1882.

2. Despatch no. 13, Vol. 12. (C.D.)

3. This year has been selected after comparison with others, because it appears to be a typical one.

metals (including hardware and cutlery); railway plant and rolling stock; silk (raw and manufactured); sugar, woollen goods, coal; liquors (wines, beer, etc.); provisions, apparel, machinery and millwork; oils (mainly kerosene).[1]

Principal articles of merchandise exported during the same period were: Animals living; articles of food and drink; metals and manufactures of metals (including hardware and cutlery); chemicals, drugs, medicines, narcotics, dyeing materials, oils, raw materials and unmanufactured articles, articles manufactured and unmanufactured.[2]

To have also a clear idea of the quantum of trade for this period it will be helpful to have a look at the total number and tonnage of the shipping of the principal nationalities other than British, engaged in the trade in one year (1885-86) as compared with say, four preceding years. This is shown in the table given on pages 134-35.[3]

Salt-petre : Around 1880 were enacted some new laws[4] by the Indian Government relative to the manufacture of salt-petre in India and it was feared that it would affect greatly the exportation of this article to the United States.

In fact, Salt-petre had always formed an important article of export from the port of Calcutta, supplying the necessary deadweight in many vessels, especially in those clearing for U.S. ports. But the laws which had just been passed were so likely to raise the price of Salt-petre as to make it difficult for the American market to buy.[5]

The production and importation of ordinary salt in India was a Government monopoly which paid heavy revenue, naturally enough the Government was most jealous in guarding it.

Wheat : The tendencies in the trade of wheat for this period were merely a continuation of those of the earlier one.

1. Despatch no. 36, Vol. 13. (C.D.)
2. Annual Consular report for the year 1885-86, Vol. 13. (C.D.)
3. From Despatch no. 36, Vol. 13. (C.D.)
4. Despatch no. 319, Vol. 12. (C.D.)
5. ibid.

The total number and tonnage of the shipping of some leading countries engaged in trade with India for the years 1881-86[1].

		1881-82	1882-83	1883-84	1884-85	1885-86
Austrian	No.	86	97	89	78	78
	Tons	112235	138215	130071	136942	137846
Belgian	No.	16	3	12	2	—
	Tons	20281	3557	15928	2646	—
Dutch	No.	13	5	39	92	127
	Tons	9699	7655	42241	95846	150060
French	No.	226	219	231	188	170
	Tons	140843	191084	286683	212039	176835
German	No.	124	238	178	156	200
	Tons	112329	213495	163081	160771	205629
Italian	No.	247	281	217	107	126
	Tons	230643	281454	248608	143904	1647888
Norwegian	No.	80	130	74	75	78
	Tons	745444	107538	67248	63402	63541
Russian	No.	12	17	11	3	2
	Tons	12502	13512	10275	2628	798

(Continued on the next page)

(continued from the previous page)

		1881-82	1882-83	1883-84	1884-85	1885-86
Swedish	No.	19	36	34	10	21
	Tons	8988	21045	18728	4069	11480
American	No.	74	73	44	52	45
	Tons	87346	85452	52033	64538	55236
Arab	No.	584	815	646	663	597
	Tons	85853	79045	102393	102215	92712
Turkish	No.	20	12	11	20	9
	Tons	14876	10315	9041	9055	5070

1. From Despatch no. 36, Vol. 13. (C.D.)

The following table is for the total export of wheat from India for five years and speaks for itself.[1]

Year	Cwt.
1880-81	7444375
1881-82	19863520
1882-83	14144407
1883-84	20956495
1884-85	15830754
1885-86	21060519

The table on the facing page shows the aggregate imports of wheat and flour into England from the several countries named for the years 1881-86.[2]

At this point of time it was genuinely being feared that U.S. had in India, a veritable competitor, so far as the production of wheat was concerned. In fact, in 1886, India was second only to the U.S. in the quantity of wheat produced.

Moreover it was to be noted that wheat growing in India was still in its infancy and its further development depended principally upon the means of transportation to the sea board. Till then British India had in operation about 12,000 miles of railway and the process of building new lines was being gradually stepped up. In fact the U.S. Consul thought the Government of England was not prepared to be content with being the great public carrier of the world but seemed to be inclined to produce her own bread stuff. With the cheap indigenous labour of India and the constantly growing facilities of transportation she could well pose a challenge to the U.S. as being a great producer of "stuff of life."[3] Moreover, at this time the surplus wheat of India was being carried to Europe in steam-ships through the Suez Canal in three or four weeks instead of going as formerly in sail-vessels around the Cape.

In conclusion then one can also look at the whole problem of economic growth in the context of the impact of rural-urban trade upon the rural sector during the period of transition which was characterised among other things by commerciali-

1. Despatch no. 36, Vol. 13. (C.D.)
2. Annual Consular report for the year 1885-86. (C.D.)
3. ibid.

Aggregate imports of wheat and flour into England 1881-86[1]

	1881-82 (Cwt)	1882-83 (Cwt)	1883-84 (Cwt)	1884-85 (Cwt)	1885-86 (Cwt)
From Russia	4089308	9659079	13398047	5494839	11986359
From U.S.A.					
Atlantic ports	31498568	26635657	23982160	22808579	21899674
Pacific ports	12278094	16302322	13417060	10168952	14107513
From Egypt	1072182	177115	1173019	1000764	109983
From India	7337924	8463174	11248988	7980951	12101963
From other countries	12229238	16060805	17248669	14945372	17083501
Total	68505314	77298152	80467943	62401457	77288993

1. Annual Consular report for the year 1885-86. (C.D.)

sation of agriculture and the monetisation of the rural economy to some extent. Trade should have caused a rise in the prices of those factors which were specific to agriculture. It should have also caused a fall in the prices of factors which are specific to industries which were threatened by the competition of machine-made products and came to have comparative disadvantage and had therefore to contract or be given up altogether. It also caused a rise in the prices of non-specific factors capable of alternative employments, for example in commerce, transportation and money-lending. Here the horizontal supply curve of labour in agriculture, for the greater part of the century, had prevented any relative rise in real earnings in agriculture. The fall in prices of factors specific to village industries had contributed to the agricultural surplus population. Thus, specialised and immobile groups of workers in the rural sector suffered heavy reductions in income. These conclusions are in line with those derived from the modern theory of international value.[1]

There is one significant aspect of India's economy in the nineteenth century which has not been discussed in this chapter viz. the Indo-American trade relations. Keeping in mind the nature of the basic source material as well was the popular belief that no such relations subsisted, worth talking about, it was thought best to deal with it under a separate chapter. This is done in the next one.

1. Ganguli, B. N. : Rethinking of Indian Economics, *Presidential address* at the 38th annual conference of Indian Economic Association.

CHAPTER VI

Facets of Indo-American Trade Relations in the Nineteenth Century

"...(an)...effort...to use such a source (American Consular Papers) to trace ...the economic condition of India in the nineteenth century....it has been one's effort to keep testing the Consular and other descriptions on the framework of such evidence as available...."

Introduction p. 9

The Backdrop

Talking of trade or commerce it might be helpful to make some formulations before an actual discussion is undertaken. The importance of a country's trade with another is a very relative affair. Especially, when one comes to such unchartered areas as Indo-American trade relations. The danger of underplaying the relationship is as much there, if not more than that of overplaying it. Some firm contours have to be kept in mind.

The importance of a country's trade may be in the mere bulk or value. It may also be in the needs of the people of the country as also the needs of other countries for the exports of a given country. What is to be remembered is that trade is basically founded on the principle of : "wherever a man might be, he should share in the productive advantage of all other men, wherever they might be." And for trade to advance and grow the population need not rise merely in number but in the average purchasing power also.

As has been pointed out earlier London was the metropolis of a whole complex of cities all round the world. Naturally in this context, as in other things also, British policy and its antecedents effected India's relationship towards other countries which included America. It might be pointed out here that England by no means imported only the things that it needed—a large part of eastern wares was transhipped in England and then exported to other European countries, so that the bullion was recovered from them. The American Declaration of Independence gave a major blow to this mercantilistic principle of English trade.

During this period (i.e. end of the 18th and the beginning of the 19th century) American ships carried nearly half of the commerce between the United States and Europe, in spite of the adverse policy of European states, designed to exclude American ships from commerce with them and with their colonies. Driven further afield by this policy, American shippers began to seek commercial connections with more distant countries, from where ware had reached them hitherto only through middlemen—and this is where India emerges on the scene. An American ship sailed for the first time to China in 1784[1]; in 1788 two ships

1. Toussaint, A. : *Mauritius Archives Publications* II, appendix 1. (Select documents)

were advertised as loading at Boston for the Isle France and India and "anybody wishing to adventure to that part of the world may have an opportunity of sending goods on freight."[1]

In the Indian sub-continent itself the natural result of measures like Pitts India Act was in course of time, indirectly to confer on the Board of Control nearly all those powers which were contemplated by Fox's measure, but possessing this great superiority, that it left the management of the commercial affairs of the Company in the hands of persons acquainted with success.[2] In spite of every effort made by the merchants of Liverpool to obtain an open trade the privileges and monopoly of the Company were extended for a period of thirty years. The Company however had lost their essential mercantile character.

For the survey of Indo-American trade relations during the period of study it might be best to chronologically divide it into segments of four and consider them all separately. These would be 1792-1833, 1834-1865, 1866-1880, 1881-1906.

1792-1833 : During the eighteenth century and a little after direct trade relations between the Indian sub-continent and the American region were not very intense. However, this is not necessarily an index of the actual nature of their trade relations. The complex around Madagascar, Mauritius, was as it were the link between the two areas and the 'exchange-house' of goods.[3] That it was so was merely because enough goods belonging to both regions were available there to make going yet further, in any meaningful way, absolutely superfluous.

Americans had been in contact with this area since an early date. Not only had Jolly Roger and others contact with Madagascar pirates but later on in the seventeenth century several ships of American origin are reported to have called here to take slaves.[4] This nature of contact continued with varying fortunes till about 1730 when the French settled firmly in this area around Mauritius and pirate activity declined. The Treaty of Amity

1. Quoted in, Day, Clive : *A History of Commerce*, p. 495.
2. Irving, B.A. : *The Commerce of India*, p. 228.
3. Gautam, Vinayshil : 'Aspects of the role of Isle de France in contacts between India and the United States of America between 1773-1810 "*proceedings volume*" thirtieth session of the Indian History Congress, 1968.
4. Johnson, Charles : *A general history of the pyrates from their first rise and settlement in the island of Providence to the present times*, p. iv, London, 1724.

and Commerce signed by France with the American colonists at the outbreak of the American War of Independence reopened Madagascar and the surrounding areas to American activity.

There was a lot of contact from the Indian side also with this area. There were persons whose whole business it was to carry goods between India and Isle de France. It is estimated that the number of arrivals in the ports of Isle de France rose to about 115 and that of clearances to nearly the same figure in about 1773. These figures continue to be the same till about 1788. They represent an average, and they were, of course, ups and downs e.g. in 1774 arrivals mounted to 283 and clearances to exactly the same figure, in 1781 the figures were 274 and 248 respectively and in 1786 only 180 and 141.[1]

Toussaint has estimated that ships known as *cabotuers* (i.e. ships engaged in the inter-island trade or the 'country trade' with India) represent about half the total number of arrivals.[2] Following the arithmetic of commerce it is easy to see the intensity of contact between India and Isle de France.

Presented with this background the role of Isle de France in contacts between India and the United States of America becomes clear. It was indeed the natural place for contacts.

There is a smooth rise in the contacts between America and Isle de France, which in our case would involve India also till around 1793—when news was received of the outbreak of war between England and France.

The Colonial Assembly which governed the island since 1790 was in the dark concerning the policy to be adopted towards neutral ships. But in August 1793 having learnt that during the previous month the British had seized French goods on board a Danish ship at Madras, it retaliated by confiscating enemy property found on all neutral ships calling at Port Louis. All American ships that arrived were consequently embargoed.[3]

The tension-fraught international situation was very evident in this region. Considerable portions of India were

1. Toussaint, A.: *Mauritius Archives Publications,* II, p. 1. (Select documents)

2. ibid, p. 1.

3. ibid, p. 8.

under the rule of British, Isle de France was under the stewardship of Britain's traditional enemy France and Americans were probing in the east with the legacy of being ex-British colonists and traditional friends of France, all these put together create the proper setting for the study of the contacts.

From April 1794 to July 1797 not less than 71[1] prize ships mainly British were brought into Port Louis by privateers. Americans thus easily got the Indian goods they wanted at Isle de France itself because these, captured as they were from English ships, were readily available. What was the need therefore to travel to India or for that matter even to China ? Not unnaturally Isle de France attracted citizens of the United States much more than places in the two latter mentioned regions—thus making it a convenient point of contact for India and the United States of America.

'So numerous and valuable were the prizes taken, and carried into the Isle de France, that the markets were overstocked with the manufactures and staple commodities of the British possessions in India.'[2] This description given in 1813 makes amply clear why some Americans took Isle de France as sufficiently important centre in its own right to make any journey to the Indian sub-continent less than meaningful. After all, the same goods were available in Isle de France which in the jargon of modern economics was indulging in 'switch trade.'

During this section of the period under survey Britons were aware of the role of the neutral shipping in spying on the movement of the British ships, consequently as time progressed they adopted a conciliatory attitude especially towards the Americans. On the whole, few of the American ships, engaged in the Isle de France trade were actually molested by British cruisers. Hence it is not difficult to see the real significance of United States of America in the affairs of India, the base for which was being provided by Isle de France.

Matters moved somewhat normally till April 1799. When news of the so-called Quasi-war between U.S.A. and France was received there, diplomatic relations were considerably strained

1. Toussaint, A.: *Mauritius Archives Publications*, II, p. 9. (Select documents)

2. Milburn, William : *Oriental Commerce : containing a geographical description of the principal places in the East Indies*. Vol. II, p. 569.

and the functions of the American Consul were suspended. However diplomatic efforts soon restored the cordial relations. In 1799-1800 only 8 American ships called at Isle de France, 19 in 1801 and 46 in 1802.[1] This thinned the Indo-American contact also.

The year 1803 is a notable point in the history of this role of Isle de France as a point of contact between India and the United States of America. It is well known that in and around this period Napoleon came into his own in France. His power not being marine based he found it difficult to attack England directly. He, consequently, thought of a new device of ruining England by ruining her trade. Thus was conceived the Continental System. By Berlin decrees he sought to enforce a blockade of the British Isle and forbade all commerce with the English. Naturally all this had its effect on the role that Isle de France had been playing uptill now.

As can be imagined the role of neutral shipping rose at once. The American ships fell under this category. It is estimated that they carried nearly half the commerce between the United States and Europe and a considerable portion of trading beyond Europe in the east was done through them. In fact, the period between 1804-1807 was of intense contact between the United States of America and Isle de France, with the number of arrivals sometimes being as high as two a week.[2] Much of the contact saw its reflection in trade with India also. It was not unnatural therefore for Englishmen, especially in India, to look upon Americans with suspicion. The previous vigil[3] on their behaviour was tightened and a policy of being on the watch which had been adopted sometime back was more rigorously implemented. There was every possibility of Isle de France being used as a base of operations by persons of anti-English sentiment.

Though there is little direct corroborative evidence on paper but circumstantially one thing is clear, grown wiser by their bitter experiences in the Western hemisphere the English

1. Toussaint, A. : *Mauritius Archives Publications*, II, pp. 75-76. (Select documents)

2. ibid, pp. 78-85.

3. Home Department, Public, O.C. 31 Jan., 1794 No. 9. N.A.I.

were increasingly worried about the potential and possible use of Isle de France as a base for hostile activity. In particular, the harbouring of Americans in Isle de France must have been particularly galling to them. This hole had to be plugged. And though externally no animosity was shown to the Americans the English seem to be determined after this period to annex Isle de France. There is a chequered record of events and documents which prove the English expectancy of the surrender of the island.[1] However, the final capitulation of the island took place only on the 3rd of December, 1810.

Hence the role of Isle de France as a point of contact between India and the United States of America can be said to be on the wane after around 1808. Yet so long as it lasted it seems difficult to deny the great international significance it had.

After 1808, of course, England used Mauritius as an advanced outpost for Indian trade and it was geared to British Indian interests. American interests there were no longer as well looked after as before.

However what is obvious is that Isle de France and its surrounding region because of its geographical location and various other factors had come to occupy a very significant place so far as the Indo-American trade relations were concerned between the year 1773-1810.

It is to be noted that for the larger part of this period there was no American Consular representation in India, nevertheless trade continued. Perhaps because of the peculiar nature of the contacts as enumerated above there was no real need for such representation.

The trade with the United States during the remaining part of this period continued to preserve some slight activity, although it materially declined from the scale to which it had once risen.

In 1818-19 the value of the imports was ninety-five Lacs of rupees and as late as 1822-23 they merely exceeded 50. In 1827-28 they were not much more than twenty-one lacs.[2] The

1. Foreign Department, Secret, Const. 31 Oct., 1809 No. 2. N.A.I.

2. Wilson, Horace Hayman : *A Review of the External Commerce of Bengal* (1830), p. 83.

only explanation to this lies in the internal condition[1] of the United States of America.

Furthermore the natural and artificial products of North America were not in request in India, and the import cargoes were made up of a variety of articles obtained from other countries, none of them of any amount except the Metals. Copper in 1827-28 was imported to the extent of one Lac and forty-six thousand rupees. Wine, Spirits, Cordage and Timber formed the most valuable portion of the remaining merchandise but the main article was always treasure. Thus in 1818-19 of the ninety-five Lacs worth of import, ninety were in Bullion and in 1829 the proportion was 17 to 21. It was chiefly in the form of Spanish and North American Dollars. The latter was worse than the former, being commonly about 7 dwts. worse than Calcutta Standard at which rate and at the usual weight, 100 would bear a mint price of about Rs. 205.14.[2]

During the years 1813-14, cotton piece goods formed one of the principal article of export of India. In 1816-17 their value was nearly thirty-six Lacs of rupees. But subsequently they were superseded here as everywhere else, partly by British and partly by North American fabrics, and amounted in 1827-28 to less than twenty-two thousand rupees. Silk piece goods entered somewhat largely into the exports of 1820s, although they subsequently fell off, being about fourteen Lacs in 1821-22 but four in 1826-27.[3] During the season that Bengal Cotton was largely exported, the Americans bore their share, the Bengal Cotton being mixed with their own and then re-shipped for London market. This article of trade subsequently ceased for many years.

Around the late twenties the Indigo trade showed signs of further decline. The recent tariff imposed heavy and annually augmenting duties, with a view to encourage the home manufacture, which was said to be successfully prosecuted in some parts of the United States. The contemporary (towards the early 30s) high prices of Indigo, artificially elevated by remit-

1. See Chapter II.

2. Wilson, Horace Hayman : *A Review of the External Commerce of Bengal* (1830), p. 84.

3. ibid, p. 84.

tance capital, was an additional inducement to the American to cultivate the Indigo plant, and a competition with them could easily have had ruinous consequences for Indian Indigo.[1]

The following tables would serve to give some idea of Indo-American exchanges during the period.

Bullion imported[2]

	From Great Britain (Son. Rs.)	From America
1813-14	32750	—
1814-15	525127	—
1815-16	1142596	4793886
1816-17	1859853	5288929
1817-18	6157981	5799449
1818-19	1216159	9059375
1819-20	15455480	4596510
1820-21	3014421	2728519
1821-22	1647458	5051178
1822-23	170758	5007652
1823-24	524032	1352331
1824-25	13250	1802632
1825-26	156978	3318210
1826-27	20180	964640
1827-28	73620	1721217

1. Wilson, Horace Hayman : *A Review of the External Commerce of Bengal* (1830), p. 84.

2. From : Wilson, Horace Hayman: *A Review of the External Commerce of Bengal* (1830), pp. 2-3 of tables.

Bullion exported[1]

	To Great Britain (Son. Rs.)	To America
1813-14	—	—
1814-15	—	—
1815-16	—	—
1816-17	—	—
1817-18	—	—
1818-19	—	—
1819-20	—	—
1820-21	4106	—
1821-22	11013500	—
1822-23	5460	—
1823-24	4414340	—
1824-25	269466	—
1825-26	48	4000
1826-27	378032	—
1827-28	4165699	—

1. From : Wilson, Horace Hayman : *A Review of the External Commerce of Bengal* (1830), pp. 2-3 of tables.

Import General[1]

	From Great Britain (Son. Rs.)	From America
1813-14	5376775	—
1814-15	4099165	—
1815-16	5752886	222768
1816-17	8051112	967099
1817-18	13562962	1149890
1818-19	15944495	503434
1819-20	8633573	132278
1820-21	11320797	159655
1821-22	15163826	290477
1822-23	18098611	243013
1823-24	15862534	113824
1824-25	11607786	307675
1825-26	12868606	374661
1826-27	12858348	199345
1827-28	18991756	454612

1. From : Wilson, Horace Hayman : *A Review of the External Commerce of Bengal* (1830), p. 4 of tables.

Export General[1]

	From Great Britain (Son. Rs.)	From America
1813-14	11963405	—
1814-15	12142283	—
1815-16	16444208	4421435
1816-17	13806966	5998251
1817-18	16912905	4891053
1818-19	13872325	7026531
1819-20	22432795	4586438
1820-21	20729084	1925079
1821-22	18968752	3853416
1822-23	24229515	3063019
1823-24	22840796	1225000
1824-25	26461457	2289719
1825-26	29810895	2610785
1826-27	24745131	664318
1827-28	30420250	1687548.

1834-1865 : During this period as in the earlier one the Americans continued to make good profit by undertaking 'carrying trade'.

Gradually as internal problems[2] resolved themselves and preoccupation with Western Hemisphere ended the Consulates were sought to be re-established in India also. But at the beginning of this period the Eastern sector of the world was getting to be a difficult one. And even where Consulates were re-established, because of the suspension of trade generally at the British East India presidencies, because of their difficulties with China, the American Consul at Bombay found his plans for mercantile transactions entirely frustrated. He was without any business whatsoever to detain him at Bombay and he decided to retire to Zanzibar having appointed an American resident by the name

1. From : Wilson, Horace Hayman : *A Review of the External Commerce of Bengal* (1830), p. 6 of tables.
2. See Chapter II.

of E. A. Webster to act as Vice Commercial Agent in his place. There was no difficulty with respect to this as he was only to be recognized by the Bombay Government as a commercial agent.[1]

The opinion of P. S. Parker while departing seems significant for he suggested to the Secretary of the State that from the small amount of American trade at Bombay, it appeared that a Consular establishment was unnecessary for its better protection. Further, that if a Consular station was desired at Bombay it would require to be filled up by some other person than one who devotes his time solely to mercantile affairs. With these sentiments he tendered his resignation on Jan. 1, 1840, from the post to which he had been appointed in October 1838.[2]

This however was no reflection on the Indo-American contacts[3] for the period, because around 1830s or so the East India Company were making experiments, seeking to introduce the American cotton as well as an improved system of cultivation in India. The latter was being expressly attempted with the help of Americans who had been induced to enter the service of the East India Company for that very purpose.

The avowed object of this movement was such an improvement in the breed of Indian cotton as would together with its greater cheapness enable it to command the markets and supply the demands of English manufactures to the exclusion of all foreign grown cotton. This was a part of the great plan of improving the cultivation of India by the introduction of the Mauritius sugar-cane, American cotton etc. This was an all out attempt to make the returns of the cultivation better; the Company also stood to gain by this because if the returns of the cultivation went up so would the revenue.[4]

The shrewd American as a third person on the scene saw through the game and observed, "the manufactures of India it is not the interest of the Government to protect or encourage,

1. Parker, P. S. in a letter to the Secretary of State, U.S., Bombay, dated Jan. 1, 1840. (B.D.)

2. ibid.

3. And so long as this continued there was bound to be some measure of trade between the two countries.

4. See Vol. 1. (B.D.)

as the revenue is derived from a tax on the soil, in some cases amounting to three-fifths of its produce. The plan of the Company is simply to make India the producing and England the manufacturing country."[1]

The policy of Continental Europe in encouraging their manufactures compelled the British Government to that course, as by the greater cheapness of French and German manufactures those of England could not on equal terms compete and it was only by securing the command of the markets of India that they were to keep this trade to themselves. The Americans had already the whole trade in coarse cottons on the western coast of Africa to themselves and from the Cape of Good Hope to the mouth of the Indus and English vessels could not dispose of a piece of that description of goods if an American vessel was in port, and even in the ports of India to which they had access the Americans began to trade to a considerable extent in coarse cloths even under the disadvantages of 7 per cent duties while British cotton paid a mere $3\frac{1}{2}$. In 1839 the Indian tariff was revised and American cotton goods were made to pay 14 per cent. But even this did not stop the importation of some kinds of goods, and on the first of January, 1841, a tariff valuation was placed on this sort of goods, of more than 40 per cent above what they were sold for in this market, and upon this advanced value 14 per cent duties were required to be paid for all cotton goods which were the manufacture of foreign countries.[2]

It is significant to note that immediately after the arrival of the planters from America the acting American Consul in Bombay made acquaintance with them and subsequently continued to correspond with them when they went to Broach, in the heart of the best cotton growing area at the mouth of river Narbuda.[3]

Soon the Consul at Bombay was to hear from them. In their letter they stated that three hundred acres of cotton which

1. Webster, E.A. in a letter to the Secretary of State, U.S., Bombay dated July 1, 1841. (B.D.)

2. Vice Consul, U.S. (Bombay Port) in a communication to the department of State, U.S., Bombay, dated July 1, 1841. (B.D.)

3. notice, ibid.

they had planted were looking as well as any they ever saw in America and they were going to plant another 100 acres as soon as the rains became lighter. They were confident of being able to raise as good cotton in Gujarat as can be grown in the United States except the Sea Island variety.

Yet because of discouragements of over-taxation, want of capital and implements for cultivating and clearing the crop after it was grown the Americans feared that the indigenous people would never be able to do it on their own.[1]

There were other difficulties also,[2] an extract from a letter from *Agra Ukhbar* on the operations in the Bundelkhand district also helps to make some very interesting points, as to how a scheme can be grandly conceived but poorly executed:

"The necessary cattle, the pivot upon which the whole undertaking turns, for without an efficient team it is impossible to begin to perform, properly, so highly an artificial cultivation as that of the American culture of cotton, more especially in the level plains of this region, where one of the greatest desiderata is to throw up a sufficient ridge to raise the cotton out of the water, in the heavy rains of the monsoon. Such cattle have not been furnished to them........"[3]

This further substantiates the hypothesis that Government sought to make India the producing country and England the manufacturing country.

There is little direct information available about Indo-American trade relations during the late forties and the early fifties of the nineteenth century but it can safely be presumed that the earlier trends carried on during this period also.

1. Webster, E.A. in a letter to the Secretary of State, U.S.A., Bombay, dated October 1, 1841. (B.D.)

2. As Mr. Finnie, one of the American cotton planters in charge of the Government Plantation at Kootsamuckeundpoor, on the banks of the Jamuna wrote to the Bombay Times, "Cotton can be produced cheaper here than in any other part of the world....India possesses a soil and climate admirably adapted for its cultivation—with abundant and cheap labour—England is ready to furnish capital—America has already provided (it is to be hoped) skill and experience—and it only requires the two latter to be brought to bear on the former to realise the most sanguine anticipations of those with whom this great national undertaking—experiment can pronounce it no longer—originated...we have received indeed everything requisite for a commencement except—aye, except a rower sufficient to break up the ground—which single exception is tantamount to having received nothing at all......" Bombay Times. (B.D.)

3. *Agra Ukhbar*, Jan. 12, 1840.

During the year 1859, 111 American ships visited Calcutta against 147 in 1858 and 159 in 1857. This was a great diminution in the aggregate of tonnage but could be accounted for by the fact that during the previous years many ships had been laid up and that a small number of American ships were being employed in carrying goods to English ports. During the year 1859, 95 ships carrying an aggregate of 161665 tonnes of goods had found cargoes from Calcutta to U.S. against 90 ships and 135469 tonnes of 1858, which also showed a large increase[1] in the amount of imports during the year, principally in the articles of piece goods and tobacco.

Americans had then two steamers each of about 500 tonnes burden plying upon the river Hooghly and a third was expected. These were principally owned by Americans and provided a profitable steam flotilla offering inducements to American capitalists. It is to be noted that the rate of freight between Calcutta and Allahabad, a distance of about 800 miles, was far greater than paid by a voyage round the Cape of Good Hope, being at the rate of $ 35 per ton.[2]

However the slavery question was soon to errupt into a Civil War in the United States of America. And this would not only very seriously affect the Indo-American trade adversely but would also raise problems of an unprecedented nature.

"There are a number of American ships trading between this port and ports in the southern states of our Union. Some of them are owned in Charlestown, New Orleans, I am informed that one of the latter is expected to arrive here in the course of a few months and that she carries a Register and sails under the flag adopted by the so-called Confederate States of America.

Under the state of feeling which exists here amongst the ship masters and other American citizens I fear that the arrival of a ship thus registered and under such flag would be the signal for violence to the ship, her officers and crew. As I am entirely destitute of instructions from you in such a case should it arise, I have to request that you will supply the deficiency at the earliest practicable moment."[3]

1. Vice Consul General for U.S. in a letter to the Secretary of State, U.S., Calcutta, dated Jan. 22, 1860. (C.D.)

2. Despatch no. 3, Vol. V. (C.D.)

3. Consul General of U.S. in a communication to the Secretary of State, U.S., Calcutta, dated July 1, 1861.

As instructions could be received from U.S. legation at London, much sooner than from Washington the Consul General also addressed a despatch to Hon. Mr. Adams, Minister to the court of St. James hoping that he might help in information or instruction in matters of this kind.

"Should a case of arrival of a ship under a Register and flag such as I have described arise I should in the absence of instructions treat her as an American ship and proceed under the view of non recognition of secession and the government formed under it.

Please instruct me whether I am at liberty to clear ships for the ports of the Southern States which newspaper accounts report in a state of blockade but of which no official information has been received by me."[1]

During this period commerce with the U.S. could be considered as extinct. No shipment of merchandise was taking place, nor there was any order in India to purchase or immediately expected by the American merchants. In 1864, four of American ships had been in the Calcutta port for months unable to obtain freight or business. Three of them unfortunately being destroyed in the terrible storm which swept over Bengal on 5 October 1864.[2] It is significant that this condition of American commercial relations with India was not something exclusive for this country but was a world-wide phenomenon. The world over American commerce was ruined, American vessels destroyed or compelled to resort to a flag, foreign, if not unfriendly for protection.[3] Naturally during these years, the British action round the world was more suspect than ever in U.S. eyes, and the U.S. Consul in India had repeatedly to assure the State department of the bona fides of his reports and the actual behaviour of the English.

In fact the quarterly reports of this period are full of the description of the depressed state of American commerce and American interest in Calcutta because of the troubles in the United States.[4]

1. Consul General of U.S. in a communication to the Secretary of State, U.S., Calcutta, dated July 1, 1861.
2. Consul General of U.S. in a communication to the department of State, U.S., Calcutta, Dec. 3, 1864. (C.D.)
3. ibid.
4. Despatch no. 9, Vol. 6. (C.D.)

However the Consul General reported that all the American citizens in Calcutta were unanimous in their loyalty to the Government.

In the early sixties a progressive increase both of exports and imports to and from the different countries of the globe had occurred with the exception of the United States. The exception was evidently due to the Civil War. The financial changes and revulsions attendant upon the consequent of the rebellion there had a correlative effect on business operations in India. Orders and Credits were withdrawn or withheld, purchase and shipments to a corresponding extent decreased. An unexpected phase of the Rebellion and one also most materially affecting American commerce was the appearance of piratical steamers on high seas, issuing out of, repairing to and refitting in British ports, whenever stress of weather, shortness of supplies or the appearance of a United States Vessel of War rendered it advisable or necessary. Several of American vessels with valuable cargoes engaged in the Indian trade were captured and destroyed by freebooters, merchants and shipowners were thus compelled to relinquish a business, the persisting in which would certainly ruin.[1]

Freights for the same reason declined to rates merely nominal. Heretofore, to the different ports of Asia, Australia, England and the Continent American vessels because of good skill and energy of their masters and the comparative quickness of their voyages had the preference.[2] But at the height of the American Civil War there were a number in port unengaged and charters with great difficulty, if at all, would be concluded for them.

American Pork, Beef, Flour and other agricultural products sold slowly and only in small quantities in Indian market, for India then like America produced more food than its inhabitants could consume. Naval stores now came from the North of Europe, being with drills and heavy sheetings too scarce and valuable in the United States for exportation. Plug tobacco was still imported, but because of bad quality and enhanced price in comparative small quantity. Kerosene oil had recently been

1. Annual Consular report for 1862-63, Vol. 6. (C.D.)
2. ibid.

introduced and as there were no religious scruples interfering with its use, was bound to make its way into general favour. Pine Mast, and Boards with Mahagonny, Ice and Copper composed the majority of American imports.[1] The value of American export was in excess and the balance was met by Bills of Exchange on London.

The few American residents in Calcutta were engaged as shipping and commission merchants as the successful prosecution of the business required. Yet there was little outlay of private capital[2], so there was but a trifling amount permanently invested in India.

It was naturally to be expected that the security upon the seas and peace in America would at once increase the value and extent of American commerce with India.

1866-1880

The period between 1866-1880 is an important one in the nineteenth century Indo-American trade relations also because in the preceding period the two polities had passed through great convulsions causing a fresh analysis if not a realignment of the fundamental norms governing the respective polities. As has been noticed the Civil War in America had been of considerable strain on United States economy in more senses than merely what a war normally is. Areas of traditional trade value were lost to the U.S. interest and goods such as cotton which had earlier stood well in the English markets were considerably edged out by the Egyptian and the Indian cotton. As compared to that 1857 had caused comparatively little dent on this (Indian) sub-continent's external trade. Perhaps this was because the healing capacity of the British Empire was considerably more than that of a comparatively new born, expanding nation which had to pass through a second Revolution to stabilise itself.

For one thing Bombay as a commercial centre of the sub-continent came to its own for the first time during this period. More and more of the produce of the Western Sea Board was directed towards this port of call and the opening

1. Consul General of U.S. in a communication to the department of State, U.S., Calcutta, dated Sept. 30, 1863.
2. ibid.

of the Suez Canal did all that was needed to give stability to the growing stature of Bombay. It is of little surprise therefore to notice Benjamin Tarnham the American Consul at Bombay not only commenting on the growing importance of Bombay but also using the plank for advancing some of his personal claims. He wrote to his headquarters: "I have the honour to inform you that this Consulate is rapidly growing in importance and as Bombay is now the commercial metropolis of all India, it appears to me that I should come under the head of 'salaried consuls' with permission to do other business. When the Inspector of Consulates was here sometime since I made known to him the fact I am now stating to you. I enclose the list of American ships now in harbour and also list those on the way due in about a month; you will perceive by this list that the Consular appointment can be no sinecure. I think the salary with permission to transact business should be $ 6000 per annum......[1] It is another matter that his recommendations were neither accepted nor did they receive due attention at the hands of the State department.

In terms of the actual volume of trade there was some hope during this period that the export of Linseed would go up but like the export of Wool it failed to register a rise. The following table relevant to the export of Linseed to the U.S.A. may serve to give an idea.[2]

Year	Cwt
1864	488,769
1865	300,257
1866	130,963
1867	127,788
1868	169,690
1869	99,348
1870	75,883
1871	295,255

1. American Consul in a despatch to the department of State, U.S., Bombay, dated August 7, 1866. (B.D.)

2. American Consul in a despatch to the department of State, U.S., Bombay, dated April 10, 1876. (B.D.)

In the case of both Linseed and Wool the extremely restrictive import duties imposed by the United States were responsible for the decline of the export of this item to America. The restrictions were, of course, placed with the understandable intention of boosting America's home industry. The U.S. Consul at Bombay had reported that, "Linseed grown in the western states of America appears to be driving East India Linseed from the American market which evidently cannot bear an import duty of 20 cent per bushel."[1] About Wool too in 1876 of the 6442 bales export, not one went to the United States.[2] But it would be incorrect to surmise from this that the Volume of Indo-American trade was either going down or that this period is to be noted for a lull in this trade relations. Kerosene Oil import from U.S. for one kept on steadily rising. The following table worked out from the Bombay despatches of November 12, 1877, October 30, 1879 and July 5, 1880 will serve to give some idea of the merchandise and treasure imported to India from U.S. and also help in comparing it to the import of some of the other countries.

	England	Italy	France	U.S.A.
	Rs.	Rs.	Rs.	Rs.
1874-75	115,302,913	949,836	775,163	664,574
1875-76	115,617,707	3,031,752	2,181,264	581,938
1876-77	156,727,279	117,225,695	2,447,557	609,474
1877-78	194,968,783	1,972,161	1,632,579	1,192,286

As can be seen the lull in years '75-'77 was more than undone and in '77-'78 America ranked above both Italy and France in terms of the total value of merchandise imported to India. Some items, as Panchanand Misra rightly points out, were also imported to India *via* England.[3]

In his article in the *Journal of Indian History*, however, Panchanand Misra has pointed out that the Government of India bore a hostile attitude towards the U.S. Consuls.[4] Even

1. American Consul in a despatch to the department of State, U.S., Bombay, dated November 12, 1877. (B.D.)

2. ibid.

3. Misra, P., 'Indo-American Trade Relations 1866-1880'. *Journal of Indian History*, Vol. XLIII, Part III, pp. 763-69.

4. ibid, p. 764.

if this statement be taken to mean that the Government was unsympathetic and unhelpful to the American needs and interests it does not appear a plausible one. The case of the collision between the French vessel *Antares* and the American vessel *Augusta*[1] which he quotes at certain length and where

1. Misra, P., 'Indo-American Trade Relations 1866-1880'. *Journal of Indian History*, Vol. XLIII, Part III. The case as Dr. Misra quotes is as follows: "...The High Court was interfering in cases which did not occur in Indian waters and wherein neither a British nor an Indian citizen was involved. Thus, complaining to the Governor of Bombay, Benjamin Tarnham wrote:

"I request to have to call your attention to the seizure of the American ship *Augusta* while lying in this harbour. The seizure has been made in the name of Her Most Gracious Majesty the Queen by an order of the High Court of Bombay. This seizure in my humble opinion is contrary to the Law of Nations and was made without trial, even of the question of jurisdiction by the Consul here, while, as I am informed, it was apparent in the plaint before which process was issued that the High Court had set jurisdiction in the matter. The pretext for this seizure is that during the passage out of Rio de Janerio, a French Barque called the *Antares* came into collision with the *Augusta* whereby the French vessel was disabled so that it is supposed she foundered at sea, the *Augusta* bringing on to Bombay the Captain and crew of the French vessel. I have yet to learn what authority the High Court of Bombay or any British jurisdiction has to interfere. I shall report this seizure to the Government I have the honour to represent and I trust you will use your authority to remove the Court's sepoys from the deck of the ship *Augusta* and allow this ship to be free. Already this seizure of the ship *Augusta* has lost her a character of five thousand pounds sterling. I do not know what steps may be necessary to take in future in regard to this seizure, but I have confidence that you will act promptly in this matter as your judgment may dictate". (Bombay Consular despatches, April 4, 1873.) The Secretary to the Government of Bombay replied, however, that "the Government is not at liberty to interfere with action of the High Court in such cases". (Bombay Consular despatch No. 182, 1873.) Benjamin Tarnham further called to the Governor's attention "the fact that the owners of the *Augusta* will practically have no remedy against the owners and master of the *Antares* for the damages that have been and will be sustained by reason to the seizure of the *Augusta* or for the costs of appearing under protest in the High Court. The High Court has not thought fit before issuing its process to take security for costs, the only person in Bombay liable for such and for the damages is the master of the *Antares* who from motives of humanity was brought to this port by the master of the *Augusta* and who has no property but the clothes on his back. Under all the circumstances I must respectfully reserve to the Government I have the honour to represent such action as it may think fit to adopt for the protection of its citizens, the owners of the *Augusta*, from the loss they will sustain by the illegal seizure of their vessel and for the wrong done to the

he suggests the unreasonableness of the Bombay High Court is not enough to justify such a conclusion. Minor irritants such as this are often known to happen even amongst countries with very pleasant diplomatic relations and certainly so in the days of distances as in the middle of the nineteenth century. The Bombay High Court's attitude need not necessarily reflect a studied policy of the Government of India and in this respect it was more likely just a whim of a judge. The fact remains that the volume of Indo-American trade does not reflect any reservations on the part of the Government of India towards America. To get a more exact picture of the incidence of Indo-American trade the following table will also be useful :

American Shipping that arrived in Calcutta[1]

Year	No. of Vessels	Total Tonnage
1866	45	41,316
1867	36	35,424
1868	58	55,458
1869	41	41,751
1870	40	43,954
1871	31	34,017
1872	53	61,310
1873	39	41,532
1874	28	28,997
1875	34	40,049
1876	30	33,151
1877	42	50,898
1878	25	31,019
1879	18	23,481
1880	23	28,816

American flag by the assumption of jurisdiction in this matter by Her Majesty's High Court. (Bombay Consular despatches, April 7, 1873.) The United States Government, however, did not take any action and the owners of the *Augusta* appointed Tarnham to fight the case in the Privy Council (Bombay Consular despatches, April 10, 1876)" pp. 764-65.

1. Calcutta Consulate in a communication to the department of State, U.S., Calcutta, dated Feb. 6, 1882. (C.D.)

This table, when processed with others shows, that there was a diversion of American ships from the port of Calcutta to Bombay and the old pattern of reaching India through the Pacific became less popular than that of reaching it through the Atlantic.

The following table shows the rise in the shipping of some European countries at Calcutta.[1]

	1859-60		1880-81	
	No.	Tons	No.	Tons
Britain	2,585	1,158,790	3,629	2,826,908
Germany	68	36,544	61	56,788
Italy	9	3,732	62	65,267
Norwegian	2	748	27	23,706

Summarising, therefore, trade with British India between 1860 and 1880, the Secretary of State, U.S.A. observed:[2]

"While the exports from the United States to India during the fiscal year 1879 amounted to about the same as the export of the year 1860, the imports into the United States from India during 1879 amount to $ 13,334,00 more than the imports therefrom in 1860. Thus it may be said that in volume our present trade with India is about equal to that of twenty years ago. But, outside of volume, this trade has undergone much change in those twenty years—all unfavourable to the United States.

In 1860 our total export to India and almost our total imports therefrom were carried in American vessels. In 1879 only a little over one-half of our exports to India and one-third our imports therefrom were carried in American vessels. The great disadvantage under which our commerce labours, in this connection, is very forcibly shown by the following extract from Consul General Litchfield's report.

'Present indications are that trade with the United States during this year will be larger than ever before. During the month of October (1879) freights to New York suddenly rose from $ 4.25 to $ 12.50 per ton, and, at one time, eighteen large iron ships, all British, were loading (at Calcutta) for that port,

1. Calcutta Consular despatches, 1880-81, p. 177.
2. ibid, 1879, p. 73.

while there were but three American ships in port at the time—a sad comment on the present condition of our merchant marine.' "[1] By and large the assessment appears coherent and acceptable.

1881-1906

Exports : The years preceding 1881 were unsettled years. What with the Afghan war or the Rumpa Rebellion in which the British had trouble with the Santhals, the general prosperity of commercial conditions, did not necessarily signify a peaceful condition all round.

Wheat : The profitable shipment of wheat depended not only upon short supplies in England from the United States, when the English harvests were deficient but also upon rates of freight and exchange.[2] It was a speculative trade and would fluctuate greatly from year to year. Its consumption in the country was limited to better classes, Rice always forming the staple food of the lower classes. The reports of the Government of India during this period speak in hopeful terms of the future of Indian wheat trade, while conceding that the general impression abroad appeared to be that the United States and Canada will be able to supply all Europe with wheat at prices which will defy competition.[3]

Coffee : In spite of an increasing cultivation of the crop the export remained more or less constant, this was because of the fact that the consumption in India among all classes was increasing year by year. The area under cultivation around 1880 was 384,198 acres.[4] The quality of the better grade of coffee from the Madras Presidency to which its cultivation was then confined compared favourably with that of Java and other coffees. The estates were owned and managed not by companies but by private European and native firms and individuals, and the results of investments were usually very remunerative. So to cite a typical case the quantity exported during

1. Calcutta Consular despatches, 1879, p. 73.
2. Report on the trade and navigation of Bengal and whole of British India, Vol. 12. (C.D.)
3. Despatch no. 352, Vol. 12. (C.D.)
4. ibid.

the year 1879/80 was 40,231,856 lbs. of which but little went to U.S.A. directly[1], though probably quite a quantity of Indian Coffee found a way into the American market via England, under different names when high values were ruling.

Tea : Very often the reduced value compared with the largely increased quantity showed the great fall in price which occurred often enough because of an overstocked London market.[2] The year 1880 was one of great anxiety to the trade and a serious crisis in the industry was feared by many. To alleviate the situation, attempts were made, with moderate success to introduce the Indian Tea into Australia. By the same token a syndicate of producers and agents for producers was formed in Calcutta for the introduction of Indian Tea not only into Australia but in a reinforced way also in America and Canada.

"Indian Tea differed from China in that it must be infused and not steeped, the latter method spoiling its good qualities. When this fact is generally understood by our people it will doubtless be appreciated in the United States as in England, and the consumption is bound to increase rapidly", wrote the American Consul at Calcutta to the Secretary of State.[3]

Oil seeds : Through the third quarter of the nineteenth century year by year less attention seemed to be paid to the cultivation of seeds, and the exports appeared to fall off gradually. The crop appeared to be relatively less and less remunerative than others, and the area under cultivation was smaller year by year. Less demand from the United States for Linseed, the most important of seeds, resulted in lower prices in India and while extremely sensitive to a strong or sudden demand in most articles, American markets rarely showed any marked fluctuation in the prices of seeds.

In oils the principal trade was in castor Oil which went largely to Australia and Liverpool. Trade to the United States in that article was very trifling by 1880-81.

Tobacco : Attempts were being made to improve the quality of Tobacco also. And although the quality of Indian

1. Report on the trade and navigation of Bengal and whole of British India, Vol. 12. (C.D.)
2. ibid.
3. ibid.

Tobacco had greatly increased the prejudice for American Tobacco in the last quarter of the nineteenth century was very strong and the Indian could be very easily distinguished from it.

Cotton : In and around 1880 the price goods trade in this country was undergoing a change in favour of the local weaving industry. This was because the indigenous cloth was cotton cloth and not a mixture of cotton and clay. As such it appeared to be a favourable time to push the sale of Indian goods.[1]

Yet at the same time with a decided superiority in quality on the part of American goods, it was by no means an easy matter to meet the preferences of the actual consumers. While in India as it happened the British importers and the indigenous middle-men were almost always able to dictate to the poor consumer what he should wear.

In the year 1878-79 England exported to British India 32,477,722 pounds of cotton yarns, valued in India at the time of entry at Rs. 27,069,054.

The portion of these yarns imported into the Bengal rural districts was 13,091,144 lbs. and the value Rs. 10,497,680.[2]

A very small portion of the yarn imported was what was known as "water twist" say about 120 Bales of No. 20s but of No. 30s throsttle spun about 250/300 Bales and about 100 Bales of No. 20s. These low counts of foreign manufacture could not compete with the local mills and imports were falling off.[3] And this too became a factor in Indo-American cotton trade balance.

General : It is curious to note that while India produced a superior quality of tea and a fair article of coffee, yet for some reason neither was much exported to the United States.[4] For the greater part of this period, the balance of trade between the two countries was largely in favour of India. The American Consulate in India was naturally seized with this problem and wanted to alter this in favour of America.

This balance of trade in favour of India vis-a-vis America was natural, because Europe with its steam ships plying through

1. Despatch no. 304, Vol. 12. (C.D.)
2. Report on the condition of the trade of cotton yarns and manufactures in India, Vol. 12. (C.D.)
3. ibid.
4. Despatch no. 36, Vol. 14. (C.D.)

the direct route of Suez Canal, supplemented by the cheap labour could furnish India with goods and wares of nearly every description, especially textile fabrics on more favourable terms than they could be procured from the United States.[1]

Maybe the American policy of protection of home manufactures had something to do with the lower quality of the American products. In open competition the quality has to be constantly raised for the article to survive. But in reality the question of tariff in the United States did not seem to have crystallized into any definite form to merit a serious discussion.

The production of fisheries was unimportant except for local consumption.[2] The forests of India were carefully preserved by the government and its teak was even then valuable as a hard wood somewhat close to be American black Wallnut. It was extensively used for building purposes as well as in the manufacture of furniture. The fragrant sandal wood was extensively used in the manufacture of ornamental boxes and cabinet ware and some of it did find its way to U.S.

Following is a list (alphabetically arranged) of the declared export to the United States from the Consular districts during fiscal year ending June 30, 1887.[3] (There were no export to the United States of any consequence from the Consular agencies subordinate to the Calcutta Consulate General except small quantities of hides and skins from Madras.)

Cinchona, coal, coffee, cocoa-nuts; coir, cotton & cotton twist and yarn, grain, pulse, rice, wheat, ivory, opium, sugar, tea, tobacco, teak, sandal, ebony wool. There is another export list available which has the following items listed:

Rubber, the quality of which article was deteriorating from year to year, checking any increase in the trade, Ginger, Turmine, Nuxvomica, Assafortida, Castor-Oil, Myrabolams, Safflower, Redwood, Bamboos, Woollen Rugs, Sursucker, an occasional shipment of rice.[4] These two put together would contain all the major exports for the period from India to the United States.

1. Despatch no. 36, Vol. 13. (C.D.)
2. ibid.
3. Consul General of U.S. in a communication to the department of State, U.S., Calcutta, dated Nov. 8, 1887. (C.D.)
4. Report on the trade and navigation of Bengal and the whole of British India, Vol. 2. (C.D.)

Imports: When the period of one's study opens one notices that the import of goods from the United States amounted in value to $ 1963,392 against $ 2,105,047 of the previous year (1879-80)[1]. The decrease was due to the falling off in grey and coloured cotton piece goods, rosin, ice, fruits and timber, however, Kerosene oil kept up a lively trade and 9½ million gallons, valued at $ 1,817,780 were received from America[2] during the year and the prospect seemed then, excellent for an immense increase in the immediate future.

While this was the shape of American Kerosene imports to India at the beginning of the period, for the better understanding of the place of this particular item in the general setting of Indian imports it would be helpful to take a composite picture.

The total importation to India during the year ending March 31,1881 amounted to more than 200 million dollars, being an increase of 20 per cent over the previous year; and out of this and 165 millions or more than 82 per cent came from Great Britain and only $ 1,963,392 or less than 1 per cent from the United States, and nearly all or $ 18,17,780 of this was from Kerosene oil leaving only the insignificant sum of $ 145,612[3] or less than one in a thousand of the general merchandise from the United States. It is true that then some American goods were imported via England by British merchants but this also proves that the market in India was not receiving the attention[4] which it merited from the American businessmen themselves.

A large field of potential market, for American goods in cheap watches and clocks, kerosene lamps, small and cheap mechanic tools of every description, electroplated goods, weighing scales, cabinets, organs, piances, sewing machines, stand patent medicines, Yanku notions, Chromopictures, paper and stationery, tobacco, umbrellas, was therefore going untapped. The success which the American Kerosene oil had in capturing the Indian market was only partially followed up in the intro-

1. Annual Consular report, Vol. 12. (C.D.)
2. Despatch no. 13, Vol. 12. (C.D.)
3. Despatch no. 35, Vol. 12. (C.D.)
4. ibid.

duction of other lubricating oils. In course of the general analysis of import potential, it was felt, that labour saving machinery would not as a rule be in demand in India[1], because labour was too cheap and plenty.

The retail trade was wholly in the hands of Indian merchants who did business in a small way and were obliged to take whatever goods were offered by the importers and jobbers. The importers were generally European merchants whose local preferences, business relations and facilities for buying naturally induced them to import European goods, and most of the American merchants were in fact only commission agents engaged in exporting Indian raw materials to the United States.[2] Hence consignment of American goods to either of this class of merchants would not naturally result in an extension of the trade. But there was a class of merchants and commission man who would gladly make a speciality of American goods provided they could obtain them on the same terms as European goods, namely easy payments or free consignments and through their agency the import would be considerable. Another method was through commercial travellers and samples. Once a Consul General had also suggested[3] a formation in America of an American Indian Company with depots at Calcutta and Madras and Bombay under Indian resident partners or agents and with experienced buyers in America to boost Indo-American trade.

While dealing with this aspect of Indo-American trade there is a very interesting despatch[4] from the Consul General Mattson to the department of State which talks of "how to promote American commerce in India"? It also takes a sociological analysis of the Indian situation and links it up rather ably with trade potential. It runs as follows :

"assuming that Western civilization which is now making fast progress in India necessarily opens the way for western industry and commerce, this country with its population of two

1. Consul General of U.S. in a communication to the department of State, U.S., Calcutta, dated May 22, 1882.

2. ibid.

3. Despatch no. 35, Vol. 12. (C.D.)

4. Mattson in a communication to the department of State, U.S., Calcutta, dated May 22, 1882.

hundred and fifty millions present at this time one of the most important fields in the world for the commerce of Western nations, and most emphatically deserves the special consideration of our American merchants and manufacturers.

It is often alleged that the conservatism and prejudice of the Hindus form a great obstacle to Western trade, but this objection has been greatly exaggerated and on the contrary it is well demonstrated of late years that the people of India readily adapt themselves to any innovations which prove advantageous to themselves. As an instance I will only mention that American Kerosene oil with its accompanying lamps has within a very short time almost entirely supplanted the native oils and vessels, not only in the homes but also in the temples of the natives in every locality where it has been introduced, simply because it proved to be cheaper and better."

Kerosene : As the indigenous people grew familiar with this oil the imports were bound to rise. The cheapness of the oil was another cause of its popularity—retailing at Calcutta at $ 1.30 to $ 1.50 per case.[1]

By then the attempt to find oil in the Borongo island of Akyab in the Bay of Bengal had been abandoned and the oil brought down from Upper Burma was used more for lubricating machinery than for illumination. Attention was then also being directed towards Baluchistan by prospectors for mineral oil, but the future was uncertain. It is true the Government of India had extended its encouragement to prospectors of mineral oils but for the purposes of illumination American Kerosene practically held the field. In fact about 96% of America's total export[2] to India consisted of Kerosene.

By a regulation of the Port Commissioners of port of Calcutta adopted during the summer of 1885, no ship (American or otherwise) laden with Kerosene oil was to be allowed to discharge her cargo above a point 16 miles below Calcutta proper, on the Hooghly river, known as "Budge Budge".

American ship masters naturally complained of the inconvenience of this arrangement on the account of the remoteness

1. Annual Consular report, Vol. 13. (C.D.)
2. ibid.

of the "Budge Budge" from their agents and consigners in Calcutta. On the other hand the Calcutta Port Commissioners claimed that the long line of ships moored at and below Calcutta for a distance of about 4 miles to a point called 'Garden Reach' would be endangered[1] by the presence of oil ships in close proximity.

For the Indian fiscal year March 31, 1886, the total imports of Kerosene oil (for illuminating purposes) were 17461875 gallons valued at Rs. 6936612. Other sorts, probably lubricating principally is set down for the same year at 2767475 gallons valued at Rs. 1076405.[2]

For the fiscal Indian year ended March 31, 1887, the total importation of illuminating oil (Kerosene) from the United States increased from 17461875 (in 1886) to 29144765 gallons valued at Rs. 11361510[3]. For the year 1887 the Kerosene or the mineral oil, classified as 'other sorts' fell off to the trifling amount of 177 gallons, caused probably by the overstocking of the market with that species of oil.

The value of imports of Kerosene during the year ended March 31, 1887 was 97·2% of the total value of all imports from U.S. to India.[4] The matter was more important than it would be ordinarily. For if America lost its export trade to India it would result in the loss of import trade to U.S., so far as the American ships were concerned, as they could not afford to come here in ballast.

Not unoften bad Kerosene oil was also shipped to India which the Consul feared would result in the ultimate loss of Indian market.[5]

Ice : It is interesting to note that Ice was an important import from America in the last three or four decades of the nine-

1. Despatch no. 36, Vol. 13. (C.D.)
2. A brief Consular report about the importation of Kerosene, Vol. 14. (C.D.)
3. ibid.
4. ibid.
5. In fact for a period American oil faced serious competition from its Russian rivals. The Government Report of the trade of India for 1886-87 bears ample evidence to this.

teenth century, into the cities of Calcutta, Bombay and Madras. There were companies coming up which would not just confine themselves to these bigger towns but open their branches into the smaller towns as well. The consumption of Ice it was noted was increasing among the middle and the lower classes.[1] The manufactured Ice appeared to be of a good quality.

Situation at the turn of the century : At the beginning of the twentieth century it was obvious that a new era in trade and commerce had begun in which England would have to fight to retain its economic status. It was certain that England would find the maintenance of her economic position far more difficult than the attainment of it proved. In fact 1901 could not be regarded as a satisfactory year for British commerce.

Questions were being asked in the British Parliament about the purchase of American locomotives by Indian Railways[2] and in general any boost to the American commerce was being strongly resented.

The total volume of the foreign trade of the United Kingdom showed a falling off in value of £7,000,000 while that of Americans registered an increase of £10,000,000.[3] In fact in the same period, Americans were making determined bids to capture the coal markets on the Mediterranean. This was again the period, and newspapers were replete with such reports, when there was great misgiving about Americans buying up British steamship lines, and combining into trusts in order to capture British markets.[4]

In fact, in 1906, U.S. Consul (Bombay) was making claims to the effect that "Bombay Consulate is one of the few in all the East where the United States sells more goods than it buys"[5]—a very impressive statement when one keeps the American involvement in China and Philippines in mind.

To boost American business prospects would, of course, be held great world fairs or expositions like the St. Louis Exposition of 1904. The occasion for such a fair was the celebration of the

1. Despatch no. 325, Vol. 12. (C.D.)
2. American Consul General in a communication to the department of State, U.S., Calcutta, dated June 12, 1901. (C.D.)
3. *Times of India*, Tuesday, Feb. 11, 1902.
4. ibid.
5. American Consul in a despatch to the department of State, U.S., Bombay, dated July 26, 1906. (B.D.)

centennial of the Lousiana purchase. The exposition was supposed to cost $ 40,000,000 and had representatives travelling all over the world.[1] One John Barrett was commissioned to explain the objects of the exposition in Asia and Australia. He visited Japan, Korea, Eastern Siberia, China, Philippines and then came to India. In fact on his visit to Bombay he was entertained by Mr. Jamsedjee Nusserwanjee Tata[2] and was at great pains to underline the deep interest of America in India.

In India too international exhibitions were organised and thus gave an opportunity to the American manufacturers to create a demand for their goods in India. Incidentally, it might be noted that these were unofficial exhibitions e.g. "The Indian Industrial and Agricultural Exhibition of the twenty-first Indian National Congress" which was to be held in the city of Benares in December, 1905.[3]

To assess correctly the American investment in Indian market and its rising gradient one needs to consider at random the value of anyone item like for instance 'Hardware and cutlery'.[4] During the decade ending in 1903 the increase under this head was over twenty-three per cent. England did not have any rise in its share of the trade while other nations like Austria, Belgium, Germany and the United States did. Alone, U.S. showed an increase of over sixty per cent, but a portion of it was due to iron oil cans, which until 1900 or so had escaped duty.[5]

An added dimension was given to the Indo-American trade relations by the active cooperation of the Americans in setting up of some industries in India. It is an interesting if relatively unknown fact that Americans were involved in J. N. Tata's scheme of establishing an industry for India to manufacture iron at less cost than elsewhere in the world. In 1902 Mr. Tata visited

1. *Times of India*, Wednesday, Nov. 26, 1902.

2. American Consul in a despatch to the department of State, U.S., Bombay, dated January 10, 1903. (B.D.)

3. American Consul General in a letter to the department of State, U.S., Calcutta, dated July 6, 1905. (C.D.)

4. It might be mentioned here that only because of lack of space other items are not being enumerated in detail, but care has been taken to select an average case.

5. Annual Report of Commerce and Industries, Bombay, India year ending March 31, 1903.

America and made a careful study of its iron manufacturing industry, with a view of applying some of the modern methods, new inventions, processes and machinery in use in the United States, to the coking of the coal, smelting and manufacturing of the iron in India. He secured the services of Mr. Christopher M. Weld and Mr. Charles P. Perin, two American mining engineers to assist him in his work.[1] Later this was to open new vistas of export-import relationship and the period 1905-1906 marks a turning point in Indian and United States history as also Indo-American trade relations in more ways than one.[2]

1. American Consul at Bombay to the department of State, despatch No. 304, dated March 30, 1905. (B.D.)

2. Gautam, Vinayshil! "Some aspects of the attitude of United States of America in India : 1901-1905," *American Government and Politics* ('72), S. Chand & Co.

Chapter VII

Epilogue

Any addition to the data available for the study of the nineteenth century Indian society and economy is welcome. In this connection American Consular Records and other reportings are of considerable value. They provide the researcher with an impressive store of information culled together by quite sophisticated minds after empirical observations by forays fairly deep into the country.

The importance of such records and evidence is manifold multiplied because, till the advent of English education in India, education did not necessarily mean literacy. This was so because to a very large extent the nature of traditional education as well as the act of imparting knowledge here was verbal. Such a state of affairs was most unconducive to 'record' formation and complicated, effectively, the task of the future generation of historians. Such records as are available of the nineteenth century are predominantly those kept by the administrative organisations which in many cases was Colonial and it is difficult to trace in it clearly the hopes and aspirations, the joys and frustrations of the people. Some other (records) represent the mind of the educated elite and as they viewed the state of affairs but there is again little which is available on the thinking process of the 'common' man. There is little which expresses those who experienced the throbs of life at a non-articulate level and while going through the pleasure and ordeal of living never put themselves down in writing. In such a situation 'third-person-account' such as in the American Consular records are of priceless evidence. Admittedly, these Records were not intended for such usage as this essay seeks to put it to but what they observed and recorded *does* lend itself to such a historical analysis. These records thus do meet our requirements upto a point.

But in order to evaluate their records, to assess their honesty, to detect their biases and to determine how far their efforts can be accepted for valid conclusions it was helpful to be aware of the nature of the influences which operated on them as also the context in which they operated. The task was complicated by the non-availability of a competent history of the American Consular Services, especially so with reference to India as also the absence of any standard work on the pattern of Indo-American relations throughout the nineteenth century. The initial problem was to set the context right and there was no other way of doing it, but in a narrative style. The attempt meant dabbling into spheres of American History and international relations where one had limited expertise. Nevertheless, the sub-plot was constructed and on that began the study of what use this particular source could be put to in the understanding of the Indian socio-economic scene in the 19th century.

The use of this type of data helped in certain theoretical formulations and model building, especially with reference to the social history of the nineteenth century. But before the conclusions are formulated it might be useful to take a quick look at the present state of one's knowledge.

Historiographically there have been changes in ideas about history itself. This can be gauzed by comparing Hume with Trevelyan. The concept of history broadened not only from the soldiers and the statesman to the people but from the state to the society. The writings on Indian history were also effected and it was a long step in the growing maturity of social history (some like to refer to it as a historical sociology) of India to pass from the first awareness of this dimension in V. Chirol's *Indian Unrest* (1910) to L. I. Rudolph and S.H. Rudolph's *Modernity of Tradition* (1969) "By the 1940's the study of Indian society cumulatively had the following components (1) a broad scale humanistically oriented tradition which emphasised the relationship between textual studies and a static model of contemporary Indian society, (2) an administrative tradition centred on the census for the study of caste which sought to see Indian society as a collection of discrete entities whose traditions and customs could be classified and studied, (3) a tradition of economic study which sought to describe the working of village economies, with some attention to the social structure of villages, (4) an anthropological tradition centred on the study of tribal peoples, and (5) an historical administrative strain which centred on the general theory of village organisation in a broad comparative framework, but without an intensive ethnographic base......consciously, or unconsciously much of the research in the period 1945 to 1955 by social and cultural anthropologists was based on the assumptions developed over the previous two hundred years as reflected by the anthropological thinking which developed during the 1930's and 1940's.

These assumptions and methods can be summarised briefly. Anthropologists study isolated or circumscribed systems, such systems in India can be found in villages, in the self-sufficient Indian village community of Munro, Metcalfe, Maine and Baden Powell. The anthropologists model of change is based on the assumption of a baseline or zero point of change. There was a time, anthropologists argue, when the system we want to study were stable or static, and anthropologists studies change by studying what happened from the postulated period of stability. In India this was to be found in villages where 'traditional India' existed. This is the Orientalist's assumption of unchanging character of Indian civilisation. Caste is the central institution of rural Indian society, it governs behaviour and values. This is the official view of caste as a 'thing' as a set of attributes. The way you study caste is to observe it in action and ask people about it.

The first publication in 1955 of two collections reporting the results of the first round of modern field work in India, *India's Villages* and *Village India* reveals the shock of recognition that great correction was needed both in the anthropologists' assumptions about India derived from the traditions of study of India and in the transfer of interests in particular subject matter, methods and theories from social and cultural anthropology as it existed in the late forties (M. B. Singer, B. S. Cohn: *Structure and Change in Indian Society*, pp. 23-25). The study of these (American Consular) sources amongst other things led me to the belief that perhaps there is a case for the re-examination of the "directions which anthropologists concerned with the study of India (began to) travel in" by these two studies noted above on the Indian village.

After all such a study is not by itself, though it may be

conducive to, a pattern formation. For the study of a vast cultural unit such as the Indian sub-continent, a viable model has to be constructed which is not merely analytical and thereby atomised but also synthetic in as much as it combines the various atoms in a meaningful way leading to a clarity of analysis of a complex society as India. It is here that perhaps all the various traditions of the humanistic oriented tradition, an administrative tradition focused on caste, a tradition of economic study focused on village economics, an anthropological tradition focused on tribal people and an historical administrative strain centred on the general theory of village organisation with an intensive ethnographic base have all to be combined together in a composite way for a viable analysis.

It is in this connection that the duality model of the 'traditional unit' and the 'colonial unit' has been put forward here. This particular source study helped substantiate the model which was attempted to be put forth. A concrete illustration would clarify the model and the point. The Bhojpuri speaking unit of Eastern India, for example, because of oneness of dialect, a fair homogeneity of culture, common exclusive set of heroes and the custom of intermarriage among the inhabitants of the region, subject to caste restrictions etc., is a traditional unit for social action and social change as also one of the numerous cultural sub-units of the country. Therefore, it holds to reason that it is not the whole truth to suggest that social loyalty in India is seldom if ever territorial. It can be at times territorial also as in the above illustrated case. Such a traditional unit being the unit of social action is also a fit unit for the study of social change. During the nineteenth century as the Consular records also help in bringing out, the stunted economic growth in the Bhojpuri speaking area, the heavy indebtedness, the progressive fragmentation of land holdings, the chronic state of industrial backwardness, the phenomena of migrant labour as also the introduction of the rule of law, and later, modern means of education and communication gave to the social development here, a peculiar character.

All this led to a particular condition of social instability when this was coupled, as it was in this region, with the relative weakness of various economic and professional organisations e.g.

trade unions etc. The situation of the colonial setting would be a significant catalyst for change in such a context.

The foreign colonial power for its own administrative needs created its own administrative units—which have been designated here as colonial units—at times quite arbitrarily. These whether at the district level or the provincial level would not unoften cut across the various traditional units and derive their sanction from the coercive power of the state. Thus unlike the traditional unit which had a moral sanction and had the agricultural-rural culture the colonial unit developed the industrial-urban culture. A few such colonial units grew around the Bhojpuri speaking unit also leading to a fit state not only of potential cultural pollination but also of conditions which might lead to social fragmentation and greater right-consciousness. The phenomena of migrant labour, amongst others, was an effective catalyst for such change.

The Consular records lend a certain amount of insight into the problem and help to underscore the varying nature of colonial units in spite of certain basic common features, throughout British India, as also the varying nature of traditional units, in spite of a certain basic common features amongst them too. Thus, it is that a possible explanation of the varying nature of response to an industrial-technological culture throughout British India is arrived at. This, of course, to a point, explains the unevenness of social evolution in present day India. A relevant point of interest in this connection is the differing types of evolution of Eastern and Western India. Having the advantage of being an All India non-governmental source, a beginning has been made to notice and study this differing pattern of social change in different parts of British India also through such a source.

The study of this change it has been suggested might possibly be carried in the three phased framework of (i) what was the Indian situation (called T_1 or $Time_1$) (ii) what were the instruments of social change and then only (iii) what was the resultant. The only difference being that T_1 or what some would imagine as the zero point of change was neither stable nor static nor for that matter even invariably decadent. T_1 in the Indian situation was at times not only vital and dynamic but also at times helped thwart or at least alter considerably the value scale of the invading industrial technological culture. Hence it is that T_3, or the resultant very often took on a peculiarly Indian texture or shape bearing little resemblance to the pristine industrial-technological value system. This would be the Indian variant of "modernism". The Consular Records, again, help to a great degree in comprehending both T_1, and the instruments of social change, because they are the results of empirical survey. In the course of the writing this has been demonstrated.

Besides, the complex nature of the Western impact and Indian response in the nineteenth century has to be noted. It is not as if the British throughout the nineteenth century had a consistent social policy in India. In fact when one notices the variations in their attitude from lingering Orientalism to Utilitarianism to Paternalism and realises the problem which the Indian society was facing for a good part of the nineteenth century, namely that of accomplishing a double revolution of liberalism and nationalism the complexity of the situation becomes almost bewildering. Source study such as this being an analysis as noted earlier, of a third-person account, also lend a limited amount of insight into the question. It ought to be remembered however, that the single largest catalyst for change in this sub-continent was the English rule and depending on whether a particular territory was a part of British, princely or just tribal India the intensity of the catalytic influence would differ.

The regional variations in the Indian response to the impact of the industrial-technological value scale have been observed and commented on already. But perhaps the researchers would like to pay some attention to the hypothesis of a social middle structure (class) termed '*meso-structure*', in the essay, which emerged in Western India and absorbed the industrial-technological value scale and passed it on into the blood stream of that segment of the Indian society but which failing to emerge—perhaps because of a far more total monopolistic system—in Eastern India made the process of such imbibing far more complicated, troublesome and in the ultimate result confusing. In all this, the Consulate Records do give an added dimension.

As in the case of the analysis of the Indian society in the 19th century so too in the case of Indian economy the lack of abundant meaningful data is a handicap. Even for an elementary understanding of the phenomena of drain there is inadequate evidence. Quantification is always a problem for after all no all-India regulatory agency like the Reserve Bank of India as today, was then existing, and so actual statistics are difficult to get hold of. Besides the agency houses then played a very significant role and their papers are also not available for processing. Hence whatever conclusion the economic historian comes to, it is inevitably semi-conjectural on partial evidence. Besides, throughout the 19th century again, there is not a uniformity of economic policy. The restraining role of free trade on imperial interests is relatively at a low key after 1857-58. These records make available a great wealth of data for the economic historian, a certain portion of which has been liberally reproduced keeping in mind the relative inaccessibility of these records. It has been further suggested that the economic situation in India was not an autonomous variable. It might help improve the methodological tools to use the sociological concepts for a fuller understanding of the economic scene.

To take the example of the problem of the drain—if the exact figures are not coming forth it should be possible to come to more plausible conclusions by locating the regions of greatest growth in terms of the middle classes and industries and see if it at all can be correlated to the reinvestment of the production surplus in that region (Ref. to pp. 94-95 for a detailed elucidation). This at least would give an added evidence of analysis and thus lead to, perhaps a more valid conclusion.

Besides, of course, the inter-relation between social developments and economic situation has been noted in the essay. This is especially so in a context like India where social, religious and cultural considerations help accelerate or retard economic growth. Certain practices may be meaningless and uneconomic in the total context of human welfare yet they may help in maintaining the stability of the society. In that case its adjustment with the economic processes become essential. The Consular records help in such an understanding. Of course, there is a possibility that the threefold segmentation of the Indian economy in the 19th century as made in the concerned chapter may not be universally acceptable as the three sections in which that century may be divided. But such evidence as the Consular sources provided lent themselves to no other classification. It is hoped not so much that this classification will be ultimately accepted as the valid classification of 19th century economy of India but that the data provided here could enrich the resources for that particular branch of history. It is also hoped that the methodological suggestions made would receive the serious attention of the researchers as well as that there may be a growing awareness of the intimate connection between the social and economic history of 19th century India.

The discussion on the nature of the Indian economy and facets of economy in the 19th century is followed by a pattern analysis of the Indo-American trade relations. It is one of the relatively less known facts of history that there were continuous and at times even intimate trade links between India and the United States from nearly the 18th century. First it was through intermediaries such as *cabeteurs* of Isle de France (Mauritius), the American goods being brought there (Mauritius) as were the Indian goods and then an exchange taking place. This intermediary station thus obviated the necessity of travelling any greater distance than was absolutely necessary. This pattern of contact continued till the second decade of the 19th century after which direct contacts became more the style. The rhythm of the trade relations has been analysed into segments of 1792-1833, 1834-1865, 1866-1880, 1881-1906, and the intensity of trade relations described and established. The second half of the century saw trade contacts between India and America again also through intermediaries but this time from the Far East consequent upon the American expansion there.

However that may be the chapter it is hoped establishes on an acceptable footing the fact of Indo-American trade relations in the 19th century.

All told these American Consular and other reportings are a heap of information and evidence which this work does not claim to have exhausted but only opened up. The occasion of the source study has led to certain theoretical formulations which have been placed before the learned audience for consideration and debate.

Of course, there were certain inherent disappointments in not finding the answers to all the problems I had set to myself at the beginning of the source study but then it opened up certain other unexpected avenues of investigation too. I intend to make no greater claim here than that of just having made a beginning.

BIBLIOGRAPHY

Primary Sources

Unpublished Primary Source Material :

Acquisition from Ames Library (Mf) N.A.I.

Acquisition from Harvard College Library, Massachusetts (Mf) N.A.I.

Acquisition from Henry E. Huntington Library & Art Gallery, San Marino California (Mf) N.A.I.

Acquisition from the United Presbyterian Church in the United States of America, Presbyterian Mission Library (Mf) N.A.I.

American Philosophical Society, papers of Philadelphia (Mf) N.A.I.

Despatches from the U.S. Consuls of Bombay (Mf), Indian Council of World Affairs Library, New Delhi

Despatches from the U.S. Consuls at Calcutta (Mf) (Personal reels)

Foreign Department, Proceedings of, N.A.I.

Indian Political Despatches to/from the Court of Directors of East India Company, N.A.I.

(Indian) Board of Trade, Proceedings of, (Calcutta, Bombay) N.A.I.

Parliamentary Papers, N.A.I.

Public Department, Proceedings of, N.A.I.

Published Primary Source Meterial :

Adams John, Inaugural Address of March 4, 1797

Adams John, Memoires

American Foreign Policy : A documentary survey, 1776-1960; Ed. Goebel, D.B.

American State Papers, Foreign Relations

Buchanan James, Inaugural Address of March 4, 1857

Congressional Globe (Ref. American House of Representatives)

Diary and Autobiography of John Adams, Ed. Butterfield, L.H.

Diplomatic Correspondences and Foreign Relationship of the United States, 1861-1899

District Report of Zila Gorakhpur, Collecti on of

Foreign Relations of the United States (United States Department of States), 1861-1945

Foreign Relations of the United States (United States Department of States), 1900-1905

General Index to the published volumes of the Diplomatic Correspondence and Foreign Relations of the United States, 1861-1899

Grant Ulysses, S., Inaugural Address (Second) of March 4, 1873

Hansards Debates

Harrison Benjamin, Inaugural Address of March 4, 1899

House Document (Ref. American Senate & American House of Representatives)

House Journal (Ref. American Senate & American House of Representatives)

House Report (Ref. American Senate & American House of Representatives)

Index to United States Documents Relating to Foreign Affairs 1828-1861

Jefferson Thomas, Inaugural Address of March 4, 1865

Life and Letters of Thomas Jefferson, Hirst F. W.

Life and Selected Writings of Thomas Jefferson, Koch, A. and Peden, W.

Lincoln Abraham, Inaugural Address (first) of March 4, 1861

Lincoln Abraham, Inaugural Address (second) of March 4, 1865

Madison James, Inaugural Address (second) of March 4, 1813

Monroe James, Inaugural Address (first) of March 4, 1817

Monroe Papers, Messages to the Congress

Opinions of Attorney Generals, Collection of (American)

Report on the Diplomatic Archives of the Department of States, 1789-1840

Treaties for the Advancement of Peace between the United States and other Powers, Brym, W. J.

Treaties and other International Acts of the United States of America, Ed. Miller Hunter

Washington Papers : Basic Selections from Public & Private Writings of George Washington, Ed. Padover S. K.

Newspapers, Reports etc. :

Newspapers :

Agra Akhbar
The Englishman
Hindu Patriot
Times of India

Reports etc. :

Calcutta Gazette (relevant volumes)
Famine Commission Report (1880)
Gazette of India (relevant volumes)
Orissa Famine Report
Report of the Committee appointed to enquire into the Indian Currency
Report of the Deccan Riot's Commission
Report of the Land Revenue Commission (1861)
Second Report of the Royal Commission appointed to enquire into changes in the relative value of precious metals
Supplement to the Calcutta price current and market report (relevant volumes)

Secondary Sources

Papers and Articles :

Atkinson, Fred J. : 'A Statistical Review of the Income and Wealth of British India' in *Journal of the Royal Statistical Society* LXV, 1902

Catanach, I. J. : Agrarian disturbances in nineteenth century India. *The Indian Economic and Social History Review*, 3

Gautam, V. : "Aspects of the role of Isle de France in contacts between India and the United States 1780-1810", *Proceedings Volume of the Indian History Congress* (30th Session), December 1968

"Some aspects of trade relations between United States of America and Mauritius (1730-1789), *Proceed-*

ings Volume of the Indian History Congress (31st Session) December 1969

"Some aspects of social change in the Bhojpuri speaking area 1858-1920 : a case study of a traditional unit in a colonial setting" *abstract of papers, 28 International Congress of Orientalists*, January 1971

"Social life in the Poona districts 1870-1880" *Maratha History Seminar Papers* ('71), Shivaji University Publications, Kolhapur

"Some aspects of folklore as an agent of nationalism in the Bhojpuri speaking area : 1917-1942, a case study of a traditional unit in a colonial setting" *abs. of papers contributed to the Seminar in Anthropology*, Ranchi, November, '71

"Some aspects of the influence of American War of Independence on India" *Journal of Historical Research*, Vol. XIV, No. 2

"A note on the use of Maratha Mission papers as a source of social history of Western India for the last three decades of the nineteenth century" *Journal of Social Research*, Vol. XV, No 1.

"Some aspects of the attitude of the United States in India 1901-1905" *American Government and Politics* ('72) S. Chand and Co., New Delhi

"Introduction to the social history of the Bhojpuri speaking area in India—as reconstructed from folk-literature" *Society and Culture*, Vol. III, No. 2

Karve, Iravati : On the Road *Journal of Asian Studies*, XXII, No. I, 1962

Kumar, Ravinder : The Deccan Riots of 1875 *Journal of Asian Studies*, XXIV, August 4, 1965

Majumdar, R.C. : Rammohun Roy and Balgangadhar Tilak on Social, Legislation, *Journal of Indian History*, Vol. XLV, No 133

Misra, P. : 'Indo-American trade relations 1866-1880' in *Journal of Indian History*, Vol. XLIII, Part III, Dec. 1965

Neale, Walter. C. : The limitations of Indian village survey data, *Journal of Asian Studies*, 17, 383-402

Ranade, M.G. : The exigencies of progress in India, *Quarterly Journal of the Poona Sarvajanik Sabha*, April 1893

Rehatsek, E. : EarlyMuslim accounts of Hindu religion, *Journal of Asiatic Society of Bombay*, 14, 418-38

Shrinivas, M.N. and T.M. Shah : The myth of the self sufficiency of the Indian village, *Economic Weekly*, 12 : 1375-78

Books :

Ahmed, A.F. Social ideas and social changes in Bengal (1818-1835)

Ahmed, Q. Wahabi movement

Al-Biruni Alberuni's India

Ambedkar, B.R. The problem of the Rupee

Anstey, Vera The economic development of India

Antrobus, H.A. A history of the Assam Tea Company, 1839-1952

Baden Powell Land system of British India, 3 Vols.

Baden Powell The origin and growth of village communities in India

Banerjee, P. Indian finance in the days of the Company, 1928

Barbosa, Duarte A description of the coast of East Africa and Malabar in the beginning of the sixteenth century

Barbosa, Duarte The book of Duarte Barbosa : an account of the countries bordering on the Indian Ocean and their inhabitants

Barker, Wharton Bimetallism

Barrier, Norman G. The Punjab alienation land bill of 1900

Basu, P.N. History of Hindu civilisation during British rule

Beale, Howard K. Theodore Roosevelt and the rise of America to world power

Bemis, B.F. The American Secretaries of State and their diplomacy

Bearce, G.D.	British attitudes towards India
Bewis, Samuel Flagg	John Quincy Adams and the foundation of American foreign policy, 1949
Bewis, S.F.	The Jay treaty, a study in commerce and diplomacy
Bhatia, B.M.	Famines in India, 1860-1905
Bhatt, V.V.	Economic change and policy in India
Bingley, A.H. and A. Nicholls :	Brahmans : Caste handbook for the Indian army
Bishop, Joseph Bucklin	Theodore Roosevelt and his time shown in his own letters
Bose, N.S.	The Indian awakening and Bengal
Bowley & Robertson	A scheme for an economic census of India
Bradley, Birt, F.B.	Twelve men of Bengal in the nineteenth century
Brant, Irving	James Madison : The President 1809-1812, 1956
Buchanan, D.H.	The development of capitalist enterprise in India, 1934
Buchnan, Francis	A journey from Madras through the countries of Mysore
Chambers, William Nisbet	Old Bullion Benton, Senator from the New West Thomas Hart Benton, 1782-1858
Chatterton, A.	Industrial evolution in India, 1912
Chintamani, C.Y.	Indian social reform
Choksey, R.D.	Economic history of the Bombay, Deccan and Karnatak, 1818-68
Chunder, Bholanath	The travels of a Hindoo
Clark, Colin	The conditions of economic progress
Cole	Senator Gerald P. Nye and American foreign relations
Colebrooke, H.T.	Remarks on the husbandry and internal commerce of Bengal
Cotton	Rice trade of the world—a report

Cunningham, W.	Growth of English industry and commerce laissez faire
Dadabhai, Naoroji	Poverty and un-British rule in India
Darling, M.L.	The Punjab peasant in prosperity and debt
Das, M.N.	Studies in the economic and social development of modern India
Dutta, K.K.	Dawn of renascent India
Datta, K.K.	Education and social amelioration of women in pre-mutiny India
Datta, K.K.	Renaissance, nationalism and social changes in modern India
David, Komph	British orientalism and Bengal renaissance
Dawson, Thomas Fulton	Life and character of Edward Oliver Wolcott
Day, Clive	A history of commerce
Dels, B.K.	Early history and growth of Calcutta
Dennett	Roosevelt and Russo-Japanese war
Digby, William	"Prosperous" British India, London, 1901
Dorman, M.R.P.	History of the British Empire in the 19th century II
Dube, S.C.	Indian village
Dube, S.C.	India's changing villages
Dumont, Louis	The "village community" from Munro to Maine
Dutt, Romesh	The economic history of India in the Victorian age
Elliot, Henry Meirs and John Dowson	A history of India as told by its own historians
Esthus	Theodore Roosevelt and Japan
Fazal, Abul	Ain-i-Akbari
Ford, Henry Jones	The Cleveland Era : A chronicle of the new order in politics
Forster, J.W.	The practice of diplomacy
Fox, Richard	Raja, kin, clan and territory

Fraser, Lovat — Iron and steel in India
Frykenberg — Land control and social policy
Gadgil, D.R. & Gayer, A.D. — The industrial evolution of India
Garraty, John A. — Henry Cabot Lodge: A biography
Ghose, Aurobindo — The renaissance in India
Gosh, A.S. — India's case for silver
Great Britain, House of Commons — Report on East India Company affairs
Guha, R. — A rule of property for Bengal : an essay on idea of permanent settlement
Gupta, A. (ed.) — Studies in Bengal rennaissance
Halhead, N.B. — A code of gentoo laws, or, ordinations of the pundits from a Persian translation, made from the original, written in the Sanskrit language
Halle, Louis J. — American foreign policy (theory and reality)
Hamilton — Works
Harrison, James L. — Biographical directory of the American Congress, 1774 1949
Hayden, R. — The senate and treaties. 1789-1817
Heimsath, C.H. — Indian nationalism and Hindu social reform
Hesseltine, William B. — Ulysses S. Grant: Politician 1957
Hollan, P.S. — A sketch of the mineral resources of India 1908
Howland, Harold — Theodore Roosevelt and his times: A chronicle of the progressive movement 1921
Hunter, W.W. — Bengal ms. records 4 vols. 1894
Hutton, J.H. — Caste in India: Its nature, function and origins
Hyde, C.C. — International law, chiefly as interpreted and applied by the United States, II
Ingham, K. — Reformers in India 1793-1833

Irving, B.A.	Commerce of India
Jain, M.S.	The Aligarh movement
Jenks, L.H.	The migration of British capital to 1875 1927
Jhonson, Charles	A general history of the pyrates from their first rise and settlement in the island of Providence to the present times
Keatinge, G.	Rural economy in the Bombay Deccan
Keynes, J.N.	Indian currency and finance
Knaplund, P.	Britain Commonwealth and Empire (1901-1955)
Knowles, L.C.A.	The economic development of British overseas empire part II
Kumar, Ravinder	Western India in the 19th century
Lach, Donald	Asia in the making of Europe
Leonard, G.S.	History of Brahmo Samaj
Leon, H. Dupriez	Economic progress
Lowis, Alfred Henry (ed.)	A compilation of the messages and speeches of Theodore Roosevelt
Lincoln, Abraham	Complete works
Lokanathan, P.S.	Industrial organisation in India
Long, J.	Adams three reports on vernacular education in Bengal and Behar
Low, D.A. (ed.)	Soundings in modern south Asian history
Loveday, A.	Indian famines
Mackenzie, Compton	Realms of silver
M'crindle, J.W.	Ancient India: as described in classical literature
Majumdar, R.C.	Glimpses of Bengal in the nineteenth century
Malloy, C.	Treaties and conventions
Malloy, W.	Treaties and conventions
Mann, Arthur	La Guardia: A fighter against his times 1882-1933
Mann, Harold H.	Land and labour in a Deccan village
Martin, R.M.	Our Indian Empire 1879

Martin, Joseph W.	My first fifty years in politics as told by Robert J. Donovan
Mathews, J.M.	The Conduct of American foreign relations
Max Muller	Rammohan to Ramakrishna
Mazumdar, B.B.	History of Indian social and political ideas (Rammohan Roy to Dayanand)
Mazumdar, Jatindra Kumar	Raja Rammohan Roy and progressive movements in India (1775-1875)
Muzumdar, R.C.	Glimpses of Bengal in the nineteenth century
Milburn, William	Oriental commerce : containing a geographical description of the principal places in the East India Vol. II
Misra, B.B.	Rise of the Indian middle classes
Mitra, Sisir Kumar	Resurgent India
Monson, T.	The economic transition in India 1911
Montgomery, Martin	History of Eastern India Vol. II
Moore, J.B.	Digest of international law
Morrison Elting E. (ed.)	The letters of Theodore Roosevelt 1868-1919 (Vols. 1-8)
Mukherjee, S.	Elites in South Asia
Mukherjee, S.N.	A history of education in India
Naik and Nurullah	A student's history of education in India
Naoroji, D.	Poverty and un-British rule in India 1876, 1901
Narain, V.A.	Some aspects of social history in India in the 19th century
Natarajan, S.	A century of social reform in India
Newton, A.P.	Cambridge history of British foreign policy
O'Malley, L.S.S.	Bengal, Bihar, Orissa, and Sikkim, Census of India 1911 (Vol. V)
Phipps, J.	History of ship-building in Calcutta etc. 1840

Pillai, P.P.	Economic conditions in India
Prain, Perid	A sketch of the life of Francis Hamilton called Buchanan : Annals of the Royal Botanic Garden
Pringle, Henry F.	Theodore Roosevelt : a biography 1931
Putnam, Carleton	Theodore Roosevelt : a biography Vol. I, 1958
Putnam, Carleton	The formative years 1858-1886
Ranade, G.	Essays on Indian Economics
Rao, V.K.R.V.	The national income of British India 1941
Reid	Indigo
Rhodes, J.F.	Mckinley and Roosevelt administrations
Rhodes, J.F.	Mckinley and Roosevelt administrations 1897-1909, 1922
Risley, H.H.	The people of India
Robertson, William	A historical disquisition concerning the knowledge which the ancients had of India
Roosevelt, Theodore	An autobiography, 1913
Rothman, David J.	Politics and Power : The United States Senate 1869-1901
Roy, B.B.	Religious movements in modern Bengal
Rudolph, L.I. & S.H.	The modernity of tradition
Sabah Al-Din'Abid Al-Rahman	Study of Hindu learning and religion in the Indo-Persian literature Indo-Iranica
Sadler, David Francis	Theodore Roosevelt : a symbol of Americans 1898-1912, 1954
Schuyler, E.	American diplomacy (N.Y. 1886)
Schuyler, E.	American diplomacy
Sen, Amit	Notes on the Bengal renaissance
Sharma, D.S.	Studies in the renaissance of Hinduism
Shirras, F.	Indian currency and banking
Shastri, Shivnath	History of Brahmo Samaj

Sinha, H.	Early European banking in India 1927
Sinha, N.K.	The economic history of Bengal, 2 Vols. Calcutta 1956, 1962
Singer, Milton	Traditional India : structure and change
Singer, Milton (comp.)	Introduction to civilization of India
Sinha, N.K.	History of Bengal
Sinha, Pradeep	Nineteenth century Bengal
Smith, Samuel Denny	Negro in Congress 1870-1901
Sound, D.S.	Congressman from India
Spear, P.	The Oxford history of India, part III
Spear, Percival	Twilight of the Moghuls
Steuart, James, Sir	The principles of money applied to the present state of the coin in Bengal, 1772
Stokes, Eric	The English utilitarians and India
Strachey, John	The end of empire
Tavernier, Jean Baptiste	Travels in India
Temple, Richard	The story of my life
Tennant, William	Indian recreation : consisting of scriptures of and rural economy of the Mohammedans and Hindus
Thorner, David	Long term trends in output in economic growth—Brazil, India, Japan
Thorner, Daniel	Marx on India and the Asiatic mode of production : contributions to Indian sociology
Tocquevelli, Alexis de	Democracy in America
Trevelyan, Charles	A report upon the inland customs and town duties of the Bengal presidency 1835
Tipathy, Amales	Trade and finance in the Bengal presidency 1793-1833, 1956
Tyson, G.W.	Bengal Chamber of Commerce and Industries 1853-1953, a centenary survey

United Nations	Measures for the economic development of underdeveloped countries
Vyas, K.C.	Social renaissance in India
Wallace, D.R.	The romance of Jute
Ward, William	A view of the history, literature and mythology of the Hindus (3 Vols.)
Whithead, H.	Indian problems in religion
Wilson, Horace Hayman	A review of the external commerce of Bengal
Wright	The control of American foreign relations
Yule, Henry & A.C. Burnell	Hobson-Jobson
Zinn, Howard	Guardia in Congress
Zacharias, H.C.E.	Renascent India from Rammohan to Mohan Das Gandhi

APPENDIX I

Despatches from the U.S. Consuls in Bombay to the department of State, U.S.A.

The volumes each of which has been microcopied on a separate roll, cover the following dates:

Roll	Volume	Inclusive Dates
1	1	Oct. 12, 1838—Nov. 16, 1857
2	2	Jan. 9, 1858—Dec. 31, 1869
3	3	Jan. 13, 1870—May 5, 1881
4	4	May 5, 1881—June 13, 1889
5	5	July 1, 1889—June 26, 1896
6	6	Aug. 13, 1896—Dec. 30, 1901
7	7	Jan. 6, 1902—Nov. 13, 1905
8	8	Jan. 5.—Aug. 11, 1906

APPENDIX II

Despatches from the U.S. Consuls in Calcutta to the department of State, U.S.A.

The volumes each of which has been microcopied on a separate roll, cover the following dates:

Roll	Volume	Inclusive Dates
1	1	1792—Dec. 12, 1850
2	2	Jan. 1, 1851—Jan. 3, 1853
3	3	April 18, 1853—Dec. 5, 1856
4	4	Feb. 15, 1854—Dec. 29, 1857
5	5	Jan. 15, 1858—Dec. 31, 1861
6	6	June 30, 1860—Sept. 30, 1863
7	7	Jan. 5, 1864—Oct. 1, 1866
8	8	Jan. 5, 1867—Feb. 18, 1869
9	9	Feb. 22, 1869—Jan. 4, 1870
10	10	Jan. 17, 1870—Nov. 24, 1875

Roll	Volume	Inclusive Dates
11	11	Dec. 6, 1875—Dec. 27, 1879
12	12	Jan. 16, 1880—Feb. 27, 1883
13	13	March 1, 1883—Dec. 27, 1886
14	14	Jan. 11, 1887—Dec. 3, 1889
15	15	Jan. 7, 1890—Dec. 19, 1894
16	16	Jan. 10, 1895—May 23, 1901
17	17	June 12, 1901—Aug. 2, 1906

INDEX